Global Migrations

This book is dedicated to
Sir Tom Devine
Mentor, Friend, Colleague
Historian of Scotland and the Scottish diaspora

Global Migrations

The Scottish Diaspora since 1600

A Tribute to Professor Sir Tom Devine

Edited by Angela McCarthy and John M. MacKenzie

EDINBURGH
University Press

Edinburgh University Press is one of the leading university presses in the UK. We publish academic books and journals in our selected subject areas across the humanities and social sciences, combining cutting-edge scholarship with high editorial and production values to produce academic works of lasting importance. For more information visit our website: www.edinburghuniversitypress.com

Edinburgh University Press Ltd
The Tun – Holyrood Road
12 (2f) Jackson's Entry
Edinburgh EH8 8PJ

First published in hardback by Edinburgh University Press 2016

Typeset in 10.5/13pt Sabon by
Servis Filmsetting Ltd, Stockport, Cheshire
and printed and bound in Great Britain by
CPI Group (UK) Ltd, Croydon CR0 4YY

A CIP record for this book is available from the British Library

ISBN 978 1 4744 10045 (hardback)
ISBN 978 1 4744 2932 0 (paperback)
ISBN 978 1 4744 1005 2 (webready PDF)
ISBN 978 1 4744 1006 9 (epub)

Contents

Figures and Tables

FIGURES

TABLES

Notes on the Contributors

Stuart Allan is Principal Curator of Scottish Late Modern Collections in the Department of Scottish History and Archaeology, National Museums Scotland. His specialism is in the national military collections reflecting the Scottish military tradition in the British armed forces. He is the co-author, with David Forsyth, of *Common Cause: Commonwealth Scots and the Great War* (2014) and in collaboration with David Forsyth he curated the exhibition of the same name. His publications include *Commando Country* (2007) and, with Allan Carswell, *The Thin Red Line: War, Empire and Visions of Scotland* (2004).

David Alston is an independent researcher with degrees in philosophy, law, and history. He has been a youth worker, school teacher, adult education organiser and museum curator. He now serves in local government as an elected Liberal Democrat member of the Highland Council. For the past fifteen years he has been exploring the historical links between the Highlands of Scotland and the slave plantations of Guyana.

Colin G. Calloway received his BA and PhD degrees from the University of Leeds and is now the John Kimball Jr. 1943 Professor of History and Professor of Native American Studies at Dartmouth College. He has written many books on Native American history, including *'White People, Indians, and Highlanders': Tribal Peoples and Colonial Encounters in Scotland and North America* (2008). He was President of the American Society for Ethnohistory in 2007–8 and was selected for the American Indian History Lifetime Achievement Award in 2011.

Ann Curthoys is an honorary professor at the University of Sydney. She has written extensively on Australian history and on historical theory and writing. Her recent publications include '"The Lying name of government": Empire, Mobility and Political Rights', in Jane Carey and Jane Lydon (eds), *Indigenous Networks: Mobility, Connections and Exchange*; 'History from Down Under: E. P. Thompson's *The Making of the English Working Class* and Australia', *Historical Reflections/*

Réflexions Historiques, and (with Ann Genovese and Alexander Reilly), *Rights and Redemption: History, Law and Indigenous People*.

David Fitzpatrick is Professor of Modern History at Trinity College, Dublin. His works include *Politics and Irish Life: Provincial Experience of War and Revolution* (1977), *Irish Emigration, 1801–1921* (1984), four chapters on Irish emigration and the Irish in Britain in *A New History of Ireland*, vols v, vi (1989, 1996), *Oceans of Consolation: Personal Accounts of Irish Migration to Colonial Australia* (1994), *The Two Irelands, 1912–1939* (1998), *Harry Boland's Irish Revolution* (2003), *'Solitary and Wild': Frederick MacNeice and the Salvation of Ireland* (2012), and *Descendancy: Irish Protestant Histories since 1795* (2014).

David Forsyth is Principal Curator, Medieval-Early Modern Collections in the Department of Scottish History and Archaeology, National Museums Scotland. His specialism is the material culture of the Scottish diaspora. He is the co-author, with Stuart Allan, of *Common Cause: Commonwealth Scots and the Great War* (2014) and in collaboration with Stuart Allan curated the exhibition of the same name. His forthcoming edited volume with Wendy Ugolini, *A Global Force: War, Identities and the Scottish Diaspora*, develops the theme of the Scottish military diaspora. He has curated a number of diaspora-related exhibitions at the National Museum of Scotland.

Erin C. M. Grant completed her PhD in 2013 with the Department of History and Art History, Department of Music and the Centre for Irish and Scottish Studies at the University of Otago, New Zealand. Under the supervision of Professor Angela McCarthy and Professor Henry Johnson, Erin investigated the previously unexplored history of women's involvement with the Great Highland Bagpipes and Scottish associational culture across the Scottish diaspora. Currently, Erin is a Research Analyst with the Government of British Columbia in Canada and is based in the City of Victoria.

David Hesse studied history and politics in Zurich and Saint Petersburg and holds a doctorate from the University of Edinburgh. He now works as a journalist for a leading Swiss newspaper. Among his publications are *Scotland and Poland: Historical Encounters, 1500–2010* (edited with T. M. Devine, 2011) and *Warrior Dreams: Playing Scotsmen in Mainland Europe* (2014).

Angela McCarthy is Professor of Scottish and Irish History at the University of Otago, New Zealand, where she teaches Irish and Scottish history and migration, and race and ethnicity in New Zealand. She is the author/editor of ten books on migration, including *A Global Clan: Scottish Migrant Networks and Identities since the Eighteenth Century* (2006), *Personal Narratives of Irish and Scottish Migration, 1921–65: 'For Spirit and Adventure'* (2007) and *Irishness and Scottishness in New Zealand* (2011). She has recently published work on migration, ethnicity, and madness and is currently writing a biography of James Taylor, 'the father of Ceylon tea'.

John M. MacKenzie is Emeritus Professor of Imperial History at Lancaster University and holds honorary professorships of Aberdeen and St Andrews universities. He is an honorary professorial fellow of Edinburgh University and is a Fellow of the Royal Society of Edinburgh. He is the author of *The Scots in South Africa* and the co-editor (with Tom Devine) of *Scotland and the British Empire*. He has been publishing on the subject of Scots and Empire since 1992 and has advocated the 'four nations' approach to British imperial history.

Andrew Mackillop is a senior lecturer in the School of Divinity, History and Philosophy at the University of Aberdeen. He is the author of *More Fruitful than the Soil: Army, Empire and the Scottish Highlands, 1715–1815* (2001), joint author of *Forging the State: European State Formation and the Anglo-Scottish Union of 1707* (2008), and joint editor of *Fighting for Identity: Scottish Military Experience, c.1550– 1900* (2002) and *Military Governors and Imperial Frontiers, c.1600– 1800* (2003). He has contributed many articles and chapters on the Scottish diaspora and Hebridean history.

Tawny Paul is Lecturer in History at Northumbria University. She has interests in the social and economic history of eighteenth-century Britain, as well as in the production and reception of public history in contemporary settings. She completed a PhD in economic and social history at the University of Edinburgh in 2011, followed by a postdoctoral research fellowship in Diaspora heritage at the Scottish Centre for Diaspora Studies. Tawny is NEH Fellow at the Huntington Library for 2015–16.

Eric Richards is Emeritus Professor of History at Flinders University in Adelaide, and in 2014 was Carnegie Trust Centenary Professor at the University of the Highlands and Islands, based at Dornoch and Inverness. His recent publications include: *Destination Australia: Migration to Australia since 1900* (2008); *The Highland Clearances: People, Landlords and Rural Turmoil* (2013); and an edited collection, *On the Wing: Mobility before and after Emigration to Australia* (2013). He is now working on the origins of mass international migration.

Iain Watson was born in Singapore and raised in the Scottish expatriate environments of Singapore, Kuala Lumpur and Penang. He has pursued a career as a global banker working in the United Kingdom, France, Yemen, Hong Kong, New Zealand and Australia. Having left the financial services industry, he is currently a PhD candidate at the University of Edinburgh where he is conducting a comparative study of Scottish migrants to Hong Kong and New Zealand since 1945. He holds degrees from the Open University (BA Hons in History) and the University of Edinburgh (MSc in Diaspora and Migration History).

Acknowledgements

W E ARE GRATEFUL TO the Scottish Government for funding the Global Migrations conference that took place in Edinburgh in July 2014 at which most of the chapters in this book were first presented. They have since been extended and revised for publication here and we are grateful to contributors for their support of the book and their swift communication with us. The July conference also formed part of the Economic and Social Research Council funded seminar series on 'Scotland's Diasporas in Comparative International Perspective' (a joint initiative of Angela McCarthy, Tom Devine and Nick Evans). We would also like to thank National Museums Scotland for providing the stimulating environment within which the conference took place and all those speakers and chairs who participated in the event including the Rt Hon. Dr Gordon Brown, Baroness Helen Liddell of Coatdyke, and Humza Yousaf, MSP.

Just prior to the conference Professor Tom Devine received word that he had been awarded a knighthood in the Queen's Birthday Honours for 'services to the study of Scottish history'. We therefore conceptualised this volume as a tribute to him, containing as it does many contributions from former colleagues and students. As with other colleagues, past and present, we are grateful to Tom for his support of our initiatives over the years, and hope he will enjoy this book in his honour.

Two contributors deserve special mention. We would particularly like to thank the leading historian of modern Ireland and its diaspora, Professor David Fitzpatrick of Trinity College, Dublin, who took on the chore of appraising several published works on Scottish diaspora history in the context of comparison with Ireland. David has characteristically provided a deep challenge to historians of Scotland's migration as they continue to advance the field. We also are deeply appreciative of Professor Eric Richards who read all the chapters in this book and provided in an Afterword his cogent thoughts on the volume and the field of study. Finally, we are grateful to Nigel Dalziel for help with the index.

Angela McCarthy and John M. MacKenzie

Sir Tom Devine speaks at the Scottish Festival in Dunedin, New Zealand, 2011. (Courtesy of *Otago Daily Times*)

A Tribute to Sir Tom Devine

John M. MacKenzie

No Scottish historian has ever had as prominent a profile as Tom Devine. And it is a profile that is as high among the Scottish public (and further afield) as it is in academia, for he has never pursued his historical activity in an ivory tower. He has always been a fully involved scholar, organically connected to the culture and society that produced him. This helps to explain why he can additionally be described as the most influential modern historian of his generation. That influence can be identified in at least four significant dimensions:

- in the writing of academic history of the highest quality
- in the raising of funds and the creation of major research institutes to develop, direct and release the research of others
- in the public presentation of Scottish history both within and outside Scotland, inspiring a following usually found only in respect of popular writers
- in providing political and social commentary which brings historical perspectives to bear on current issues such as Scottish devolution and the 2014 independence referendum debate.

In the pursuit of all of these, Tom has been indefatigable in his involvement in public bodies; in delivering notable lectures not only in Scotland, but elsewhere in the United Kingdom as well as in Canada, the United States, New Zealand and throughout Europe; in writing in newspapers, recently particularly *The Herald*; and in media appearances on radio and on television. When we put into the mix highly influential positions in three Scottish universities (including a deputy principal-ship), adjunct professorships in both Canada and the United States, and a striking collection of prizes, medals, honours and honorary degrees from universities in Scotland and Northern Ireland, it becomes hard to believe that he has managed to cram it all into one career.

This tribute could very easily become a series of rather boring lists, for staggeringly long listings, all of them reflecting successfully accomplished projects and publications, constitute the bulk of Tom's curriculum vitae. Just to take the research topics he has undertaken, we find that they cover thirty-two themes. These range from Glasgow merchants and colonial trade, together with the effects of that trade on the Scottish economy, to various aspects of rural life and agrarian change (including illicit whisky making); from famine in Scotland to comparative studies of the social and economic history of Ireland; from the history of Glasgow and issues of urban expansion to elites and landowning in the Highlands; from mortality in Scottish coalmining to Irish immigration; from women workers to radical reform; from general histories of Scotland to the Scottish diaspora and what may be called the Scottish Empire; and most recently, from Scotland and the Union to Scotland and slavery.

He is the originator of the influential and felicitously named 'Devine paradox', the conundrum as to why Scottish emigration could only be rivalled by that from Ireland and Norway, despite Scotland's status (unlike them) as an advanced industrial economy. All of this reveals a formidable range, yet this brief survey fails to cover it all. In the pursuit of all of this, he has raised a staggering amount of research money, amounting to more than £4.5 million between 1976 and 2013. This includes the remarkable sums he secured to found the AHRC Research Centre for Irish and Scottish Studies at the University of Aberdeen, Irish-American funds and the support of the Glucksman family for the endowment of the chair that would continue this Centre's work, various awards for the Scottish Centre for Diaspora Studies at the University of Edinburgh and many other grants and bequests. And when Tom founds research centres, he always ensures that they swiftly reach a high standard of international excellence and are hailed as such.

It has undoubtedly been his recent major trilogy, the best-selling *The Scottish Nation* (1999), *Scotland's Empire* (2003) and *To the Ends of the Earth: Scotland's Global Diaspora* (2011), which has helped to seal Tom's dominance in Scottish historical studies. *The Scottish Nation*, when first published, covered the years from 1700 to 2000, enabling him to set the scene in pre-Union Scotland, deal with the major political, social, agricultural and urban changes of the eighteenth century in which he has long been expert, as well as examine the dramatic transformation of the nineteenth and the problems of decline in the twentieth. The book ends on a note of optimism, with the final chapter entitled 'A Nation Reborn?' Its concluding sentences suggest that with the meeting of the new Scottish parliament in July 1999, 'the Scottish nation undeniably embarked on another exciting stage in its long history'. But we should note the word 'nation'. Tom has always been alert to the fact that since 1707 Scotland has been a nation without a state. Perhaps it was this which led him increasingly in the direction of examining the global significance of the Scots with their extraordinary export of their culture and civil society throughout the world.

Scotland's Empire also covered a long period, in this case from 1600 to 1815. The first chapter, 'A Nation of Emigrants', picked up on that striking propensity of the Scots for apparently restless mobility, first of all in the Low Countries, Scandinavia, the Baltic regions and eastern Europe, later throughout the globe. The book proceeded to chart the social and economic reasons for this, including of course a marginal environment, poverty, stereotyping as a naturally martial people, educational attainment and perhaps (but low down the list) the spirit of adventure. By the end of the work, Tom is uncompromising. Having examined the manner in which 'Highlandism', associated with Jacobitism and the influence of Sir Walter Scott, forged Scottish identity in the nineteenth century, he asserts that 'virtually every other sphere of Scottish life, from economy to emigration, from rural transformation to political development, was fashioned in large part by engagement with empire'. Thus the Scots were indeed very far from being 'absent-minded imperialists'. And he could have added that 'Highlandism' was thereby exported throughout the world, re-forging Scottish identities in global contexts.

But these were among the many themes he took up in *To the Ends of the Earth: Scotland's Global Diaspora*, covering the years 1750 to 2010. This is a book which is about a great deal more than the migrations suggested by the title. One chapter constituted a significant return to the question of slavery, which Tom recognised that he had earlier neglected. It examined trade and industry in their imperial dimensions, as well as dealing with geographical destinations (the United States as well as imperial), relationships (sometimes violent) with indigenous peoples, as well as occupational categories such as traders, missionaries and soldiers. He was also concerned to examine the reciprocal effects upon Scotland, not least the ways in which overseas opportunities and success could be contrasted with social deprivation, the mal-distribution of wealth and class distinctions to be found in Scotland itself. And that offers a clue to a key theme which has run through so much of his work: the condition of the people. Tom has always been concerned with the full range of social classes, not least with the common people. Title after title of his early work proves this to have been the case.

It is now time to return to these earlier publications, so we asked the Historiographer Royal of Scotland, Professor Emeritus Christopher Smout, for his assessment:

Tom was, of course a highly distinguished Scottish economic and social historian long before he first became involved in the diaspora project. It is forty years since his Strathclyde PhD was published in 1975, as his first book, *The Tobacco Lords*. As suggested above, he refers to it now with a note of apology because it failed to mention the slavery on which the trade was based, but it remains pivotal, the only book-length treatment of the subject by a Scottish scholar (*and* he has recently set about making handsome amends on the slavery front). Alongside the works of the great American historian Jacob Price from the same decade, it is still where we start and finish in the history of that first post-union economic success story.

Economic history at that time was obsessed by the eighteenth-century origins of the industrial revolution, which in Scotland also encompassed very dramatic, and interlinking, agrarian and commercial changes, all themes on which, in particular, Henry Hamilton of Aberdeen and Roy Campbell of Glasgow had already written fluently. Tom threw himself into the debate in a series of articles and contributions to volumes of essays, including several books edited or co-edited by himself, increasingly reaching over into the nineteenth century. He dealt acutely with several subjects, ranging from the exceptional pace of Scottish urbanisation to the relative passivity of Scottish rural society (the latter a notion which made people cross), from the political economy of the union to the temporary and seasonal migration of Highland workers. When he became head of department at Strathclyde, he made the seminars there a point of national energy for Scottish economic and social history, and a number of edited volumes were its fruits.

Not least in his achievements were his contributions to the Scottish–Irish seminars which tried to compare and contrast the economic and social experience of the two countries in their relationship with England, especially in the eighteenth and nineteenth centuries. It also involved their relationship with each other, leading to an edited volume on *Irish Immigrants and Scottish Society in the Nineteenth and Twentieth Centuries* in 1991, the first modern account of the matter. All this work was ultimately recognised by his election to the Royal Irish Academy, and it led later to a national discussion in Scotland on the extent to which anti-Catholic discrimination still existed as a cultural force. This was a particular personal interest of Tom's, both as a Catholic and as the descendant of Irish immigrants, though he himself felt that such discrimination was largely a thing of the past. He has always seen the burning relevance of history to the present day, and never hesitated to give his opinion on modern as well as historical matters of culture and politics.

Perhaps it was this awareness of the experience of another Celtic society that drew him into a book on *The Great Highland Famine*, published in 1988. It was to infuriate those who regarded the Clearances as a form of cultural genocide carried out against a helpless peasantry by malevolent lairds, since Devine, on the basis of detailed research into government and estate papers, attributed the economic deterioration that preceded the famine not to wickedness but largely to external economic forces, to internal demographic circumstances manifested in the rise of population since 1750, and to the misjudgement of lairds. His critics accused him of 'History from Above', as though it was a crime to read the contemporary documents and the printed record, rather than just to listen to 'traditional' songs and stories from the dispossessed. He did, however, also illuminatingly discuss the racism of Lowland commentators and the prejudice of British civil servants who regarded Celts as their biological and moral inferiors. His work is in the tradition of Eric Richards and Malcolm Gray but is unlikely ever to be flavour of the month at Sabhal Mòr Ostaig.

In my own opinion, however, his most important early book was *The Transformation of Rural Scotland: Social Change and the Agrarian Economy, 1660–1815*, of 1994, an exploration of the Lowland agricultural revolution again marked by the depth and design of research, and acuity of observations. Its particular strength was to use well-chosen local studies, from estate papers, to test the generalisations of improving writers, and thereby to work out the timing, scale and scope of change. He had much to say about dispossession (a topic which the improvers themselves shied off), showing how among farmers dispossession was modest in scale and steady rather than abrupt in timing, but among cottars the experience was often more traumatic, like that which overwhelmed the Highlands. This has popularised the notion of Lowland Clearances – not a particularly happy term, as it tends to lump everyone together as victims and to deny any positive pull of the towns. Agrarian economic history is no longer in fashion, and perhaps the most glaring gap left in all Scottish history of recent centuries is a volume to follow up this masterpiece by covering the century after 1815, a time when Scottish farming was a model to the European world.

The general public, however, would probably name his enormous narrative account written for Penguin in 1999 – it ran to 696 pages – *The Scottish Nation, 1700–2000*, as his greatest achievement of these years. It certainly took Scotland by storm in the best-seller lists, bought far beyond the universities and their students. This was the more remarkable as it is by no means an easy read: it is serious, well argued, carefully documented and impressively wide-ranging in its scope. Plainly it hit the public wish for authoritative history, a volume by a scholar who was deeply informed, clear about his opinions and quite free from the sentimentality and romance popularly associated with the name of Scottish history.

With it Tom shot to national fame, moved first to Aberdeen and then to Edinburgh: he became a public intellectual and greatly enjoyed himself affixed to the national firmament. No one deserved academic stardom more, but there was no resting on any laurels. His drive and originality were to lead him to a whole new area hitherto almost completely neglected in modern scholarship in Scotland, diaspora studies, and what followed is the matter of this book.

Let us now return to Tom the man, his personality and character, as well as his plans for the future now that he has entered his eighth decade. To say that Tom is one of the most energetic historians around would be something of an understatement. He attends and presents papers at conferences (frequently also organised by him) and gives many distin-guished named lectures in Scotland, Ireland and elsewhere across the world (notably in North America). His propensity to lecture without notes is always impressive. His membership and chairmanship of com-mittees, of boards of governors, councils and trustees, as well as of edi-torial boards, academic consultancies and advisory panels also presents a formidable list, but they include (in no particular order) the National Museum of Scotland, Historic Scotland, the Historical Association of the United Kingdom, the Royal Society of Edinburgh, the British Academy, the Economic and Social Research Council, Trinity College Dublin, the Saltire Society, *The Scotsman, Scotland on Sunday*, as well as advisory roles for the United Kingdom, Irish and Scottish governments. When we add to this the host of undergraduates he has taught (in some fourteen courses covering British, Scottish, Irish, economic, cultural and global history), his twenty-seven postgraduate supervisions, external examiner-ships and the many university committees that oppress us all, it becomes all the more extraordinary that his scholarly output has been so prolific. Perhaps not the least of his skills is that he is also good at delegation.

But Tom is of course also active in his church, in the Scottish Catholic History Society, and in his local community. Above all he is a family man, a devoted husband, father and grandfather, who has had his share of tragedy as well as triumph (*The Scottish Nation* is dedicated to the memory of his son John, while *Scotland's Empire* hails the arrival of his grandson). He is highly sociable, loving to debate, and sometimes argue, over a drink in the pub. He is a generous friend and host who combines an occasional gruffness of manner with affectionate good humour and banter. He is an active collaborator, sending comments on chapters or articles in what feels like minutes after their receipt. Modern technology has ensured that he can answer emails literally in seconds wherever he is, even when the messages constitute commiseration on health problems or congratulations on his honours and knighthood. He is naturally and justifiably proud of his achievements, not least of the unique honour of his triple fellowships of the British Academy, the Royal Society of Edinburgh and (in an honorary capacity) the Royal Irish Academy. His knighthood was all the more remarkable because it was the first ever granted to a scholar for 'services to the study of Scottish history'.

It is something of a relief to find that he spends as much time as he can at his cottage on the Isle of Mull, for which he clearly has a considerable affection. Tom, given his origins and lived experience, has always seemed like an intensely urban person, but it was on Mull that he was photographed in almost romantic and certainly countrified poses for, of all journals, the *Scottish Field*. This, the magazine of the 'green welly' rural, horsy, huntin', shootin' and fishin' fraternity, seemed like a highly unlikely vehicle for a profile of the radical, city-bred Devine. But it is perhaps also an outlet for those who love Scotland in all its guises, not least in promoting its distinctive identity. The writer of the article, Kevin McKenna, described himself as 'chastened and scolded by Scotland's most eminent historian' for daring to produce a callow explanation for the lack of any revolution in Scotland against the British state. McKenna was more perceptive about Tom himself and is worth quoting:

> The creases on his face could only belong to someone for whom mirth and laughter are not chores, though they hint at pain too. He is endlessly gossipy and wants to hear the latest about the newspaper world, Celtic FC and all the news that's unfit to print about those who occupy our parliament.

In the interview, Tom was both revealing and moving about his Irish grandparents, who migrated to Scotland from Donegal and Cavan in the 1890s, surely providing him with his empathy for all migrants, as he was about his own upbringing and pride that his father was one of the first working-class Catholic graduates from an Irish background. He also described his slow conversion towards the study of history and his eventual realisation that it is (one of his favourite phrases this) the 'Queen of Disciplines'. McKenna responded by calling him not only a prince of Scottish historians, the man who has done more than anyone to connect Scots with their past, but also as someone who, through his work on identities, could be described as a sort of 'father of the nation'.

Tom also proclaimed the extent to which he believes Scotland has moved on from its days of intense anti-Catholic discrimination. And that reminds me of one of my own memories of Tom. We were attending a conference together and suddenly he said to me, 'You'll never guess who rang me last night'. 'Right, Tom: I'll never guess.' 'The Cardinal', he responded with that characteristic hint of triumph mixed with jollity (this was Thomas Winning), 'threatened me with excommunication, he did'. 'Go on, Tom, he must have been joking!' The distinguished composer (now Sir) James MacMillan had given an Edinburgh Festival lecture in which he had suggested that there was still some discrimination against Catholics in Scotland. Inevitably, the media had been straight on to Tom, who had denied it. Hence the Cardinal's call requesting that he toe the party line!

But Tom has never toed party lines. And that was perhaps why, after a period of teasing, he announced his conversion in 2014 to the Yes vote in the Scottish independence referendum. He had already been a prominent commentator, but he was, quite naturally, instantly everywhere, from television news programmes to Radio 4's 'Any Questions?', the UK national newspapers as well as the Scottish ones, and some overseas as well.

Quotes about Tom are legion but perhaps it is appropriate to end with some highly pertinent ones: *The Herald* described him as 'Scotland's chronicler' in 1999. Colin Kidd in the *Times Literary Supplement* suggested that he had brought 'Scottish historiography into rigorous and unsentimental alignments with developments internationally'. Two Harvard professors contributed their sound bites. Niall Ferguson, whose politics must be miles away from Tom's own, described him as 'the pre-eminent historian of modern Scotland' while David Armitage announced that he was 'the undoubted doyen of the field'. Most strikingly, Martin Kelly asserted that Tom is not only 'Scotland's greatest living historian, but should also be regarded as our principal man of letters'. In 2014 Tom was listed at number sixteen in the top twenty of the *Herald* newspaper's 100 most powerful and influential people in Scotland: 'The nation's preeminent historian, a towering and fearless intellect . . . an academic tornado from early in his career (who has) reshaped the way the Scottish past is viewed.' The following year the Catholic journal *The Tablet* placed him seventh out of the top 100 Catholics in the United Kingdom. Tom has also indulged in public debates with senior politicians, leading to remarkable compliments from figures such as ex-prime minister Gordon Brown, current prime minister David Cameron and cabinet secretaries in the Scottish government.

All this provides more than enough comfortable praise for Tom to rest on, but there is no sign of that. He is involved in a collaborative project to examine the Scottish influence on the Ceylonese (Sri Lankan) tea industry and has just produced books on Scotland and slavery, and the Union. The former in particular contains some surprises for an orthodox English historiography on the subject. Despite achieving the biblical three score years and ten in 2015, there is no sign of Tom slowing down. Nor would we want him to. All historians look forward to continuing to be stimulated, intrigued – and sometimes irritated (in a constructive way) – by his work and his comments for some time to come. No doubt there are more 'Devine paradoxes' in the making.

1

Introduction
Global Migrations:
The Scottish Diaspora since 1600

Angela McCarthy and John M. MacKenzie

SINCE THE SEVENTEENTH CENTURY, an estimated 3.6 million Scots have left their homeland. This mobility was built on movement since the Middle Ages. During the past two decades, historians have increasingly sought to map the volume, chronology and profile of this migration, conceptualised by some as Scotland's diaspora.[1] The rate of migration (including that to the rest of the United Kingdom) was surpassed in some periods only by Ireland, Norway and Italy and, most strikingly, net out migration continued until the 1990s. Faced with this notable phenomenon, early studies concentrated on motives for migration and the Scottish influence and contributions – particularly economic and cultural – in new lands. More recent work has endeavoured to explore the experiences of migrants including key themes of retention of ethnic characteristics and identities.[2]

Several broad outlines emerge from these studies. First, Scottish mobility can be seen as global, not simply imperial, with the destinations to which Scots gravitated changing over time. Early mobility, for instance, was centred on Europe (especially Scandinavia, the Baltic and Poland), with Scots moving there as soldiers, pedlars and traders. From the seventeenth century, however, Scots began to colonise Ireland in considerable numbers and from the 1650s could be found in the Caribbean and the thirteen eastern colonies of North America. Only after the 1750s, however, did Scottish sojourners and settlers really begin to penetrate North America, the West Indies, Asia, Australasia and Africa.[3] Second, the size of the outflow differed over time. Emigration in the seventeenth century was more voluminous than the eighteenth. But with improved communications, transport and vast new opportunities in the host lands in the nineteenth century, population outflows increased exponentially. The era of mass migration between 1815 and 1930 resulted in at least 50 million people (but more likely 60 million) leaving Europe. Britain and Ireland's portion of this mobility comprised around 18.7 million, which was approximately 36 per cent of all European migrants (at a time when Britain and Ireland constituted between 10 and 11 per cent of Europe's total population). Scotland's share was around 2 million.[4] Third, the motives for migration from Scotland changed in very broad terms, when judged at the macro level, from deprivation to aspiration. Fourth, Scottish distinctiveness in contributions to new lands is visible in such areas as economic enterprise, environmental transformation and missionary activity.[5]

This volume seeks to extend our knowledge of this striking mobility. It engages with key themes that have resonance to wider scholarship – including cross-cultural encounters, slavery and empire. Three areas of analysis, however, stand out across the volume: ethnicity, relationships with indigenous peoples, impact at home and comparative frameworks. To each of these we now turn.

ETHNICITY AMONG THE MIGRANT AND MULTIGENERATIONAL GROUPS

Ethnicity – encompassing both migrants and the multigenerational descent group – is a key issue within studies of migration. Yet historians have tended to be sceptical about claims to Scots exceptionalism. They have been anxious about such notions as the myth of the enterprising Scot, or of the capitalistic Scot, bred in Weberian Calvinism, or the alleged myth of the educated and literate Scot. To these we can add such notions as the martial race Scot and the 'exotic' Scot, apparently obliterating a distinctive and valued culture in favour of the Highland forms of the defeated Jacobites. Additionally, there are the supposed myths of the intellectual and Enlightened Scot and of the radical Scot. Each has perhaps smacked too much of the self-regarding 'Here's tae us, wha's like us?' school. And it may be said that the kernel of truth at the centre of these myths sometimes becomes more apparent in the global setting. Yet can we agree with Eric Richards, in his thoughtful Afterword to this volume, that 'the quest for distinctive markers is now yielding diminishing returns'?

In this book, Angela McCarthy utilises a case study of James Taylor, 'father of the Ceylon tea enterprise', to raise questions regarding the role of his Scottish origins in shaping his achievements abroad. In particular, she highlights his educational background and agricultural and industrial developments in Scotland as being just as important to consider as factors in Ceylon. In doing so, McCarthy provides an alternative perspective to David Fitzpatrick's emphasis in Chapter 13 on opportunities

in new lands and his claim that 'home skills were often unexportable'.
Stuart Allan and David Forsyth, meanwhile, seek to explain the stronger
Scottish military tradition among the expeditionary forces of Canada
and South Africa during the First World War compared with Australia
and New Zealand. Despite such divergence, there were attempts among
troops of all countries to maintain a Scottish identity, particularly in the
piping and drumming tradition. Iain Watson, on the other hand, examines identity among 'sojourners' and 'settlers' in Hong Kong and New
Zealand, and the descent group in the latter through the use of questionnaires and oral interviews. Both migrant groups cited the significance
of the bagpipes, music and dancing, and history, tradition and customs.
For migrants in Hong Kong, however, food, drink and the environment
were more distinctive than family, hospitality and humour as cited by
their counterparts in New Zealand. These migrants are, however, selective about the aspects of a Scottish identity they deploy and their usage
varies in many ways.

Beyond this great exodus of people, ethnicity encompasses others
including the multigenerational descent group. Watson's chapter is
intriguing for his comparisons between migrant and descent perceptions of Scottish identity. One particularly striking finding emerges
from his question to respondents as to what distinctive event defines
Scotland and Scottish migration. Migrants chose Bruce, the Wars of
Independence, the Union of the Crowns and/or Parliaments, Culloden
and the Jacobites. Descendants, on the other hand, placed great emphasis on the Clearances. International students with Scottish ancestry
who spent four months in Edinburgh in 2013 are the focus of Tawny
Paul's assessment of the encounter between their imagined heritage,
based in part on family stories, and the 'real' Scotland. Capturing their
observations in written, oral and visual forms, these young folk held
a perception of Scottishness tied to the pipes, castles and clans of the
Highlands rather than urban Edinburgh. Through their encounters with
Edinburgh's past and present, they were forced to reconsider their perception of Scotland. Erin Grant, meanwhile, draws on her research with
female pipers descended from Scottish migrants to argue that their personal expressions of Scottish identity emerged more from their personal
ties to Scotland than their involvement with pipe bands.

We might also include 'affinity Scots', those with an attachment to
Scotland but without genealogical roots. David Hesse explores these
Northern Europeans in the period after 1945 when musicians, athletes,
re-enactors and commemorators conveyed enthusiasm for Scotland in
several ways. Influenced by film, novels, the media and Scottish nation-

alism, Hesse argues that these affinity Scots chose to identify with Scotland as their own heritage was unavailable, bland or too problematic. Yet the Scotland they did identify with was a selective – and highly romantic – one.

Ethnicity is likewise at the heart of chapters by Colin Calloway and Ann Curthoys, which seek to examine Scottish relations with indigenous peoples. The evidence indicates that Scots were no different than other ethnicities in their frontier behaviour, participating in violence, dispossession and sexual abuse against native peoples. Importantly, Colin Calloway shows here and elsewhere that indigenous peoples did identify different ethnicities and draw parallels with the Scots. So too did Scots draw parallels with indigenous peoples as evident in works on the Scots in Africa and New Zealand.[6] Research also points to Scots being more prepared to learn from Maori environmental practices.[7] In these ways Scots were distinctive from English migrants where research has yet to indicate any affinity. We might therefore hypothesise that some migrant connections to indigenous peoples, imagined or otherwise, emerge from a sense of oppression felt by minority groups. Evidence elsewhere, for instance, points to Jewish migrants in New Zealand similarly identifying with Maori.[8] Parallels were also drawn between indigenous peoples and Irish Catholics.[9]

Such an explanation, however, misses other reasons for migrant connections to different peoples, especially cultural factors. In his chapter, John MacKenzie suggests that, although a variety of different Scottish diasporas can be identified in the case of Africa, the contribution of Scots was invariably distinctive. The Presbyterian church and Scottish missions appeared in different parts of the continent and, in each case, were significant in both the medical and educational fields, most notably on the eastern Cape and in Malawi. Where they settled, as in southern Africa, they brought different skill sets to bear, in the press, in the creation of financial institutions, in frontier farming and as artisans in construction and in mining. Their ethnicity was marked out both by governors (who considered that they suited frontier conditions) and by indigenous Africans, who distinguished them from the English, strikingly in the competitive dance troupes which emerged both in East and in South Africa. This demonstrates that when we focus on the cultural dimensions, distinctive ethnicities do become salient.

IMPACT AT HOME

Despite two important edited collections about return migration and Tom Devine's argument that interactions and relationships between homeland and destination be incorporated in any study of mobility, this avenue of investigation is still an overlooked aspect within studies of Scotland's diaspora.[10] The influence of migration on the Scottish homeland is then a second important theme addressed in this book. Andrew Mackillop offers a wide-ranging assessment of profit and loss to Scotland between 1600 and 1800. As well as considering the repatriation of monies, goods and assets, he also draws attention to human capital and the intellectual and cultural benefits for Scotland of migration. Two key findings emerge here. In the period before 1700 Scottish migrants tended to integrate, which explains the minimal reverse impact of these migrations on Scotland. For the period between 1700 and 1800, by contrast, that impact was greater, despite a smaller outflow of people. David Alston, meanwhile, uses behavioural economics to posit an explanation for the apparently dangerous choice of Highland Scots moving to such a risky environment as Guyana. Assessing the prospective losses or gains for those receiving information in Scotland he emphasises that negative views received back in Scotland had no traction given the emphasis on stories of success. Whether such a theory can be applied to the decisions made by other ethnicities or Scots in different environs is clearly an issue for future research.

While we do not have for the nineteenth century onwards a similar account to Mackillop's profit and loss exploration, some pertinent points can be made. The first is that Scotland's diasporas cannot be separated from the history of investment, trade and finance since migration and settlement are clearly bound up with economic knowledge of and responses to the outer world. We therefore have to think in terms of financial institutions in Scotland, in particular the global significance of Scottish banks and bankers, of the distinctive role of Scottish law and of Scots solicitors in putting investors in touch with overseas borrowers. And to these we must add important Scots financial innovations, such as mutuality (the ownership of insurance companies, for example, by all the investors), which Scots carried with them around the world. These appealed to Scottish investors in spreading risks, offering a sense of ownership, while also securing expert advice. At any rate, the scale of investment was striking, growing from £60 million in 1867 to £200 million in 1913. An extra dimension here is the extent to which women became prominent investors in overseas ventures. In 1913, Scottish women held 21 per cent of overseas investments. But if the scale of investment seems clear, what happened to the returns on those investments is much more obscure.[11]

Connected with this is the extent to which Scottish specialities, for example in engineering, or in skilled trades, such as stonemasons, carpenters, foresters and so on, produce opportunities not only for the migrants, but also for the social and economic contexts which supported them. Glasgow supplied engineers throughout the world, notably to Argentinian and Indian railways. Aberdeen produced stonemasons for construction works, for example in ports, throughout the British Empire and beyond. Scottish estate foresters carved out careers for themselves in India and elsewhere. Such sectors produced opportunities for individuals, for those who replaced them, and for the services which supported them. Moreover, if we accept that Scots exported their civil society around the world, it may be that the global significance of Scots expertise had effects upon the Scottish universities, promoting disciplines such as medicine, public health, botany, forestry, anthropology and theology. Thus, Scottish universities, despite their innate conservatism, developed disciplines that were strikingly innovative in the late nineteenth century, and often ahead of their English counterparts. The Scottish publishing industry also benefited, with book and journal exports finding Scottish diasporic markets. This helps to explain the emergence of Glasgow and Edinburgh as major publishing centres, as well as key producers of cartography. The logistics of migration would have stimulated this publishing sector, as well as others both small and large scale, from agencies to shipbuilding. Associational culture throughout the formal and informal empires helped to promote 'brand loyalty' in respect of many Scottish exports from whisky and beer to iron products. Moreover, great entrepreneurs, such as the shipowners Sir William Mackinnon, Sir Donald Currie and others, brought major orders to Scottish shipyards and their ancillary industries.

The massive outflow of funds from Scotland was inevitable in a global private enterprise economy. But to what extent was the considerable investment overseas a promoter of underdevelopment and underemployment at home? By the 1870s, most informed commentators agreed that there was a surplus of capital at home after the end of the vast railway boom in the preceding three decades and the continuing surge of worldwide profits from Scottish manufactured exports. Interest rates abroad were much more attractive than earnings at home. Yet there were indeed great social needs for investment in Scotland, not least to tackle the appalling problems of Scottish working class housing at the time. But the

financial returns were too trifling and the risks too great to attract investors compared with the opportunities to be had in funding the railways of
Canada, building the cities of the United States and resourcing the sheep
runs of New Zealand and Australia. Profits on external investments,
then, were much greater than internal investment.[12]

Or was the export of population a means of avoiding even greater
social deprivation? It appears to be the case in very broad terms that
Scottish migration in the earlier period was skewed towards the poorer
in Scottish society and later towards the semi-skilled and skilled with
a significant minority of professional migration occurring in parallel.
Moreover, we need to consider the extent of individual migrant remittances back to families at home. The post office records have been used
to reveal the extraordinary scale of such remittances to Cornwall.[13] This
might constitute a significant element on the profit side, although such
remittances may have helped to develop further family serial migration.
It is also often forgotten that the large contingent of Scottish migrants in
the modern period must have also channelled capital abroad. Most had
some means when they left Scotland, especially the skilled and professional classes who were a key part of the exodus in the nineteenth and
twentieth centuries. Moreover, the rate of return migration to Scotland
in the late Victoria era of around one third (less than levels for Italy,
Spain and Sweden) did not compensate for the overall haemorrhage of
resources especially when the national funding of the education of the
migrants in taken into account.[14] At a later date, the development of
'roots tourism' has been a significant factor in the twentieth century,
starting from relatively small beginnings and developing to a much
greater extent as the twentieth century wore on, culminating in the
concept of 'Homecoming' in modern times.

But most importantly, it is clear that Scottish industry became dangerously dependent on foreign markets, developing a high degree of
vulnerability. This was true in terms of textile manufacture where disruptions in the supply of raw material as well as import substitution
in imperial territories led to serious decline in linen, cotton and jute.[15]
The Scottish dependence on heavy industries became more pronounced
and this led to serious consequences in the twentieth century as Scots
exported their technologies to countries, particularly in the Far East,
which were able to reduce labour and other costs such that Scottish
production was priced out of the market. But finally it may be said that
there was a certain psychic return upon the Scots global presence, one
which certainly fed into the developing nationalism from the 1930s
onwards.

COMPARATIVE APPROACHES

The third key contribution of this volume is the deployment of comparative frameworks to advance our knowledge of the Scottish outflow particularly from the twentieth century onwards. Such comparisons to date, however, have mostly focused on similarities and differences between the Scots and the Irish. Comparing the movement of the Catholic Irish with the Scots to the United States in the nineteenth century, Devine concludes that 'divergence rather than convergence was often the norm'.[16] He identifies several key differences to explain the more positive reception of the Scots: their Protestantism, dispersed settlement and skill base. By contrast, the Irish were negatively typecast for their Catholic faith, poverty, the scale of their migration and their unskilled occupations.[17] Meanwhile, the key variable contributing to 'differentiation in the immigration experience' derives, Devine reckons, from the 'contrasting paths of development of the countries from which they had come after the 1850s'. Scotland, more industrial than Ireland's rural agricultural economy, supplied a more skilled workforce.[18] McCarthy's exploration of the personal testimonies of Scottish and Irish migrants who ventured to a range of destinations in the twentieth century, meanwhile, points to 'subtle differences rather than yawning cultural gaps . . . similarities in attitude and expectation are more common than divergent or unique experiences'.[19] Where England fits into these comparisons remains to be seen.

This agenda of examining comparative migration from Scotland and Ireland emerged out of a broader legacy of comparison between the domestic histories of these societies which began from the late 1970s with a series of edited collections. Much of the earlier work focused on the differing economies and social structures of the two societies.[20] Comparisons were made of agricultural productivity, trade, cities, banking, income, landed society, wages, unrest, Poor Law, industries and policy, among other themes. More recent comparisons incorporate cultural aspects including literature, cinema and language.[21] Such was the success of these comparative initiatives that centres for Irish and Scottish Studies emerged in the northern and southern hemispheres.[22]

Explicit comparison between the Scots in different destinations, by contrast, has less readily been undertaken. Instead, studies incorporating the Scottish experience in diverse new lands tend to examine each destination on its own terms, thereby failing to tease out similarities and differences.[23] Two recent postgraduate theses, by contrast, point to what can be achieved in this respect. Kim Sullivan's investigation of Scottish associational culture in North America and Australasia showed that early migration to North America and the consequent hardships generated a benevolent focus while ethnic associations in Australasia, emerging during a later period, were culturally oriented. She also considered transnational communications, finding that although Scottish societies in New Zealand and Australia were more inclined to pursue such networking, most contact was 'transitory and casual in nature'.[24]

Erin Grant likewise included a comparative framework to examine female pipers in Scotland and its diaspora. She found that these pipe bands possessed similar qualities in terms of their hierarchy, multigenerational membership, music and performances. Differences, however, were gleaned in respect of the extent to which these bands travelled and their participation in competitions. As with Sullivan's assessment of the origins of Scottish associational culture, Grant similarly points to the origins of these female pipe bands being in the diaspora before developing in Scotland.[25] The comparisons she undertakes in this book highlight similarities rather than differences. Female pipe bands in the countries she considers all had strong ties to other Scottish associations and female pipers around the diaspora held similar expressions of personal ethnic identity and connections to Scotland. Other historians, meanwhile, have sought to identify key contrasts between Scottish associations and those of their Irish counterparts. Such research reveals that Scottish societies were products of the diaspora, had cultural and social rather than political and religious aims, and did not form part of an international fraternal movement.[26] The clan societies founded in the twentieth century did, however, develop an international flavour.

In this volume a comparative focus is most firmly adopted in three chapters. First is Allan and Forsyth's examination of Scottish identity in the military culture of the expeditionary forces of Canada, South Africa, Australia and New Zealand during the First World War. Their explanation for differences in the expression of a Scottish identity in the forces lies with the imperial politics of pre-war military administration and the organisation and local circumstances of mobilisation. Comparison is also at the heart of Watson's assessment of twentieth-century migrants to Hong Kong and both migrants and the multigenerational descent group in New Zealand. He outlines various contrasts to questions surrounding the distinctive features of Scottish culture and events, what historical books are read and how well-informed these groups are about Scotland. His key argument is that Scottishness across all groups is individually constructed and manufactured. For migrants, it is used as a tool to facilitate integration with environment and time from departure influencing perceptions. For the descent group, such perceptions are more romantic, shaped by both time and distance from the homeland.

The third and most expansive comparative chapter is David Fitzpatrick's robust challenge towards the end of this book. With characteristic panache and an enviable deployment of statistical evidence to compare Scotland with Ireland and England, he calls into question claims of a distinctive Scottish diaspora. His argument is centred around six prongs of 'diaspora': its scale; its economic push factors; whether a shared national culture affected performance; success; functioning as an ethnic group; and its impact on Scotland. In all these areas Fitzpatrick contends that the Scots were not distinct from the English. It is a convincing argument on many levels.

We might, however, critique Fitzpatrick's argument in two key ways. First, the term 'diaspora' is hotly contested in various disciplines, but Fitzpatrick provides no justification for his selection of his six 'measures' of diaspora by which to assess Scottish distinctiveness. Other scholars, for instance, have conceptualised diaspora in different ways and Scottish migration is seen as adhering to such formulas. We might think here, for instance, of Rogers Brubaker's 'three core elements that remain widely understood to be constitutive of diaspora': dispersion in space; orientation to a 'homeland'; and boundary-maintenance.[27] Second, by focusing on a largely quantitative approach, Fitzpatrick misses core aspects of a distinctive Scottish diaspora emerging from qualitative data. There is no doubt, as the contributions to this volume attest, that Scottish migrants perceived themselves and were perceived by others as different. Collectively, then, these chapters provide an alternative assessment to Fitzpatrick's argument. It puts the case that there *is* a Scottish diaspora that is distinctive from other national migrations while sharing some features with them. We do, however, firmly support Fitzpatrick's call for comparative compilation and assessment of quantitative datasets to provide statistical evidence for many assumptions of Scottish over-representation and disproportionate achievements in the British world. His chapter constitutes an important corrective which all historians of the Scottish diaspora need to take account of. As Eric Richards points out in his Afterword to this volume, these and other debates will continue to radiate across Scotland's empire.

NOTES

1. For example, T. M. Devine, *To the Ends of the Earth: Scotland's Global Diaspora, 1750–2010* (London: Allen Lane, 2011).
2. For summaries of Scottish migration see chs 7, 16, 22, and 27 in T. M. Devine and Jenny Wormald (eds), *The Oxford Handbook of Modern Scottish History* (Oxford: Oxford University Press, 2012), pp. 500–32. See also John M. MacKenzie and T. M. Devine, 'Introduction', in John M. MacKenzie and T. M. Devine (eds), *Scotland and the British Empire* (Oxford: Oxford University Press, 2011), pp. 1–29.
3. Broad overviews of these points can be found in T. M. Devine, *Scotland's Empire, 1600–1815* (London: Allen Lane, 2003), chs 1 and 2, and Devine, *To the Ends of the Earth*, chs 1 and 4.
4. Dudley Baines, *Emigration from Europe, 1815–1930* (Basingstoke: Macmillan, 1991).
5. See especially John M. MacKenzie and T. M. Devine, 'Introduction', in MacKenzie and Devine (eds), *Scotland and the British Empire*, pp. 9–19.
6. John M. MacKenzie with Nigel R. Dalziel, *The Scots in South Africa: Ethnicity, Identity, Gender and Race, 1772–1914* (Manchester: Manchester University Press, 2007); Angela McCarthy, *Scottishness and Irishness in New Zealand since 1840* (Manchester: Manchester University Press, 2011), ch. 7; Angela McCarthy, 'Scottish migrant ethnic identities', in MacKenzie and Devine (eds), *Scotland and the British Empire*, pp. 139–40.
7. Tom Brooking, '"Green Scots and Golden Irish": the environmental impact of Scottish and Irish settlers in New Zealand – some preliminary ruminations', *Journal of Irish and Scottish Studies*, 3:1 (2009), p. 52.
8. Leonard Bell, 'Introduction', in Leonard Bell and Diana Morrow (eds), *Jewish Lives in New Zealand: A History* (Auckland: Godwit, 2012), p. 16.
9. See, for instance, Graeme Morton and David A. Wilson (eds), *Irish and Scottish Encounters with Indigenous Peoples: Canada, the United States, New Zealand, and Australia* (Montreal and Kingston: McGill-Queen's University Press, 2013), and McCarthy, *Scottishness and Irishness in New Zealand*, ch. 7.
10. Marjory Harper (ed.), *Emigrant Homecomings: The Return Movement of Emigrants, 1600–2000* (Manchester: Manchester University Press, 2005); Mario Varricchio (ed.), *Back to Caledonia: Scottish Homecomings from the Seventeenth Century to the Present* (Edinburgh: Birlinn, 2012).
11. Christopher Schmitz, 'The nature and dimensions of Scottish foreign investment, 1860–1914', *Business History*, 39:2 (1997), pp. 42–68; Eric Richards, 'Australia and Scotland: the evolution of a long-distance relationship', *Australian Journal of Politics and History*, 56:4 (2010), pp. 485–502. See also R. C. Michie, *Money, Mania and Markets: Investment, Company Formation and the Stock Exchange in Nineteenth-century Scotland* (Edinburgh: John Donald, 1981).

12. Devine, *To the Ends of the Earth*, pp. 248–50.
13. Gary B. Magee and Andrew S. Thompson, 'The global and the local: explaining migrant remittance flows in the English-speaking world, 1880–1914', *Journal of Economic History*, 66 (2006), pp. 177–202, and Magee and Thompson, 'Lines of credit, debts of obligation: migrant remittances to Britain, c. 1875–1913', *Economic History Review*, 59 (2006), pp. 539–77.
14. Devine, *To the Ends of the Earth*, p. 237.
15. See, for example, Bruce Lenman, Charlotte Lythe and Enid Gauldie, *Dundee and its Textile Industry* (Dundee: Abertay Historical Society, 1969), and Jim Tomlinson, *Dundee and the Empire: 'Juteopolis', 1850–1939* (Edinburgh: Edinburgh University Press, 2014).
16. Devine, *To the Ends of the Earth*, p. 126.
17. Ibid. pp. 142–3.
18. Ibid. pp. 143–4.
19. Angela McCarthy, *Personal Narratives of Irish and Scottish Migration, 1921–65: 'For spirit and adventure'* (Manchester: Manchester University Press, 2007), p. 222. See also McCarthy, *Scottishness and Irishness in New Zealand*.
20. T. M. Devine and David Dickson (eds), *Ireland and Scotland, 1600–1850: Parallels and Contrasts in Economic and Social Development* (Edinburgh: John Donald, 1983); Rosalind Mitchison and Peter Roebuck (eds), *Economy and Society in Scotland and Ireland, 1500–1939* (Edinburgh: John Donald, 1988); R. J. Morris and Liam Kennedy (eds), *Ireland and Scotland: Order and Disorder, 1600–2000* (Edinburgh: John Donald, 2005).
21. Liam McIlvanney and Ray Ryan (eds), *Ireland and Scotland: Culture and Society, 1700–2000* (Dublin: Four Courts Press, 2005).
22. For example, centres at the University of Aberdeen, Trinity College Dublin, and University of Otago.
23. See, for example, Devine, *Scotland's Empire*; Marjory Harper, *Emigration from North-East Scotland*, vol. 1: *Willing Exiles* (Aberdeen: Aberdeen University Press, 1988); Tanja Bueltmann, *Clubbing Together: Ethnicity, Civility and Formal Sociability in the Scottish Diaspora to 1930* (Liverpool: Liverpool University Press, 2014); Tanja Bueltmann, Andrew Hinson and Graeme Morton, *The Scottish Diaspora* (Edinburgh: Edinburgh University Press, 2013).
24. Kim Sullivan, 'Scots by association: Scottish diasporic identities and ethnic associations in the nineteenth–early twentieth centuries and the present day', unpublished PhD thesis, University of Otago, 2010, p. 252.
25. Erin C. M. Grant, 'The Ladies' Pipe Band diaspora: bands, bonnie lassies and Scottish associational culture, 1918–2012', unpublished PhD thesis, University of Otago, 2013, pp. 225–6.
26. Tanja Bueltmann and Gerard Horn, 'Emigration and ethnic associational culture in a colonial capital: a comparative study of Wellington's Irish Protestant and Scottish immigrant communities to 1910', in Jennifer Kelly

and R. V. Comerford (eds), *Associational Culture in Ireland and Abroad* (Dublin: Irish Academic Press, 2010), pp. 85–104; Angela McCarthy, *Scottishness and Irishness in New Zealand*, ch. 5.

27. Rogers Brubaker, 'The "diaspora" diaspora', *Ethnic and Racial Studies*, 28:1 (2005), p. 5.

2

'As Hewers of Wood, and Drawers of Water'? Scotland as an Emigrant Nation, c. 1600 to c. 1800

Andrew Mackillop

THIS ATTEMPT TO RETHINK how early modern Scottish emigration might be conceptualised began life as part of a conference which explored the theme of whether the movement overseas of its people worked to Scotland's profit or to its loss.[1] Leaving aside for a moment the entirely legitimate concern that such a complex human phenomenon cannot be so easily reduced to a simple dichotomy, there is little doubt that contemporaries understood the significance of the migrations which seemed such a recurrent feature of Scottish society between the 1603 and 1801 unions. If many commentators at the time wrestled with what to make of the propensity of Scots for mobility, it is unsurprising that some chose to emphasise the positive or negative consequences. In this sense at least, framing the topic in terms of 'profit' or 'loss' is perhaps less anachronistic than might at first seem the case. Take, for example, the sentiments expressed in a pamphlet published in Edinburgh in 1695. Ostensibly, the tract concerned itself with recent trends in the lucrative Europe-to-Asia trades. In explaining Scotland's international standing, the author offered a blunt assessment of the kingdom's experience of emigration since the uniting of the Scottish and English crowns. The conclusion was unequivocal. Despite the migration since the early 1600s of tens of thousands to Ulster, the Scandinavian kingdoms, the Polish–Lithuanian Commonwealth, the Dutch Republic, England and her Atlantic colonies, Scotland had not prospered – the opposite in fact. The pamphlet's preface concluded: 'we had some who raised their fortunes . . . yet still we have been hitherto advancing our neighbours, but securing no colonies, or settlement for ourselves . . . as hewers of wood, and drawers of water.'[2]

The powerful biblical image drawn from *Joshua 9:23* of a faithless people cursed to be forever slaves to others chosen by God would have been immediately clear to any Scot capable of reading the pamphlet in the first place. The laying down of a profound spiritual question mark over a society forced into the large-scale dispersal of its people points to the need to better recapture the religious and rhetorical discourses, alongside the better known socio-economic explanations, by which Scots sought to make comprehensible the departure of so many. What is inescapable in this particular example is the palpable sense that emigration worked to the advantage of other societies but not always, or even usually, for Scotland itself. The point was made all the more cogent by the candid acknowledgement that, for a few, mobility had undoubtedly brought material success. An enhanced understanding of the scale of movement to mainland Europe and Ireland and the ways in which Scots accessed the state apparatus and economies of a range of host societies confirms that early modern mobility could indeed reward and enrich. Individual Scots and their networks of associates had done well throughout the seventeenth and early eighteenth centuries, acquiring landed estates and noble titles as far afield as Sweden, Ulster and New Jersey, or rising to financial and mercantile prominence in entrepôts such as Stockholm, Danzig, Rotterdam, Amsterdam, London and Boston.[3] All this the pamphlet author did not deny. The point was a deeper, structural one. The focus was not on individuals or even larger groupings abroad but on the domestic and material condition of Scottish society as a whole, not least in comparison to the seemingly greater capacity for affluence in the places to which so many Scots moved. The success of the few cast into greater relief the disquieting reality that mass emigration did not seem to give domestic Scottish society demonstrable benefits commensurate with the substantial dissipation of a key national resource. Was the commentator's pessimism justified: did human mobility during the age of mercantilism and empire involve migrant Scots contributing to other societies but not substantially or consistently to their own?

Adopting a cost–benefit analysis of early modern Scottish emigration involves a shift away from some of the basic frameworks by which mobility is interpreted. The subject has been conceived of mainly in terms of quantities, geographies, the forces at work in Scotland and in the receiving society prompting movement, and the different dynamics produced by issues of proximity and the type of emigrant involved.[4] There is also a striking emphasis on what factors maintained Scottish distinctiveness in the host societies, how the original immigrants and successive generations networked and assimilated over time, and what effects their presence had upon the development of the countries they moved to.[5] One consequence of these approaches is the tendency to break up early modern migrations into discrete geographic theatres and particular streams of movement. This finds its most obvious expression in the conventional assessment that until about the 1730s to 1740s, Scotland's migratory horizons were largely continental European, Irish and English in focus, as indeed befitted a medium-sized north European kingdom. Thereafter Scottish emigration became more obviously Atlantic and imperial in nature. This explains why analysis has stressed how the old European destinations gave way via Ulster to the opportunities afforded by connections to England and, after 1707, Britain's empire in the Caribbean, North America and Asia.[6] Matters were, of course, never that neat. Periods of simultaneous multiple movements and gradual organic change, rather than dramatic shifts, characterised geographic realignment during the 1600 to 1800 epoch.[7] The half century between c. 1680 and c. 1730 may well have marked a crucial age of overlap, with established European routes retaining and enhancing their attraction even as links with the Atlantic and Asia worlds developed slowly and intermittently, though ultimately to massive effect.

Ironically, the most obvious destination in terms of continuity over the whole of the early modern age – England – is the one place historians of Scotland have done least to address. Whatever the cause of such striking neglect – the prosaic 'near diaspora' nature of cross-border mobility, the difficulties of tracing Scots in a broadly similar society, or methodological ambivalence towards overly incorporating the history of Scotland into that of her larger neighbour – the upshot is a glaring gap in knowledge.[8] Yet even allowing for the imperative to integrate England into understandings of early modern Scottish migration, the use of this perspective alone perpetuates an understanding of migration as a bilateral, geographically defined movement. It does little to address the specific theme of profit and loss. Assessing the extent of gain or detriment for Scotland requires moving away from explaining only changes in location and asking instead what sort of emigrants left, with what motivations and, crucially, whether they or the proceeds they acquired returned in ways that clearly affected their homeland.[9] This entails a fundamental reconsideration of how mobility is understood in relation to the society and economy from which it emanated. Too often migration is conceptualised as an essentially reactive phenomenon, manifesting itself in response to specific political, military, social or economic conditions. This separating out of human mobility into a discrete process is a mistake which fails to grasp the fact that migration was viewed in early modern Scotland as an export activity in and of itself. In other words, emigration should be understood as the deployment of human capital and as a method by which Scottish society sought to diversify the means of acquiring wealth.

Talk of emigrants as human capital brings to mind the self-regarding adage that Scotland's best export is its people.[10] Leaving aside the 'wha's like us' tone, this maxim relates to the supposedly positive effects Scots had upon the societies they journeyed to, not the impact their departure may have had on Scotland. Thinking of people as wealth in and of themselves changes how emigration can be understood. Human movement becomes an investment strategy, the substituting of venture capital to enhance wealth generating potential. Human capital has been defined as the qualities acquired by or believed by others to be invested in a given individual.[11] Like conventional forms of affluence such as money or tradable goods the human version can be extremely valuable and, crucially, easily transferred by means of migration or emigration.[12] The notion of people and their social networks as a form of capital in their own right is conceptually useful in a Scottish context precisely because societies which lack monetary resources retained the option of deploying the human variety as an alternative form of wealth. The implications for the historic image of a poverty-stricken early modern Scotland are profound, arguably even transformative. Although relatively poor in that it lacked large reserves of venture finance, a range of political, social and economic levers existed that could facilitate the mobilisation of the human variant of wealth. Viewed in this way Scotland was considerably richer or, more precisely, had a much greater potential to generate profits than judgements based on conventional measures of monetary wealth would suggest.

Conceiving of emigration in this way helps to foreground the specific theme of 'profit' and 'loss', although a better starting point is to think in terms of the variable degrees of productivity inherent in all human movement. The concept of human capital can provide an overarching framework within which the many migrant streams emanating from Scotland from the 1600s to 1800s can be considered holistically and comparatively. All the numeric totals suggested for the two centuries from 1600 to 1800 are to all intents and purposes guesstimates. In the context of this dubiety there is a telling general consensus which views the movements of the early 1600s to early 1700s as numerically larger and drawn from a smaller overall population than would be the case between c. 1700 and c. 1800. The eighteenth century is known for the burgeoning of large-scale migrations to North America as a consequence of landlord-induced changes in rural society and the emergence of global forms of sojourning to places as diverse as the Caribbean, South Asia and China.[13] The understandable attention that the onset of 'clearance' and the globalisation of Scottish migration attracts belies the fact that the eighteenth century witnessed a noticeable slowing down of mass, large-scale departures. This era lay sandwiched between an epoch of greater rates of exodus from around the 1600s to the 1700s and again in the century between the end of the Napoleonic Wars and the outbreak of the Great War.[14]

Overall departures for the 100 years after the regal union have been placed in a necessarily broad band of between roughly 160,000 to a liberal estimate of about 240,000.[15] Some of the totals mooted for movement to places such as Ireland, Poland and Sweden are extremely large indeed for a sending society boasting a population of little more than 1 million at any one time. While figures of 30,000 moving to Poland in the early decades of the century are now considered excessive, any potential drop in the overall Scottish rate has been more than compensated for by suggestions that levels of military migration during the Thirty Years War (1618–48) were higher than previously thought. Figures of around 50,000–60,000 form the latest thinking, with the majority serving in the armies of Sweden.[16] In the absence of even basic figures for England, Ireland emerges as the single most important seventeenth-century receiving society. Ulster in particular absorbed large numbers at the beginning and at the end of the century; perhaps as many as 14,000 by the early 1630s, a second pulse in the 1650s, before another, even larger wave during the 1690s and early 1700s. In the latter case warfare, related economic dislocation and famine may have sparked an exodus as high as c. 50,000.[17] If the less dramatic but constant streams of military, commercial, intellectual and episodic migrations to England and the Dutch Republic are factored in, it is understandable how such large overall totals are arrived at. Allowing for a necessary degree of caution, these figures underpin judgements which stress seventeenth-century Scotland's high position in the European emigration league table.[18]

The best informed estimates for the century or so after the British Union of 1707 are somewhere in the order of c. 100,000 to c. 120,000 – again, with figures to England awaiting a systematic effort at recapture. It is interesting that compared to the cautionary injunctions surrounding some of the large accumulative totals for the seventeenth-century, there has been noticeably less debate over whether the post-1707 figures represent excessively high or conservative assessments.[19] They do not, for example, incorporate substantive movements to places like the West Indies, a location that over the course of the second half of the eighteenth century alone attracted c. 12,000 to c. 21,000 Scots.[20] In light of these omissions it is possible that conventional understandings of the total volume of migration over the course of the eighteenth century are too conservative. Yet even allowing for an upward adjustment, alongside the potential for the seventeenth-century calculations being too high, it is clear that fewer Scots moved abroad in the later period. This can be said with some confidence in per capita terms, given that Scotland's population increased from approximately 1 million in 1707 to just over 1.6 million by 1800.[21] If overall patterns evolved slowly, with no sudden dramatic shifts, the end result by the 1750s still represented a fundamental reshaping of the frameworks within which Scotland's emigration history unfolded. Although the seventeenth century witnessed several simultaneous large-scale migration streams, for example in the 1610s to 1630s to Poland, Ulster and Scandinavia, the succeeding century entailed more dramatic geographic dispersal and the maintenance of multiple and concurrent branches of migration for decades at a time. Overall volume declined, but the range of destinations increased, as did the tendency for greater numbers to move across truly oceanic distances. By the 1750s and 1760s this diversification meant sustained if not necessarily large-scale human mobility from Scotland to England, the Caribbean, Asia and both the temperate and Arctic zones of North America.[22] Scottish human capital acquired a far broader range of investment markets through the empire in particular.

These basic structural distinctions are relevant to an analysis of how Scottish human capital produced tangible dividends by dint of emigration. Viewed in this framework it is difficult to avoid the conclusion that much of the large-volume movements of the seventeenth century did not deliver commensurate material benefits to Scotland – exactly the point the 1695 author lamented. This does not mean that these earlier migrant streams did not work to the country's advantage; they clearly did so in a variety of ways and at important historical junctures. The key point is in what degree to the numbers leaving. Attempting a balanced appraisal of the domestic impact of migration under the blunt terms of 'profit' or 'loss' is complicated by the reality that contemporary priorities are difficult to recapture and collate into a homogenised whole. Emigrants were first and foremost individuals and networks of individuals, and what brought them profit could be detrimental for other Scots or ensure little or no gain for Scottish society more generally.[23] Nothing better illustrates this ambiguity than the interaction between Scottish migration and the Covenanting movement. One of the most decisive instances of emigrants clearly influencing Scotland involved the return home of around 300 veteran officers from Swedish service in 1637–8. Many were senior figures with command experience in one of Europe's most advanced military machines. The best known was Alexander Leslie, a

highly capable officer with the rank of field marshal. The arrival back
of a range of junior commissioned officers, forty captains, and at least
twenty-four field officers at the ranks of major, lieutenant colonel and
colonel enabled the rapid development of a cutting edge regimental
system with Scottish manpower raised through the usual proprietary
mechanisms. This shaping of the armies of the Covenant played a central
role in securing Ulster in the early 1640s and was to prove vital in key
English parliamentarian victories in the mid-1640s.[24] Whether all this
was to Scotland's profit or loss does of course depend on perspective. It
is highly unlikely that royalists would have viewed such returns in positive terms; but the influence is indisputable.

The political effects on pre-1707 Scotland of mass migrations to
Ulster underline the difficulties in assessing matters in terms of simple
profit or loss. The consequences of a migratory connection changed
over time as new circumstances and successive waves of movement
added additional complexities and depth. Fear over the possible spread
of Covenanting unrest into Ulster explains in part the punitive policies
of the Restoration regime in Scotland during the 1660s and 1670s.[25]
Conversely, the Ulster link may well have worked to the advantage
of a key interest group in Scotland during the 1706–7 union negotiations. With major military commitments on the continent, English
governments had good reason to view in a conciliatory way the con-
stitutional status of the Presbyterian Kirk for the simple reason they
could ill afford the outbreak of sympathetic unrest among the now
inflated Scottish emigrant communities in the north of Ireland. As one
prominent anti-union tract noted in 1706: 'The Scots in Ireland will not
see their Mothercountry [sic] overpowered with unconcerned Looks'.[26]
However unrealistic these implied threats appear in retrospect, their
existence demonstrates how migration inflected the tone of the union
question in ways that were doubtless noted in London. Could it be that
one of the unintended legacies of the previous century of Scots movement into Ulster was a pragmatic recognition by the English political
elite of the need to accept the Kirk's established status within the proposed union settlement?[27]

It is also difficult to gainsay the proposition that seventeenth-century
emigration patterns benefited Scotland in intellectual and cultural terms.
The departure between 1680 and 1730 of just over 1,000 Scots students
to the great Dutch universities amounted to a strategy of enhancing
human capital. It provided Scottish lawyers, clerics and doctors with
the very latest thinking from one of Europe's most progressive societies.[28] There can be little doubt that the early Enlightenment in Scotland

owed part of its character and timing to this intellectual mobility. This underlines the need to think more capaciously about how various forms of social wealth accumulated in pre-union Scotland beyond monetary or financial resources, and how the legacies of the continental era of emigration shaped key aspects of the country's eighteenth-century history. Indeed, by contributing directly to the emergence of Edinburgh as a primary centre of British-world medicine by the 1750s, the old links with the Dutch Republic influenced the scope and scale of Scots medical migration across the British Empire for 100 years after the original connections had withered.[29]

Before turning to conditions and contrasts with the later period, one remaining subject requires consideration: this relates to the return flow of material wealth generated by migrants. Repatriation of monies, goods and other tangible assets from the continent during the seventeenth and early eighteenth centuries is a topic where much of the research is still in its early stages.[30] While some studies have begun to show particular instances of return flows, surviving evidence for the seventeenth century is neither as systematic nor as accessible if compared with the material available for the next century. As a result, the scale of the dividend from the European era of mobility can be easily underestimated and is certainly difficult to reconstruct other than through a limited number of legal and financial records in one country that often lack an equivalent for the other destinations. Any overall evaluation must therefore tread carefully and strike a balance between the disguising effects of a fragmentary evidence base and any tendency to over-inflate what examples do survive.

The question of returning migratory wealth ties into broader debates on the general state of pre-union Scotland. On the one hand, the pre-1707 kingdom has been viewed as experiencing relative if uneven economic decline and persistent underdevelopment, a societal feature which both caused and was in turn compounded by mass emigration.[31] Countervailing interpretations stress the innovative and dynamic characteristics of Scottish emigration and how human mobility contributed both directly and indirectly to a better overall economic position than is often recognised.[32] In one scenario emigration was a manifestation of underlying problems; the counterclaim is that human mobility and migrant networks helped ease the country's lack of economic diversity and mitigate its weak mercantile and fiscal position. These contrasting positions are encapsulated in the uncertainty surrounding the consequences of the large-scale movement of Scottish pedlars into England and along the Baltic littoral and Scandinavia throughout the sixteenth and seventeenth centuries. One school of thought stresses the extent to which these itinerant trading emigrants became progressively disconnected from the domestic Scottish economy. They increasingly relied on local goods and a diverse range of foreign imports in ways that reduced their capacity or inclination to vent Scottish-sourced goods across north Europe.[33] The contrary emphasis argues that Scots merchants operating out of the main European ports continued to import typical Scottish wares such as wool and leather, often using pedlars at both ends of the supply chain. Having acquired these products from locally based small-time traders across rural Scotland, merchants used commodity stores to supply emigrant Scots pedlars operating in the rural hinterlands of Poland, Prussia and Sweden.[34] The sheer number of individuals involved makes it difficult to conceive how the Scottish economy would not have benefited; but again the question is one of proportion. The nature of this particular form of economy, with its atomised supply and distribution mechanisms, may have militated against its benefits manifesting themselves in a concentrated and obvious way back in Scotland. If so, then the extent of the profits could well have been masked by the perception that emigration did not appear to bring sufficiently demonstrable economic results.

If tracing the flow of goods outward is tricky, then quantifying returning emigrant wealth is a similar methodological challenge. An obvious indicator of successful wealth accumulation was the capacity to purchase land back in Scotland. What seems clear from the available examples is that, given the very large number of migrants involved, a surprisingly small number of estates seem to have been acquired by Scots returning from the European destinations. Prominent émigrés such as Alexander Leslie, who acquired the estate of Balgonie in Fife, or William Forbes of Menie and Craigievar, a successful merchant based in Danzig who bought several other properties in the north east, stand out as atypical, although certainly not exceptional.[35] Successful entrepreneurs based on the Continent continued to buy estates well after the age of mass migration to the continent had tailed away.[36] But processes of integration and assimilation into host societies meant the number of properties in Scotland acquired in this way was noticeably smaller in comparison to the purchasing patterns of sojourners returning from imperial locations in the eighteenth century. To these continental examples should be added the properties and profits acquired by Scots based in or returning from London. In the 1710s James Fraser of Chelsea purchased the estate of Wester Moy in Easter Ross and, because his metropolitan income maintained him independently, he was able to use its rental (about £60

sterling per annum) to assist his Inverness-shire kin and invest in education infrastructure.[37] There were of course others, and further research
will in time reveal a range of examples. The number of landed estates
acquired by mercantile and professional returnees over the course of the
seventeenth and early eighteenth centuries was dwarfed by the acreage
obtained in Ireland during the plantation era. Given the draconian
nature of landlord power in early modern Scotland, the conditions of
tenure in Ulster represented a major avenue of upward social mobility
for thousands of Lowland Scots and clearly constituted an individual
and collective process of profiting by emigration.[38]

On occasion the link between Scots expatriates and wealth transfer could be obvious. In 1650–1, in an effort to re-acquire his royal
patrimony, Charles II sought and obtained the right to levy a 10 per
cent property tax on British subjects living in the lands of the Polish
Crown. This produced a return of around £10,000, although little
found its way into the use for which it was intended.[39] The Polish tax
is a clear example of the significant potential for wealth transfer back
into seventeenth-century Scottish and British societies. Aberdeen civic
society seems to have been particularly alert to the possibilities of
drawing on expatriate wealth. Between 1699 and 1703 Marischal
College launched two appeals 'To all our generous and Charitable
Countrey-men within the Cityes of Dantzick, and Konings-berg and
the Kingdom of Poland' for funds to renovate and rebuild. In the
end the effort raised the substantial sum of £1,500.[40] However, it
was more usual for profits to seep back into Scotland in prosaic and
unseen ways, be it in the form of non-monetary assets such as jewels,
endowments to churches and educational institutions, or investment
in commercial development such as shipping, docks or textile manufacturing. As the examples of James Fraser and Marischal College
indicate, wealth acquired through emigration could be used to enrich
the value of potential human capital at home by investment in education and social provision. Schools and hospitals, such as Robert
Gordon's in Aberdeen in 1732, which benefited from a colossal
bequest of £10,000, confirm that the country's wider social–educational infrastructure could and did benefit.[41] This back flow encompassed most regions of Scotland and percolated down the hierarchy
of migrants, from service elites such as Alexander Leslie and soldiers
and civilian labourers.[42] There is no need for counter-factualism
to understand how different and less affluent pre-1707 Scotland
would have been without the mass movement of its people abroad.
In this sense the commentator in 1695 failed to acknowledge the

positives and the profits which the country's tradition of migration delivered.

None of these examples of returning wealth should surprise. The scale of seventeenth-century movement to such a diverse range of locations (often indeed the most sophisticated states and economies in Western Europe) means it would have been remarkable if some substantive political, economic, social and cultural impact and profit were not apparent. But bar the development of a dense set of reciprocal links with Ulster, which shaped Scotland's domestic and imperial development over the whole span of time covered here, what is surprising about the continental emigrations of the era before c. 1700 is their relatively intermittent, hard to trace and ultimately muted effects.[43] In material terms, the incidence of large fortunes, systematic investment, enhanced credit and financial returns do not seem a proportionate return for the numbers involved. Had Scottish society committed its reserves of human capital for a relatively low return, reduced in fact to the international equivalent of 'a hewer of wood and drawer of water'? Part of the answer to that question lies in reflecting upon the sort of emigrants leaving and to what sort of receiving societies. In human capital terms seventeenth-century Scotland functioned as a high-volume export economy. Very large numbers of its emigrants were ordinary soldiers in Danish, Swedish, Dutch and increasingly, English service.[44] The social typology of this sort of mobility directly affected the capacity to accrue material gain for the sending society. The blunt truth was that much of this human wealth was lost. The nature of seventeenth-century warfare combined with the inability of states in that period to consistently feed, house, clothe and pay their soldiers meant death rates were appalling.[45] Thousands simply disappeared into the maw of protracted conflicts in the Low Countries, the German kingdoms and Ireland. These losses represented individual and familial tragedies. But viewed in terms of the deployment of human assets they also represented the dissipation of profit potential in a manner similar to the much better known capital losses suffered by the Company of Scotland. But there are positive reasons, too, why the venting of such large migrant numbers did not accrue to Scotland in proportion. Many of the merchants, pedlars and military personnel integrated and eventually assimilated into their host societies in ways that loosened and then eventually severed connections with Scotland. This might take a generation or two but is probably the key reason why such a relatively small trace of the very large continental emigrations were to be found in Scotland, even by the 1750s. The process amounted in effect to the gradual but ultimately sustained loss of human capital.

The contrast with the later emigrations of the 1700s to 1800s, particularly after about 1740, is striking. The extent and intensity of Scotland's migratory and commercial engagement with Britain's increasingly global empire is well known.[46] But the growing streams of human mobility to North America, to the slave colonies of the West Indies and the conquest empire in India constituted far more than just a change of location. Increasingly, the dispersal of Scottish human capital evolved from its old high-volume characteristics to one of qualitative human capital and a correspondingly reduced reliance on substantial numbers. These structural characteristics changed the operating principles and the resulting productivity of Scotland's migration economy. This does not mean that substantial numbers of Scots did not move overseas or to England. They did: but increasingly they were of a different type and to the sort of destinations that meant reciprocal links with Scotland's economy and society were more consistently retained. As a consequence the country began profiting from its human capital mobility in more comprehensive, consistent and demonstrable ways.

Even where large numbers were still involved, as with the new military economy of the post-Culloden Highlands, it became possible to better perfect the exchange of human capital for its monetary equivalent. In some respects the movement of Scottish manpower to imperial theatres mirrored the earlier commitment of large numbers into major conflicts such as the Thirty Years War and the Nine Years War of 1688–97: by 1758, for example, 4,200 men (17.5 per cent) of the 24,000- strong British army in North America had been recruited in the Scottish Highlands.[47] There, however, the broad parallels end. Military migration in the eighteenth century was far smaller in numeric terms than a century earlier and yet produced longer-term gains for both the individuals involved and the societies from which they were drawn. A defining reason for this change lay in the radically different nature of the state and its resources. While kingdoms like Sweden constructed military machines of devastating effectiveness, financial and logistical support structures were underdeveloped in comparison to the highly sophisticated fiscal–military states created by the global conflicts of the eighteenth century.[48] In 1775, in response to the outbreak of hostilities in North America, the British Crown raised two new Highland battalions. These units cost £47,000 – just shy of Scotland's entire annual land tax. This was the deployment of large volumes of human capital in exchange for guaranteed state monies and income. For ordinary soldiers, too, the profits could be substantial. In 1784 alone, soldiers from Highland regiments demobilised in what remained of British North

America were granted as their property a total of 54,300 acres in Nova Scotia and Quebec.[49] At a total of eighty-five square miles these lands were equivalent to over one third of the entire island of Islay. An additional round of military resettlement in Nova Scotia entailed a further 300 demobilised Highland soldiers and their families obtaining 19,400 acres – almost the same acreage as the whole island of Tiree.[50] These arrangements entailed outright acquisition of land ownership, not the tenancy arrangements practised in Ulster under the Plantation regime. Scotland's transatlantic military economy delivered massive upward social mobility to thousands from a rung of society usually viewed as the victims of empire, not its beneficiaries. It could reasonably be asked if these new centres of Highland landownership in North America were to Scotland's profit or loss given they entailed the drain of populations out of the Highlands and undoubtedly facilitated further chain migration.[51] Yet these communities, some of which survive to the present day, provided a vital alternative source of material security – a safety net in effect – which enabled Gaels to attempt negotiations for better terms of tenure with their landlords at home.[52]

The case of the West Indies, the transatlantic tobacco trade, the commercial–territorial empire of the English East India Company, and the activities of the Hudson's Bay Company underscore how patterns of Scottish migration increasingly did not involve vast numbers but did entail substantive material returns. The crucial lesson to be drawn from the mid- to later eighteenth century is that it did not take mass movement to accrue large profits. In this respect it was not just geography that marked this century out from that which preceded it. It is the simultaneous existence and persistence of the four major commercial–migratory branches that secured a far more obviously profitable dynamic for the sending society. These major imperial theatres spanned the globe and constituted the ideal framework for the investment of qualitative human capital in the form of literate and numerate sojourners, merchants, plantation clerks and overseers, lawyers, military and marine officers and doctors.[53] This was not an economy of large numbers but of high-end human capital, and the returning financial dividends altered Scotland in profound and lasting ways.

The significance of the West Indies in Scottish migration and economic history is covered in greater detail in another chapter, so only some of the basic features of returning profits will be noted here. Slave and sugar wealth percolated widely through Scottish society. This involved investment in landed estates in most areas of Scotland, civic philanthropy for the purposes of school and hospital construction, as well as major injections of liquidity through credit in the banking sector.[54] The most accurate calculations put Scottish human mobility to the Caribbean over the last half of the century at c. 20,000. In light of these figures, the sector secured one of the highest per capita monetary returns on human capital investment.

A marked feature of the eighteenth-century phase of migration was its regional diversity. Different parts of the country contributed human assets in niche and specialised ways. The example of the Highlands and military manpower is well known.[55] Less well appreciated is the case of the Orkneys. Detailed research has confirmed the observations of contemporary commentators regarding how closely this part of north Scotland interconnected with the Hudson's Bay Company.[56] By 1800 fully 80 per cent of the fur trading corporation's 524 personnel were Orcadians.[57] Compared to the volume of those leaving for European destinations in the previous century this total can appear numerically insignificant. However, this assumes a crude correlation between quantity and returning impact. Annual salary remittances home from the Company's bases in Arctic North America by the 1790s ran at roughly £4,800 per annum.[58] The sum may appear trivial, but as a percentage of overseas income it ensured the islands ranked as one of the most 'imperial' regions of Scotland.

Few other sectors of the empire better illustrate the mobilisation of high end human capital than Scottish involvement in Asia. Best estimates suggest that approximately 2,500 Scots were involved in the English East India Company's elite areas of employment between 1690 and 1815.[59] This again is a noticeably small numeric total by earlier seventeenth-century standards. The deployment of ordinary Scots soldiers in Asia was also on a small scale – usually less than 1,500 per decade.[60] Those involved were army officers, merchants, mariners and medics. Unlike their seventeenth-century predecessors in Europe, few ever intended to stay. If they died in Asia, and many did, their monies were often remitted home.[61] The result was a substantial injection of profits from one of Scotland's numerically smallest emigrant streams. Leaving aside monies spent on estate purchases, sasine records make it possible to identify the presence across all the major regions of Scotland of wealth acquired in Asia. In Fife, lending of Asia profits totalled £132,000 between 1780 and 1810; in the small county of Kirkcudbright, the sum was £34,455 for the same period.[62] No fewer than 208 landed estates were purchased across every major shire. Five hospitals – in Inverness, Elgin, Aberdeen, Stirling and Dumfries – were built either exclusively with Indian profits or in conjunction with other overseas wealth.[63]

In this respect Asia profits were directly akin to those from the Caribbean in that both were widely dispersed across the whole country. Meanwhile tobacco wealth tended to circulate more narrowly within the confines of the trade itself and in the subsidiary mercantile and manufacturing sectors that supported it. Profits were highly concentrated in the west coast of Scotland, a pattern confirmed by the fact that the vast majority of the 145 estates purchased by Glasgow's mercantile elite were located in and around the counties surrounding the city.[64] There is an obvious contrast to be drawn with the difficult-to-trace effects of the large-scale pedlar economy of the earlier period. No fewer than ninety manufacturing concerns in Scotland (the vast majority in and around Glasgow) benefited from colonial merchant investment between 1700 and 1815.[65] This ensured that Scottish society became far more self-consciously aware of the overseas connection. In other words, there developed a perception that emigration worked obviously to the country's advantage in ways that had not seemed so self-evidently true in the earlier era. If the profits of the West and East Indies trades are combined with those of fur trading, tobacco and slave fortunes, there can be little doubt how comprehensively eighteenth-century Scotland's economy of sojourning human capital worked to the country's material advantage.

Yet concluding with such an obvious contrast between the different phases of Scottish human mobility would constitute a failure to reflect on whether viewing emigration as a matter of profit and loss is in fact particularly helpful. It inevitably involves both. If seventeenth-century Scotland did not benefit in proportion to the tens of thousands that left, emigration still offered real respite from land pressure, endemic poverty, economic constraint, occasional famine and religious persecution. As a relatively underdeveloped society in finance–capital terms, emigration offered early modern Scotland an absolutely vital form of economic diversification. The pre-1730 returns may have seemed low given the numbers involved, but without emigration there can be no doubt the country would have faced ongoing problems of socio-economic marginalisation and capital accumulation. It is the striking difference with the demonstrable profits accruing from human mobility in the eighteenth century which points to the wider significance of the Scottish example. A key reason which makes studying Scottish emigration in the early modern period of international relevance and significance is that the country's trajectory constitutes a telling example of an economy heavily reliant on human capital shifting from its European locus into genuinely global forms of activity. The noticeable reliance on people, as opposed to more conventional monetary forms of capital, offers a glimpse of an alternative mode of expansion that can contribute to current conceptual models of the historic phases of globalisation.[66]

It is important to acknowledge that material gains are easier to quantify: the extent, nature and significance of the various losses involved less so. If the varying ability over time of emigration to bring profit to Scotland has formed the central concern of this chapter, then it is perhaps fitting to end on the theme of loss. Throughout the 1600s to 1800s, Scots of all social classes migrated and contributed to other societies, augmenting the armies and labour pools of a diverse range of kingdoms and countries. Scots migrants formed dynamic trading communities all over Europe and increasingly Britain's worldwide empire, connecting economies and swapping goods and services over continental and finally oceanic distances. The drain of tens of thousands from a domestic economy with an already straitened capacity for domestic demand doubtless shaped and perhaps even inhibited the country's overall rate of development.[67] Emigration certainly hastened social rupture and displacement. Entire communities, be these in the Border uplands or in localities like Glenquoich in Inverness-shire, are now largely gone.[68] That reality is a difficult thing to quantify on a credit and debit column. Lastly, even as new modes of human capital migration took Scots across Britain's global empire, to the country's obvious material benefit, there were surely still moral dimensions at play. However, these were of a radically different kind to the fears raised by the pamphlet author in 1695. The mobility of Scots increasingly meant other peoples faced their own cultural and social version of being reduced to 'hewers of wood and drawers of water'. Conspicuously missing from this chapter are the Irish peasants displaced by Scots immigrants to Ulster, the Algonquin and Iroquois peoples whose lands were appropriated by Highland soldiers, the Africans whose enslavement helped improve Scotland, or the South Asians faced with the relentless aggression of the English East India Company's military complex in which so many Scots were to be found. How are those on the receiving end of early modern Scotland's culture of emigration to be placed in the balance of profit and loss?

NOTES

1. 'The global migrations of the Scottish people since 1600', National Museum of Scotland, Edinburgh, 4–6 July 2014: http://www.ed.ac.uk/schools-departments/history-classics-archaeology/news-events/global-migrations-2014/provisional-programme (accessed 10 December 2014).

2. M. Charpentier, *A Treatise Touching the East Indian Trade* (Edinburgh: Andrew Anderson, 1695), preface.
3. Elsa-Britta Grage, 'Scottish merchants in Gothenburg, 1621–1850', in T. C. Smout (ed.), *Scotland and Europe, 1200–1850* (Edinburgh: John Donald, 1986), pp. 112–15; D. Catterall, *Community Without Borders: Scottish Migrants and the Changing Face of Power in the Dutch Republic, c. 1600–1700* (Leiden: Brill, 2001), pp. 3–15; Alexia Grosjean and Steve Murdoch (eds), *Scottish Communities Abroad in the Early Modern Period* (Leiden: Brill, 2005); Leos Müller, 'Scottish and Irish entrepreneurs in eighteenth-century Sweden', in David Dickson, Jan Permentier and Jane Ohlmeyer (eds), *Irish and Scottish Mercantile Networks in Europe and Overseas in the Seventeenth and Eighteenth Centuries* (Ghent: Academia Press, 2007), pp. 148–53; William Brock, *Scotus Americanus* (Edinburgh: Edinburgh University Press, 1982), pp. 6–7; Ned Landsman, *Scotland and its First American Colony, 1683–1765* (Princeton, NJ: Princeton University Press, 1985), pp. 100–1; Justine Taylor, *A Cup of Kindness: The History of the Royal Scottish Corporation, a London Charity, 1603–2003* (East Linton: Tuckwell Press, 2003), pp. 1–55.
4. T. M. Devine, 'A global diaspora', in T. M. Devine and Jenny Wormald (eds), *The Oxford Handbook of Modern Scottish History* (Oxford: Oxford University Press, 2012), pp. 160–1.
5. Tanja Bueltmann, Andrew Hinson and Graeme Morton, *The Scottish Diaspora* (Edinburgh: Edinburgh University Press, 2013), pp. 6–9; Alexia Grosjean and Steve Murdoch, 'Introduction', in Grosjean and Murdoch (eds), *Early Modern Scottish Communities*, pp. 6–12; D. Catterall, 'At home abroad: ethnicity and enclave in the world of Scottish traders in northern Europe, c. 1600–1800', *Journal of Early Modern History*, 8 (2004), pp. 319–56.
6. T. M. Devine, *Scotland's Empire* (London: Allen Lane, 2003), pp. 2–25; David Armitage, 'Diaspora Scotland', in Jenny Wormald (ed.), *Scotland: A History* (Oxford: Oxford University Press, 2005), pp. 282–99; Stephen Conway, *Britain, Ireland and Continental Europe in the Eighteenth Century* (Oxford: Oxford University Press, 2011), pp. 7, 136–7, 214.
7. Steve Murdoch and Esther Mijers, 'Migrant destinations, 1500–1750', in Devine and Wormald (eds), *The Oxford Handbook of Modern Scottish History*, pp. 320–37.
8. R. A. Cage, 'The Scots in England', in R. A. Cage (ed.), *The Scots Abroad: Labour, Capital, Enterprise, 1750–1914* (London: Croom Helm, 1985), p. 30; Steve Murdoch, 'Scotland, Europe and the English "missing link"', *History Compass*, 5 (2007), pp. 890–913; R. A. Houston, 'Eighteenth-century Scottish studies: out of the laager', *Scottish Historical Review*, 73 (1994), p. 66; Stana Nenadic (ed.), *Scots in London in the Eighteenth Century* (Lewisburg: Bucknell University Press, 2010); Jerry White, *London*

in the Eighteenth Century: A Great and Monstrous Thing (London: Bodley Head, 2012), pp. 17–81.

9. Mark Wyman, 'Emigrants returning: the evolution of a tradition', in Marjory Harper (ed.), *Emigrant Homecomings: The Return Movement of Emigrants, 1600–2000* (Manchester: Manchester University Press, 2005), pp. 21–4.

10. Gordon Donaldson, *The Scot Overseas* (Edinburgh: Robert Hale, 1966), p. 201.

11. Pierre Bourdieu, 'The forms of capital', in John G. Richardson (ed.), *Handbook of Theory and Research for the Sociology of Education* (New York: Greenwood, 1986), pp. 243–8; G. S. Becker, *Human Capital: A Theoretical and Empirical Analysis* (Chicago: University of Chicago Press, 1993), pp. 11–24.

12. Jean-Pierre Vidal, 'The effect of emigration on human capital formation', *Journal of Population Economics*, 11 (1998), pp. 589–600; D. J. Siddle, 'Migration as a strategy of accumulation: social and economic change in eighteenth-century Savoy', *Economic History Review*, 50 (1997), pp. 1–20.

13. Devine, *Scotland's Empire*, pp. xxvi–xxviii; James Horn, 'British diaspora: emigration from Britain, 1680–1815', in P. J. Marshall (ed.), *The Oxford History of the British Empire*, vol. II: *The Eighteenth Century* (Oxford: Oxford University Press, 1998), pp. 40–6.

14. Angela McCarthy, 'Scottish migrant ethnic identities', in John M. MacKenzie and T. M. Devine (eds), *The Oxford History of the British Empire: Scotland and the British Empire* (Oxford: Oxford University Press, 2011), pp. 120, 144–6.

15. T. C. Smout, N. C. Landsman and T. M. Devine, 'Scottish emigration in the seventeenth and eighteenth centuries', in Nicholas Canny (ed.), *Europeans on the Move: Studies on European Migration, 1500–1800* (Oxford: Oxford University Press, 1994), pp. 76–95.

16. Peter Paul Bajer, *Scots in the Polish-Lithuanian Commonwealth, 16th–18th Centuries: The Formation and Disappearance of an Ethnic Group* (Leiden: Brill, 2012), pp. 77–92; Steve Murdoch, *Scotland and the Thirty Years' War* (Leiden: Brill, 2001), pp. 9–20.

17. Nicholas Canny, 'The origins of empire: an introduction', in Nicholas Canny (ed.), *The Oxford History of the British Empire*, vol. I: *The Origins of Empire* (Oxford: Oxford University Press, 1998), pp. 12–17; Patrick Fitzgerald, 'Scottish migration to Ireland in the seventeenth century', in Grosjean and Murdoch (eds), *Scottish Communities Abroad*, pp. 28–9; Karen Cullen, *Famine in Scotland: The 'Ill Years' of the 1690s* (Edinburgh: Edinburgh University Press, 2010), pp. 172–9.

18. Smout, Landsman and Devine, 'Scottish emigration', p. 76.

19. Murdoch and Mijers, 'Migrant destinations', pp. 326–7.

20. Douglas Hamilton, *Scotland, the Caribbean and the Atlantic World, 1750–1820* (Manchester: Manchester University Press, 2005), p. 23.

21. R. A. Houston, 'The demographic regime', in T. M. Devine and Rosalind Mitchison (eds), *People and Society in Scotland*, vol. I, *1760–1830* (Edinburgh: John Donald, 1988), pp. 12–13; Geoffrey Holmes and Daniel Szechi, *The Age of Oligarchy: Pre-industrial Britain, 1722–1783* (London: Longman, 1993), p. 350.

22. Beultmann, Hinson and Morton, *Scottish Diaspora*, pp. 154–62, 173–6, 189–97, 223–9.

23. Steve Murdoch, *Network North: Scottish Kin, Commercial and Covert Associations in North Europe, 1603–1746* (Leiden: Brill, 2006), p. 239.

24. Alexia Grosjean, *An Unofficial Alliance: Scotland and Sweden, 1569–1654* (Leiden: Brill, 2003), pp. 165–73; David Stevenson, 'Leslie, Alexander, first earl of Leven (*c.*1580–1661)', *Oxford Dictionary of National Biography*, Oxford University Press, 2004; online edn, October 2007 (http://www.oxforddnb.com/view/article/16482, accessed 13 January 2015).

25. Keith M. Brown, 'Reformation to Union, 1650–1707', in R. A. Houston and W. W. J. Knox (eds), *The New Penguin History of Scotland from the Earliest Times to the Present Day* (London: Penguin, 2001), pp. 254–6.

26. Patrick Abercromby, *The Advantages of the Act of Security, Compar'd with these of the Intended Union* (Edinburgh: s.n., 1706), p. 28.

27. George Ridpath, *A Discourse Upon the Union of Scotland and England . . . Humbly Submitted to the Parliament of Scotland, by a Lover of his Country* (Edinburgh: s.n., 1702), p. 113; Jeffrey Stephen, *Scottish Presbyterians and the Act of Union 1707* (Edinburgh: Edinburgh University Press, 2007), pp. 54–5.

28. R. Feenstra, 'Scottish-Dutch legal relations in the seventeenth and early eighteenth centuries', in Smout (ed.), *Scotland and Europe*, pp. 128–33; E. Mijers, 'Scottish students in the Netherlands, 1680–1730', in Grosjean and Murdoch (eds), *Scottish Communities Abroad*, pp. 303–9.

29. *An Address to the College of Physicians, and to the Universities of Oxford and Cambridge; Occasion'd by the Late Swarms of Scotch and Leyden Physicians & etc.* (London: M. Cooper, 1747), pp. 1–30; D. G. Crawford, *A History of the Indian Medical Service, 1600–1913*, I (London: Thacker, 1914), pp. 134–97; Mark Harrison, *Medicine in an Age of Commerce and Empire* (Oxford: Oxford University Press, 2010), pp. 5–7, 85.

30. Catterall, *Community Without Borders*; Steve Murdoch, 'Children of the diaspora: the "homecoming" of the second-generation Scot in the seventeenth century', pp. 66–70, and Alexia Grosjean, 'Returning to Belhelvie, 1593–1875', in Harper (ed.), *Emigrant Homecomings*, pp. 218–21; Steve Murdoch, 'The repatriation of capital to Scotland: a case study of seventeenth-century Dutch testaments and miscellaneous notarial instruments', pp. 34–55; Siobhan Talbott, '"If it please god, I come home": Scottish return migration from France in the long seventeenth century', pp. 56–72; and Kathrin Zickermann, 'Scottish return migration from northwest Germany during the early modern period', pp. 73–89, all in Mario Varricchio (ed.),

Back to Caledonia: Scottish Homecomings from the Seventeenth Century to the Present (Edinburgh: Birlinn, 2012).

31. T. C. Smout, *Scottish Trade on the Eve of Union, 1660–1707* (Edinburgh: Oliver and Boyd, 1963), pp. 130–251; Christopher A. Whatley, 'The issues facing Scotland in 1707', *Scottish Historical Review*, 87 (2008), pp. 11–13.

32. T. M. Devine, 'The Union of 1707 and Scottish development', *Scottish Economic and Social History*, 5 (1985), pp. 25–6; Allan I. Macinnes, *Union and Empire: The Making of the United Kingdom in 1707* (Cambridge: Cambridge University Press, 2007), pp. 46–7; Murdoch, *Network North*, p. 240.

33. Smout, *Scottish Trade*, p. 95.

34. Laurence Fontaine, *History of Pedlars in Europe* (Durham, NC: Duke University Press, 1996), pp. 9–11, 14–15, 27, 119–20; Murdoch, *Network North*, pp., 127–43.

35. Murdoch, *Network North*, pp. 232–3; Bertram of Nisbet, National Records of Scotland, Edinburgh [hereafter NRS], GD 5/176.

36. Abercairney Muniments, NRS, GD 24/1/670, GD 24/1/23; NRS, Minute Books of the General Register of Seisins, RS62/18: 3 January 1763–29 December 1770: 12 June 1767: William Stewart; 28 May 1768: George Carnegie; Register of Sasines, Angus (711–713); Dundee City Archive, Wedderburn of Pearsie Muniments, GD 131/25: Pearsie 18 December 1774: Katherine Wedderburn to Ensign Charles Wedderburn.

37. Probate Court of Canterbury, The National Archive, Kew [hereafter TNA], PROB 11/644, pp. 168–70.

38. L. Soltow, 'Inequality of wealth in land in Scotland in the eighteenth century', *Scottish Economic and Social History*, 10 (1990), pp. 39–56; T. M. Devine, *The Transformation of Rural Society: Social Change and the Agrarian Economy, 1660–1815* (Edinburgh: Edinburgh University Press, 1994), pp. 14, 62.

39. Bajer, *Scots in the Polish-Lithuanian Commonwealth*, p. 7.

40. Mary Pryor, 'Picturing the divisiveness of Union', in Andrew Mackillop and Micheál Ó Siochrú (eds), *Forging the State: European State Formation and the Anglo-Scottish Union of 1707* (Dundee: Dundee University Press, 2009), pp. 162–4.

41. Shona Vance, 'Schooling the people', in E. Patricia Dennison, David Ditchburn and Michael Lynch (eds) *Aberdeen Before 1800: A New History* (East Linton: Tuckwell Press, 2002), p. 322; R. A. Houston, *Social Change in the Age of Enlightenment Edinburgh, 1660–1760* (Oxford: Clarendon, 1994), p. 246.

42. Macinnes, *Union and Empire*, p. 234; Murdoch, *Network North*, pp. 228–40; Murdoch, 'The repatriation of capital to Scotland', pp. 37–47.

43. For Ulster's crucial role in shaping the trajectory of the Scottish economy see Devine, *Scotland's Empire*, pp. 25, 31.

44. H. Dunthorne, 'Scots in the wars of the low countries, 1572–1648', in G. G. Simpson (ed.), *Scotland and the Low Countries, 1124–1994* (East Linton: Tuckwell Press, 1996), pp. 104–21; J. Migglebrink, 'The end of the Scots-Dutch Brigade', in S. Murdoch and A. Mackillop (eds), *Fighting for Identity: The Scottish Military Experience, c. 1550–1900* (Leiden: Brill, 2002), pp. 83–103; Murdoch, *Scotland and the Thirty Years' War*, pp. 19–20; Grosjean, *Unofficial Alliance*, pp. 23–67, 106; Stephen Conway, 'Scots, Britons and Europeans: Scottish military service, c. 1739–1783', *Historical Research*, 82 (2009), pp. 114–30.

45. Grosjean, *Unofficial Alliance*, p. 59.

46. John M. MacKenzie, 'Empire and national identities: the case of Scotland', *Transactions of the Royal Historical Society*, sixth series, 8 (1998), pp. 221–2.

47. P. J. Marshall, 'A nation defined by Empire, 1755–1776', in A. Grant and K. Stringer (eds), *Uniting the Kingdom? The Making of British History* (London: Routledge, 1995), p. 210; Stephen Brumwell, *Redcoats: The British Soldier and War in the Americas, 1755–1763* (Cambridge: Cambridge University Press, 2002), p. 266.

48. John Brewer, *The Sinews of Power: War, Money and the English State, 1688–1783* (London: Unwin Hyman, 1989).

49. Haldimand Papers, British Library [hereafter BL], Add MS 21828, fos. 29–151.

50. Colonial Office Papers, TNA, C.O. 700/Nova Scotia/50, 54 and 67.

51. Eric Richards, 'Scotland and the uses of the Atlantic Empire', in B. Bailyn and Philip D. Morgan (eds), *Strangers within the Realm: Cultural Margins of the First British Empire* (Chapel Hill and London: University of North Carolina Press, 1991), pp. 89–91.

52. Allan I. Macinnes, Marjory-Ann D. Harper and Linda G. Fryer (eds), *Scotland and the Americas, c.1650–c.1939: A Documentary Source Book* (Edinburgh: Lothian Print, 2002), pp. 108–11.

53. R. B. Sheridan, 'The role of the Scots in the economy and society of the West Indies', in V. Rubin and Arthur Tude (eds), *Comparative Perspectives on Slavery in New World Plantations Societies* (New York: Kraus-Thomson, 1977), pp. 94–8; A. I. Karras, *Sojourners in the Sun: Scottish Migrants in Jamaica and the Chesapeake, 1740–1815* (Ithaca, NY: Cornell University Press, 1992), pp. 11, 125–9; Douglas Hamilton, 'Scotland and the eighteenth-century empire', in Devine and Wormald (eds), *The Oxford Handbook of Modern Scottish History*, pp. 426–38.

54. David Hancock, *Citizens of the World: London Merchants and the Integration of the British Atlantic Community, 1735–1785* (Cambridge: Cambridge University Press, 1995), pp. 279–381; Hamilton, *Scotland, the Caribbean and the Atlantic World*, pp. 195–220; T. M. Devine, 'Did Slavery make Scotia great?', *Britain and the World*, 4 (2011), pp. 40–64; Stephen Mullen, 'A Glasgow-West India merchant house and the imperial

dividend, 1779–1867', *Journal of Scottish Historical Studies*, 33 (2013), pp. 196–233.

55. Andrew Mackillop, *'More Fruitful than the Soil': Army, Empire and the Scottish Highlands, 1715–1815* (East Linton: Tuckwell Press, 2000).

56. J. S. H. Brown, 'A parcel of upstart Scotchmen', *The Beaver: Exploring Canada's History*, 68 (1988), pp. 4–11; J. S. H. Brown, *Strangers in Blood: Fur Trading Company Families in Indian Country* (Vancouver: University of British Columba Press, 1985), pp. 26–41.

57. Suzanne Rigg, *Men of Spirit and Enterprise: Scots and Orkneymen in the Hudson's Bay Company, 1780–1815* (Edinburgh: John Donald, 2011), pp. 11–37, 174–5.

58. The Statistical Account of Scotland, Parish of Orphir, Orkney: http://stat-acc-scot.edina.ac.uk/link/1791-99/Orkney/Orphir/19/407/ (accessed 5 February 2015); Rigg, *Men of Spirit*, p. 139.

59. George McGilvary, *East India Patronage and the British State: The Scottish Elite and Politics in the Eighteenth Century* (London: Tauris, 2008), pp. 209–32; Andrew Mackillop, 'Locality, nation and empire: the Scots in Asia, 1695–1813', in MacKenzie and Devine (eds), *Scotland and the British Empire*, pp. 65–71.

60. Embarkation lists, 1753–63, British Library (BL), India Office Records, L/MIL/9/85; Embarkation Lists, 1775–1784, BL, L/MIL/9/90.

61. P. J. Marshall, *East Indian Fortunes: The British in Bengal in the Eighteenth Century* (Oxford: Oxford University Press, 1976), pp. 12, 229–50; A. Mackillop, 'Europeans, Britons and Scots: Scottish sojourning networks and identities in Asia, c.1700–1815', in Angela McCarthy (ed.), *A Global Clan: Scottish Migrant Networks and Identities Since the Eighteenth Century* (London: Tauris Academic Studies, 2006), pp. 19–47.

62. Register of Sasines, Kirkcudbright, 1781–1813 (1-3062), NRS; Mackillop, 'Locality, nation and empire', p. 80.

63. Andrew Mackillop, 'The Highlands and the returning nabob: Sir Hector Munro of Novar, 1760–1807', in Harper (ed.), *Emigrant Homecomings*, pp. 233–61; George McGilvary, 'The return of the Scottish nabob, 1725–1833', in Varricchio (ed.), *Back to Caledonia*, pp. 99–101.

64. T. M. Devine, 'Colonial commerce and the Scottish economy, c.1730–1815', in L. M. Cullen and T. C. Smout (eds), *Comparative Aspects of Scottish and Irish Economic and Social History, 1600–1900* (Edinburgh: John Donald, 1977), p. 178; T. M. Devine, 'Glasgow colonial merchants and land, 1770–1815', in J. T. Ward and R. G. Wilson (eds), *Land and Industry: The Landed Estate in the Industrial Revolution* (Newton Abbot: David and Charles, 1971), pp. 207–35.

65. T. M. Devine, 'The colonial trades and industrial investment in Scotland, c.1700–1815', *Economic History Review*, 29 (1976), p. 4.

66. A. G. Hopkins, 'Introduction: globalization – an agenda for historians', in A. G. Hopkins (ed.), *Globalization in World History* (London: Pimlico,

2002), pp. 2–7; C. A. Bayly, *The Birth of the Modern World, 1780–1914* (Oxford: Blackwell, 2004), pp. 37–48.

67. Richard Saville, 'Scottish modernisation prior to the industrial revolution, 1688–1763', in T. M. Devine and J. R. Young (eds), *Eighteenth Century Scotland: New Perspectives* (East Linton: Tuckwell Press, 1998), p. 13.

68. Marianne MacLean, *The People of Glengarry: Highlanders in Transition, 1745–1820* (Montreal: McGill-Queen's University Press, 1993); Edward J. Cowan, 'From the southern uplands to southern Ontario: nineteenth-century emigration from the Scottish borders', in T. M. Devine (ed.), *Scottish Emigration and Scottish Society* (Edinburgh: John Donald, 1992), pp. 61–83.

3

'You Have Only Seen the Fortunate Few and Draw Your Conclusion Accordingly': Behavioural Economics and the Paradox of Scottish Emigration

David Alston

EARLY IN 1800 A group of sixteen young men left Inverness hoping to make their fortunes from the cotton plantations of Demerara and Berbice on the north coast of South America. In April of the following year a carpenter named James Fraser, who had been in Berbice since the mid-1790s, wrote home reporting the death of one of them, his own brother Sandy, who had had to borrow the five pounds he needed to make the journey, and he added the warning that 'there is only two of the fifteen who came out with him in life'. By September, James Fraser himself was dead and the news in Inverness was that all but one of the sixteen young men had 'dropt into their Graves'. Yet, despite this, a third and last brother, Simon, was on his way to the colony. That the deaths of so many did not deter others is the paradox of much Scottish involvement in the Caribbean.[1]

Since 1796, when British forces had accepted the surrender of the three adjoining Dutch colonies of Essequibo, Demerara and Berbice – which would unite as British Guiana in 1831 and now form the Republic of Guyana – the region had held an allure which, notwithstanding these and many other deaths, continued to draw young men to it. According to Henry Dalton, the British colony's first historian writing in the 1850s, many who came were 'of the Gaelic race' and 'of humble extraction, uneducated, and glad to accept any opening that presented itself'.[2] Charles Waterton, an eminent naturalist whose family were plantation owners and who himself spent time in Guyana, later recalled how 'shoals' of poor Scotsmen had arrived in Berbice hoping for sudden wealth and of how once, according to what he has heard, 'forty of them lay on the beach and drank rum until they were all dead'.[3] No doubt this was an exaggeration but the story suggests that the influx of young Scots had left its mark on the popular imagination. It was common to call these men 'adventurers' and, because a number of the 'early adventurers' had come from northern Scotland, the attraction of Guyana was especially strongly felt in and around Inverness, the largest town in the Highlands.

The tropical coast of South America, and Berbice in particular, was an especially dangerous place for white Europeans, largely because of the prevalence of yellow fever, which had been introduced from Africa to the Caribbean with the slave trade and to which Europeans, unlike enslaved Africans, had no inherited, albeit partial, immunity. It was, indeed, an Inverness doctor, Colin Chisholm, who had first concluded, on the basis of his observations, that what he called 'malignant pestilential fever' had spread with the slave ships.[4] The danger of disease throughout the British colonies was certainly recognised by some in Scotland, such as John Downie, the parish minister of Urray (Ross-shire), who published a pamphlet in 1797 urging the development of manufactures in the Highlands so that 'our young men of education and spirit would find employment at home [and] we should not be under the necessity of sending them to the East or West Indies, where the climate destroys at least three of every four'. Yet young men continued to choose to run these risks, including Downie's own sons Hector and Murdo, who both went out to Demerara.[5]

It is important to pause and recognise that such behaviour is a puzzle, albeit one which will be found in many other situations where people act against their better interests, risking their lives, health, friendships, relationships and capital, hoping against the odds for a successful outcome. Simply to say that this is how people commonly behave, while true, is a weak explanation, lacking a conceptual framework and providing no signposts to the features of their situation to which we should attend in order to deepen our understanding.

The argument put forward in this chapter is that, as historians, we need the insights of the new discipline of behavioural economics in order to provide fuller and richer explanations. This will be explored through the example of Guyana, a place where Scots operated at the edge of empire, where higher risks were being taken, where the system was being pushed to breaking point in pursuit of profit, and consequently where the question 'Why did people act as they did?' is especially pressing.[6]

BEHAVIOURAL ECONOMICS

Over the past three decades the emerging discipline of behavioural economics has fundamentally changed the way in which economists conceptualise the world. Its achievement has been to provide an account of features of decision making which are left unexplained in the standard, or classical, economic framework.[7] It has done this by drawing on insights from the social sciences, particularly psychology, and with the increased realism of this underpinning, it has enriched the explanatory power of economic theory. It is notable that Daniel Kahneman, the co-founder with Amos Tversky of the discipline, is not only a Nobel laureate in economics but has also been described as 'the most important psychologist alive today'.[8]

Richard Thaler and Cass Sunstein, who have both developed the study of behavioural economics and written popular works on its application, have characterised the contrast with classical economic theory as a difference between what they call 'econs' and humans. Econs are 'the efficient calculators imagined in economic theory, able to weigh multiple options, forecast all the consequences of each, and choose rationally'. In contrast, humans 'operate by rules of thumb that often lead them astray . . . they are too prone to generalise, biased in favour of the status quo, [and] more concerned to avoid loss than make gains, among other shortcomings'.[9] Behavioural economics allows us to develop a systematic understanding of the ways in which humans, as distinct from 'econs', make choices – and it is human choices and actions which are the subject matter of history.

Kahneman makes the same distinction by describing two systems of thought and the continual 'psychodrama' of their interaction. What he calls system 1 operates automatically and quickly, with little effort and no sense of voluntary control. It is 'a machine for jumping to conclusions' which has evolved as a remarkably efficient tool allowing us to act, generally effectively, on the basis of minimal information. Because we often have little more than minimal information, much of our life and interaction with others relies on system 1 and, in evolutionary terms, we have only got where we are today because of our ability to jump quickly to conclusions which are for the most part, in our natural evolutionary environment as hunter gatherers, accurate and helpful. But system 1 can, and does, lead us astray because of its innate and necessary 'heuristics and biases', without which it would not be 'fast thinking'. System 2, in contrast, is the reflective and 'slow' thought that requires 'attention to . . . effortful mental activities . . . including complex computations'. This can correct for the errors of system 1 but only by sustained effort and attention – and therefore only to a limited extent. The fallacy of classical economic theory is to believe that system 2 is the predominant, or only, system of thought. In the words of Thaler and Sunstein:

> The false assumption is that almost all people, almost all of the time, make choices that are in their best interest . . . We claim that this assumption is

false – indeed, obviously false. In fact, we do not think anyone believes it on reflection.[10]

Kahneman makes the further point that 'when we think of ourselves, we identify with System 2, the conscious, reasoning self that has beliefs, makes choices, and decides what to think about and what to do'. In retrospect we will therefore wish to see our decisions, and the decisions of others, as complying with this model of rational choice. However, extensive experimental data make it clear that the heuristics and biases of system 1 are not easily eliminated and an account of human decision making which does not take them into account will be, at best, incomplete.[11]

BEHAVIOURAL ECONOMICS AND MIGRATION

A key insight of behavioural economics is that, in evaluating options, prospective losses count for more than prospective gains. This insight alone can help to build on existing historical analysis. In *Scotland's Empire*, Tom Devine summarises the academic debate on the causes of Highland emigration before 1815.[12] He rejects the simple view that 'emigration was a consequence of a rising population in an impoverished society' because, reviewing the evidence, he concludes that 'all this hardly suggest a people driven by the inexorable pressure of demographic forces from their native land'. He also argues against the alternative perspective, as expressed by J. M. Bumsted in *The People's Clearance*, that 'the Highlander *chose* to come to America, of his own free will and usually to improve his situation rather than to escape grinding oppression',[13] because this view does not take into account the 'extraordinary scale and intensity of the broader social and economic changes which were sweeping across the Highlands'. Devine then focuses on the prospects which faced tenants in the Highlands, rather than on the immediate pressures, and on how these prospects were understandably perceived. He is surely correct, for example, in his observation that 'fear of clearance in the future may have been as potent a factor as actual eviction in promoting emigration'. Devine concludes that in these circumstances 'emigration was a much more rational choice for those who could afford it' and that this was 'a movement [of people] which involved a degree of calculation and a careful weighing of prospects'.[14]

Behavioural economics grew from what Tversky and Kahneman called 'prospect theory'. Keeping, for the time being, with their central insight of loss aversion, we can see that in the human (as opposed to the 'econ') 'calculation and . . . careful weighing of prospects' in Highland migration, prospective losses will count for more than gains. Devine rightly attends to the prospects which faced tenants in the Highlands. But prospect theory suggests that the actual gains may well not outweigh the actual losses; the decision reached may not stand up to retrospective scrutiny; and, in such circumstances, there will be a tendency to preserve the appearance of rationality by exaggerating the losses which migrants faced. We need to attend to how prospects appeared to people – how the options were framed – and how they came to be seen in that way. Only then can we understand their decision making.

This also applies to the paradox of migration to the West Indies. Devine recognises the dangers to Europeans in the Caribbean and suggests that 'desperation as much as the search for opportunities explains why so many were willing to hazard their lives in the lethal environment of the West Indies'.[15] This may be true if 'desperation' refers to the subjective state of mind of migrants but, again, an objective loss which was much less than a prospective gain would often lead to the decision to 'search for opportunities'.

In order to reach a deeper understanding we must attend to how things appeared to prospective migrants, how their options were framed and what, for them, counted as prospective losses or gains. To do this, we need to make use of further aspects of behavioural economics.

THE AVAILABILITY HEURISTIC

In 1970–1 Daniel Kahneman and Amos Tversky sought an answer to the question 'what do people actually do when they wish to estimate the frequency of a category' and concluded, from their experiments, that 'instances of the class will be retrieved from memory, and if retrieval is easy and fluent, the category will be judged to be large'. They named this the availability heuristic and identified three factors, other than actual frequency, which will tend to make instances readily retrievable from memory, namely events of a kind which attract attention, dramatic events and instances which are vivid because of personal or direct experience.[16] In the 1790s, those with the opportunity of investing or working in Guyana were faced with the immediate question: What are the chances of success and how frequently do 'adventurers' in Demerara and Berbice succeed? This was a difficult, perhaps impossible, question to answer accurately and their conclusions were influenced by the availability heuristic.

This can be seen in the decision made in 1801 by a consortium of merchants and Highland landowners, led by Lord Seaforth, the chief of Clan Mackenzie, to purchase the lands of the Berbice Society. The deal was concluded in 1801 and after subsequent divisions this created eighteen new cotton plantations on the Berbice coast. Their correspondence prior to the purchase shows that they had all come to see the opportunity to invest in Berbice in such a positive light that they believed they were almost certain to succeed in making large gains. Indeed, not to invest would be a lost opportunity. One of Seaforth's partners, Fraser of Reelig, enthused, 'What an asylum for those of broken fortunes from other colonies . . . What an opportunity to rival the French in Domingo . . . [and to] supply the deficiencies of our own wearing out islands.'[17]

Their judgements were entirely focused on the financial prospects. Fraser referred to the Irish planter Lambert Blair, who had recently 'paid about 20,000 florins [c. £1,666] for each lot and sells for 60,000 [c. £5,000]', and to George Porter, who had bought lots 'in 1782 for £500, worth £5000 in 1800 and £7000 in 1801 – all for uncultivated land'. The consortium's confidence was bolstered by the belief that they had inside information, two of the partnership had travelled in secret to Holland to complete the negotiations, and they felt that they had now stolen a march on Blair. When their purchase had been completed, Fraser remarked that 'Mr Blair heard through blabbing and expressed his disappointment at having missed the speculation, declaring it worth £100,000. If so, it is tolerably cheap at £20,400.'[18]

This correspondence was strictly confidential and the parties were concerned to convince only themselves of the prudence of their investment. Fraser of Reelig summarised their prospects with a list of nineteen reasons why investing in Berbice was likely to be successful, a list which he made available to Seaforth and the other partners.[19] Being asked to list a large number of instances of a category will, in fact, tend to lead to a judgement that the likelihood of occurrence is less – because examples become increasingly difficult to call to mind – but Fraser was something of an obsessive compiler of lists and so perhaps immune to this effect. For the others he provided assurance, which appeared authoritative, that the reasons were many and various, although, in fact, Fraser had systematically underestimated the problems and overestimated the benefits.[20]

In a memorandum, intended for the Duke of Portland, which argued for continued British control of Dutch Guiana and was therefore intended for circulation beyond the confines of the partnership, Seaforth wrote in similarly confident terms:

> [Guiana's] operation in creating very rapid and splendid fortunes to
> Individuals is very apparent ... my attention was very early drawn towards
> this subject, from several Gentlemen in my neighbourhood being among the
> first speculators in Guiana. Of these, some never had any fortune, & others
> had exhausted what little fortune they were possessed of, yet, with very few
> exceptions ... they all returned speedily with larger & some of them with
> immense fortunes.[21]

With Kahneman and Tversky's conclusions in mind, we can readily see
that the examples of success were 'readily retrievable from memory'
because 'splendid fortunes' could hardly fail to attract attention, because
they were dramatic instances of 'rapid' success and of reversals in
fortune, and because they were based on personal and direct experience
of 'Gentlemen in my neighbourhood'.[22] Seaforth and his partners had
convinced themselves but, as events were to prove, they had overestimated the frequency of success.

It is well recognised that strong, kin-based networks gave Scots, especially Highland Scots, an advantage in pursuing the opportunities offered
by the expanding British Empire. Douglas Hamilton, in relation to the
Caribbean, concludes that 'networks based on ties of kinship (broadly
defined) and local association underpinned virtually all Scottish activity
in the West Indies in the later eighteenth century'.[23] Douglas Catterall
makes similar points in relation to the Americas in general, where 'the
practices established by Scots enclaves, nourished by kinship-based networks, carried Scots ... and moved with them'.[24] Andrew Mackillop
observes that even in the Anglocentric world of British India, the fact
that 'Scottish networks were nonetheless the norm ... underlines the
adaptability of the associative methods used by Scots overseas'.[25] But,
because these were networks of communication, strongly influencing
what information was available, did they perhaps make Scots more open
to the distortions of the 'availability heuristic'? It was all too easy to
jump to conclusions when word spread through family networks, as in a
letter written from India in 1804 in which Lachlan Mackintosh referred
to 'the large Invernessian fortunes made [in Demerara]'.[26]

The letters written home by 'adventurers' in the West Indies both
communicated information and were a means by which those who had
ventured abroad sought to make sense of their own experience. Some
historians, such as David Gerber, argue that migrants' letters are of such
a personal nature, concerned with 'the immigrant's existential hunger
for continuity' and the construction of their new identity, that they are of
little value as evidence for broader attitudes.[27] Others would dispute this
and Eric Richards suggests that such a constrained approach 'empties

out the baby with the bath water'. Although migrant letters present fragments of evidence, not a social survey, Richards points out that 'historians always deal in fragments of evidence' and that there are exemplars
'of precise and incisive scholarship' such as David Fitzpatrick's use of
the correspondence exchanged between Ireland and Australia in *Oceans
of Consolation*.[28] But even if Gerber were correct, the experimental evidence of behavioural economics shows that most decisions are, in fact,
based on fragments of evidence and what was presented in such letters,
however limited in perspective, would have been influential in framing
choices for prospective migrants. The availability heuristic makes this
doubly significant – it was not simply that news spread but, by making
examples of success come readily to mind, judgements as to the likelihood of success were distorted.

This process extended to many ranks in society and the apparent
opportunities were frequently communicated by letters to friends in the
Highlands. Donald Mackintosh, who had become bankrupt about 1790
attempting to establish a bleach-field at Dunain, outside Inverness, had
come to Berbice where he became manager of plantation Golden Fleece.
In 1796 he wrote:

> I see many young men here in a prosperous way who came but few years
> ago to the Country as bare as I did . . . I believe there is hardly any place
> where money may be made with more facility than here, the great difficulty
> is once to have a little; but when that little is in hand it can be increased by
> a rapid progression.[29]

The flames of enthusiasm were also fanned by locally respected individuals such as Inverness-born Dr Colin Chisholm, who published works in
which he spoke with authority from his time in the West Indies and who
believed that the emigration to Demerara promised 'to render [it] the
most wealthy and flourishing colony in the western world'.[30]

The wealth of those who had succeeded and returned to the Highlands
also came readily to mind because it was manifested in the splendid
new residences of those few successful adventurers who came home.
There was Drakies House, on the outskirts of Inverness, built by Robert
Gordon on his return to Inverness in 1803; Belladrum, eleven miles
outside the town, where, in the same year, James Fraser had lavished
£20,000 of profits from his plantations on 'adorning his house'; and
Innes House, near Elgin, bought in 1798 by Thomas Cuming, who had
left the north as a poor sixteen-year-old thirty years before and now
styled himself 'Cuming of Leuchars'.[31] Even though some of these individuals had concerns about their prospects in Guyana, these were only

privately expressed, while their grand houses stood as public manifestations of their success.

There were other voices but it was difficult for them be heard because
they were at odds with the spirit of enthusiasm for these 'adventures
abroad'. Seaforth's phrase 'rapid and splendid fortunes' was echoed in
a letter written the following year by Thomas Fraser, in St Vincent, to
his cousin Simon Fraser, a baker in Inverness, in which he acknowledged
that 'your Demerara planters have certainly made a large and rapid
fortune'. But Fraser advised his cousin:

> Now look at the poor adventurer who goes there to do his best by his indus-
> try only, he gets a grant of several hundred acres of Swampy boggs he com-
> mences draining with a few negroes he takes the spade often and works to
> forward the Settlement but alas all his endeavors to combat difficulties only
> serves to ruin his health and too often the poor man sinks under his distress
> before he gets a crop to compensate his labour ... *you have only seen the*
> *fortunate few and draw your conclusion accordingly*[.][32]

Thomas Fraser wanted to discourage emigration to the West Indies,
earlier expressing his view that 'there is too many here already which
makes the wages very poor for all kinds of trades', but his was probably
a more balanced assessment of the prospects in Guyana.[33] However,
because it did not cohere with the optimistic view which had been
formed around Inverness, it had no traction. As has been observed in
relation to other manias for investment and subsequent financial crashes,
'there is nothing so disturbing to one's well-being and judgement as to
see a friend get rich'[34] and, until things began to go dramatically wrong
for some more prominent individuals, it was still the 'fortunate few' who
came to mind when one thought of Demerara.[35]

Kahneman has referred to a further aspect of system 1 thinking as
'WYSIATI: what you see is all there is'. Minimal information, once
formed into a coherent 'story', is remarkably resistant to the consideration of further evidence. So, because Highland investors and prospective 'adventurers' in Guyana could weave a coherent story from
the limited information available to them, information which was also
easily retrieved from memory, they remained confident and gave no
attention to other information which might have disturbed them, such
as the high death rate. This information might as well not have existed
and so Fraser of Reelig's analysis of the prospects for investment in
Berbice made no mention of the risk of disease and death.

Only outsiders were likely to be able to offer a more objective view.
Revd James Macgregor in Pictou, Nova Scotia, had received letters

from James Forbes, a man from the Inverness area who had arrived in Demerara before 1805, saying that 'he had a good deal of sickness there at first, but that now he enjoys good health' and that he intended 'to return home after a year or two with a small fortune'. This was typical of the aspirations of young migrants. However, Macgregor, writing to relations in Inverness, commented:

> A vain intention indeed! How many have made the same resolution, but could never put it in execution! Every man promises to be content with a little fortune while he has it not, but as soon as he gets it, it is nothing, and it requires more to make a little fortune, till old age or death comes. Besides how many drop off especially in the unhealthy climate of Demerara, and the West Indies, before a year or two run their round! Alas! few have the wisdom to know they have enough. Fortune hunters are among the chief of fools.[36]

STEREOTYPES AND THE REPRESENTATIVENESS HEURISTIC

Kahneman and Tversky also concluded from their studies that judgements as to the frequency of a category were influenced by the extent to which particular examples were taken to be representative of a class. This is, in effect, the question of stereotypes. In the case of Guyana, once a stereotype of a successful Demerara planter had become established then the appearance of such individuals reconfirmed the view that success was common. If others could identify with the stereotype, then this further bolstered the belief that their own success was likely. And a stereotype had certainly been established in the Highlands. Earlier sections of this chapter have quoted references to 'the large Invernessian fortunes made [in Demerara]' and to 'a large and rapid fortune' made by 'your Demerara planters'; and by 1803 Edward Fraser of Reelig could simply say, in a letter of written to Lord Seaforth, who was then in Barbados, that he was looking forward to Seaforth's return 'as rich as a Demerary man'.[37]

Integral to the stereotype was the sense that success was the result of the effort and character of the Demerary men and this allowed the local stereotype to nest within, and be reinforced by, a more general sense of Britishness. Linda Colley suggests that, from the mid-eighteenth century, 'a cult of commerce became an increasingly important part of being British' and Lord Seaforth, in 1800, was insistent that 'the sudden accumulation of fortunes [in Guiana] was ... *Not* built on dishonourable means but on the Energy of British Capital and British Industry'.[38] In 1807 a young clerk, Henry Bolinbroke, expressed the almost identical view that 'British capital, industry, and perseverance, had accomplished in eight years, what would not have been done by any other means in half a century'.[39]

Only when Guyana lost its allure did another view begin to form. In 1810 Fraser of Reelig wrote ruefully to Seaforth saying that he was 'determined to bring home my sons after 10 years unsuccessful trial'. He had considered going to Guyana himself, as had Seaforth, but 'at your age and mine what should we do . . . we should have to compete with low cunning characters versed in every subterfuge and ravelling'.[40] His son Edward had seen the reality of what made a successful planter from the moment he arrived in the colony in 1803, describing the manager under which his brother worked as 'a harsh disagreeable vulgar little creature, though a very good planter'. But, at the time, this had formed no part of his father's image of the colonies, being only a few months after his reference to Seaforth returning 'as rich as a Demerary man'.[41] The positive stereotype endured for some years in the north of Scotland. In 1811, William Young, the factor on the Sutherland estates, writing to Lady Sutherland, readily referred to a John Grant, who was sending remittances home to his mother in Golspie, as a 'Demerara man'.[42] But by 1815 the situation had changed decisively and Alexander Alexander, a former soldier who arrived in Demerara looking for work, found that many of the coastal plantations in Berbice had been abandoned. He was frequently mocked and ridiculed, often by fellow Scots, described Georgetown as 'filled with a race of people, everyone on the catch' and lamented that 'I a stranger . . . I met with nothing but ill usage and insult'.[43]

ANCHORING EFFECTS

An anchor is a piece of information, which may be neither accurate nor relevant but which nevertheless biases judgement because of its associative affect. An anchoring number can either have a priming effect or can result from the process of starting with a 'best guess' followed by a process of inadequate adjustment, which typically stops short because of uncertainty. It is disturbing that even a randomly generated number, with no rational connection to the question, can have a priming effect. One of the most alarming of Kahneman's examples is that of an experiment with a group of German judges, all with more than fifteen years' experience. They were presented with a fictitious case of a woman caught shoplifting and then told to roll a pair of dice. The dice were loaded so that all rolls resulted in either a three or a nine. They were then asked if they would sentence the offender to a term in prison more or less, in months, than the number on the dice. Finally they were asked what sentence they would impose. Those who had thrown a three handed down a sentence, on average, of five months; those who has thrown a nine an average sentence of eight months. This is a further salutary reminder that all of us are prone to the distortions of the heuristics and biases inherent in our 'fast', automatic thinking as humans.[44]

The judgement of those who considered either financial investment in Guyana or going to one of the colonies was prone to influence by the sums bandied about in local gossip and conveyed in letters. There were not only reference to fortunes which were, variously, 'large', 'immense', 'rapid' or 'splendid', but also specific sums. In 1801 James Fraser of Belladrum was 'said to have made £40,000' from his most recent time in Guyana, while a shoemaker and assistant were told they might hope to make 'twenty or thirty shillings per day'.[45]

Primed by such numbers, relatives often had inflated ideas of what they would receive on the death of adventurers in Guyana and this led to some bitter disputes. Donald Mackay, an Invernessian in Demerara, had agreed to act under a power of attorney to deal with the executors of the carpenter, James Fraser, mentioned at the beginning of this chapter. Fraser, who died in 1801, had at some point led his relatives to believe that 'he considered himself worth about 5,000 stg' but in 1803 Mackay observed that 'In this Country in particular it is very true that it is the death of a man that throws the best light on his affairs'. In 1804 he wrote to Inverness saying, 'I am extremely sorry that imaginary calculations should have led the heirs to expect £1000 each & consequently incur debts on the faith of it'. After an increasingly bitter dispute, they received nothing.[46]

LOSS AVERSION AND FRAMING EFFECTS

The examples above show the way in which networks of communication had a powerful influence on how options were framed, both on what was attended to as prospective losses or gains and on the assessment of the likelihood of success. In Guyana reality quickly reasserted itself and forced a change of perspective, but still one in which losses and gains were framed in a particular way. Edward Fraser, the second son of the Reelig family, who was in Berbice from 1803 until 1811 attempting to make a success of his family's investment and so help to ensure that they could keep the family estate, quickly saw things differently. In many personal letters to his mother, he reflected on his situation.[47] He was well aware of the dangers, frequently reported the death of friends and acquaintances, opposed slavery and detested the country and its ethos. But, although he felt that he 'would rather live in the bleakest part of the Highlands than [in Berbice]', he was well aware of his father's optimistic view of the prospects for cotton planting and recognised that 'if one is industrious [one] may make some money [here]'. He also believed, given the pressure to support his family in their struggle to maintain their Scottish home, that 'to return home little better than I came out would be for me more dreadful than never to return'. That prospective loss weighed heavily on him and the chance, albeit small, of large gains in Berbice led him to accept that 'this is the country for us for perhaps 20 years'.

Loss aversion kept Fraser and others in the colonies, and maintained investments, long after their interests would have been better served by accepting their losses. Peter Fairbairn arrived in Berbice in November 1801 to manage the land bought by Lord Seaforth and his partners, and, contrary to all his expectations, remained in Guyana until his death in 1822. He had never intended to stay. In 1808 he hoped to return the following year 'after 8 years abroad' and felt, at this date, that he had stayed for the previous two years against his own interests and to the injury of his family and children. By July 1809, however, he was still unable to leave: 'In vain I attempted to close my arrangements to quit this country and find it impossible until I see results of the ensuing crop.' In 1810 he was still there and expressed his regret that he had not left in 1806. But there were further losses to be avoided because he had recently 'laid out £100 on 40 barrels of American beans' for the slaves and so he concluded '[I] cannot leave yet'.[48] And so it continued.

BEHAVIOURAL ECONOMICS AND THE PARADOX OF SCOTTISH EMIGRATION

The argument of this chapter is that Kahneman's development of a rounded account of 'human judgment and decision-making under [conditions of] uncertainty', using the insights of experimental psychology, makes behavioural economics especially relevant, and indeed essential, to the study of migration.[49] In his introductory essay to *Scottish Emigration and Scottish Society*, published in 1992, Devine identified what he called 'the essential paradox of Scottish emigration'. While there was migration on a large scale in the nineteenth century from almost all European countries, these were for the most part agricultural economies, with migrants moving to urban, industrialising centres. In Scotland, however, substantial emigration occurred as Scotland was itself rapidly becoming more urban and more industrialised. It was accompanied by extensive migration into Scotland particularly from Ireland. The majority of migrants from Scotland were from urban, rather than rural areas, and the migrants often had skills which were in demand in Scotland.[50] In this, and in more detail in later studies, Devine has drawn attention to the importance of the prospects facing those who chose to migrate, the negative effect not so much of immediate poverty but of 'the economic insecurity [which] was basic to emigration' and, on the other hand, the prospect of 'more "opportunity", independence and . . . [of] aspirations which . . . could not easily be satisfied in Scotland itself'.[51] Devine concludes that 'what comes through strongly from the evidence is the central importance of individual human choice and decision, albeit powerfully fashioned by the prevailing structural forces of society, ideology and economy'.[52] But understanding the nature of these individual choices and decisions – understanding them as human choices and decisions – requires the new insights of behavioural economics into 'decision making under conditions of uncertainty'.

This will also provide a sounder basis for understanding the wider 'social psychologies' of emigration, which Eric Richards, among many others, has drawn attention to and of which the rush of Highlanders to Guyana is but one example:

> The idea that emigrants have been gripped by a collective obsession, a powerful imitative pattern of behaviour, recurs . . . Where it manifested itself it was usually diagnosed as 'madness' by opponents of emigration . . . The vocabulary of emigration is full of these manias, humours, frenzies, deluges, mass delusion, suggesting odd and compulsive psychic states which take hold of entire communities prior to emigration. Yet in the nineteenth century landed interests also complained of the opposite psychology, namely the immovable inertia of the rural population and their refusal to respond to the obvious benefits and incentives of emigration.[53]

Behavioural economics suggests that such collective 'madness' and collective inertia, and vacillations between them, are not the product of what might appear 'odd and compulsive psychic states' but of the inherent heuristics and biases of human decision making.

NOTES

1. James Fraser (Demerara), 12 April 1801, Highland Council Archive [HCA], D122/2/3; Stephen Foster, *A Private Empire* (Millers Point, NSW: Murdoch Books, 2010), p. 119, quoting Simon Fraser of Fairfield to Alexander Macpherson, 29 September 1801, Macpherson of Blairgowrie archive;

Simon Fraser (Demerary), to Alexander Fraser, Inverness, 9 September 1802, HCA, D122/2/3.

2. Henry Gibbs Dalton, *A History of British Guiana*, 2 vols (London: Longmans, 1855), vol. i, p. 306.

3. Julia Blackburn, *Charles Waterton* (London: Vintage, 1997), p. 27, quoting conversations recorded in the notebooks of Sir Norman Moore, National Register of Archives, 29440.

4. Colin Chisholm, *An Essay on the Malignant Pestilential Fever introduced into the West Indian Islands from Boullam, on the coast of Guinea, as it appeared in 1793 and 1794* (Philadelphia: Thomas Dobson, 1799), p. 89.

5. Revd John Downie, *Hints Towards the Improvement of the Counties of Ross and Cromarty* (Edinburgh: J. Dickson, 1797); for Hector and Murdo Downie see the author's website: <http://www.spanglefish.com/slavesandhighlanders> (accessed October 2015).

6. David Alston, '"The habits of these creatures in clinging one to the other": enslaved Africans, Scots and the plantations of Guyana', in T. M. Devine (ed.), *Recovering Scotland's Slavery Past: The Caribbean Connection* (Edinburgh: Edinburgh University Press, 2015), pp. 99–123.

7. Colin F. Camerer, George Loewenstein and Matthew Rabin (eds), *Advances in Behavioural Economics* (Princeton, NJ: Princeton University Press, 2004); Peter Diamond and Hannu Vartiainen (eds), *Behavioural Economics and its Applications* (Princeton, NJ: Princeton University Press, 2007).

8. Daniel Kahneman, *Thinking, Fast and Slow* (London: Allen Lane, 2011). The description of Kahneman is by Steven Pinker, Harvard College Professor and Johnstone Family Professor in the Department of Psychology at Harvard University.

9. Lawrence M. Mead, 'Econs and humans: a review of *Nudge*', *Claremont Review of Books*, 9:2 (2009), <www.claremont.org/crb/article/econs-and-humans> (accessed October 2015).

10. Richard Thaler and Cass Sunstein, *Nudge: Improving Decisions About Health, Wealth and Happiness* (London: Penguin, 2009), p. 10.

11. Kahneman, *Thinking, Fast and Slow*, pp. 20–4.

12. T. M. Devine, *Scotland's Empire, 1600–1815* (London: Allen Lane, 2003), pp. 135–9.

13. J. M. Bumsted, *The People's Clearance* (Edinburgh: Edinburgh University Press, 1982), p. 63.

14. Devine, *Scotland's Empire*, p. 138.

15. Ibid. p. 232.

16. Kahneman, *Thinking, Fast and Slow*, p. 129.

17. Edward Fraser to Lord Seaforth, 1800, National Records of Scotland [NRS], GD46/17/14, fo. 386. For further detail see Finlay McKichan, 'Lord Seaforth: Highland proprietor, Caribbean governor and slave owner', *Scottish Historical Review*, 90:2 (2011), pp. 204–35.

18. Alston, '"The habits of these creatures"', Table 5.1 and Table 5.2, pp. 104–5; Edward Fraser to Lord Seaforth, 10 April 1801, NRS, GD/46/17/14.
19. Edward Fraser to Lord Seaforth, 1800, NRS, GD46/17/14, fo. 386.
20. Kahneman, *Thinking, Fast and Slow*, pp. 131–5. For examples of Fraser's lists see Edward Satchwell Fraser, 'Emigration from the Highlands and Islands of Scotland', National Library of Scotland [NLS], MS9646.
21. Draft memorandum from Lord Seaforth to the Duke of Portland, NRS, GD46/17/14, fo. 337.
22. Ibid.
23. Douglas Hamilton, *Scotland, the Caribbean and the Atlantic World, 1750–1820* (Manchester: Manchester University Press, 2010), p. 221.
24. Douglas Catterall, 'The worlds of John Rose: a northeastern Scot's career in the Atlantic world, c1740–1800', in Angela McCarthy (ed.), *A Global Clan: Scottish Migrant Networks and Identity Since the Eighteenth Century* (London: Tauris Academic Studies, 2006), p. 71.
25. Andrew Mackillop, 'Europeans, Britons, and Scots: Scottish sojourning networks and identities in Asia, c1700–1815', in McCarthy (ed.), *A Global Clan*, p. 39.
26. Letter book of Lachlan Mackintosh of Raigmore, NLS, MS6360, fo. 73.
27. David A. Gerber, *Authors of their Lives: The Personal Correspondence of British Immigrants to North America in the Nineteenth Century* (New York: New York University Press, 2006).
28. Eric Richards, 'Australian colonial mentalities in emigrant letters', available online at <http://www.nla.gov.au/openpublish/index.php/australian-studies/article/viewFile/1757/2132> (accessed October 2015): original version presented to the British Australian Studies Association (7 September 2006); David Fitzpatrick, *Oceans of Consolation: Personal Accounts of Irish Migration to Australia* (Ithaca, NY: Cornell University Press, 1994).
29. Donald Mackintosh to Colonel Baillie of Dunain, 24 May 1796, HCA, D456/A/10/49; John Shaw, *Water Power in Scotland, 1550–1870* (Edinburgh: John Donald, 1984), p. 238.
30. Colin Chisholm, *An Essay on the Malignant Pestilential Fever* (London: J. Mawman, 1801), vol. ii, p. 190.
31. Letters of Donald Mackay to James Grant, NRS, GD23/6/391/4; for Thomas Cuming see the author's website available at: <http://www.spanglefish.com/slavesandhighlanders> (accessed October 2015).
32. Thomas Fraser (St Vincent) to Simon Fraser (Inverness), 24 April 1801, HCA D238. Emphasis is mine.
33. Thomas Fraser (Grenada) to Simon Fraser (Inverness), 3 August 1771, HCA D238.
34. Charles P. Kindleberger, *Manias, Panics and Crashes: A History of Financial Crisis* (New York: John Wiley & Sons, 1989), p. 19.
35. James Grant to Evan Bailie Esq., MP for Bristol, 27 June 1803, NRS, GD23.

36. George Paterson, *Memoir of the Reverend James MacGregor* (Philadelphia: Joseph M. Wilson, 1859), p. 337.

37. Fraser (Inverness) to Seaforth, 30 April 1803, NRS, GD46/17/23.

38. Linda Colley, *Britons: Forging the Nation, 1707–1837* (New Haven: Yale University Press, 1992), p. 61; Draft memorandum to the Duke of Portland, NRS, GD46/17/14.

39. Henry Bolinbroke, *A Voyage to the Demerary* (London: Richard Phillips, 1806), p. 186.

40. Fraser to Seaforth, 30 November 1810, NRS, GD46/17/35, fo. 332.

41. Edward Fraser (Berbice) to his mother, 13 November 1803, National Register of Archives of Scotland [NRAS], 2696.

42. William Young, factor, to Lady Sutherland, 1 June 1811, NLS, Dep313/1574, no. 16.

43. Alexander Alexander, *The Life of Alexander Alexander*, 2 vols (Edinburgh: William Blackwood, 1830), vol. i, pp. 286, 385.

44. Kahneman, *Thinking, Fast and Slow*, pp. 119–28.

45. Edward Fraser of Reelig to Lord Seaforth, 18 June 1801, NRS, GD46/17/20; Donald McRae (Demerary), to Simon Fraser, shoemaker (Church Street, Inverness), 24 July 1801, HCA, D122/2/3.

46. Copy letters Alexander Fraser (Inverness), to Donald Mackay (Demerary), 25 August and 24 October 1804, HCA, D122/2/3; Donald Mackay (Demerary), to James Grant (Inverness), 15 February 1803, NRS, GD23/6/391/3; Donald Mackay (Demerara) to Alexander Fraser, merchant (Inverness), 25 August 1804, HCA, D122/2/3.

47. Fraser of Reelig papers, NRAS, 2696.

48. Fairbairn to Seaforth, 7 April 1808, NRS, GD46/17/31; Fairbairn to Seaforth, 29 July 1809, NRS, GD46/17/35; Fairbairn to Lady Seaforth, 1 February 1810, NRS, D46/17/35; Fairbairn to Seaforth, 24 May 1810, NRS, GD46/17/35.

49. For general comment on the application of behavioural economics to migration studies see Mathias Czaika, 'Migration and economic prospects', *Journal of Ethnic and Migration Studies*, 41:1 (2015), pp. 58–82.

50. T. M. Devine, 'Introduction: the paradox of Scottish emigration', in T. M. Devine (ed.), *Scottish Emigration and Scottish Society* (Edinburgh: John Donald, 1992), pp. 1–15.

51. T. M. Devine, *To the Ends of the Earth: Scotland's Global Diaspora, 1750–2010* (London: Allen Lane, 2011), p. 105.

52. Ibid. p. 106.

53. Richards, 'Australian colonial mentalities'.

4

Scottish Diasporas and Africa

John M. MacKenzie

THE PLURAL IS IMPORTANT. There have been several Scottish diasporas to Africa, not just in the sense of different periods and regions,
or in terms of the movement of people as sojourners and settlers, but
also in respect of religious and cultural influences, and then again in the
realm of perceptions, of both intellectual and popular ideas. It might be
thought that there would be a curious asymmetry in charting the connections between one small and poor society in north-western Europe
and an entire continent with a host of different peoples and contrasting
environmental regions. Yet the nature of the imperial period was such
that a study of the inter-penetration of Scotland and Africa is essential,
not least in terms of the reciprocal influences stimulated by the relationship. This reciprocity has to be understood, for the influence of Africa
on Scotland and Scottish self-perceptions is itself important. Imperial
influences were never one-way and cannot be examined solely through
the dissemination of people, faiths and ideas. Empire was always about
exchanges, negotiations, interactions, and the relationship of Scotland
and Africa well reflects this. Moreover, the reciprocities occurred within
Africa itself, for there were some intriguing ways in which African
societies seem to have adopted Scottish forms into elements of, for
example, their dance traditions. All of this indicates the manner in which
Scottish ethnicity was undoubtedly seen as being distinct from that of
the English. Moreover, the Scottish influence upon Africa certainly took
different forms from that of other Britons.

The movement of Scots to Africa was different in kind from migrations to Canada, Australia and New Zealand. Although those three territories of settlement all had indigenous societies, whites overwhelmed
them in terms of sheer numbers, backed by unstoppable military and
political power. In British-controlled Africa, land alienation and indigenous dispossession took place in the territories that became the Union
of South Africa, in Southern and Northern Rhodesia (Zimbabwe and

Zambia), as well as in Nyasaland (Malawi) and Kenya. Most migrants to Africa were either professionals or people with capital, although many migrants to South Africa were working class. All migrants experienced an immediate boost to social status since whites were seldom involved in manual labour. They suddenly found themselves in supervisory roles, controlling low-paid African workers, as well as living with servants. In the professional and managerial spheres, Scots tended to occupy networks associated with the missionary societies and universities, commercial and shipping organisations, specific professions such as medicine and teaching, as well as mining and agricultural sectors. This short chapter can only offer a few pointers to the ways in which these diasporas created distinctive relationships with Africa and Africans, as well as demonstrating the importance of the theme of mutuality.

Scottish migration to Africa has only recently come under close scrutiny by historians.[1] Those to Canada, the United States, Australia and New Zealand have always been subject to much more attention, partly because of the numbers involved and partly because of the strength and visibility of the continuing Scottish associational culture in these countries. The connection with the Highland Clearances (often more prominent that it should be), the active recruitment of migrants, the enigmatic relationship with the cyclical fluctuations of the Scottish economy and the significance of the shipbuilding and shipping industries in these movements all contributed to the importance of such studies. Africa seemed to be in a different category, partly because it was thought that the flows of people there were relatively slight while the connections seemed to be largely of a professional and religious nature. Nevertheless, there was always an awareness that the Scottish interest in Africa was long-standing. This has been re-emphasised by the manner in which the involvement of Scots in the slave trade has increasingly become a significant focus of historical research, while there have also been studies of the visibility of Scots in the plantation economies of the West Indies.[2] Recent studies have additionally revealed the extent to which Scots were involved in the campaign for the abolition of the slave trade as well as in the acquisition and administration of territory in West Africa for the resettlement of slaves.[3]

But Scottish connections with Africa seemed fragmentary. Attention to Scots in Africa has invariably focused upon the activities of celebrated Scottish explorers, such as James Bruce (1730–1794), Mungo Park (1771–1806), Alexander Gordon Laing (1794–1826), William Balfour Baikie (1825–1864) and, above all, David Livingstone (1813–1873). Interestingly, these figures already demonstrated a number of the characteristics of the Scots involvement with the continent. Bruce reflected commercial concerns since, as a wine merchant, his interest emerged from his connections with Spain and Portugal. Park, Baikie and Livingstone were all doctors. Laing was a military man. All of them were highly literate and Bruce, Park and Livingstone wrote celebrated books that not only drew attention to the interior of Africa but helped to frame the perceptions of the continent that were influential in the nineteenth and twentieth centuries. All of them had an interest in natural history as well as human sciences such as philology and proto-anthropology. In addition, Livingstone was of course a missionary precursor whose heroic death stimulated one of the great legendary myths of Victorian times, one which had incalculable effects on subsequent missionary expansion and extensive activities in the continent.[4] Although Livingstone influenced many Christian denominations both in Britain and elsewhere in Europe, it was inevitably Scots who claimed to be particularly energised by his explorations, his publications, and the extraordinary power of his reputation. Although some missions in Africa, either with Scottish personnel or specifically of the Scottish churches, predated the outburst of activity associated with his death, still the aura of Livingstone, confirmed by his burial in the national Valhalla of Westminster Abbey, came to be associated with all of them. A good example of this is the United Presbyterian (as it became) Calabar Mission in southern Nigeria, which had its origins in Jamaica, and was led by Hope Waddell and William Anderson. Through the arrival of Mary Slessor (1848–1915) in 1876, it immediately associated itself with Livingstone's reputation. Slessor herself was absorbed into the colonial administration of the law and was certainly a protagonist of the extension of the British Empire in the region.[5] The missions on the eastern Cape in southern Africa and, above all, those of the Established and Free Churches of Scotland in the region that later became Nyasaland (Malawi) were respectively incorporated into the Livingstone legend or were directly inspired by him.[6]

Indeed, the prominence of the Malawi missions as well as of commercial activity associated with them, for example by the African Lakes Company, led the territory of Nyasaland to be regarded almost as a Scottish colony. One popular missionary biographer regarded Scottish activities around Lake Nyasa as offering compensation for the disaster of the Darien Scheme of the 1690s, that is the failed Scottish attempt to set up a colony in Central America which, through the loss of so much Scots capital, helped to move the country towards the Union of 1707.[7] Moreover, Scots were fearful of Portuguese encroachment on this supposedly Scottish colonial territory. Within a few years of the founding of these missions, Scots were campaigning to oppose what they saw as the dangerous prospect of a Portuguese takeover of what they regarded as their territory in southern Malawi. Portuguese ambitions – or desire to re-establish what they saw as their historic rights – became apparent in 1888. Immediately anxieties were expressed in Scotland. In 1889, Sir Harry Johnston was sent to Lisbon to negotiate a treaty and the resulting draft agreement confirmed the worst of Scottish fears. Meetings produced memorials and petitions all over Scotland and the press repeatedly asserted that public opinion would not tolerate any danger to the work of Livingstone.[8] When Archibald Scott, the convenor of the Church of Scotland Foreign Mission Committee, presented a 'monster petition' to the prime minister, he announced 'My Lord, this is the voice of Scotland'.[9] It was a public outcry that successfully pressured the government of Lord Salisbury to decline to ratify the treaty. Although Salisbury may well have been happy to manipulate this pressure for his own purposes, this celebrated incident reveals the manner in which Scots (though with English allies) were prepared to agitate in favour of the retention of a region they had come to see as, in some senses, their own, hallowed by the name of Livingstone. Southern Malawi remained in British hands.

All of these effects of what may be called the exploratory and missionary diaspora of the Scots are well known, but the much greater complexity of the relationship of Scotland with Africa has become better understood in recent years. The various Scots diasporas can be identified as including the appearance of professionals in many parts of Africa, including specific Scots specialisms such as medicine and education, often but not exclusively associated with missionary endeavour.[10] In the colonial era, surveyors, engineers and later foresters and agronomists have to be added to this list, as well as numbers of Scottish administrators who came to work in the colonial administrative service. Moreover, if attention is focused upon southern Africa we find that Scots were long involved in the region, even when the Cape remained under Dutch control. There were many Scottish migrants in the Netherlands who moved on to the Cape, not least in the Scots Brigade which constituted a key component of the Dutch military defence forces in the region. Scots merchants were also prominent. Two of the most celebrated plant hunters in southern Africa in the eighteenth century were Scots, Francis Masson (1741–1805) and William Paterson (1755–1810), who made the remarkable Cape flora more widely known. Whether or not Masson and Paterson were involved in espionage, as the Dutch suspected, the fact is that when the British did attack the Cape in 1795, the invasion had the appearance of being a Scottish enterprise. The Scottish secretary of state for war, Henry Dundas, Viscount Melville, sent a Scottish admiral, George Keith Elphinstone, and a general with a Scottish background, James Henry Craig, to take the colony. After its return to the Dutch in 1802, the Cape was taken again in 1806 by another Scottish general, Sir David Baird. Scottish regiments, the Argyll and Sutherland Highlanders, the Seaforth Highlanders and the Highland Light Infantry, were closely concerned with these occupations. The Dutch forces at the Cape surrendered without a fight, advised by their Scottish-Dutch commanding officer Colonel Robert Gordon, who was a royalist and therefore had no time for Napoleonic rule in the Netherlands. He encountered so much hostility that he subsequently committed suicide.[11]

From this time onwards the Scots became very prominent at the Cape. Lists of names of residents include many that appear to be Scottish, although they could have arrived there via the Netherlands, Ireland or England. Although names provide slippery evidence, there can be little doubt that there was a major Scottish presence, embracing shipping and mercantile interests, as well as sectors associated with education, banking and insurance, the press, and religious and missionary activity. Scots fought for press freedoms from the autocratic governor, Lord Charles Somerset, as well as for legal amelioration for indigenous inhabitants.[12] However, such legal amelioration is fraught with ambiguities. The principle of 'mutuality' was introduced into banking and insurance by John Fairbairn, while the founder of a South African literary tradition in English was the Borders settler, radical and poet, an associate of Sir Walter Scott, Thomas Pringle.[13] The numbers of Scots among the white colonists was boosted by the Scottish contingent in the 1820 settlement introduced to 'settle' the eastern frontier. The governor, Somerset, anxious to maintain aspects of social control over the Dutch through the strengthening of the Dutch Reformed Church, introduced many Scots ministers, who received some training in language and theology in the Netherlands and soon became highly influential within the Afrikaner community. Cape law was Roman Dutch, closer to Scots law then to the English common law. Consequently some Scottish lawyers also became significant. By the middle of the century, there can be little doubt that many of the characteristics of an anglophone Cape had been, for good or ill, initiated by Scots. After 1843, the new colony of Natal became an important destination for Scots migrants. Some Scots were recruited for specific projects, such as Aberdonian stonemasons who arrived to work on the Durban harbour works. Indeed, the arrival of so many Scottish artisans and professionals aroused the anger of English colonists.

Scots brought with them major cultural and intellectual influences. The adherence of some Scots to the free trade principles of Adam Smith was certainly influential at the Cape, not least in overturning East India Company monopolies. The Scottish military spread both Presbyterianism and freemasonry, while Scottish divines introduced a politically committed theology. The missions of the eastern Cape were significant in many economic, social and cultural ways, introducing western building techniques, industrial training for Africans and a print culture with printing presses disseminating religious materials, books and magazines. Scots may also have had a particular affinity for linguistic activity.[14] Above all, they created educational institutions and medical provision which, while reflecting racial hierarchies and dominant patriarchal ideologies, laid the foundations for the emergence of a westernised African elite. The first ordained African minister, Revd Tiyo Soga, received his theological training in Scotland and married a Scots woman. Later, such radicalism dissipated and these missions can be seen as becoming increasingly compromised in accepting and working within racially divisive and discriminatory policies. They served to entrench white power, confirming new social hierarchies and creating a 'blue-collar' intermediate class to service white economic and administrative activities. But many future African leaders and nationalists were nurtured at these institutions.

The discovery and exploitation of diamonds to the north-west of the Cape from the early 1870s and the rapid development of gold mining in the Transvaal in the later 1880s transformed the economic and social conditions of southern Africa. Cities grew rapidly, roads and railway lines were developed, shipping services massively improved, migrants were sucked in and cheap African migrant labour came to be the essential workforce of the mining industry. Among the cohorts of immigrant whites, Scots featured prominently, now arriving to make money rather than find adventure or contribute to missionary endeavour.[15] The mining boom in southern Africa coincided with depressed conditions in North America and this helped to divert migrants to the region. Scots migration to southern Africa rose suddenly in the 1880s and the region soon became a significant destination. As elsewhere, the Scottish component was disproportionate to the relative populations within the United Kingdom. The 1911 Union of South Africa census reveals that 20 per cent of UK-born white settlers were Scots, considerably higher than the 12 per cent constituted by their population within Britain. Thus Scots, their numbers boosted by involvement in the 1899–1902 Anglo-Boer War and subsequent settlement schemes, constituted a surprisingly high proportion of the anglophone white population of the new Union.

Scottish chemists were indeed vital for the vast development of the Rand gold mines. The essential characteristic of these mines was that the ore was of exceptionally low grade. The extraction of the gold was problematic and older mercury techniques were much too expensive. Three chemists, John Stewart MacArthur and brothers Robert and William Forrest, working in the Tennant laboratories in Glasgow, succeeded in creating the cyanide extraction process in 1887. This MacArthur-Forrest process was crucial once it was introduced to the Rand by 1890. Many more low-grade mines then came into production.

Another celebrated Scot was able to exploit the sudden and dramatic growth in both passenger and freight traffic to and from southern Africa. Greenock-born Donald Currie (1825–1909) rose rapidly in the Cunard shipping company and in 1862 founded his own Castle Line to serve Liverpool and Calcutta.[16] Spotting the coming rapid expansion of southern Africa he concentrated the Union–Castle Line on serving Cape Town and other ports. In 1876 it shared the mail contract with the rival Union Line and in 1900 the two lines merged under Currie's management to become one of the celebrated imperial shipping lines. Currie used his resulting wealth to buy three estates in Glen Lyon, Perthshire. He was a Liberal and Liberal Unionist MP in Perthshire for twenty years (1880–1900), acted as an adviser to government on South African and shipping affairs, and invested a great deal of his profits in Perthshire, Edinburgh University and Belfast (where he spent part of his boyhood). At his death, his shipping line possessed forty-seven ships totalling almost 300,000 tons. Currie used his ships to forward imperial interests, including the carrying of troops for various conflicts, including the Anglo-Boer War.

Scots in South Africa soon developed all the aspects of associational culture which are to be found elsewhere. These included Presbyterian churches, freemasonry, Caledonian and St Andrew's societies (with highly visible meetings and dinners), as well as dance and musical activity, Highland Games and various sports. Many Scots involved in these associations were middle-class professionals and commercial entrepreneurs who valued the opportunities for networking, as well as providing private social security arrangements. A magazine, *The South African Scot*, was founded, although its survival period was relatively short, perhaps 1905–7. Above all, Scots became heavily involved in the labour force of the mining industry, taking on skilled tasks and supervisory roles in respect of the great mass of black labour. In the pursuit of its own interests, white labour invariably adopted a racially exclusive approach to trade union and socialist activity. Jonathan Hyslop has charted the complexities of the distinctive form such radicalism took in the racial contexts of South Africa. Hyslop's work has, however, shown that there was never a monolithic approach to the politics of the left (let alone of other parts of the spectrum) among Scots.[17]

The life of Dundee-born James Thompson Bain (1860–1919) demonstrated the international character of the socialist and labour ideas that came to bear upon South Africa.[18] Bain was active in radical politics in Edinburgh and may have encountered celebrated international figures such as William Morris, Prince Peter Kropotkin, Annie Besant and others. He joined the British army and fought in the Zulu War. He also served in India and may well have visited Argentina. He later became increasingly radicalised in South Africa, moving to Kimberley and then to the Rand. As a republican, he sympathised with the Afrikaners in the Transvaal in their opposition to the British. During the Boer War, his Transvaal citizenship prevented him from being shot as a traitor to the British cause. Sent to Ceylon to a Boer prisoner of war camp, he soon emerged as a leader of the agitation for prisoner rights. Back in South Africa, he became closely associated with a socialist coterie of Scots who were helping to develop trade unions and the Labour Party. Bain was concerned to protect white workers against competition from cheaper Chinese and Africans, so he came to symbolise a specific South African radicalism. He was closely involved in the controversial visit of the early Labour leader James Keir Hardie to South Africa in 1908[19] and was a major organiser of the Rand mining strike of 1913–14, as a result of which he was deported to Britain. Other Scots, such as Alexander Seaton Raitt (1867–1907) and Robert Cruikshank Graham (1869–1950) took different positions. Raitt fought in the Anglo-Boer War on the British side and was nominated to city and legislative councils by the high commissioners Milner and Selborne. Although that appears to mark him down as an imperial collaborator, his concern with workers' rights led him to attempt to establish workers' compensation schemes (which failed), oppose Chinese labour, and also demonstrate a sympathetic approach to the plight of black workers. Yet all three of these figures (even Bain in his later years) believed in the socially redemptive power of the British Empire, facilitating international labour connections with unionisation elsewhere in the Dominions, rather than the alternative force of a 'foreign' international socialist movement. In South Africa, many people have either clung to Scottish identities, if in different ways, or have rejected them. But an awareness of something distinctively Scottish in cultural, religious and political terms has continued down to modern times.

The complexity of Scottish affiliations is neatly illustrated in the ways in which South Africa displayed examples of the Scottish military tradition through the founding of the Cape Town Highlanders and the Transvaal Scottish (respectively in 1885 and 1902). These regiments used Scottish uniforms and pipe bands, maintaining links with Scottish counterparts. They fought in campaigns against indigenous Africans, such as the Zulu, in imperial wars against the Boers, and in the First World War. They were also deployed (sometimes under duress) to help put down the Rand mine strikes in 1913–14 and 1919. Yet, partly through the Scottish influence in the Dutch Reformed Church, the Afrikaans community developed an affection for Scottish symbolism, perhaps because it seemed to stand out against the English. The Scots regiments survived through the apartheid period, often featured at the state openings of the South African parliament, and remain as infantry reserve units within the South African army today, now with many kilted African soldiers. They may also have helped to spread variants of Scottish dress, together with dance forms, into African societies. Thus, Scottish immigrant culture acquired a whole variety of meanings in African contexts. There may indeed be other examples of the influence of Scottish dancing, as there are on other continents.[20]

British imperial advance into East Africa also had a distinctly Scottish element. The Imperial British East Africa Company (IBEAC) was one of three African chartered companies used as an 'arm's length' device for British involvement in the partition of Africa. The principal mover here was another Scottish shipowner, Sir William Mackinnon (1823–93), who was already well versed in promoting imperial interests.[21] Born in Campbeltown, Mackinnon left to work for mercantile and shipping interests in Glasgow. In 1847 he went to India and, with former school friend Robert Mackenzie, founded the Mackinnon Mackenzie Company, which was to become one of the greatest agencies and mercantile firms in the East with branches stretching from the Persian Gulf to India, Ceylon, Burma, South-East Asia and the Far East. Involved in the coastal trade of the Bay of Bengal, he was soon providing shipping for the developing advance of the British into Burma. From the 1860s, he was closely associated with Sir Bartle Frere, Governor of Bombay, in establishing a service to the Persian Gulf to extend British influence. The death of Livingstone and developments connected with Zanzibar led him to look across the Indian Ocean. In 1888 he founded the IBEAC to help frustrate German ambitions in the region. The directorship of this company represented its mix of business, imperial and philanthropic interests, with a strong Scottish element, including Sir John Kirk (Livingstone's doctor and botanist on the Zambezi expedition),

Sir Donald Stewart, A. L. Bruce (son-in-law of David Livingstone), the Marquis of Lorne and Sir George Mackenzie. The latter became the administrator in Mombasa and wrote 'Thank God, we are all Scots here'.[22] Why he wrote that might arouse some discussion. While the IBEAC helped to achieve the government's objectives, it was grossly under-capitalised and collapsed in 1896.

Mackinnon (like Currie) was a member of the Free Church, as was the case with so many Glasgow industrialists who financed the mission in northern Malawi. The Free Church missionary Alexander Murdoch Mackay was educated in Edinburgh and Berlin and had a particular aptitude for practical activities associated with the founding of missions, such as mechanics, carpentry, farming and road building. Despite his Free Church background he joined the Church Missionary Society, went to Zanzibar in 1876 and on to Uganda in 1878, where he died of malaria in 1890.[23] His early death helped him to become yet another inspirational force in the missionary push into Africa. Starting from 1891, a number of Scots missionaries arrived in Kenya to found Presbyterian mission stations among the Kikuyu and other peoples. Dr James Stewart, the celebrated Lovedale missionary from the eastern Cape, arrived to take charge. After the First World War, a presbytery of East Africa was founded and African elders appointed, followed by African pastors in the later 1920s. The Presbyterian Church became the fastest growing church in East Africa, but it has been suggested that a process of decolonisation from Scotland is reflected in a recent wave of Pentecostalism, the leaders of which set about destroying alleged connections with freemasonry and other symbols of a Scottish past.[24] Scots inevitably appeared as both settlers and sojourners in other areas of settlement in Africa, notably Kenya, Southern and Northern Rhodesia (Zimbabwe and Zambia) and Nyasaland (Malawi). Presbyterian missions in all of these became significant in establishing educational and medical services for Africans.

West Africa tends to be particularly associated with the shipping interests and trades of Liverpool, with the palm oil that made the fortunes of Lever Brothers. However, there was a Presbyterian presence in Ghana, albeit a relatively weak one.[25] It was stronger in Nigeria where the Presbyterians became influential among the people of the Central Belt just south of the Muslim north. It has been suggested that these Presbyterians, given their Scottish background, encouraged the resistance of the people in that region to the efforts of the imperial government in rationalising its administration into that of the north, which Central Belt peoples saw as alien.[26] Presbyterians famously flourished in south-eastern Nigeria, where there are alleged to be well over 3 million members today, in 2,000 congregations.

The Scottish cultural diaspora has produced some intriguing manifestations. Some elements of Scottish dancing have been identified among African dancers in both eastern and southern Africa. On the East African coast they were known as Scotchi, dressed in kilts and later using bagpipes.[27] Scots constituted a considerable proportion of the population of Mombasa and Africans must have been aware of elements of Scottish culture through their St Andrew's Day and Caledonian Society events. The Scottish military tradition was also in evidence. These African dance societies, part of the Beni dance society tradition which fielded ngomas or team dancers, had divided into two intense rivals, Kingi and Scotchi, representing English and Scots. A British administrator reported that in 1910 he had seen a fifty-strong dance troupe, calling themselves Scotchi and wearing military uniforms and kilts marching in Mombasa. They carried dummy wooden rifles and marched to a bugle band, attracting a very large audience. By 1919 the Scotchi had become even more prominent. The same division between Kingi and Scotchi turned up further north in Lamu, where the Scotchi tradition lasted for at least fifty years and where the dancers wore kilts, sporrans and bonnets. Ranger has analysed these dances as a creative response to European idioms, as an adaptation of a competitive dancing tradition that ran deep in Swahili society. The dances constituted a response by young men to modernisation, a means of grappling with the modern world and, in some instances, of engaging in protest, even against elite leadership. What is clear is that Africans on the Kenyan coast sought to reproduce in their own competitive and politically intense dancing the perceived distinctions between English and Scottish ethnicities, even placing them in an oppositional mode.

Elements of Scottish dancing have also been taken up, presumably independently, by various African groups in South Africa, including Zulu people in the Nazareth Baptist Church. The Scottish contingent of dancers (one of several groups), wearing kilts and topis and known as isikoshi, seems to have been originally founded by the first prophet of this church, Isaiah Shembe, at the end of the First World War. The tradition has continued, passing through various modifications, down to modern times. The isikoshi remain highly inventive and very popular, prominent at the annual festivals of this church. A whole range of explanations have been suggested for this incorporation of supposed Scottishness into Zulu dance traditions. It is certainly the case that the kilt offers considerable freedom of movement. It may be that it was seen

on Scottish soldiers or at Highland Games events and may have been
immediately related to Zulu traditional garments. Magnus Echtler has
suggested that the dance started out in some senses as an expression of
anti-colonialism, but that in modern times it has become a vehicle for
youthful resistance to the power of the elders who control the church.[28]
Yet another Scottish dance group has been identified among the Pedi
people of the northern Transvaal (now Limpopo province).[29] They seem
to have their origins around the 1960s and are known as Maaparankwe.
They wear expensive kilts purchased from the Johannesburg Caledonian
Society shop and have developed a dance style or kibu, which again
may be associated with military identity and social cohesion, perhaps
a form of escapism, and even an association with a people, the Scots,
who seemed to constitute a minority, sometimes resistant, but bearing
with them this strangely attractive cultural identity. As in East Africa,
Africans identified Scots as a wholly different ethnicity whose cultural
forms could be incorporated in appealing ways.

Such expressions of Scottishness have served to maintain a wider sense
of Scottish identity enhanced by its global manifestations. Moreover, the
Scots attitude to Africa and Africans over the years has reflected Scottish
ideas in general. There were black people in eighteenth-century Scotland
and some of them can be identified through their appearance in the
Scottish courts, cases that seem to reveal a degree of even-handedness
in the judicial system of the time.[30] Famously, Scots judges were doubt-
ful about the status of black slavery in Scotland and more widely in
Britain. The remarkable case of Tiyo Soga reflects the lack of racism
in the early nineteenth century. Moreover, when he was ordained, the
moderator of the United Presbyterian Church indulged in an attack
on the British government in respect of its prosecution of the frontier
wars.[31] Scots were already revealing a degree of dissidence from national
politics that would be recreated in the twentieth century. But Scots were
undoubtedly swept up into the more pronounced racism of the later
nineteenth century, racism that was itself developed through the writings of Scots such as Robert Knox. Henry Drummond's book *Tropical
Africa*, written after a visit to the Lake Nyasa region at the invitation
of the African Lakes Company, was highly influential, disseminating his
social Darwinism and his suggestion that Africa required to be 'pitied
and redeemed'.[32] While such a patronising view of the continent must
have been common at the time, any reading of other popular works by
Scottish missionaries, their memoirs and biographies reveals a complexity of views of Africa and Africans, many sympathetic and some admir-
ing. Yet it is undoubtedly true that, despite missionary disapproval,

when it came to violent acts of dispossession in the settler territories of Africa, or in the highly destructive suppression of resistance and revolt, Scots were no different from other colonialists.

In any case, by the 1880s West African students were appearing in the Scottish universities, notably Edinburgh, Aberdeen and Glasgow, often studying medicine. They were invariably active in student politics and developed their sense of radicalism and proto-nationalism, as well as pan-Africanist ideals, while in Scotland.[33] Many academics and fellow students must have revised their views of Africa. Moreover, there can be little doubt that Africa became highly prominent in the last few decades of the century. The founding of the Royal Scottish Geographical Society, with branches in Aberdeen, Dundee, Edinburgh and Glasgow, contributed to this, but this was also true of the press and of the cockpits of publishing in Glasgow and Edinburgh.[34] Scotland had also become a centre of cartographical publishing contributing to knowledge of and ideas about Africa.[35] Evidence derived from the catalogue of one notable Scottish library set up in 1898 reveals the extent to which Africa was prominent in its purchasing policy.[36] In the same decade, the three Botswanan chiefs who visited Britain in 1895, Bathoen, Sebele and Khama, received a particularly warm welcome in Scotland, notably in their visits to Edinburgh and Glasgow, which included civic receptions, visits to industrial units and shipyards, churches and Glasgow University.[37] The chiefs' visit was designed to lobby for the inclusion of their territory in the British Empire to avoid incorporation into the white-ruled Cape, but it also had the effect of raising the profile of Africa and Africans. They were seen as dignified and civilised, although such favourable views were achieved through allowing themselves to be partially incorporated into British norms.

While there were notorious race riots in Glasgow in 1919, resulting from the post-war recession and the social disruption caused by the war,[38] there can be little doubt that what was seen as the special Scottish relationship with parts of Africa contributed to the Scots cultural and political revival of the era. Nationalist writers highlighted the separate contribution of Scots to the British Empire as contributing to a sense of Scottish distinctiveness, the global expression of the 'stateless nation'. This was promoted by the continuing power of the reputation of David Livingstone and the realisation that his memory was celebrated and honoured by Africans. These phenomena received a considerable boost at the time of the creation of the Central African Federation of Northern and Southern Rhodesia and Nyasaland in 1953. This was self-evidently a vehicle for the spread of southern African white racism and the suppression of African nationalist politics. After the emergencies of 1959, particularly in Malawi, the Church of Scotland (though not without dissent) became active in opposing the policies of the Westminster government. In many respects this activity has fed into the modern development of the Scotland-Malawi partnership which intriguingly sees the devolved government of Scotland as developing a separate aid and diplomatic policy in relation to Africa, Malawi in particular, despite the reservation of these functions to Westminster.[39] In many cases, the decolonisation of the Presbyterian churches of many parts of Africa after the Second World War preceded that of political decolonisation – regional and independent Presbyterian churches were established with autonomous synods and assemblies freed from the authority of the parent churches in Scotland.

In the same period, the numbers of Africans arriving in Scotland to be educated and to work rose tremendously. While discrimination remained, attitudes were changing. The decline of empire, the brutal campaigns of the final years of British rule (such as so-called Mau Mau in Kenya) kept Africa in the public eye through the press and other media, not least because of the involvement of Scottish regiments.[40] Yet, in the same period many in the churches and in education sought to promote the notion that there was a 'special relationship' between Scottish society and certain regions of the continent. It is clear that the manifestations of this relationship confirm the instrumentality of the ethnic and cultural diversity of British migrants. The argument for the cultural absorption of migrants in their new homes generally does not work in the case of Africa. Thus, although a great deal of further research needs to be done, it is apparent that the reciprocal relationship of Scotland and Africa is richly complex. It was important to several parts of Africa, not least in the provision of educational and medical opportunities, as well as being unquestionably significant for Scots' estimations of themselves in respect of the wider world.

NOTES

1. An excellent early example of a regional survey was J. D. Hargreaves, *Aberdeenshire to Africa: Northeast Scots and Overseas Expansion* (Aberdeen: Aberdeen University Press, 1982). More recently, John M. MacKenzie with Nigel R. Dalziel, *The Scots in South Africa: Ethnicity, Identity, Gender and Race, 1772–1914* (Manchester: Manchester University Press, 2007).
2. Douglas Hamilton, *Scotland, the Caribbean and the Atlantic World, 1750–*

1820 (Manchester: Manchester University Press, 2005); Eric J. Graham, *Burns and the Sugar Plantocracy of Ayrshire* (Ayr: Ayrshire Archaeological and Natural History Society, 2009); T. M. Devine (ed.), *Recovering Scotland's Slavery Past; The Caribbean Connection* (Edinburgh: Edinburgh University Press, 2015).

3. Iain Whyte, *Scotland and the Abolition of Black Slavery, 1756–1838* (Edinburgh: Edinburgh University Press, 2006); Catherine Hall, *Macaulay and Son: Architects of Imperial Britain* (New Haven: Yale University Press, 2012).

4. John M. MacKenzie, 'David Livingstone: prophet or patron saint of imperialism in Africa; myths and misconceptions', *Geographical Journal*, 129:3–4 (2013), pp. 277–91.

5. W. P. Livingstone, *Mary Slessor of Calabar: Pioneer Missionary* (London: Hodder and Stoughton, 1916). The literature on Slessor has grown considerably. For a recent African evaluation, see Oluwakemi A. Adesina and Elijah Obinna, 'Invoking gender: the thoughts, mission and theology of Mary Slessor in southern Nigeria', in Afe Adogame and Andrew Lawrence (eds), *Africa in Scotland, Scotland in Africa: Historical Legacies and Contemporary Hybridities* (Leiden: Brill, 2014), pp. 203–27. See also J. H. Proctor, 'Serving God and the empire: Mary Slessor in south-eastern Nigeria, 1876–1915', *Journal of Religion in Africa*, 30:1 (2000), pp. 45–61.

6. MacKenzie with Dalziel, *Scots in South Africa*, ch. 4; John McCracken, *Politics and Christianity in Malawi, 1875–1940* (Cambridge: Cambridge University Press, 1977).

7. W. P. Livingstone, *Laws of Livingstonia: A Narrative of Missionary Adventure and Achievement* (London: Hodder and Stoughton, 1921), p. 9. Livingstone suggested that it was 'a more noble undertaking' than Darien, 'more in line with the higher genius of the people . . . to realise the life-aims of Livingstone'.

8. The Scottish press covered these meetings prominently, e.g. *The Scotsman*, 25 July 1888, p. 5; 22 December 1888, p. 6; 29 December 1888, p. 6; 24 April 1889, p. 6; 30 May 1889, p. 6, and many others.

9. W. P. Livingstone, *A Prince of Missionaries: the Rev. Alexander Hetherwick of Blantyre* (London: James Clarke, n.d.,), p. 52. The memorial was signed by 11,000 ministers and elders. The prospect of Uganda being abandoned by the IBEAC produced a similar agitation in churches throughout Britain, together with a large public meeting at Exeter Hall in London, in 1892.

10. For education in Nigeria, for example, see W. H. Taylor, 'The Presbyterian educational impact in eastern Nigeria', *Journal of Religion in Africa*, 14:3 (1983), pp. 223–45.

11. This and succeeding paragraphs (except where otherwise referenced) are based on MacKenzie with Dalziel, *Scots in South Africa*.

12. John M. MacKenzie, '"To enlighten South Africa": the creation of a free

press at the Cape in the early nineteenth century', in Chandrika Kaul (ed.), *Media and the British Empire* (Basingstoke: Palgrave, 2006), pp. 20–36: Andrew Ross, *John Philip (1775–1850): Missions, Race and Politics in South Africa* (Aberdeen: Aberdeen University Press, 1986).

13. Another Scottish poet was Charles Murray. Jonathan Hyslop, 'Making Scotland in South Africa: Charles Murray, the Transvaal's Aberdeenshire poet', in David Lambert and Alan Lester (eds), *Colonial Lives Across the British Empire: Imperial Careering in the Long Nineteenth Century* (Cambridge: Cambridge University Press, 2006), pp. 309–34.

14. See, for example, Vicky Khasandi-Telewa, '"She worships at the Kikuyu church": the influence of Scottish missionaries on language in worship and education among African Christians', in Adogame and Lawrence (eds), *Africa in Scotland*, pp. 287–306.

15. Henry Drummond, *Tropical Africa* (London: Hodder and Stoughton, 1889), p. 1.

16. Andrew Porter, *Victorian Shipping, Business and Imperial Policy: Donald Currie, the Castle Line and Southern Africa* (Woodbridge: Boydell, 1986). Porter, however, fails to understand the Scottish dimension. Typical of Currie's enterprise was his establishment of the *Union-Castle Guide to South Africa* in the late 1890s (later including East Africa). Its cover announced that its information was for 'tourists, sportsmen, invalids and settlers'. Issued annually, it had considerable sales.

17. Jonathan Hyslop, 'Archie Gibb's Zulu war dance: biographical explorations in South African military identity'. Available at <http://www.academia.edu/1481365/Archie_Gibbs_Zulu_War_Dance_Biographical_Explorations_in_South_African_Scottish_Military_Culture> (accessed October 2015).

18. Jonathan Hyslop, *The Notorious Syndicalist: J. T. Bain, a Scottish Rebel in Colonial South Africa* (Johannesburg: Witwatersrand University Press, 2004).

19. Jonathan Hyslop, 'The world voyage of James Keir Hardie: Indian nationalism, Zulu insurgency and the British labour diaspora, 1907–1908', *Journal of Global History*, 1 (2006), pp. 343–63. See also Hyslop, 'Scottish labour, race and Southern African empire, c. 1880–1922: a reply to Kenefick', *International Review of Social History*, 55 (2010), pp. 63–81.

20. For example, the Inuit in parts of Canada adopted dance forms from Scots whalers, complete with fiddle and accordion accompaniment. They still practice such dancing today.

21. J. Forbes Munro, *Maritime Enterprise and Empire: Sir William Mackinnon and his Business Network, 1823–1893* (Woodbridge: Boydell, 2003); John S. Galbraith, *Mackinnon and East Africa, 1878–1895* (Cambridge: Cambridge University Press, 1972).

22. Quoted in Andrew Dewar Gibb, *Scottish Empire* (London: Alexander Maclehose, 1937), p. 147.

23. *A. M. MacKay: Pioneer Missionary of the Church Missionary Society in Uganda*, by his sister (London: Hodder and Stoughton, 1893).

24. Damaris Seleina Parsitau, 'Pentecostalising the Church of Scotland? The Presbyterian Church in East Africa and the Pentecostal challenge in Kenya, 1970–2010', in Adogame and Lawrence (eds), *Africa in Scotland,* pp. 228–50.

25. Michael Kweku Okyerefo, 'Scottish missionaries in Ghana: the forgotten tribe', in ibid. pp. 251–62.

26. Musa A. B. Gaiya and Jordan S. Rengshwat, 'Scottish missionaries in central Nigeria', in ibid. pp. 263–86.

27. T. O. Ranger, *Dance and Society in Eastern Africa, 1890–1970* (London: Heinemann, 1975), pp. 25–8 and 145–51, and passim.

28. Magnus Echtler, 'Scottish warriors in Kwazulu-Natal: cultural hermeneutics of the Scottish dance (Isikoshi) in the Nazareth Baptist Church, South Africa', in Adogame and Lawrence (eds), *Africa in Scotland,* pp. 326–48.

29. Hyslop, 'Archie Gibb's Zulu war dance', pp. 14–16.

30. Ian Duffield, 'Identity, community and the lived experience of black Scots from the late eighteenth to the mid-nineteenth centuries', *Immigrants and Minorities*, 11:2 (1992), pp. 105–29.

31. MacKenzie with Dalziel, *Scots in South Africa*, pp. 116–17.

32. Drummond, *Tropical Africa*, p. vii. And see ch. 4.

33. Marika Sherwood, 'Two pan-African political activists emanating from Edinburgh University', pp. 103–36, and Marrku Hokkanen, 'Missionaries, agents of empire and medical educators: Scottish doctors in late nineteenth century southern and east central Africa', pp. 77–89, in Adogame and Lawrence (eds), *Africa in Scotland.*

34. John M. MacKenzie, 'The provincial geographical societies in Britain, 1884–1914', in Morag Bell, Robin Butlin and Michael Heffernan (eds), *Geography and Imperialism, 1820–1940* (Manchester: Manchester University Press, 1995), pp. 93–124.

35. James McCarthy, *Journey into Africa: The Life and Death of Keith Johnston, Scottish Cartographer and Explorer (1844–79)* (Latheronwheel: Whittles, 2004).

36. The Inglis Memorial Library, Edzell, Angus. The printed catalogue, which I have examined, reveals the prominence of African publications at the time. J. Smedley, *Inglis Memorial Hall and Library, Edzell* (Edzell: Zeldel Publishing, 2015).

37. Neil Parsons, *King Khama, Emperor Joe and the Great White Queen: Victorian Britain Through African Eyes* (Chicago: University of Chicago Press, 1998), pp. 180–4. There was no time to fulfil a fervently requested visit to Dundee, p. 157.

38. Jacqueline Jenkinson, *Black 1919: Riots, Racism and Resistance in Imperial Britain* (Liverpool: Liverpool University Press, 2009).

39. John M. MacKenzie, 'David Livingstone, the Scottish cultural and politi-

cal revival and the end of empire in Africa', in Bryan S. Glass and John
M. MacKenzie (eds), *Scotland, Empire and Decolonisation in Africa in
the Twentieth Century* (Manchester: Manchester University Press, 2015),
pp. 180–99. See also the articles by McCracken and Ross in Adogame and
Lawrence (eds), *Africa in Scotland*, pp. 42–73 and 309–25, and Bryan S.
Glass, 'Protection from the British empire? Central Africa and the Church
of Scotland', *Journal of Imperial and Commonwealth History*, 41:3 (2013),
pp. 475–95.

40. Bryan S. Glass, *The Scottish Nation at Empire's End* (London: Palgrave,
2015).

5

'Have the Scotch no Claim upon the Cherokees?' Scots, Indians and Scots Indians in the American South

Colin G. Calloway

IN APRIL 1847, AFTER the potato crop failed in the Western Highlands and Islands of Scotland, John Ross, the principal chief of the Cherokee Nation, wrote a letter to the editor of the *Cherokee Advocate*: 'It is said that there are not less than 300,000 Scotch on the Highlands and Islands, who must through charity, be fed during the ensuing summer or die of famine', he said. He urged the Cherokee people to do something for this 'benevolent and Christian cause'. 'Have the Scotch no claim upon the Cherokees?', Ross asked. 'Have they not a very especial claim? They have.' Ross called on the Cherokee people to hold a meeting at the capital, Tahlequah, to take steps to raise money. The meeting appointed a 'Relief Committee' and in May, Ross sent a bank draft for $190 'for the relief of those who are suffering by the famine in Scotland'.[1] It was more than many Cherokees could afford. In 1847, the Cherokee Indians in what is now Oklahoma and Arkansas were just beginning to emerge from more than twenty years of crisis. They had become divided into bitter factions, been driven from their homelands in Georgia and endured civil war within their nation. And John Ross had never set foot in Scotland. So what explains the Cherokees' generosity and empathy for people 4,000 miles away whose sufferings can have seemed no greater than their own?

Romantic assumptions that a natural affinity existed between Scots and American Indians as clan-based peoples do not suffice as an answer. Scottish General John Forbes, who had both Cherokees and Highland Scots in his army as he marched against the French Fort Duquesne (renamed Fort Pitt) in 1758, described them as cousins;[2] but just a couple of years later, with Britain now at war against the Cherokees, Highland troops burned Cherokee villages, destroyed Cherokee crops and killed Cherokee people. The explanation for the Cherokees' response to the Highland famine lies instead in the enduring presence of Scots and their descendants in the Indian nations of the south-eastern United States.

HISTORICAL AND HISTORIOGRAPHICAL BACKGROUND

The experiences and images of Scots driven from their homelands by the Hanoverian government's suppression of the Jacobite rebellions, the dismantling of the ancient clan system and the Highland Clearances dominate historical writing and popular memory, and some authors argue that emigrant Scots empathised – and may even have identified – with indigenous peoples who, like them, suffered from colonial oppression. In reality, most Scots who migrated did so to pursue new opportunities rather than escape oppression, and scholars taking a hard look at the involvement of Celtic peoples in British imperialism and settler colonialism around the globe question whether being Scottish – or Irish – affected colonists' attitudes to indigenous peoples, and whether ethnic background and country of origin mattered as much as did frontier conditions and the specific circumstances of encounter in determining how colonists dealt with Native people.[3] Many Scots found advancement in the British Empire, became avid colonisers themselves and forged new opportunities out of diaspora. Scotland itself became an imperial nation within the British state.[4] In colonial North America, Scottish educators were prominent in colonial society and the Society in Scotland for the Propagation of Christian Knowledge, founded in 1709 for the education of Highlanders, continued its educational and assimilative efforts among Native Americans.[5] Scottish and Scottish-trained ministers dominated the Episcopalian and Presbyterian churches, and Scottish doctors dominated the medical profession in the American colonies. Scottish soldiers fought for new territories, Scottish settlers occupied them and Scottish merchants formed commercial cliques.[6] Scottish colonial governors, soldiers, traders and settlers were probably as likely as their English or American counterparts to exploit, shoot, cheat and dispossess indigenous peoples. People who had experienced dispossession and displacement themselves seem to have had few qualms about dispossessing and displacing other people.

At the same time, however, John Ross's question reminds us that, at least in certain times and places, there was something distinctive about Scots relations with Indian peoples. The migration of Scots to North America and the recurrent relocation of indigenous peoples meant that Scots and their descendants encountered Native peoples across virtually the whole of North America. Subsuming those Scots into a larger 'English' category risks missing an important dimension of colonial–Indian relations: the difference between Scots and English matters today; it mattered more in the eighteenth century, and Indian people noted the distinction.[7] And although Scots–Indian relations cannot be simply explained as the shared sufferings of oppressed peoples, their encounters do need to be understood in the context of – and as a product of – the workings of capitalism and colonialism on both sides of the Atlantic. In Scotland and America colonial expansion transformed tribal homelands into contested borderlands and the rise of the nation state entailed the destruction of kin-based systems of social and political organisation.[8] New market forces broke old communal bonds and disrupted old ways of life as capitalist forces subordinated tribal societies and incorporated tribal resources into new economic systems. Kin-ordered modes of production gave place to capitalist systems where wealth controlled labour, means of production and distribution.[9] Communal landholding practices gave way to commercial management of property. Industrialisation and commercialisation of agriculture demanded the appropriation and exploitation of land, and reorganising land required relocating populations.[10] Resources extracted from American lands, such as tobacco, deerskins and cotton, fuelled developments in Scotland and England; displaced peoples from Scotland who gravitated to the American frontier met Indian people using the products of the industrial revolution. Indians in the North American fur trade overhunted to buy blankets made by children working fourteen hours a day in Yorkshire textile mills that used wool from sheep grazing on the lands of displaced Highland Scots, some of whom made careers in the North American fur trade.

SCOTS AND INDIANS IN THE FUR AND DEERSKIN TRADES

Everywhere in North America the fur trade depended on Indians, and almost everywhere in the trade there were Scots. Service in the Hudson's Bay Company and the Northwest Company brought men from the Scottish mainland, the Hebrides and the Orkneys into contact with Native peoples, from eastern Canada to the Pacific Northwest, from the Arctic to the Great Plains. Scots also dominated the deerskin trade with the Creek, Cherokee, Choctaw, Chickasaw, Seminole and other smaller tribes in what is now the south-eastern United States. By 1764 the south-eastern Indian trade was producing 800,000 pounds of deerskins per year, and many Scots traders made their fortunes in it.[11]

Scots and Indians understood the fur and deerskin trade in rather different ways. Indian people, whose societies operated along networks of kinship, sharing and reciprocity, viewed trade as an exchange built on cooperation rather than competition, a way to build alliances and establish mutual obligations, not just to gain material goods. For Scots, as for other Europeans, trading was business, the opportunity to accumulate wealth by buying and selling. Scottish traders who lived and operated in Indian societies were instrumental in introducing new concepts of property and reorienting those societies to a market economy.[12] They injected capitalist values and practices into the Indians' world even as capitalism was transforming the clan world back in the Scottish Highlands. Scots traders surely generated tensions as they tried to conduct business according to market demands and values, and Indian societies experienced strains as they shifted from ritual exchange to commercial hunting. As Scots traders and Indians interacted, often on a daily basis, they borrowed from each other's cultures. Clothing styles reflected the mix. South-eastern Indians adopted linen shirts, woollen and cotton cloth, sometimes tartan, and silver jewellery. Creek and Seminole men's clothing incorporated so many elements and styles of Highland dress that, with each passing decade, their dress 'seemed more like that of Highland lairds'.[13] Indians were being pulled into the commercial networks of the Atlantic world; Scots were being pulled into the communal networks of the Indian world.

Panton, Leslie and Company and its successor John Forbes and Company came to dominate the south-eastern trade and were active in Indian affairs. The original partners were all from northern Scotland. Panton, Leslie and Forbes were born in the coastal area east of Inverness overlooking the Moray Firth. As loyalist traders they took refuge in St Augustine during the American Revolution. Spain took over Florida by the terms of the Peace of Paris in 1783, but allowed the merchants to stay on. The Spanish colonial authorities permitted the company to sell British guns, goods and cloth to help keep the Creeks and Seminoles in the Spanish (and out of the American) orbit. By the late eighteenth century, the Creeks depended upon steady supplies of manufactured goods via trade and Panton, Leslie and Company worked closely with the Creek chief, Alexander McGillivray, who issued the licenses traders needed to operate in Creek towns. McGillivray's position in Creek society depended in part on his connections with Panton, Leslie and Company; Panton, Leslie and Company prospered in part because of their connections with McGillivray. Centring their business empire at Spanish Pensacola, the company extended their operations from Nassau in the Bahamas to western Tennessee and effectively controlled the whole south-eastern trade. Panton, Leslie and Company and John Forbes and Company sent Scottish boys to live with Indian families and learn their languages and cultures. Panton said his company exported at least 124,000 deerskins every year from 1783 to 1799.[14]

When the deerskin trade declined, Panton, Leslie and their succes-
sors continued to find opportunities. As the United States spread across
the south – removing Indians to make way for cotton and slaves – they
were instrumental in negotiating the transfer of Indian lands to the
United States. William Panton and John Forbes bought at discount the
debts individual Indian hunters owed small traders and then aggregated
the debts into one lump sum. They then exerted their influence to have
the tribes make treaties with the United States. The tribes sold millions
of acres of land to the United States, and the United States diverted
substantial sums from the purchase price to the traders. In 1805, for
example, the United States bought 8 million acres of Creek land for
$380,000, of which more than $77,000 went to Forbes and Company
to settle the Indians' debts. In this way, 'thousands of small, face-to-face
exchanges between traders and hunters were transmuted by a multina-
tional company and an expanding nation-state into massive land cessions that affected an entire people.'[15] Leveraging Indian debts to secure
Indian lands in this way was standard practice in Thomas Jefferson's
Indian policy but Scottish traders also employed the practice.

In areas and eras where the fur and deerskin trades predominated,
Scots and Indians coexisted and cohabited. Scots built new lives in
Indian country even as they brought changes to the Indians' world and
many also built Indian families. Sexual relations between Indian women
and non-Indian men were omnipresent in the fur trade. American frontiers were dangerous places for Indian women, who commonly suffered
sexual abuse and violence in a world where colonialism imposed new
gender relations and demanded the domination, and even degradation,
of Indian women and their bodies.[16] The fur trade was no exception.
Traders in Canada routinely abandoned their Native wives and families
with apparently little concern when they returned east or to Britain, a
practice known as 'turning off'. Scotsman George Simpson, governor
of the vast Hudson's Bay Company territory in the early 1800s, was
notorious for his casual and cynical exploitation of Native and Métis
women. He encouraged traders to form 'connubial alliances' as good
for business and 'the best security we can have of the good will of the
natives', but he regarded such liaisons as temporary and referred to
Native women in disparaging terms, using and casting off one 'bit of
brown' after another. An illegitimate son himself, he fathered at least
five children by four different women before he married an eighteen-
year-old cousin in London in 1830.[17]

But the fur and deerskin trades depended on Indian cooperation deep
in Indian country where the power dynamics often favoured the Indian

participants more than in other colonial situations. Where Scots and Indians lived side by side and slept side by side they often developed deeper relationships and more enduring connections than Simpson and his kind ever envisaged. In many Indian societies, sexual intercourse and marriage were ways of incorporating outsiders as kin, bringing potentially dangerous and disruptive strangers into the community.[18] Intermarriage between Scots and Indians, and between Scots and the Indian daughters of other Scots, produced Scots-Indian families and sometimes even Scots-Indian communities. They produced a population in both Canada and the United States that traced descent from Scottish clans as well as from Indian tribes and generated complicated webs of allegiance and identity that persist to this day. In the north-west, James Hunter has traced the many generations of the family descended from Hudson's Bay Company trader Angus McDonald who married a Salish and part Mohawk wife, Catherine, and who died on the Flathead Reservation in Montana in 1889.[19]

In the south-east, said Scotsman and South Carolina Indian agent Thomas Nairne as early as 1708, it was 'the easiest thing in the world . . . to procure kindred among the Indians'.[20] Indian wives gave traders connections and extended kinship ties in the community where they did business. Traders who married into Indian societies usually did so according to Native custom and, among the matrilineal and matrilocal tribes of the south-east, usually took up residence in their wife's town, where they adapted to, and sometimes adopted, Native ways of living and organising families.[21] Marrying a trader could enhance a woman's status by giving her family access to new sources of wealth and manu- factured goods that were becoming necessities (although at a cost: the source of the wife's status and identity 'came to derive from her husband rather than her mother, brother, lineage, or clan').[22] As in the fur trade of the north-west, intermarriage in the deerskin trade of the south- east produced extensive and sometimes complicated family lineages. Robert Grierson, a Scottish trader in the late 1700s, married a Creek Indian woman called Sinnugee, who was a refugee from Spanish Florida and therefore was likely part Spanish, Mesoamerican and African. They settled in what is now Alabama, had eight children and owned slaves. Their descendants today 'number in the thousands' and 'live in Oklahoma, Tennessee, Washington, California, Texas, Kansas, Hawaii, and probably just about every other state'.[23]

SCOTS INDIANS IN THE SOUTH-EAST

Scots traders and their offspring exerted an influence disproportionate to their numbers during turbulent and transitional times in south-eastern Indian–white relations. They built networks of power and influence that stretched from Indian villages to colonial capitals; they acted as cultural intermediaries between colonial governments and Indian societies; and they often played important roles in tribal affairs. By the time the United States instituted a national policy of Indian removal in 1830, people of Scots-Indian descent were ubiquitous among the tribes of the south-east.

Scotsman James Logan Colbert settled in Chickasaw country in 1729, lived there for forty years, married three Chickasaw women in succession, and had half a dozen sons. Working through tribal forms and institutions, the Colberts were 'the principal Chickasaw spokesmen for well over a century'. In a period of intense change and American expansion across the south, they generally sided with the Americans. Some fought with Andrew Jackson in the Creek War of 1813–14; a couple served as negotiators when the Chickasaws signed treaties of removal; and one, Levi Colbert, became principal chief of the Chickasaws.[24]

Traders named McGillivray and McIntosh played crucial roles in Creek country.[25] Lachlan McGillivray migrated from Dunmaglass, Inverness-shire, in 1736 as an indentured servant, and entered the Indian trade in the 1740. (The largest Indian trading company in the south-east was run by a kinsman, Archibald McGillivray, until his retirement in 1744.) Lachlan McGillivray learned to speak Muskogee, the dominant Creek language, participated in the purgative black drink ritual, cultivated relationships with Creek chiefs, and mastered the subtle arts of intercultural diplomacy. He married well, taking as his wife Sehoy Marchand, the Creek daughter of a French officer; she was a member of the prestigious Wind Clan and sister of a Creek chief named Red Shoes. McGillivray spent a dozen years at the Creek town of Little Tallassee and became an influential figure in British–Indian relations and in colonial Georgia. He named his first son Alexander, after the clan chief who fell at Culloden, and, although Alexander inherited his mother's Wind Clan identity and was raised Creek, Lachlan saw to it that that he received a formal education in Charles Town, South Carolina.[26]

When Alexander McGillivray returned to his mother's people, he was literate and widely read: he had studied Greek, Latin, English history and literature. He owned and managed a large plantation, owned slaves and functioned effectively in the Atlantic commercial world. During the American Revolution, he supported the British cause and had an appointment in the British Indian department. After the Revolution, this Scots Indian emerged as the most prominent chief in the Creek nation – actually a loose confederacy of more than fifty autonomous towns stretching across northern Florida, western Georgia, northern Alabama and eastern Mississippi – and perhaps the most prominent individual in the Indian south-east. Chronically ill but an astute politician and an agile diplomat, he balanced Creek relations with the state of Georgia, with the United States and with Spain in an era and area of intense international competition. As a silent partner in Panton, Leslie and Company, he also controlled the flow of trade goods into Creek country.

One of George Washington's first challenges as president was to insert the federal government into relations between Georgia and the Creek confederacy in an effort to avoid an all-out Indian war and the possibility of international conflict. Doing so involved asserting the authority of the national government over Georgia's assertions of state rights and winning the allegiance of Alexander McGillivray, who had made a treaty of alliance with the Spaniards at Pensacola. Washington first attempted to secure a treaty with McGillivray by dispatching commissioners to Creek country but negotiations foundered. McGillivray dismissed one of the treaty commissioners as a puppy and 'a great boaster' and declared, 'by G— I would not have such a Treaty cram'd down my throat'.[27] The commissioner told Washington that McGillivray had 'the good sense of an American, the shrewdness of a Scotchman, & the cunning of an Indian'.[28] Washington then sent a special envoy to invite McGillivray to New York. McGillivray and a delegation of almost thirty Creeks travelled north by land and spent nearly a month in the nation's temporary capital. There were endless meetings, informal conferences and lavish dinners, and they saw the sights. McGillivray's delegation attracted crowds and his negotiations attracted international attention. At the Treaty of New York, signed in August 1790, McGillivray ceded disputed land on the Oconee River but secured a trade agreement with the United States that bolstered his position in Creek country. A secret article commissioned McGillivray a brigadier general in the United States Army with an annual pension of $1,200, more than the stipend he received from Spain. The treaty was intended to wean McGillivray from his alliance with Spain and bring peace to the frontier in Georgia. It did neither. Georgians continued to encroach on Creek land; Creeks continued to resist, and McGillivray went back to his Spanish alliance.[29]

Like his father, he wanted his son (also named Alexander) to receive a formal education. After Alexander senior died young in 1793, William Panton honoured his friend's wishes and sent the boy to Inverness, where he was reunited with his Highland grandfather and studied under a tutor. Unfortunately, the young man never returned to Creek country: he died of pneumonia in 1802.[30]

The McGillivrays were not the only descendants of Clan Chattan who functioned as intermediaries, culture brokers and chiefs in Creek country. James McQueen, a native of Scotland, entered the Creek trade in the 1750s and married a woman of the Wind Clan. His son, Peter McQueen, rose to the position of head warrior of Little Tallassee.[31] He was a leading 'Red Stick' in the Creek War, and moved to Florida to continue the fight against the United States. William Weatherford, a grandson of Lachlan McGillivray, was also a Creek resistance leader in the Creek War.

Not all Scots Creeks had the Creeks' best interests at heart. William McIntosh, whose Creek name was Tustunnuggee Hutkee, or White Warrior, was born in the Lower Creek town of Coweta. Like Alexander McGillivray, he was a member of the Wind Clan through his Creek mother and of Clan Chattan through his Scottish father, an officer. Like McGillivray, he was prominent in Creek government and had Scottish relatives who were prominent in Georgia affairs. But McIntosh pursued a different path from McGillivray. He led the pro-American faction in the Creek War and fought as an ally of Andrew Jackson at the Battle of Horseshoe Bend in 1814, where 800 Creeks died. He helped the Americans, and himself, in a series of shady land deals. On one occasion he tried to bribe John Ross and other Cherokee chiefs into selling Cherokee land to the United States, which got him summarily expelled from the Cherokee Council meeting. In 1825, in blatant violation of a Creek law prohibiting further land sales, he and a handful of minor chiefs signed the Treaty of Indian Springs, selling virtually all remaining Creek land in Georgia in exchange for a payment of $200,000. A 'special, and secret' compensation paid McIntosh $25,000. He was assassinated by Creek warriors, some of whom had Scottish names. (The United States annulled the treaty to avoid open war between the Creeks and Georgia but quickly obtained the land by other treaties.)[32]

Scots who developed their ties with Indians by marriage and trade also strengthened their ties with each other by marriage and patronage – as they did elsewhere – a practice that non-Scots disparaged as 'clannishness'. Alexander McGillivray owed his appointment in the department to the superintendent of Indian affairs in the south, John Stuart.

SCOTS INDIAN AGENTS IN CHEROKEE COUNTRY

The son of an Inverness merchant who had supported the Jacobite rebellion, Stuart emigrated to Charles Town in 1748. In the late 1750s and 1760s, he formed a lasting friendship with the Cherokee chief Attakullakulla, or Little Carpenter, who saved his life at the siege of Fort Loudon in 1760 and later adopted him. Attakullakulla did not make friends with every Scot he met – General John Forbes called him a great 'Rascal'[33] – but he and Stuart worked together to develop a British–Cherokee alliance. In 1761, Attakullakulla urged the lieu-tenant-governor of South Carolina to appoint Stuart as agent to the Cherokees. 'All the Indians love him', he said, 'and there will never be any uneasiness if he is here.' Stuart was appointed British superinten-dent of Indian affairs in the South, with responsibility for the Creeks, Cherokees, Catawbas, Choctaws and Chickasaws, and assigned agents to each of the nations to cultivate good relations and British allegiance. He held the post until his death in 1779, by which time he owned extensive lands in South Carolina, Georgia and East Florida, and 200 slaves. Stuart and many other Scots in the imperial administration saw British–Indian cooperation and alliance as the key to peace and order on the frontier. In their view colonists, more than Indians, must be con-trolled; whites, not Indians, constituted the main threat to peace. Stuart got the Cherokee chief Oconostota elected to the St Andrew's Society of Charles Town and called him his 'old friend'; the Cherokees called the red-headed Stuart 'bushy head'. Stuart had a Scottish wife, but he had many Cherokee children. Bushyhead became a common Cherokee surname.[34]

Stuart appointed two fellow Scots, Alexander Cameron and John McDonald, as his deputies in Cherokee country. Alexander Cameron had migrated to Georgia in 1738. He served in the French and Indian War and against the Cherokees in 1761 and was awarded 2,000 acres by the crown for his services; he built a plantation he named Lochaber. But he lived and traded with the Overhill Cherokees, married a Cherokee woman, and they had three children.[35] Oconostota referred to Cameron as 'Brother Scotchie', and asked that he be permitted to remain as the Cherokees' commissary. 'He has long lived amongst us as a beloved Man. He has done us Justice and always told us the truth. We all regard him and love him and we hope he will not be taken away from us.' By the time of the Revolution, Cameron had lived with the Cherokees so long that he 'had almost become one of themselves'. Hated by Americans who blamed him for instigating Cherokee attacks on the frontiers, Cameron was a marked man. He took refuge deep in Cherokee country and the Cherokees refused American demands to give him up.[36] The British appointed Cameron superintendent of the Choctaws and Chickasaws but he died in Savannah in December 1781. His Scots-Cherokee children went to Britain: in 1787 George was living with Cameron's brother, Donald, and the two girls attended school in England under their uncle's guardianship.[37]

John McDonald, Stuart's other appointee as Cherokee agent, was born in Inverness. He migrated to South Carolina at the age of nineteen and worked for a trading house before he became Stuart's deputy and commissary in Cherokee country. McDonald married a Cherokee woman. During the Revolution he fought alongside the Cherokees against the Americans. John Norton, himself of Scots and Cherokee parentage (and an adopted Mohawk), who visited McDonald's home early in the nineteenth century, said McDonald entertained him 'with the hospitality of an ancient Caledonian or a modern Cherokee'. By that time, McDonald had lived for forty years among the Cherokees and spoke their language 'elegantly'.[38]

In most cases, sons and daughters of Scottish fathers lived with their mother's people and in matrilineal Cherokee society they inherited membership in their mother's clan. The clan was the basic unit of Cherokee society. All Cherokees belonged to one of seven clans and clan ties bound autonomous Cherokee towns together as one nation and one people. Clan membership determined one's place and identity in society and kinship ties determined both personal and social relations. Clan members were obligated to care for, protect, and if necessary avenge the deaths of clan relatives.[39] Scottish fathers who lacked membership in a Cherokee clan lacked a place in the Cherokee social structure, although often they might be given honorary membership or adopted. The key relationship was that between the mother and child: children were the mother's relatives, not her husband's. The influential male figure in the child's life was not the father but the mother's brother, who had responsibility for teaching and disciplining her children; the father who belonged to a different clan, or to no clan, was a 'legal stranger' to the child and might even invoke clan retaliation if he attempted to inflict punishment on his offspring.[40]

John McDonald married Annie Shorey, the daughter of trader and interpreter William Shorey and a Cherokee woman named Ghigooie, who was a member of the Bird Clan. Annie was therefore a member of the Bird Clan, and her children were likewise members of the Bird Clan. One of them, Mary, married Daniel Ross, another Scot. Their son, John

Ross, was therefore seven-eighths Scottish. But since eighteenth century
Cherokees reckoned identity by clan, not by 'blood', he was Cherokee
and Bird Clan through his maternal line.[41] He was also principal chief
of the Cherokee Nation during the Removal crisis – or what we might
call the Cherokee Clearances.

THE CHEROKEE CLEARANCES AND THE SCOTTISH CLAIM

The Cherokees during the eighteenth century endured escalating
warfare, plummeting populations and loss of lands to encroaching colonial powers. In the American Revolution, they saw their villages burned
and their homeland further diminished. In the late eighteenth and early
nineteenth century they rebuilt their lives and their tribe. Many adopted
American-style agriculture (farming by Cherokee men using ploughs
instead of by Cherokee women using hoes); some built plantations;
some owned slaves. Elite Cherokee planters now discussed the price of
cotton at dinner and sent their sons to American schools. The Cherokees
adopted a constitution modelled on that of the United States and printed
their own newspaper, the *Cherokee Phoenix*, in both Cherokee and
English. By the 1820s the Cherokees were a modernising Indian nation.

But that did not save them from American land hunger and from
the aggressions of the state of Georgia. In 1830 Congress passed the
Indian Removal Act, authorising the president to negotiate treaties by
which Indian tribes east of the Mississippi would give up their lands
and relocate west of the Mississippi – ethnic cleansing, American-style.
Removal was not new, but now it was national policy. 'Doubtless it will
be painful to leave the graves of their fathers', president Andrew Jackson
acknowledged, but it was no more than others had done before them.
'To better their condition in an unknown land our forefathers left all
that was dear', he said, invoking his own Scotch-Irish roots.[42]

After gold was discovered in Cherokee country, Georgia ramped up
its pressure on the Cherokees, to make their situation so intolerable
that they would make a treaty of removal with the federal government.
The state extended its laws over Cherokee country, harassed Cherokee
people, closed down the Cherokee printing press, arrested Cherokee
leaders and distributed Cherokee land to its citizens by lottery. Despite
a landmark case in the US Supreme Court, *Worcester* v. *Georgia*, in
1832 – which declared that Georgia had no jurisdiction over Cherokee
country within its state boundaries – the assault was relentless and the
federal government did nothing to protect the Cherokees. By 1835, a
group of Cherokees, convinced that removal was now the only chance

of survival, signed a treaty that sold the Cherokees' remaining land to the United States for $5 million and committed all Cherokees to move across the Mississippi. The treaty signers moved west voluntarily; the rest of the Cherokees were rounded up, interned in stockades and marched west under guard in 1838. Some 4,000 people – one quarter of the nation and including John Ross's wife – died during what became known the Trail of Tears.

After reaching the west, the Cherokee National Council passed death sentences on the men who had sold land in defiance of Cherokee law, and the leading treaty signers were assassinated. One, John Ridge, was dragged from his bed and beaten to death in front of his wife and children. The assassinations sparked a cycle of revenge killings and plunged the Cherokees into a state of virtual civil war. Things became so bad that President James Polk recommended permanently dividing the Cherokee Nation, which forced the two sides to patch together an uneasy truce in 1846 and try to rebuild their shattered economy, society and government. For the Cherokees in 1847, post-traumatic stress disorder was a way of life.

Meanwhile, racial dynamics were changing. By the nineteenth century, notions of white racial superiority were becoming firmly established in Britain.[43] As white women, Christian missionaries and Victorian and racist attitudes reached fur trade communities in Canada, Indian and Métis women alike were relegated to an increasingly inferior status and an increasingly vulnerable position. As happened elsewhere in the British Empire, men who had commonly married Native women, then Métis wives, now dismissed both for white wives as part of the 'domesticating' of the empire.[44] In the United States, racial lines hardened as Cherokees, Creeks and Choctaws were cleared out of their homelands to make way for American cotton fields worked by African slaves. Some of Robert Grierson's and Sunnugee's children had children with African partners but, in the increasingly rigid racial hierarchy of the south, such multiracial families and communities were no longer tolerated. Racist attitudes became entrenched, driving a wedge between the Grierson family.[45] White men who married Indian women became disparaged as 'squaw men'.

But Cherokee–Scottish connections and family ties that were forged in Georgia and the Carolinas in the eighteenth century survived the Cherokee Clearances and endured in Arkansas and Oklahoma in the nineteenth century. Many Cherokees who had trekked west along the Trail of Tears were children and grandchildren of people who had migrated from Scotland and they had Scottish surnames. For Cherokees with names like McDonald, McIntosh, Bushyhead and Ross, the famine-stricken Scots did indeed have a special claim on them.

NOTES

1. Gary Moulton (ed.), *The Papers of Chief John Ross*, 2 vols (Norman: University of Oklahoma Press, 1984), 2: p. 321.
2. Alfred Proctor James (ed.), *Writings of General John Forbes Relating to his Service in North America* (Menasha, WI: Collegiate Press, 1938), p. 117.
3. Studies of Scots-Indian relations that place varying degrees of emphasis on their similarities in background and experience include: Colin G. Calloway, *White People, Indians, and Highlanders: Tribal Peoples and Colonial Encounters in Scotland and America* (New York: Oxford University Press, 2008), from which some of the material in this essay is drawn; Margaret Connell Szasz, *Scottish Highlanders and Native Americans: Indigenous Education in the Eighteenth-Century Atlantic World* (Norman: University of Oklahoma Press, 2007); Michael Newton, *We're Indians Sure Enough: The Legacy of the Scottish Highlanders in the United States* (Richmond, VA: Saorsa Media, 2001); Tom F. Cunningham, *The Diamond's Ace: Scotland and the Native Americans* (Edinburgh: Mainstream, 2001); and James Hunter, *Glencoe and the Indians* (Edinburgh: Mainstream Publishing, 1996) – published in the United States as *Scottish Highlanders, Indian Peoples: Thirty Generations of a Montana Family* (Helena: Montana Historical Society Press, 1997). Like Calloway in his work on Highland Scots and American Indians, Irishman Michael Coleman feels 'strong "resonances" between Indian and Irish histories'; Michael C. Coleman, *American Indians, the Irish, and Government Schooling: A Comparative Study* (Lincoln: University of Nebraska Press, 2007), p. 1. The essays in Graeme Morton and David A. Wilson (eds), *Irish and Scottish Encounters with Indigenous Peoples* (Montreal: McGill-Queen's University Press, 2013), challenge and qualify assumptions that shared backgrounds and common experiences linked Celtic and Native peoples in North America and Australasia.
4. Neil Davidson, *The Origins of Scottish Nationhood* (London: Pluto Press, 2000), ch. 5; Angus Calder, *Scotlands of the Mind* (Edinburgh: Luath Press, 2002), pp. 21–5, 163, 191.
5. Szasz, *Scottish Highlanders and Native Americans*.
6. T. C. Smout, N. C. Landsman and T. M. Devine, 'Scottish emigration in the seventeenth and eighteenth centuries', in Nicholas Canny (ed.), *Europeans on the Move: Studies on European Migration, 1500–1800* (New York: Clarendon Press, 1994), p. 99; Arthur Herman, *How the Scots Invented the Modern World* (New York: Crown, 2001).
7. For example, in their otherwise fine studies Kirsten Fischer, *Suspect*

Relations: Sex, Race, and Resistance in Colonial North Carolina (Ithaca, NY: Cornell University Press, 2002) and Michelle LeMaster, *Brothers Born of One Mother: British–Native American Relations in the Colonial Southeast* (Charlottesville: University of Virginia Press, 2012), make little or no distinction between Scots and English.

8. These issues are explored further in Calloway, *White People, Indians, and Highlanders,* and Allan I. Macinnes, *Clanship, Commerce and the House of Stuart, 1603–1788* (East Linton: Tuckwell Press, 1996).

9. Eric R. Wolf, *Europe and the People Without History* (Berkeley: University of California Press, 1982), ch. 3.

10. Allan I. MacInnes, 'Scottish gaeldom: the first phase of clearance', in T. M. Devine and Rosalind Mitcheson (eds), *People and Society in Scotland*, vol. 1: *1760–1830* (Edinburgh: John Donald Publishers, 1988), p. 70; John C. Weaver, *The Great Land Rush: Making the Modern World, 1650–1900* (Montreal: McGill-Queens, 2003).

11. Edward J. Cashin, *Lachlan McGillivray, Indian Trader: The Shaping of the Southern Colonial Frontier* (Athens: University of Georgia Press, 1992); Katherine E. Holland Braund, *Deerskins and Duffels: The Creek Indian Trade with Anglo-America, 1685–1815* (Lincoln: University of Nebraska Press, 1993), pp. 56–7, 62, 70, 87, 98.

12. Claudio Saunt, *A New Order of Things: Property, Power, and the Transformation of the Creek Indians, 1733–1816* (Cambridge: Cambridge University Press, 1999), ch. 3.

13. Dorothy Downs, 'British influences on Creek and Seminole men's clothing, 1733–1858', *Florida Anthropologist*, 33 (June 1980), pp. 46–65; Dorothy Downs, *Art of the Seminole and Miccosukee Indians* (Gainesville: University Press of Florida, 1995), chs 1–2, plate 22; J. Leitch Wright, Jr, *Creeks and Seminoles: The Destruction and Regeneration of the Muscogulge People* (Lincoln: University of Nebraska Press, 1986), quote at p. 36.

14. William S. Coker and Thomas D. Watson, *Indian Traders of the Southeastern Spanish Borderlands: Panton, Leslie and Company and John Forbes and Company, 1783–1847* (Pensacola: University of West Florida Press, 1986); Braund, *Deerskins and Duffels,* ch. 9; Panton's deerskin figures at pp. 72, 98.

15. Coker and Watson, *Indian Traders of the Southeastern Spanish Borderlands*, pp. 228–9, 366, 370, and ch. 12; map of 1805 cessions at p. 264; figures at pp. 265, 271–2; Joel W. Martin, 'Cultural contact and crises in the early republic: Native American religious renewal, resistance, and accommodation', in Frederick E. Hoxie, Ronald Hoffman and Peter J. Albert (eds), *Native Americans and the Early Republic* (Charlottesville: University Press of Virginia, 1999), pp. 244–6 (quote).

16. Fischer, *Suspect Relations,* ch. 2; Andrea Smith, *Conquest: Sexual Violence and American Indian Genocide* (Boston: South End Press, 2005).

17. E. E. Rich (ed.), *Journal of Occurrences in the Athabasca Department by*

George Simpson, 1820 and 1821, and Report (Toronto: Champlain Society, 1938), pp. 392, 396; Jennifer S. H. Brown, *Strangers in Blood: Fur Trade Company Families in Indian Country* (Norman: University of Oklahoma Press, 1996), pp. 115–30; Silvia Van Kirk, *Many Tender Ties: Women in Fur Trade Society, 1670–1870* (Norman: University of Oklahoma Press, 1980), pp. 161–2.

18. Julianna Barr, *Peace Came in the Form of a Woman: Indians and Spaniards in the Texas Borderlands* (Chapel Hill: University of North Carolina Press, 2007), pp. 69–71.

19. Hunter, *Glencoe and the Indians*.

20. Thomas Nairne, *Nairne's Muskhogean Journals: The 1708 Expedition to the Mississippi River*, ed. Alexander Moore (Jackson: University Press of Mississippi, 1998), pp. 60–1.

21. Braund, *Deerskins and Duffels*, pp. 83–4; Theda Perdue, *'Mixed Blood' Indians: Racial Construction in the Early South* (Athens: University of Georgia Press, 2003), p. 25; LeMaster, *Brothers Born of One Mother*.

22. Braund, *Deerskins and Duffels*, pp. 84–5; Theda Perdue, *Cherokee Women: Gender and Culture Change, 1700–1835* (Lincoln: University of Nebraska Press, 1998), p. 83.

23. Claudio Saunt, *Black, White, and Indian: Race and the Unmaking of an American Family* (New York: Oxford University Press, 2005), quotes at p. 3.

24. Arrell M. Gibson, *The Chickasaws* (Norman: University of Oklahoma Press, 1971), p. 65; James R. Atkinson, *Splendid Land, Splendid People: The Chickasaw Indians to Removal* (Tuscaloosa: University of Alabama Press, 2004).

25. Amos J. Wright, Jr, *The McGillivray and McIntosh Indian Traders on the Old Southwest Indian Frontier, 1716 to 1815* (Montgomery, AL: New South Books, 2007).

26. Braund, *Deerskins and Duffels*, pp. 43–6; Cashin, *Lachlan McGillivray*.

27. John Walton Caughey, *McGillivray of the Creeks* (Columbia: University of South Carolina Press, 2007; first published 1938), pp. 251–4.

28. 'From David Humphreys', Presidential Series (24 September 1788–30 September 1794), volume 4 (8 September 1789–15 January 1790), in *The Papers of George Washington*. Available at <http://rotunda.upress.virginia.edu/founders/GEWN-05-04-02-0059> (accessed October 2015).

29. J. Leitch Wright, Jr, 'The Creek-American Treaty of 1790: Alexander McGillivray and the diplomacy of the old southwest', *Georgia Historical Quarterly*, 51 (1967), pp. 379–400.

30. Cashin, *Lachlan McGillivray*, pp. 308–10; Wright, *The McGillivray and McIntosh Traders*, pp. 269–76.

31. Braund, *Deerskins and Duffels*, p. 183.

32. Benjamin W. Griffith, Jr, *McIntosh and Weatherford, Creek Indian Leaders* (Tuscaloosa: University of Alabama Press, 1988); Michael D. Green, *The*

Politics of Indian Removal: Creek Government and Society in Crisis (Lincoln: University of Nebraska Press, 1982), pp. 54–7, 69–97.

33. James (ed.), *Writings of General John Forbes*, p. 233.

34. J. Russell Snapp, *John Stuart and the Struggle for Empire on the Southern Frontier* (Baton Rouge: Louisiana State University Press, 1996), pp. 45–53, 55–7, 87; W. Stitt Robinson (ed.), *North and South Carolina Treaties, 1756–1775*, in Alden T. Vaughan (gen. ed.), *Early American Indian Treaties and Laws, 1607–1789*, vol. 14 (Bethesda, MD: University Publications of America, 2003), p. 336; Nadia Dean, *A Demand of Blood: The Cherokee War of 1776* (Cherokee, NC: Valley River Press, 2012), pp. 27–9.

35. John L. Nichols, 'Alexander Cameron, British agent among the Cherokee, 1764–1781', *South Carolina Historical Magazine*, 97 (1996), pp. 94–114; wife and children at p. 100.

36. K. G. Davies (ed.), *Documents of the American Revolution, 1770–1783*, 21 vols (Shannon: Irish University Press, 1972–1982), 12: p. 194; 17: pp. 232–4; William L. Saunders and Walter Clark (eds), *The Colonial and State Records of North Carolina*, vol. 10 (Raleigh: State Printer, 1890), p. 767.

37. Nichols, 'Alexander Cameron', p. 100.

38. Carl F. Klinck and James J. Talman (eds), *The Journal of Major John Norton, 1816* (Toronto: Champlain Society, 1970), pp. 58, 76.

39. Perdue, *Cherokee Women*, pp. 41–2, 46–7; John Phillip Reid, *A Law of Blood: The Primitive Law of the Cherokee Nation* (New York: New York University Press, 1970), ch. 5.

40. Perdue, *Cherokee Women*, pp. 49, 54; Reid, *A Law of Blood*, pp. 39–41.

41. Theda Perdue, 'Race and culture: writing the ethnohistory of the early south', *Ethnohistory*, 51 (2004), p. 703.

42. Andrew Jackson, 'State of the union address, Dec. 6, 1830', extracts reprinted in Theda Perdue and Michael D. Green (eds), *The Cherokee Removal: A Brief History with Documents* (Boston: Bedford/St Martin's Press, 1995), pp. 119–20.

43. Roxann Wheeler, *The Complexion of Race: Categories of Difference in Eighteenth-Century British Culture* (Philadelphia: University of Pennsylvania Press, 2000), p. 33.

44. In the British Raj wives were brought to India specifically to help limit familiarity between colonising men and colonised women. In that sense, 'white wives blighted racial harmony'. See Ronald Hyam, *Empire and Sexuality: The British Experience* (Manchester: Manchester University Press, 1990), ch. 5, quote at p. 207; Margaret MacMillan, *Women of the Raj: The Mothers, Wives, and Daughters of the British Empire in India* (London: Thames and Hudson, 1988), pp. 110–11.

45. Saunt, *Black, White, and Indian*.

6

Conflicts of Interest, Crises of Conscience: Scots and Aboriginal People in Eastern Australia, 1830s–1861

Ann Curthoys

THIS CHAPTER RESPONDS TO two challenges. One is John MacKenzie's suggestion that in our studies of empire and settler colonialism we ought to deconstruct the terms 'British' and 'British settler' into their component parts – English, Scottish, Welsh and Irish.[1] The other comes from Australian historian Ann McGrath, who urges historians to work harder than they have done so far to disentangle the component ethnicities that made up the category 'white' that is so foundational to whiteness and settler colonial studies.[2]

In setting out to understand the ethnic dimensions of British settler colonialism, as these two historians wish us to do, this chapter focuses on the relationships between Scots and Aboriginal people in the eastern Australian colonies – New South Wales (NSW), Victoria and Queensland – from the mid 1830s to the early 1860s.[3] This was a period of intense pastoral expansion, high immigration and rapid political change. In these decades, a set of struggling British colonies under direct British rule, mostly dependent on convict labour, and occupying relatively small regions in a vast continent, were nearly all transformed into a set of large, free, self-governing democratic colonies. It was the period when some regions experienced intense frontier conflict and violence, while others saw its end and the emergence of a post-frontier society characterised by a mix of Aboriginal employment, poverty, institutionalisation and interaction with the newcomer populations. For the settlers, my focus is both on Scottish pastoralists, often known as squatters, and their Scottish-Australian critics, often the educated middle class, including journalists, politicians, amateur ethnographers, and men of the church. In the course of exploring these diverse relationships, this chapter considers some key individual Scots in the Australian colonies, including the explorer Thomas Mitchell, pastoralists Niel Black, Angus McMillan and the Archer brothers, writers Katherine Kirkland and Mary McConnel, newspaper editor Thomas McCombie, missionary John Green, and perhaps most significant of all, Presbyterian minister, editor and writer John Dunmore Lang. It also considers those Aboriginal individuals and communities who encountered these Scots, from the Kurnai in the south to the Kabi Kabi and Wakka Wakka peoples in the north.[4]

In exploring the interactions between Scots and Aboriginal people in eastern Australia, we confront the question of whether there were any significant differences between Scottish and other settlers in terms of their ideas about Aboriginal people and especially their actions towards them. In writing about Scottish Highlander settlers in the United States, Colin Calloway is firm that there are none:

> Highland traders, soldiers, and settlers often displayed the same prejudices, sentiments, and behaviour as other European traders, soldiers and settlers when dealing with Indians ... Highland governors, soldiers, and traders were probably just as likely as their English or American counterparts to exploit, shoot, and cheat Indians, and Highland settlers proved as eager as anyone else to occupy Indian land.[5]

Can we say the same of the Australian colonies, either of Scottish Highlanders specifically or of Scottish settlers more generally? There is little existing literature to guide us, whether on Scots in Australian colonial history in general or on their relation to Aboriginal people in particular. While we do have studies of individual Scots of importance, including various governors, politicians, newspapermen, and clerics, general analytical studies are rare.[6] Malcolm Prentis has written on both Scottish and Aboriginal history, but only occasionally does he bring the two studies together.[7] There is only one major book specifically on Scottish–Aboriginal interactions, and that is Don Watson's excellent and now thirty-year-old *Caledonia Australis: Scottish Highlanders on the Frontier of Australia*.[8] He traces what happened when a group of Highlanders migrated in the 1830s to the south-eastern districts of NSW, part of what later became the colony of Victoria, and in subsequent decades made good their claim to Aboriginal land. It is a brilliant book, written as both irony and tragedy.

In addition, there are some studies of individual Scots and their relationship with Aboriginal people, such as D. W. A. Baker's exploration of the interactions between the explorer Thomas Mitchell and Aboriginal people, and Stephen Foster's story of the Macpherson family's engagement with the British Empire over five generations; it has several chapters on one family member who settled in NSW including a revealing chapter entitled 'War with the Blacks'.[9] Of the six women Barbara Dawson examines in her recent book on white women's views of Aboriginal people, three are Scots.[10] Beyond these there is very little. We can sympathise with Tom Devine's sense of frustration with the paucity of Australian work on Scots and Aboriginal people. Significantly, though, there is no paucity at all of work on settler–Aboriginal relations in Australia more generally; it is a focus on Scots, or for that matter, English, specifically, that is missing.[11]

An important reason for the scarcity of scholarship on Scots and Aboriginal people is that there is little pressure from Aboriginal people for a better understanding of Scottish–Aboriginal interactions. While there are a good number of people of mixed Scottish and Aboriginal descent, who in their own bodies represent a historical interaction, they rarely identify in that way. Most regard themselves as Aboriginal, not as Scottish-Aboriginal. As Ann McGrath points out, while some prominent people of Aboriginal and Irish descent do refer publicly to their Irish ancestry, 'It is rare indeed to hear of anyone identifying as "Aboriginal English", "Aboriginal Scots" or "Aboriginal Welsh".'[12] One reason for this is that people of mixed Irish and Aboriginal descent see both sides of their family tree as arising from an inheritance of colonial oppression. Britain is understood as the colonial oppressor of the Irish; furthermore, Irish migrants, who came to Australia in much greater numbers than Scots, were usually Catholic, poor and likely to remain working class. Despite some knowledge of the Highland Clearances, Scotland is not understood in the same way, and Scottish migrants are more likely to be classed with the English as oppressors and colonisers.

Because of this perception, there has been little push so far from the descendants of Aboriginal–Scottish marriages and sexual relationships to explore that particular history. Victoria Grieves, an Aboriginal historian of Scottish and Aboriginal (more specifically, Worimi) descent, writes about mixed race marriages and families, including her own. She mentions where her own ancestors came from, such as James and Agnes McClymont, who came from Ayr in 1823, and traces their son William's marriage to Anne Butler, a Worimi woman. She also draws attention to Agnes's second marriage, to another Scot, Henry Carmichael, and Carmichael's involvement in local Scottish conflicts and alliances. Though Grieves's work is in many ways ground-breaking, it is more interested in the nature of race relations under settler colonialism than in distinguishing the various settler ethnicities from one another.[13]

SCOTS AND ABORIGINAL PEOPLE IN NEW SOUTH WALES IN THE 1830s

The process of dispossessing Aboriginal people of their land and largely replacing them with British settlers took a long time, starting in 1788 in Sydney Cove and arguably ending in the Northern Territory in the 1930s. Scottish soldiers were an integral part of this ongoing bloody process. They shared with their English, Welsh and Irish counterparts a desire to serve and in many cases a hope that they might subsequently make good in the colony. Some of the convicts, and increasingly some of the free settlers, were Scots. While Scottish farmers who had lost their lands and hoped to gain new lands went mainly to North America, from the 1820s they turned to the Australian colonies too. Though they did not migrate in large groups and set up new Scottish settlements, they did concentrate in certain areas at certain times, such as the Port Phillip district in southern NSW in the 1840s, or New England to the north-west and Moreton Bay to the north in the 1850s.[14] These concentrations were the result of surges in Scottish migration coinciding with the extension of settlement on to newly encountered Aboriginal lands.

As the number of Scots slowly grew, Aboriginal people began to notice them. Jessie Mitchell tells of a revealing conversation in 1834 between a young Wiradjuri girl, Geanil, and William Watson, a missionary, originally from Yorkshire, in NSW:

> *Geanil*: Who is that white master, Mr Watson, is he an Englishman?
> *Mr W*: No.
> *Geanil*: O. He is an Irishman then?
> *Mr W*: No. He is a Scotchman. He comes from another country, but it also belongs to my King.
> *Geanil replies*: All about master belong to your King, King William.[15]

Geanil's puzzlement tells us that she is not yet used to the Scots; it also reminds us of how much British officials, missionaries and settlers stressed to Aboriginal people the power of the monarch and his or her representative, the governor.

Aboriginal people became more familiar with the Scots in the late 1830s, when the rate of Scottish migration to the colonies grew as a direct result of the rapid increase in Scottish companies interested in pastoral development and investment.[16] One reason for the rise in the number and size of such companies at this time appears to have been the vast sums spent by the British government compensating slave-owners for the loss of their slaves in the Caribbean after the abolition of slavery in British settlements in 1833.[17] Whether wealthy pastoralists, middle class overseers or labourers, many of these Scottish migrants in the late 1830s and early 1840s came to NSW to establish or work upon pastoral runs.

Squatters sometimes found lands appropriate for pastoralism themselves, but more often, they came in the wake of professional explorers, some of whom were Scots. Major Thomas Mitchell entered extensive Aboriginal lands in the west and south of NSW in the 1830s, and William Landsborough did the same in Queensland in the 1860s. In his third long expedition in 1836, Mitchell, originally from Craigend in Stirlingshire, and by this time Surveyor General of New South Wales, followed the rivers down to the south-west until he reached the Western District of Port Phillip. He publicised it as 'one of the finest regions on earth'.[18] On his return, he reported that on 24 May 1836, at a place he called Mount Dispersion, on the Murray River near its junction with the Darling River, he ambushed a large group of Aboriginal people, leading a 'considerable number' to be killed and the rest to flee.[19] His report referred to the Aboriginal people as 'treacherous savages', and described exultingly the way his party had pursued them and shot as many as they could.[20] The executive council later conducted an inquiry, which condemned Mitchell for insufficiently attempting conciliation and for the intemperate language of his report, though not the massacre itself.[21]

Mitchell's reports of the vast pastoral land available in the Western District of Port Phillip helped speed up the flow of new settlers to the region, first of pastoralists from both north and south, and then directly from Britain. Of the many Scottish migrants, one of the pastoralists, Niel Black, is well known, primarily because of the valuable journal he kept in 1839–40.[22] A Highlander from Argyll, Black arrived in Sydney in 1839, which he soon left for Port Phillip. He much preferred Melbourne to Sydney, he wrote, since it was 'a Scotch settlement'.[23] As a squatter struggling to establish himself on the land, his journal records with unusual directness the approach squatters, Scots and English alike, took to the Aboriginal people they would inevitably encounter. Before venturing into new country, they warned him as a 'new chum', he would need to be prepared to slaughter natives 'without remorse'.[24] In the end, he chose to take up an established pastoral run in the belief that after the previous superintendent had led a massacre of more than thirty-five men, women and children, the 'poor creatures are now terror stricken and will be easily managed'.[25] He renamed the station Glenormiston, employing Scottish labourers and recent arrivals, and focused on making money. It seems he subsequently took little interest in the Aboriginal people who remained; in this, as Margaret Kiddle points out, he was not unusual.[26]

Katherine Kirkland, from Glasgow, was also part of the wave of Scots arriving in Port Phillip in the late 1830s, termed by one local resident 'the Glasgow invasion'.[27] Kirkland returned to Britain in September 1841, and nine months later, her anonymous memoir, *Life in the Bush*, appeared serially in *Chambers's Edinburgh Journal*.[28] As Barbara Dawson points out, the account gives valuable insights into Wathaurong reactions to the pastoral invasion that was soon to lead to so much death and social destruction.[29] Kirkland describes a welcoming ceremony held by around 100 Wathaurong, meeting the women and children, and women's food-getting and childcare practices.[30]

JOHN DUNMORE LANG

While some Scots were in the forefront of the displacement of Aboriginal people from their land, others expressed concern. Visitors, travellers, journalists, middle class radicals and liberals, and missionaries at various times questioned the prevailing orthodoxy. One Scotsman, Thomas Walker, born in Leith and at this time a successful businessman who had arrived in NSW in 1822, recorded in a journal his month in the bush in 1836, visiting a large number of newly established pastoral stations. He reports on the Aboriginal people he met with a sympathetic ethnographic eye, and notes that *their* imperative to 'resist our encroachments' was just as great as *our* necessity 'of finding a place of refuge for the teeming increase of our own over-peopled country'. We should ask ourselves, he says, whether we have done enough to mitigate the effects of our 'trespassing and encroaching upon the soil of their inheritance and birthright'.[31]

For some, there was a keenly felt tension between a belief on the one hand in the settler's right, and indeed obligation, to take and develop the land, and a concern on the other at the destructive effects of such actions on Aboriginal people. One of those who most clearly exhibits that tension is the somewhat perplexing figure of the Revd John Dunmore Lang, one of the best-known Scots in Australian history. Lang's career in colonial politics and religious affairs was long, fractious, contradictory and controversial. Born in Greenock, west of Glasgow, Lang was a graduate of the University of Glasgow. He arrived in NSW as a young man in 1823 to join his brother, who had been granted Wonnarua land in the Hunter district north of Sydney, and soon became leader of the Presbyterian Church in the colony. Lang did more than anyone to publicise the opportunities in the Australian colonies among Scots and to pressure the Colonial Office to ensure that a good proportion of assisted migrants came from Scotland.[32]

His approach to missionary work among the Aboriginal people of NSW is mixed, and historians have been somewhat divided in their interpretation of what this volatile man thought and did in relation to Aboriginal people.[33] Lang is a complex figure: he was an ardent coloniser who yet recognised the shocking effects of colonisation on Aboriginal people, and a Presbyterian minister who was a trenchant and destructive critic of actual missionary endeavour in the colony. A landowner himself, he was not necessarily opposed to the taking of Aboriginal land per se, but rather to the brutal manner in which squatters typically took it, and to the behaviour of settlers and especially convicts, who brought alcohol, made sexual demands and introduced disease. When Fowell Buxton was pressing for the establishment of a House of Commons Select Committee on Aborigines in British Settlements, he asked Lang in 1834 to present evidence to the forthcoming committee. Lang provided Buxton with a letter on the condition of Aboriginal people in NSW. Although acknowledging that usurping Aboriginal people's lands would have undermined their conditions of life in any case, he goes on to insist that the presence of convicts made the situation much worse. An ardent proponent of free Protestant immigration, Lang in this letter hovers between suggesting that free settlers got on well with Aboriginal people and acknowledging that they had been involved in 'murderous expeditions', developed low opinions of Aboriginal people's capacity to be 'improved', and done nothing to assist in their civilisation and conversion to Christianity. Lang concluded that so fast was the loss of Aboriginal population from infanticide, intemperance and European diseases, it was only 'through the influence of Christianity, brought to bear upon the natives by the zealous exertion of devoted missionaries, that the progress of extinction can be checked'.[34] The following year Buxton was successful in getting his committee; its report in 1837 was to recommend some significant changes to Aboriginal policy in Britain's settler colonies.[35]

Yet if Lang saw missionary endeavour as the only hope for saving the lives and souls of Aboriginal people, he was in fact highly critical of the existing missions at Lake Macquarie and Wellington Valley, telling Buxton they were achieving little despite government funding. He was especially scornful of the mission at Lake Macquarie run by Congregational minister Lancelot Threlkeld, which the London Missionary Society had supported from 1824 to 1828, but which was at this point dependent upon government financial support. In a series of articles in November 1835 in his own newspaper, *The Colonist*, Lang bitterly attacked Threlkeld. As Anna Johnston discusses in her detailed account of the articles and the court case that ensued, he had a number of criticisms: Threlkeld did not send itinerant missionaries to accompany the mobile Aboriginal people; in addition, he put 'civilising' before 'Christianising', failed to convert anyone, and was wasteful with government funding. Unsurprisingly, Threlkeld sued for libel, and the court case over two days in March 1836 attracted major press and public interest. The trial ended in something of a stalemate, with Lang found guilty, and Threlkeld awarded damages of only a farthing.[36] This episode did nothing to assist missionary work in NSW, which was already struggling and strongly opposed by settlers on the grounds that its project of converting Aboriginal people to Christianity was a hopeless one.

Soon afterwards, Lang was involved in missionary enterprises of his own. In 1837, he lobbied the Scottish Missionary Society to establish a mission in Moreton Bay in the northern districts of NSW. With the penal settlement there scheduled to close, the area was ripe for free immigration, which in Lang's view, should be accompanied by missionary endeavour. Yet since Scots were scarcely represented in early missionary activity in the Australian colonies, Lang was unable to find any and arranged to bring German missionaries, mainly Lutherans, to Moreton Bay. Their mission, at Zion Hill, near present day Brisbane, opened between April and June 1838, with a large staff. It was to last for eight years.[37]

Through 1838, Lang was involved in the public debates that were then preoccupying the colony over matters of Aboriginal policy. After the House of Commons Select Committee Report of 1837, the Colonial Office had instructed the new governor, Sir George Gipps, to institute a policy of stronger protection of Aboriginal people on the frontiers of settlement. Not only should he enforce the rule of law, with perpetrators of massacres of Aboriginal people brought to trial, but he would be required also to oversee a new class of official called 'protectors', soon to be sent to areas of conflict over land. Settlers and newspapers received this news with considerable anger, insisting that it was the settlers, not Aboriginal people, who needed protection. The whole debate was inflamed by Governor Gipps's insistence that the men who had conducted a massacre of Aboriginal people at Myall Creek in north-western NSW earlier that year be brought to trial.[38]

As the debate over the protection policy and the impending Myall

Creek trial raged, Lang chaired the first meeting of the Aborigines Protection Society, which sought to put a pro-Aboriginal case before the public.[39] Another Scot, the sevety-one-year-old Alexander McLeay, former Colonial Secretary of New South Wales, chaired the second meeting as president of the new organisation.[40] Soon afterwards, Lang delivered a sermon that constituted one of his most outspoken statements on the responsibility of the colonists for Aboriginal deaths. The current drought, he said, was a visitation from on high.[41] He drew a parallel between the Gibeonites as the remnant of the ancient Aboriginal inhabitants of the land of Israel and 'the wretched Aboriginal inhabitants of this land'. We have taken their land, he said, given them vice and disease, and their blood is on the hands of many colonists.

> Not only have we despoiled them of their land, and given them in exchange European vice and European disease in every foul and fatal form, but the blood of hundreds, nay of thousands of their number, who have fallen from time to time in their native forests, when waging unequal warfare with their civilized aggressors, still stains the hands of many of the inhabitants of the land![42]

Lang then warned his congregation that the Lord would

> avenge the blood of the wretched Aborigines of this territory ... They are still bone of our bone and flesh of our flesh – formed originally after the image of God, like ourselves, and guilty only, as far as we are concerned, of an Ethiopian skin, and an untutored soul.

The present drought might indeed be God's punishment for the killing of Aboriginal people.

Lang came back to the question of settler responsibility for Aboriginal deaths later, in his book *Cooksland* (1847), which strongly advocated emigration to Moreton Bay (later Queensland). He commented that the squatter approach was 'tantamount to a sentence of confiscation, banishment, and death to the unfortunate aborigines'. What the colony needed, he said, was a way of ameliorating squatting's effects so that 'the white and black races may co-exist in harmony and peace'.[43] Though he came back to the troubling issue from time to time throughout his life, he never found a way to reconcile his enthusiasm for colonisation with his recognition of its disastrous consequences for Aboriginal people.

THE KILLING TIMES: THE 1840s

Around the same time as Lang was mourning Aboriginal deaths, another Scot came to the colony who was to figure largely in its subsequent history. Angus McMillan, originally from Skye, travelled in 1839–40 from Sydney down to the south-east corner of the colony, Kurnai country, which he named 'Caledonia Australis', but which officials renamed Gippsland, after the governor.[44] It was land, he wrote, 'sufficient to feed all my starving countrymen'.[45] He established his own station at Bushy Park and employed Highlanders almost exclusively.[46] When Kurnai men, seeking to drive the settlers away from their land, killed the nephew of a leading Scottish squatter, Lachlan Macalister, local Scots formed a company under McMillan's leadership known as the Highland Brigade.[47] Watson suggests that McMillan was involved in massacres between 1840 and 1843; one, the Warrigal Massacre, described by Watson as 'a very Scottish affair', led to the deaths of up to 150 Kurnai.[48] These and other actions were successful in putting an end to violent Kurnai resistance; Kurnai people subsequently turned to other means of protest in defence of their lands.

It is tempting to think that the Scots, themselves often the victims of land loss, including in the Clearances, may have been a little more aware than their English counterparts of Aboriginal people's desire to keep their land. Yet there is no evidence of this in Port Phillip, and none later in the northern regions of NSW that separated to form the new colony of Queensland, two areas where there were higher than usual concentrations of Scots. There *were* differences between the pastoralists in their approach to Aboriginal people, but these were not on ethnic lines. They had much more to do with levels of access to cheap convict or immigrant labour and thus with degrees of interest in employing Aboriginal labour in pastoral work. While some squatters kept Aboriginal people away from the newly established pastoral stations, and responded to any stealing or physical attacks with ferocity, others, who wanted to employ Aboriginal people as stockmen and labourers, encouraged friendly relations.

Two historians, John Mackenzie-Smith and James Lergessner, have contrasted these different styles through their studies of Scottish squatter families, especially the Archers and the Mackenzies, in the Moreton Bay area.[49] The Archer brothers came originally from Perth, Scotland, but since 1825 had been resident at Larvik, Norway. Their extensive journals and letters to their parents now provide a rich source for Scottish-Australian history. Seeking new pastoral lands, David and Thomas

Archer went north to a place they named Durundur. Unable to attract free labourers to the region, they decided to employ Aboriginal people rather than convicts.[50] Their approach was to develop close relationships with a particular clan, to exclude other Aboriginal people and groups, and to employ some of the clan in return for food.[51] Nearby, Evan and Colin Mackenzie, who had arrived from Edinburgh with their own workers as bounty passengers, had taken up the Kilcoy run in May 1841.[52] Their labour force also included some assigned convicts, ticket-of-leave labourers and free workers from Sydney.[53] Unlike the Archers, they were not seeking Aboriginal labour and their main aim was to keep Aboriginal people away from the station. When a large group of Giggabarah people approached the station in December and threateningly sought food, sheep and equipment, the shepherds laced the flour with arsenic and strychnine. Because responsibility was harder to determine, poisoning had since the Myall Creek hangings become a more common method of removing Aboriginal people from their land. In his detailed account of these events, local historian James Lerghessner says between fifty and seventy people died as a result of the poisoning.[54] The owner of the pastoral station, Evan Mackenzie, was widely blamed for the massacre (for years Aboriginal people in the region knew arsenic and strychnine as 'Mackenzie'), though, given his temporary absence from the property when the poisonings occurred, precise responsibility is disputed.[55]

Sometimes squatters and their families developed an interest in Aboriginal people and culture, even while wary of them in frontier conditions. A few years after the poisonings at Kilcoy, David McConnel, one of the many Scots to settle in the upper Brisbane River valley in 1840, returned to Edinburgh, married Mary MacLeod, and returned to the colony in 1849. The McConnels came on one of Lang's chartered ships, part of Lang's scheme to encourage emigration and settlement through the growth of cotton. McConnel, from a wealthy cotton merchant family, established a cotton farm on the Brisbane River, and years later Mary's memoir described in some detail her relations with the women and children on the station, particularly as her domestic servants, and their responses to white women's clothing and customs. Although a Presbyterian evangelical, she had no success in converting any of the Aboriginal people who lived with and worked for her to Christianity.[56]

NEW GOVERNMENTS AND NEW POLICIES IN THE 1850s

As frontier violence receded, both settlers and Aboriginal people developed new modes of dealing with one another. Though Port Phillip witnessed particularly destructive frontier violence, it also saw the British humanitarian tradition continue to influence public discourse. Another Scot, Thomas McCombie, who arrived from Aberdeenshire in 1841, became over the next two decades an outspoken advocate for a new approach to Aboriginal policy. In an essay published in 1845, he wrote of the inability of the Protectorate to protect Aboriginal people from loss of land and livelihood, and wondered whether the British government had any right to 'take possession of the country'. The question now was, he wrote, 'what the ultimate fate of the blacks is to be'.[57] He returned to the question over a decade later, when the Port Phillip district had been separated from NSW, renamed Victoria, and experienced a new wave of Scottish migration during the gold rushes.[58] By 1858, the colony was a thriving democratic colonial society, having gained responsible government and, soon afterwards, universal male suffrage.

By this time a member of the legislature, McCombie chaired a select committee to investigate the condition of Aboriginal people in the colony.[59] Its report recommended greater government intervention, including the establishment of a central board of respectable citizens who would help ensure that Aboriginal people were protected, and the establishment of new reserves for agriculture, pastoralism and missionary work, something Aboriginal people themselves were seeking.[60] Assisting them in their bid for land was another Scot, John Green, who was to play a major role in Victorian Aboriginal history for the next three decades. Green had arrived with his wife, Mary, from Aberdeen in late 1857, and while working as a Presbyterian 'bush missionary' amongst Europeans on the goldfields had formed close relationships with the Kulin. Bain Attwood attributes his unusual sensitivity to the wishes of Aboriginal people to his Scottish Presbyterian background, speculating that his familiarity with the history of the Highland Clearances made him suspicious of English and Anglican hegemony.[61] As we have seen, though, familiarity with that history did not necessarily produce sympathy for Aboriginal people. While John and Mary's Scottish background may have indeed influenced their thinking, many other factors were involved.

Responding both to the select committee and possibly to Aboriginal pressure as well, the colonial government of Victoria in 1860 established a system of rationing and reserves, overseen by a body called the Central

Board Appointed to Watch Over the Interests of the Aborigines.[62] In keeping with his status as a gentleman, Angus McMillan was appointed in 1860 as one of those correspondents. The Kulin, with whom Green was closely associated, continued to press for a reserve and in March 1863 trekked with the Greens to their desired land, named it Coranderrk, and successfully campaigned to make it a permanent reserve.[63] The subsequent history of the Board, in 1869 renamed the Aborigines Protection Board, was to prefigure much of the history of humanitarian activity in the Australian colonies, in that desires to protect, educate, 'civilise' and convert gradually became more secular in nature, and overwhelmingly became a project of government management and control.

SCOT VERSUS SCOT ON ABORIGINAL MATTERS IN QUEENSLAND, 1861

The situation in the northern districts was very different from that in Victoria, but again some of the leading figures in the development of Aboriginal policy were Scots. In 1859, Britain separated these districts from NSW and granted the new colony responsible government, though its settler population, at 26,000, was small and most of the land was still clearly in Aboriginal hands. With frontier violence rife, the new settler government used the Native Police as a principal means of dispossession, with a far larger loss of life than in any other colony. Ray Evans and Robert Orsted-Jensen have estimated that the number killed could be over 66,000, well over the 20,000 Henry Reynolds famously estimated for the six Australian colonies taken together.[64]

In 1861, only two years after the creation of Queensland as a self-governing colony, an event occurred which highlights the variety of Scottish behaviour on the Australian frontier.[65] A select committee of the legislative assembly was appointed to inquire into allegations of the murder of Aboriginal people in several regions in south-east Queensland, the organisation and management of the Native Police force, and the condition of Aboriginal people in the colony. The man who moved to establish the committee and became its chair was Robert Mackenzie, a pastoralist born to a wealthy family in Ross-shire, Scotland, and now the new colonial treasurer. Mackenzie's motion appears to have been in response to a paid advertisement in the *Moreton Bay Courier*, placed there by another Scot, John Mortimer, from Aberdeenshire, alleging murderous behaviour by the Native Police on and around his station, Manumbar.[66] At around the same time, the coroner, Dr Henry Challinor, an Englishman who had arrived in Moreton Bay accompanying a group of Scottish migrants, reported that three Aboriginal people had been killed by the Native Police on a property at Fassifern, fifty miles south-west of Brisbane, with the property manager and local police magistrate also implicated. When the attorney general refused to lay blame, Challinor, like Mortimer, gave information to the *Courier*.[67]

Charged with investigating both the Manumbar and Fassifern incidents along with two others, the committee was controversial from the beginning, composed as it was only of men who supported the Native Police force and opposed attempts to protect and support Aboriginal people.[68] Given its composition, it is not surprising that its final report concluded that while some of the allegations of murder by the Native Police were justified, these were unrepresentative of the force as a whole. When the assembly adopted the report, the way was clear for the Native Police to continue with its punitive expeditions.[69]

CONCLUSION

This story of killings in Queensland in 1861 and the responses to them encapsulates some of the themes of this chapter. Colonists were divided over how they should relate to Aboriginal people, in both 'new' and established settlements. There were clear differences between pastoralists and their critics, and both groups differed considerably amongst themselves. Scots, like the English, were present on all sides.

Has it been worth it, then, taking up the challenge to address the question of ethnic origins and traditions within Australian colonial history? I think it has, not because I have discovered a particular Scottish approach to colonising and its ethical dilemmas but rather because I have not. To assess fully Scottish distinctiveness would take a more directly comparative project, one that considered as ethnic groups the English, Welsh and Irish, as well as Scots, than has been possible here. What *is* possible, however, at this point is an assessment of the Scots in relation to the now quite extensive body of work on British settler colonialism in eastern Australia. Whether we consider squatters, preachers, writers and editors or politicians, we find that Scots thought about and interacted with Indigenous people in the eastern Australian colonies in ways that are entirely familiar to us from this broader scholarship. Until further research is undertaken, we can conclude provisionally that despite Scotland's distinctive history and the importance of Scottish diasporic connections in colonial life, Scots who joined imperial endeavours in the Australian colonies appear to have taken on the British imperial project with very much the same enthusiasm, confusion, contradiction and class tensions as their English counterparts.

NOTES

1. John M. MacKenzie 'Irish, Scottish, Welsh and English worlds? A four-nation approach to the history of the British Empire', *History Compass*, 6:5 (2008), pp. 1244–63.
2. Ann McGrath, 'Shamrock Aborigines: the Irish, the Aboriginal Australians and their children', *Aboriginal History*, 34 (2010), p. 63.
3. 'Indigenous' is often the preferred term, but I use the term 'Aboriginal' since that is used in so many of the sources I quote.
4. See also my related chapter, 'Scottish settlers and indigenous people in colonial Australia', in Alison Scott Inglis (ed.), *For Auld Lang Syne: Images of Scottish Australia from First Fleet to Federation* (Ballarat: Art Gallery of Ballarat, 2014), pp. 83–102.
5. Colin Calloway, *White People, Indians, and Highlanders: Tribal Peoples and Colonial Encounters in Scotland and America* (New York: Oxford University Press, 2008), p. 18.
6. For biographies see D. W. A. Baker, *The Civilised Surveyor: Thomas Mitchell and the Australian Aborigines* (Melbourne: Melbourne University Press, 1997); D. W. A. Baker, *Days of Wrath: A Life of John Dunmore Lang* (Melbourne: Melbourne University Press, 1985); Malcolm Ellis, *Lachlan Macquarie: His Life, Adventures, and Times* (Sydney: HarperCollins Publishers, 2010 [1947]); Harry Dillon and Peter Butler, *Macquarie: From Colony to Country* (Sydney: William Heinemann Australia, 2010). General works include David Macmillan, *Scotland and Australia, 1788–1850: Emigration, Commerce and Investment* (Oxford: Clarendon, 1967); Museum of Scotland (ed.), *That Land of Exiles: Scots in Australia* (Edinburgh: Her Majesty's Stationery Office, 1988); Malcolm Prentis, *The Scots in Australia* (Sydney: University of New South Wales Press, 2008 [1983]).
7. See Malcolm D. Prentis, 'John Mortimer of Manumbar and the 1861 native police inquiry in Queensland', *Journal of the Royal Historical Society of Queensland*, 14:11 (1992), pp. 466–80.
8. Don Watson, *Caledonia Australis: Scottish Highlanders on the Frontier of Australia* (Sydney: William Collins, 1984).
9. Stephen Foster, *A Private Empire* (Sydney: Pier 9, 2010), pp. 234–51.
10. Barbara Dawson, *In the Eye of the Beholder: What Six Nineteenth-century Women Tell Us about Indigenous Authority and Identity* (Canberra: ANU Press, 2014).
11. T. M. Devine, *To the Ends of the Earth: Scotland's Global Diaspora, 1750–2010* (London: Allen Lane, 2011).
12. McGrath, 'Shamrock Aborigines', p. 72.

13. Vicki Grieves, 'The McClymonts of Nabiac: interracial marriage, inheritance and dispossession in nineteenth century New South Wales colonial society', in Alison Holland and Barbara Brookes (eds), *Rethinking the Racial Moment: Essays on the Colonial Encounter* (Cambridge: Cambridge Scholars Publishing, 2011), pp. 125–56.

14. Prentis, *The Scots in Australia*, p. 94.

15. Jessie Mitchell, *In Good Faith? Governing Indigenous Australia through God, Charity and Empire, 1825–1855* (Canberra: ANU Press, 2011), p. 80.

16. Macmillan, *Scotland and Australia*, p. xvii.

17. Legacies of British Slave-Ownership, UCL, available at <https://www.ucl.ac.uk/lbs/> (accessed October 2015). See also Nick Draper, *The Price of Emancipation: Slave-Ownership, Compensation and British Society at the End of Slavery* (Cambridge: Cambridge University Press, 2009).

18. Alexia Howe, 'It was a vast blank', in Museum of Scotland, *That Land of Exiles,* p. 60.

19. D. W. A. Baker, 'Thomas Mitchell', *Australian Dictionary of Biography*, <http://adb.anu.edu.au/biography/lang-john-dunmore-2326> (accessed 23 March 2015); Zoe Laidlaw, 'Richard Bourke: Irish liberalism', in David Lambert and Alan Lester (eds), *Colonial Lives across the British Empire: Imperial Careering in the Long Nineteenth Century* (Cambridge: Cambridge University Press, 2006), p. 129.

20. Laidlaw, 'Richard Bourke', p. 129.

21. Ibid. p. 130.

22. See Maggie MacKellar, *Strangers in a Foreign Land: The Journal of Niel Black and Other Voices from the Western District* (Melbourne: Miegunyah Press, 2008); Penny Russell, *Savage or Civilised? Manners in Colonial Australia* (Sydney: New South Books, 2010), p. 84.

23. Margaret Kiddle, *Men of Yesterday: A Social History of the Western District, 1834–1890* (Melbourne: Melbourne University Press, 1961), p. 43.

24. Russell, *Savage or Civilised?*, p. 92.

25. Ibid. p. 94.

26. Kiddle, *Men of Yesterday*, p. 128.

27. Nathan F. Spielvogel, 'When white men first looked on Ballarat', NLA MS 3776, quoted by Dawson, *The Eye of the Beholder*, p. 77.

28. Ibid. p. 74.

29. Ibid. p. 75.

30. Ibid. pp. 93–4.

31. Thomas Walker, *A Month in the Bush of Australia* (London: J. Cross, Simpson, and Marshall, 1838), p. 32. See W. Joy, 'Thomas Walker', *Australian Dictionary of Biography*, <http://adb.anu.edu.au/biography/walker-thomas-1101> (accessed 23 March 2015).

32. The most detailed biography is Baker, *Days of Wrath*, also available in abridged form as *Preacher, Politician, Patriot: A Life of John Dunmore*

Lang (Melbourne: Melbourne University Press, 1998). See also Anna Johnston, *The Paper War: Morality, Print Culture, and Power in Colonial New South Wales* (Perth: University of Western Australian Publishing, 2011), pp. 160–7.

33. See Meredith Lake, '"Such spiritual acres": Protestantism, the land and the colonisation of Australia 1788–1850', unpublished PhD thesis, University of Sydney, 2008, ch. 8; Paul Pickering, 'The highway to comfort and independence: a case study of radicalism in the British world', *History Australia,* 5:1 (2008), pp.6.1–6.14; Anne O'Brien, 'Humanitarianism and reparation in colonial Australia', *Journal of Colonialism and Colonial History,* 12:2 (2011), <http://muse.jhu.edu.ezproxy1.library.usyd.edu.au/journals/journal_of_colonialism_and_colonial_history/v012/12.2.o-brien.html#f62-text> (accessed 4 March 2015).

34. House of Commons, 'Report of the select committee on Aborigines (British settlements),' *British Parliamentary Papers,* 7:425 (1837), p. 11.

35. There is an extensive literature on this report; see Alan Lester and Fae Dussart, *Colonization and the Origins of Humanitarian Governance* (Cambridge: Cambridge University Press, 2014), pp. 80–104.

36. Anna Johnston, '"A blister on the imperial antipodes": Lancelot Edward Threlkeld in Polynesia and Australia', in Lester and Lambert (eds), *Colonial Lives,* p. 76; Johnston, *The Paper War,* pp. 160–7.

37. Anna Johnston, '"God being, not in the bush": the Nundah Mission (Qld) and colonialism', *Queensland Review,* 4:1 (1997), pp. 71–80.

38. Alan Atkinson and Marian Aveling (eds), *Australians 1838* (Sydney: Fairfax, Syme & Weldon Associates, 1987), pp. 55–61, 390–4.

39. *The Colonist,* 3 October 1838, p. 3.

40. Ibid. p. 2. See also the *Sydney Herald,* 24 October 1838, p. 2.

41. *The Colonist,* 29 December 1838, p. 4; Lake, 'Such spiritual acres', p. 287.

42. *The Colonist,* 29 December 1838, p. 4.

43. John Dunmore Lang, *Cooksland in North-Eastern Australia* (London: Longman and Co, 1847), p. 469. See discussion of this text in Pickering, 'The highway to comfort and independence', pp. 06.9–06.10; Lake, 'Such spiritual acres', p. 293.

44. Adrian Howe, '"Those who make money are generally Scotchmen"', in Museum of Scotland, *That Land of Exiles,* p. 93.

45. Watson, *Caledonia Australis,* p. 112.

46. Ibid. p. 141.

47. Ibid. pp. 165–6.

48. Ibid. p. 167.

49. John Mackenzie-Smith, 'The Scottish presence in the Moreton Bay district, 1841–1859', unpublished PhD thesis, University of Queensland, 1999; see also John Mackenzie-Smith, *Moreton Bay Scots, 1841–59* (Nudgee, Qld: Church Archivists' Press, 2000); James Lergessner, *Death Pudding: The Kilcoy Massacre* (Brisbane: Schuurs Publications, 2007).

50. Lergessner, *Death Pudding*, p. 159.
51. Mackenzie-Smith, 'The Scottish presence in the Moreton Bay district', p. 62.
52. Lergessner, *Death Pudding*, p.159; John Mackenzie-Smith, 'Kilcoy, the first six months – Sir Evan Mackenzie's albatross', *Journal of the Royal Historical Society of Queensland*, 13:12 (1989), pp. 429–44.
53. Lergessner, *Death Pudding*, p. 175.
54. Ibid. p. 197.
55. Mackenzie-Smith, 'Kilcoy, the first six months', pp. 429–44.
56. Dawson, *The Eye of the Beholder*, pp. 102, 119.
57. McCombie, *Adventures of a Colonist*, no pagination.
58. Malcolm Prentis, 'Lowland Scottish immigrants until 1860', in James Jupp (ed.), *The Australian People* (Cambridge: Cambridge University Press, 2001), p. 764.
59. Leigh Boucher and Lynette Russell, '"Soliciting sixpences for township to township": moral dilemmas in mid-nineteenth century Melbourne', *Postcolonial Studies: Culture, Politics, Economy*, 15:2 (2012), pp. 149–65.
60. *Argus*, 27 January 1859, p. 7. Richard Broome, *Aboriginal Victorians: A History since 1800* (Sydney: Allen & Unwin, 2005), pp. 122–3.
61. Bain Attwood, *Rights for Aborigines* (Sydney: Allen & Unwin, 2003), p. 12.
62. Broome, *Aboriginal Victorians*, p. 125.
63. Jane Lydon, *Eye Contact: Photographing Indigenous Australians* (Durham, NC: Duke University Press, 2005), pp. 60–3; Attwood, *Rights for Aborigines*, p. 9; Diane Barwick, *Rebellion at Coranderrk* (Canberra: Aboriginal History Monographs, 2001), pp. 41, 51, 58; Broome, *Aboriginal Victorians*, pp. 124–5.
64. Raymond Evans and Robert Orsted-Jensen, '"I cannot say the numbers that were killed": assessing violent mortality on the Queensland frontier', 2014. Available at SSRN <http://ssrn.com/abstract=2467836> or <http://dx.doi.org/10.2139/ssrn.2467836> (accessed October 2015).
65. Prentis, 'John Mortimer of Manumbar'. There is a discussion of this episode in Jessie Mitchell and Ann Curthoys, 'How different was Victoria? Aboriginal "protection" in a comparative context', in Leigh Boucher and Lynette Russell (eds), *Settler Colonial Governance in Nineteenth-Century Victoria* (Acton, ACT: ANU Press and Aboriginal History Inc., 2015), pp. 183–201.
66. *Moreton Bay Courier*, 16 March 1861, p. 3; Denis Cryle, *The Press in Colonial Queensland: A Social and Political History, 1845–1875* (St Lucia: UQP, 1989), pp. 67–8; Prentis, 'John Mortimer of Manumbar', p. 474.
67. Rosalind Kidd, *The Way We Civilise: Aboriginal Affairs, The Untold Story* (Brisbane: UQP, 1997), p. 13.
68. 'Report from the select committee on the native police force and the condition of the Aborigines generally', *Queensland Votes and Proceedings of*

the Legislative Assembly, 1861, available at <http://www.nla.gov.au/apps/
doview/nla.aus-vn529131-p.pdf> (accessed 23 March 2015). See the report
from Brisbane correspondent, *The Argus*, 8 August 1861, p. 5; Prentis,
'John Mortimer', pp. 474–5.

69. 'Report from the Select Committee on the Native Police Force', p. 5.

7

The Importance of Scottish Origins in the Nineteenth Century: James Taylor and Ceylon Tea

Angela McCarthy

R ECENT OVERARCHING STUDIES OF the Anglophone world present migrants as an undifferentiated mass, so potentially marginalising their individual ethnicities, cultural influence of the homelands, and their varied engagement with the countries where they settled.[1] In part this reflects many studies of the British Empire which continue to elide ethnic differences, despite John MacKenzie stating that the 'ethnic mix from the United Kingdom ... [is] the great hidden story of imperial rule'.[2] Both MacKenzie and T. M. Devine have sought to rectify this in respect of the Scots.[3] And, as Devine reinforces in a recent global overview of Scottish migration,

> individual nations of Britain still do merit specific consideration in their own right as part of the broader British dynamic. This is true in terms of the nature of their emigration, migrant identities and global impact because of the distinctive nature of their own economic, social and intellectual structures.[4]

It is within this context that this chapter examines the life of James Taylor, 'the Father of the Ceylon tea enterprise' (Figure 7.1), to examine the importance – or not – of his Scottish background. Later in this book, for instance, David Fitzpatrick argues that 'home skills were often unexportable' and 'background and origin are much less important ... than differential opportunities in the host countries'. This chapter disputes that claim and shows the ways in which Taylor's origins were important in his achievements abroad. But why is Taylor a useful case study? First, despite acclaim in his adopted land, he never accumulated vast wealth or recognition in the land of his birth.[5] As he put it in 1874, 'Some how or other I was born apparently to do good for others without much benefitting myself.'[6] Taylor therefore enables us to consider the fate of a migrant who had minimal financial assets at the outset of his departure from Scotland at sixteen years of age. Second, a focus on Taylor is

Figure 7.1 James Taylor (dressed in white), 'the father of the Ceylon tea enterprise', with unidentified friend in Ceylon, c. 1863. (Courtesy of T. J. Barron)

facilitated by the serendipitous survival of his correspondence spanning forty years, his published letters and his photograph albums.

ACKNOWLEDGED INFLUENCES

In 1967, in his centenary study of Ceylon tea, D. M. Forrest assessed James Taylor's contribution to the tea economy with a focus on factors in South Asia. In particular, Forrest noted early experimentations in tea cultivation and manufacture in Ceylon and India which were abandoned due to the costs involved.[7] Taylor, by contrast, was the first to make good tea on a commercial scale, his first tea field comprising nineteen acres (Figure 7.2). Taylor certainly acknowledged the influences of others, including Mr Noble, 'an Indian tea planter from Cachar', who showed Taylor how 'to pluck and wither and roll tea with a little leaf growing on some old tea bushes in my bungalow garden ... He told me about fermenting and panning and the rest of the process as then in vogue.' Later, Taylor learned too from Mr Baker, 'a tea planter from Assam', as to how to prune sufficiently while he copied Mr Cameron's practice of finer and regular plucking.[8] Jenkins, 'an old assam Tea planter', had visited to 'see how my Tea was growing, and so on, and showed me how to manufacture it'.[9] Taylor also visited the Darjeeling tea district in 1874[10] and in 1876 summarised in a letter to his brother and sister:

> I had no help nor information about it except what I could pick up from books and papers and one or two tea planters I met. I learned a good deal from this old Assam tea planter and how it is we have so beaten him in quality of tea I don't know. We are now trying Cardamons and Cinnamon.[11]

But central to his employers (Messrs D. G. B. Harrison and Martin Leake) entrusting him with cultivating Assam-hybrid tea seeds was Taylor's earlier experiments and success with cinchona (a medicinal plant, the bark of which was used to produce quinine which treated malaria). Another factor, acknowledged by Taylor but not by later commentators, is that he learned about coffee growing from the local workforce. As he confessed to his father shortly after his arrival in Ceylon, if his employer, George Pride, 'had not coolies that understood better than I do I could not do at all'.[12] This indigenous knowledge of coffee cultivation was, however, less transferable with the emergence of tea.[13] There is, then, no question that factors in South Asia contributed to Taylor's achievements in Ceylon. Yet these are only one part of the story. Influences from his Scottish background are also critical to consider.

Figure 7.2 The first nineteen acres of tea at Loolecondera, still cultivated to this day. (© National Museums Scotland, James Taylor

EDUCATION IN SCOTLAND

John M. MacKenzie argues that the accomplishments of Scots abroad and migrant interactions with new environments were shaped by nineteenth-century Scotland's religious, ethical, intellectual and educational traditions.[14] The orthodoxy holds that Scots had a democratic education system open to all regardless of class and with it a breadth of curriculum.[15] While recent work indicates that the quality of education in the nineteenth century was variable and attendance sometimes poor, there remained notable differences with education in England and most other parts of Europe, including a national system of schools and the professional status of schoolmasters.[16] Moreover, pupils in later years at school were taught basic mathematics and natural philosophy while developments in Scottish agriculture at the time saw it become ever more 'precise and progressive'.[17] Strikingly, the north-east, from where Taylor hailed, had the best literacy rates and schooling in nineteenth-century Scotland.

James Taylor's life provides insight into these educational aspects. He was born in March 1835 at Mosspark on the Monboddo estate near Auchenblae in the civil parish of Fordoun in Kincardineshire, in eastern Scotland. Fordoun parish, with a population in 1831 of 2,238, was noted for its rich cultivation while its inhabitants were said to be of a 'highly respectable class'. Taylor's wheelwright father Michael was 'a respectable hard-working man' (Figure 7.3), who had married Margaret Moir two years before Taylor's birth.[18] The marriage resulted in a further three children while another two children were produced after the death of Taylor's mother in 1844 and his father's remarriage. Margaret Taylor's death was considered 'a bitter sorrow and irretrievable loss' and with his father's remarriage 'home life became almost unbearable to the young lad who was no favo[u]rite with his stepmother.'[19] Perhaps this situation contributed to Taylor's love of learning which was claimed to be more appealing than 'the drudgery of farm-life'.[20] Recollected by his minister as 'a quiet steady-going lad with prominent eyes and eyebrows, and a heavy but thoughtful expression', Taylor was educated at the Fordoun parish school at Auchenblae.[21] As well as Latin and Greek, he learned reading, writing, and arithmetic.[22]

By 1849, at the age of fourteen, James Taylor had become a pupil-teacher at the Free Church School of Fordoun under the master, David Souter, 'a good man but a slow and far from able man'.[23] Souter was to instruct Taylor in teaching and in return Taylor would receive lodging, food and medical attendance.[24] In later years, Taylor reflected on this

Figure 7.3 Michael Taylor, James's father, c. 1875–6. (Courtesy of T. J. Barron)

initial profession in letters sent to his father from Ceylon. He recollected his father's belief that teaching was 'a lazy sort of existence and of little importance compared to work', prompting Taylor 'to feel qualms that I should not succeed in the world so well as if I had been learning a trade [and] made me feel less respect for my education which I was engaged in and so less interest in it and less spirit in pushing it'.[25] A remembrance from 'an Edinburgh correspondent' after Taylor's death similarly observed that 'his father had no sympathy with his son's eager pursuit after all kinds of solid and useful learning'.[26]

It is within this context of concerns about his profession and the relationship with his stepmother, together with the influence of a relative in Ceylon, that Taylor made the decision to migrate to Ceylon. He is said to have conferred at Fettercairn with his mother's cousin Henry Stiven (a grandson of Charles Stiven, the famous snuffbox maker). In October

1851 the cousins travelled to London, 'a nasty, smoky hole', to sign a contract to serve as assistant superintendents on George Pride's coffee estates. Following their preparations in London the cousins set sail on the ship *Sydney*. They arrived at Colombo on 20 February 1852 after a four month passage and were hosted by the Mackwood family. Four days later, 'after a fine ride through some fearful scenery', they arrived at Kandy. Henry Stiven set off for the Ancoombra estate at Matale, while Taylor went to Naranghena estate at Hewaheta Lower. Six weeks later, Taylor was transferred to Loolecondera, a neighbouring estate, though he continued to manage both Naranghena and Waloya.

Extant evidence suggests that Taylor's successful commercial cultivation of coffee, cinchona and tea in Ceylon was due partly to his deep interest in learning. Outlining a typical day on a coffee estate in 1852, the year of his arrival, Taylor informed his father that in the evening he tried to learn the local language and study maths, algebra, geometry, Latin and Greek, while Sundays were spent reading.[27] He considered himself the most learned of his employer's superintendents and contemplated becoming a surveyor.[28] He told his father that 'I measure the land myself that is being planted which saves the expences of surveying'.[29] His education and penmanship likewise stood him in good stead in keeping Loolecondera's accounts.[30] He wrote regularly to the newspapers and exchanged ideas with other planters about planting matters, some of which generated heated debates.[31] As Tom Devine has stressed, Scottish penetration of empire was not simply due to 'limited opportunities at home but it was also facilitated by the training they had received in basic numeracy, literacy and often in an impressively wide range of vocational skills.'[32] That Taylor emerged from a modest rural trade background characterised by continuity of residence further aided his education.[33]

AGRICULTURAL IMPROVEMENT

But Taylor's formal education, shaped by his Scottish background, is only part of the story. The broader developments in Scotland's agriculture are also very relevant. Agrarian 'improvement' in Scotland since the 1760s had resulted in more effective land use, the organisation of labour, and deployment of capital resources and commercial expertise.[34] The Scottish Enlightenment was formative in this transformation of agrarian Lowland Scotland through 'rational, systematic and planned intervention.'[35] Such reorganisation was managed by 'the proprietor and his factor' and 'demanded a practical versatility'.[36] Scots were important in this respect as they were accustomed to working for landlords and tenant farmers were generally viewed as a 'compliant labour force'.[37] Moreover, as Tom Devine has put it, 'the Scottish agricultural system was attracting international attention for its excellence' and 'was widely copied elsewhere'.[38] And north-east Scotland was one of the epicentres of excellence in this regard.

Taylor's arrival in Ceylon in 1851 occurred four years after a general collapse in the coffee economy due to spiralling costs, unscientific estate management, inadequate superintendents, neglect of systematic weeding, poor methods of manufacture and storage and, finally, blight.[39] As a result, around one tenth of Ceylon plantations were abandoned and a further third sold at nominal rates.[40] T. J. Barron, in his study of Ceylon's coffee planters, notes that the early planters 'were conspicuously lacking in any kind of agricultural scientific expertise' and even those who were aware 'were not necessarily able to respond accordingly'. This was a natural consequence of prioritising short-term profits rather than the longer-term application of science.[41] Early investors were frequently the country's military officers, judges and civil servants who did not take into account the soil and methods of cultivation, thereby losing heavily in the 1840s, at a time when Britain also experienced financial difficulties.[42] By contrast, the new era of the 1850s was characterised by scientific methods of cultivation, careful estate management (including weeding, manuring and pruning), road improvement and railway planning.[43] Investors at this time sought those with relevant background skills to tend the estates and scientific methods of cultivation were introduced.[44] And Scots were instrumental in this respect.

Barron highlights the importance of this agricultural expertise gained in Scotland. Robert Boyd Tytler, for instance, encouraged those with agricultural skills from his east Aberdeenshire home area to serve apprenticeships in Ceylon. Other agencies followed his practice.[45] According to a planter in Ceylon in the 1850s, 'agricultural enterprise' pursued in north-east Scotland aided developments in tropical Ceylon's agriculture.[46] Barron stresses that 'practical day-to-day observations and experiences' were vital in developments and some planters such as Arthur Sinclair were exemplary in this respect. According to Sinclair, 'my planting experience was acquired in Aberdeenshire. What I had chiefly to learn in Ceylon was the nature of the different localities on an island where every few miles gave a change of soil and climate'.[47]

Having lived on the Monboddo estate back in Scotland, Taylor would have been familiar with trade and agricultural practices before arriving in Ceylon where he tried his hand at growing plants and other products including chocolate, nutmegs, cloves and vanilla.[48] He constructed Scottish cross-drains, still evident at Loolecondera, claiming as a result that his roads were the best in the district and 'It is the same with all my work it lasts for ever'. His roof thatching, he attested, was good for five years without a drop whereas others only lasted a year 'and few can make a roof without drops'.[49] The dry stone dykes (walls) that he erected without mortar replicated practices in the Scottish Lowlands and are still evident at Loolecondera. Such practices reflected the skills prevalent in Lowland Scotland where small farmers and tradesmen thatched their houses and devised their own tools.[50]

TECHNOLOGY

As well as his education and knowledge of agricultural techniques, Taylor's achievements can also be situated in the industrialisation of Scotland from the 1760s. A range of factors, including market demand, the provision of capital, natural endowment and a rich economic heritage, generated 'a quite unprecedented series of technological innovations'. Moreover, the agricultural revolution did not simply lead to the mushrooming of agricultural skills, but also an expansion of trades associated with agriculture. Vital, as Tom Devine states, was 'a labour force which had already developed skills in engineering, mining and textiles and, crucially, had become accustomed to more rigorous time and work disciplines of industrial capitalism'.[51] Taylor, as noted, focused on his education but his father was a wheelwright and Taylor would have been alert to the skills of his father's trade. William Taylor, also a tenant on the Monboddo estate and either Taylor's grandfather or great-grandfather, was known as the earliest maker of farm fans which 'were well-compacted machines, in good demand in their day'.[52] Such skills and knowledge may have been transferred generationally, facilitated by the continuity of residence available to rural Lowland tradesmen.[53] Taylor would also have been aware of the Luther Water, a river providing water power for Auchenblae's mills.[54]

Certainly, evidence from Ceylon points to Taylor's experimentations with machinery. In 1857 he told his father 'I put up all my own machinery' which, together with his store and pumping house, were 'the neatest and most convenient I seen'. His bungalow, meanwhile, he claimed, 'is the envy and admiration of all the chaps in the district'.[55] Taylor's education and technical skills were also admired by others. The 'ingenious arrangement of a water duct' that Taylor built 'showed considerable engineering skills' which he carried out in a 'quiet, unobtrusive per-severing way'.[56] As contemporaries further noted, 'a more intelligent, practical planter does not exist', while Taylor's employer, Martin Leake, stated, 'He is a man who, of all whom I have known, is the most entirely devoted to his work. Self-advancement has been, I believe, as nothing in his eyes.'[57]

These developments may also have contributed to the tea factory that Taylor established. In January 1873 he reported that 'The Tea house is finished and I have been making Tea in it for a month nearly now'. He further revealed, 'It is all my own contrivance but is very much thought of by Mr Jenkins and another Tea Planter I had a visit of the other day from Cachar' (Figure 7.4).[58] According to a planter in Ceylon who visited Taylor regularly, the early tea factory 'was in the bungalow. The leaf was rolled on the veranda by hand, *i.e.*, from wrists to elbow, while the firing was done in *chulas*, or clay stoves, over charcoal fires, with wire trays to hold the leaf.'[59] By 1872, however, Taylor wrote of invent-ing a machine to roll tea: 'This has often been tried in India but without success I believe. However I think my machine will do it. I tried various ways to do it by a machine without success before I hit on my present idea.'[60] The following year he continued in another letter to his father:

Tea rolling machines have been invented in Assam & Cachar and perhaps elsewhere but none of them I have yet heard of are thoroughly successful so as to dispense altogether with hand rolling. Mine may do so, but it is hard to say till we see it at work. I suppose the chances are all against it. It is entirely different in everything from any of the machines I have yet heard of.[61]

The rolling machine was essential to crush the leaves to release the juice and enzymes that provided the flavour for tea. It was linked to a water-wheel six metres in diameter, to supply power.[62]

Taylor's mention of rolling machines in India presumably refers to the Kinmond tea roller invented in 1867 which used animal power then engines and boilers to drive the machines.[63] Taylor's invention may have drawn on his knowledge of this machine but also reflected his practi-cal experience. His machine was, however, more likely to have been inspired by technological developments in Ceylon, with its substantial history of machine and building design which began in the early nine-teenth century, but became critical with the more heavily mechanised tea economy.[64] Indeed, Barron argues that it is the development of techno-logical expertise which is the most 'outstanding omission' in studies of agricultural enterprise in Ceylon and which 'gave the Ceylon planters a world-wide reputation in the nineteenth century'.[65] Such mechanisation,

Figure 7.4 James Taylor's house and the first tea factory at Loolecondera. (© National Museums Scotland, James Taylor photo album, K.2000.200)

he attests, was crucial to the tea and cinchona economies and was one factor which differentiated planter and indigenous knowledge.[66] The Scottish factor in such developments was presumably critical but more research is required in this regard. Nevertheless, it points to the importance of community cultural capital in providing Taylor with the skills, knowledge and attributes which would prove critical after his settlement in Ceylon. Pierre Bourdieu's concept of social capital – the resources based on relationships and networks – is also important in assessing Taylor's accomplishments, and it is to this we now turn.

SCOTTISH NETWORKS

James Taylor moved to Ceylon within an established migration trail from Scotland, especially regional mobility from the north-east. Ranald Michie identified this aspect, noting that Ceylon's coffee economy benefited from north-east Scottish agricultural expertise and networking. This dominant Scottish influence lasted, he estimates, from the 1830s through to the 1870s, with many early arrivals being individuals who were involved in the East India Company.[67] And, as Andrew Mackillop has indicated, during the eighteenth century migrants from east and central Scotland were disproportionately involved in the East India Company.[68] Ceylon, then, can arguably be seen as an extension of that original eastern Scotland hegemony in India.

Contemporaries in Ceylon certainly testified to this north-east influence. Writing in 1840, Ceylon's Governor James Alexander Stewart Mackenzie requested labour from specific areas in Scotland. He implored Alexander Bannerman at Aberdeen to 'send me out a good ploughman (who can milk cows – is that quite out of the question?) build Dikes, bring out with him, and work a pair of Aberdeenshire Oxen – a plough & Harrow, such as he is in habit of using?'[69] Yet Mackenzie did not limit this quest to those from the north-east. In 1838, desiring road overseers, he rhetorically asked James McAdam, '[S]hall I say I would prefer Scotch people?'.[70] Those in later decades similarly testified to the north-east character of the Scottish presence in Ceylon. As John Ferguson reminisced in 1893, 'Not so far back, two-thirds of our planters were Scotchmen, and, again, two-thirds of these hailed from the north-eastern counties of which Aberdeen is the capital'.[71] Arthur Sinclair, a fellow of the Royal Colonial Institute, commented on the 'the patient, plodding Aberdonian' who, 'famous for agricultural enterprise at home', has contributed successfully to Ceylon's agriculture.[72] Scots in Ceylon, then, resembled their counterparts in other destinations within the Scottish diaspora by drawing on their personal networks and identities.[73]

Yet these regional connections also owed something to the Scottish participation in earlier tropical plantations. As Barron puts it, 'the first generation of planters were the inheritors of nearly 200 years of planting experience'.[74] He does not, however, stress the *Scottish* dimension of this prior involvement although Scots had considerable experience in this respect. They were, for instance, prominent in the tobacco plantations in Virginia, Maryland and the Carolinas where personal relationships by marriage or kinship proved critical to transatlantic trading.[75] Scots were likewise 'disproportionately numerous in the Caribbean', where 'The practice of employing relatives of associates from the same part of Scotland as overseers or managers was widespread'.[76] Their literacy and numeracy skills stood them in good stead as planters and clerks, among other occupations, in the sugar, coffee and cotton trades.[77] Indeed, Robert Boyd Tytler was 'quietly shipped . . . off to Jamaica, where, upon learning all that was necessary, his valuable services were transferred to Ceylon.'[78] Such networking practices, then, did not simply emerge in the nineteenth century but were built upon similar characteristics of prior movements, though the extent to which individuals and ideas circulated from and around these regions is little studied and remains an area of future research. Nevertheless, the north-east gravitation to Ceylon echoes regional linkages found in earlier centuries (such as the Highland Scottish presence in Guyana discussed in this volume).

Taylor's movement to Ceylon was made within this networking context. Described in his youth as 'a big-headed, large-chested, burly lad, looking a picture of robust health', Taylor was lured to Ceylon by his mother's cousin Peter Moir, an agent for Ceylon coffee estates.[79] Taylor certainly acknowledged in 1872 that 'Peter got me out here', while fellow planter Hugh Blacklaw recollected in 1907:

> The late Mr Peter Moir, who came from the same place as I did, had come out to Ceylon in 1843. He was manager of Messrs Hadden's properties out here, and enticed a lot of young people from our small town to come out. It was through his influence that my brothers and I came to Ceylon. It is a very small town, ours. It is St Laurencekirk, Kincardineshire, with a population of about 2,000 souls, yet at one time there were as many as fourteen St Laurencekirk men in Ceylon. There were my four brothers and I, the four Moirs, James Taylor of Golconda, pioneer of tea and cinchona, Robertson, father of Robertson of the G.P.O., Petrie, the two Bissets and Stiven of Ancoombra, Matale West, who afterwards went to Kandanuwara and died at the Galle Face Hotel in 1868.[80]

It is perhaps not surprising then that Taylor concluded in 1859 that those of Scottish origin made the best planters in Ceylon:

> Really neither the English nor the Irish in this part of the world are nearly so good as Scotchmen with few exceptions. Even English proprietors try to get Scotch superintendents as for example Pride (my old master and his brother says he thinks them the most useful people in the world and the Messrs Hadden proprietors of the Moirs' places have found scotchmen serves them better than any other manager in the country perhaps of any class would have done. When ever any estate is doing well it is a Scotchman that is on it. If we speak with a Scotchman it is about estate matters and wives if with an Englishman his whole heart and soul is in dogs and horses and I think the few Irish that I know seem generally to give themselves precious little trouble about anything. I see little of the wit they are famed for and terrible little practical sense.[81]

While this statement appears to be ethnic conceit, evidence presented in the form of a novel, from the viewpoint of the wife of an English planter, echoes Taylor. The author recalls that early coffee planters were 'cunning Scotchmen', some of whom sold out with moderate returns and went home.[82] English planters, by contrast, 'were University men' who 'knew absolutely nothing of agriculture . . . They knew nothing of manuring and draining, roading and planting . . . There was no preparation in England, either at school or at home, for the colonist's life in Ceylon, and everything had to be learnt from the beginning.'[83] Later planters, such as Thomas Villiers, recollected that 'it was largely from Scotland that the original settlers came out', with the English 'following up the pioneer work of the Scotch' about forty years later.[84] And such was the extent of the Scottish presence in Ceylon that the nomenclature of many estates was strikingly Scottish.[85]

PERSONAL QUALITIES

The final consideration in Taylor's achievements is his personality and abilities, together with what may be termed his emotional capital. This, as Helga Nowotny, terms it, is the 'knowledge, contacts and relations as well as the emotionally valued skills and assets, which hold within any social network characterised at least partly by affective ties'.[86] Here we might extend Nowotny's private realm focus to the public sphere to incorporate the emotional capital of Taylor's fellow planters. They considered him 'an upright, industrious superintendent' who carried out 'intelligent, careful, and successful experiments in the cultivation and preparation of both cinchona and Tea'.[87] Being 'a man in a thousand'

and 'a slave to his work', Daniel Morris, the assistant director of the Royal Botanic Gardens at Kew, observed that 'Taylor, in his plodding, careful way, worked out unaided, the details of tea manufacture'.[88]

After his death, Taylor was noted as being a 'fine specimen of a Scotch Colonial' and praised for his life of 'unceasing labour . . . restless energy in seeking out facts, and his telling of them to his fellow-planters, freely, and to the best of his knowledge'. Assessment of this colonial knowledge production is still to be undertaken, but holds promise in contributing to the wider historiography on the ways that information was created, circulated, and contested.[89] In sum, Taylor was remembered as

> the noblest of men. The kindest of friends, the gentlest, the wisest, and the most experienced of planters . . . simple, lovable, charitable, and possessed of extreme modesty – such was the Father of the Ceylon Tea enterprise; a man whose kindnesses will live in many a planter's memory, and whose name will stand high in the archives of this Colony for ever.[90]

This colonial knowledge, however, would have been redundant to a large extent if Taylor did not possess the emotional capital to also obtain the respect and obedience of his workforce. In 1892, the year that Taylor died, a revealing extract appeared in the *Tropical Agriculturalist* setting out the ideal planter's qualities:

> A young man properly graduating as a planter in Ceylon is bound to acquire much practical knowledge respecting the best treatment of the plant and soil on which he is engaged; in regard to the proper management of coloured labour – (and nowhere are labourers treated more kindly) – including the learning to speak the coolies' language colloquially; he is expected to understand not only the mysteries of seed nurseries, of planting, draining, and road making; but to be able to design and superintend buildings, whether in wattle and daub for coolly lines, or in brick and stone for his own bungalow and factory, and the more he is, or becomes, of a practical engineer, land surveyor, and even physician for his coolies, the better.[91]

Certainly Taylor adhered to such qualities and in 1872 he was one of the planters who advocated the appointment of a doctor in the district. As he commented:

> A properly qualified Doctor in this District would be a great blessing to many of the coolies and to myself . . . In cases when the best has not been done, and proper medical attendance not been procured, if the cooly dies, which is frequently the case, the result is very unsatisfactory for one's conscience.[92]

In 1890 the *Tropical Agriculturalist* noted:

One small fact will show how conscientiously careful Mr. Taylor is in his work. Strict cleanliness is of much importance in the preparation of tea; and when coolies are seen dressed in specially clean clothing, the remark made is, 'Some of Taylor's tea coolies'.[93]

CONCLUSION

This brief look at James Taylor's life has attempted to illuminate some aspects of the social, cultural and economic world of Scotland which contributed to his achievements in Ceylon's tea enterprise. His love of learning and experimentation is set in the broader context of educational, engineering and agricultural developments that transformed Scotland during the nineteenth century. This cultural capital was crucial but so too was social capital. His experiments were influenced by a range of individuals, and owed something to the longer history of Scottish engagement in the tropical environments. Taylor was likewise part of a considerable out-migration from north-east Scotland to Ceylon and India. These factors are all important in light of recent studies of the Anglophone world and the British Empire which elide the ethnic composition of Britons.[94] Also critical was Taylor's diligence and perseverance. While other experiments in tea would similarly bear fruit, Taylor's persistence meant that he was the first to succeed in cultivating commercially Ceylon's new commodity and was recognised by his contemporaries and later generations of tea planters in Sri Lanka for that achievement.

But is the example of Taylor exceptional or do we find similarities among other comparative examples? We might here consider briefly the development of tea in India. In Darjeeling, Scotsman Robert Fortune is known as the 'father of tea' after he stole tea seeds from China. Like Taylor, Fortune was educated at parish level and had no formal higher education schooling. His knowledge of horticulture arose from practical application but was supplemented through trade qualifications in horticulture. Key, however, as his biographer claims, is that 'to be a great gardener demanded great patience'.[95] Fellow Scotsman Archibald Campbell, meanwhile, is known as the 'guardian' of tea in Darjeeling. He too emerged from a modest rural Scottish background, obtained a basic parish level education, and was initially a local gardener before obtaining a medical education which saw him become a naval surgeon.[96] We might also briefly consider Charles Alexander Bruce, who is credited with learning to grow and make tea in Assam. He was criticised for lacking practical or theoretical knowledge but was a 'zealous, hard-working person'. Like Taylor he learned from others, in his case tea makers from China, but, unlike Taylor, produced poor tea.[97] Although a tentative sample, these examples show similarities including the importance of cultural capital such as a primary education and a modest trade/artisan background, factors which this article argues cannot be elided when assessing the achievements of these Scots abroad. Yet, as the descriptions above also testify to, the personal attributes of individuals need to be incorporated. While further research on individuals and groups is required to test the hypotheses proposed here, the chapter demonstrates the need to go beyond a focus on influences from the new world after settlement to also incorporate the background of British and European individuals who sought new lives in South Asia.

NOTES

The author wishes to thank the Royal Society of Edinburgh for funding the research for this chapter and the following for their helpful comments on an earlier version: Tom Barron, Tom Devine and John M. MacKenzie.

1. James Belich, *Replenishing the Earth: The Settler Revolution and the Rise of the Anglo-World, 1783–1939* (Oxford: Oxford University Press, 2009); elides distinctions between 'Britons'.
2. John M. MacKenzie, *Empires of Nature and the Nature of Empires: Imperialism, Scotland and the Environment* (East Linton: Tuckwell Press, 1997), pp. 64–5.
3. John M. MacKenzie and T. M. Devine (eds), *Scotland and the British Empire* (Oxford: Oxford University Press, 2012).
4. T. M. Devine, *To the Ends of the Earth: Scotland's Global Diaspora, 1750–2010* (London: Allen Lane, 2011), p. xvi.
5. Anon., 'The Late Mr James Taylor of Loolecondera', 4 May 1892, Papers of James Taylor, planter in Ceylon, National Library of Scotland (hereafter NLS), MS 15908.
6. James Taylor (Loolecondera) to his father Michael Taylor (Mosspark), 25 January 1873, Taylor papers, NLS. The only proprietary interest in land that Taylor ever had was in Lover's Leap, Nuwara Eliya, which he opened as a cinchona plantation before it was taken over by mortgagees; see 'Pioneers of the planting enterprise in Ceylon', p. 4.
7. D. M. Forrest, *A Hundred Years of Ceylon Tea, 1867–1967* (London: Chatto and Windus, 1967), ch. 3.
8. James Taylor (Loolecondera) to Secretary of the Planters Association (Kandy), September 1891, reproduced in *Ceylon Mail*, 21 October 1891, Taylor papers, NLS.
9. James Taylor (Loolecondera) to his father Michael Taylor (Mosspark), 25 January 1873, Taylor papers, NLS.

10. Taylor wrote to his father from Darjeeling in March 1874 and reflected again on his visit in a letter from Loolecondera dated 11 April 1875.
11. James Taylor (Loolecondera) to his brother and sister, 5 November 1876, Taylor papers, NLS.
12. James Taylor (Naranghena) to his father Michael Taylor (Mosspark), 11 April 1852, Taylor papers, NLS.
13. T. J. Barron, 'Science and the nineteenth-century Ceylon coffee planters', *Journal of Imperial and Commonwealth History*, 16:1 (1987), p. 20.
14. John M. MacKenzie, 'Scots and the environment of empire', in MacKenzie and Devine (eds), *Scotland and the British Empire*, pp. 147–75.
15. Lindsay Paterson, 'Traditions of Scottish education', in Heather Holmes (ed.), *Scottish Life and Society: Institutions of Scotland: Education* (East Linton: Tuckwell Press, 2000), p. 23.
16. R. D. Anderson, *Education and the Scottish People, 1750–1918* (Oxford: Clarendon Press, 1995), p. 23.
17. Laurence James Saunders, *Scottish Democracy, 1815–1840: The Social and Intellectual Background* (Edinburgh: Oliver and Boyd, 1950), p. 38.
18. 'Pioneers of the planting enterprise in Ceylon: James Taylor', *The Tropical Agriculturalist*, 14, 2 July 1894, p. 1.
19. Ibid. p. 1.
20. Ibid. p. 1.
21. Ibid. p. 1.
22. These subjects were all taught at the school in 1831, at which time the parish had six schools. See *New Statistical Account of Scotland*, vol. XI: *Forfar – Kincardine* (Edinburgh: W. Blackwood and Sons, 1845), p. 105.
23. James Taylor (Loolecondera) to his father Michael Taylor (Mosspark), 17 September 1857, Taylor papers, NLS. Souter's name is also rendered 'Soutar'.
24. Teaching indenture, 1 April 1849, in Taylor papers, NLS.
25. James Taylor to his father, undated letter, Taylor papers, NLS.
26. 'Pioneers of the planting enterprise in Ceylon', p. 2.
27. James Taylor (Loolecondera) to his father Michael Taylor (Mosspark), 23 June 1852, Taylor papers, NLS.
28. Ibid. 9 March 1854, Taylor papers, NLS.
29. Ibid. 17 September 1857, Taylor papers, NLS.
30. Ibid. 23 June 1852, Taylor papers, NLS.
31. See, for instance, the following articles on pruning in the *Colombo Overland Observer*, South Asian newspapers online: Taylor's article on the pruning of coffee, pp. 11–12, and the response from 'A Planter', pp. 2, 129, in the digital edition dated 5 June 1865; Taylor's response to 'A Planter' in the same publication, digital edition dated 17 June 1865, p. 10; and a further response in the digital edition dated 3 July 1865, p. 9.
32. T. M. Devine, *The Scottish Nation, 1700–2000* (London: Penguin Books, 2000), pp. 99–100.

33. Gavin Sprott, 'The country tradesman', in T. M. Devine (ed.), *Farm Servants and Labour in Lowland Scotland, 1770–1914* (Edinburgh: John Donald, 1984), p. 144.

34. T. M. Devine, *The Transformation of Rural Scotland: Social Change and the Agrarian Economy, 1660–1815* (Edinburgh: John Donald, 1994), p. 165.

35. Ibid. p. 65.

36. Saunders, *Scottish Democracy*, p. 17.

37. Alastair Orr, 'Farm servants and farm labour in the Forth Valley and south-east Lowlands', in Devine (ed.), *Farm Servants and Labour*, p. 29.

38. T. M. Devine, 'Scottish farm service in the agricultural revolution', in ibid. pp. 1, 4.

39. Lennox A. Mills, *Ceylon Under British Rule, 1795–1932* (London: Oxford University Press, 1933), pp. 229–30, 236.

40. Ibid. p. 235.

41. Barron, 'Science and the nineteenth-century Ceylon coffee planters', p. 7.

42. G. C. Mendis, *Ceylon Under the British* , 2nd edn (Colombo: Colombo Apothecaries' Co. Ltd, 1946), p. 46. See also Mills, *Ceylon Under British Rule*, p. 77.

43. Mills, *Ceylon Under British Rule*, pp. 237–40.

44. Ibid. p. 238.

45. Barron, 'Science and the nineteenth-century Ceylon coffee planters', p. 12.

46. Ranald C. Michie, 'Aberdeen and Ceylon economic links in the nineteenth century', *Northern Scotland*, 4 (1981), p. 70.

47. Barron, 'Science and the nineteenth-century coffee planters', p. 18.

48. James Taylor (Loolecondera) to his sister and brother, 5 November 1876, Taylor papers, NLS.

49. James Taylor (Loolecondera) to his father (Mosspark), 9 September 1860, Taylor papers, NLS.

50. Sprott, 'The country tradesman', p. 144.

51. T. M. Devine, 'Industrialisation', in T. M. Devine, Clive Lee and George Peden (eds), *The Transformation of Scotland: The Economy since 1700* (Edinburgh: Edinburgh University Press, 2005), pp. 41, 58.

52. Charles A. Mollyson, *The Parish of Fordoun: Chapters in its History, or Reminiscences of Place and Character* (Aberdeen: John Rae Smith, 1893), p. 154.

53. Sprott, 'The country tradesman', p. 144.

54. Mollyson, *The Parish of Fordoun*, pp. 154, 149.

55. James Taylor (Loolecondera) to his father Michael Taylor (Mosspark), 17 September 1857, Taylor papers, NLS.

56. *Ceylon Mail or Weekly Independent*, 21 October 1891, in Taylor papers, NLS.

57. Cited in Forrest, *A Hundred Years*, pp. 74, 66.

58. James Taylor (Loolecondera) to his father (Mosspark), 25 January 1873, Taylor papers, NLS.

59. William H. Ukers, *All About Tea*, 1 (New York: Tea and Coffee Trade Journal Company, 1935), p. 197.

60. James Taylor (Loolecondera) to his father Michael Taylor (Mosspark), 18 March 1872, Taylor papers, NLS.

61. Ibid. 25 January 1873, Taylor papers, NLS.

62. A later roller, known as the 'Loolecondera Standard' and supplied from India, was subjected to a patent case in the 1890s. See *Tropical Agriculturalist*, 1 March 1892, pp. 654–74.

63. H. A. Antrobus, *A History of the Assam Company, 1839–1953* (Edinburgh: T. A. Constable, 1957), pp. 292–3.

64. Barron, 'Science and the nineteenth-century Ceylon coffee planters', p. 14.

65. Barron, 'Sir James Emerson Tennent', p. 13.

66. Barron, 'Science and the nineteenth-century Ceylon coffee planters', p. 20.

67. Michie, 'Aberdeen and Ceylon', pp. 69–82.

68. Andrew Mackillop, 'Locality, nation, and empire: Scots and the empire in Asia, c.1695–c.1813', in MacKenzie and Devine (eds), *Scotland and the British Empire*, pp. 66, 70.

69. James Alexander Stewart Mackenzie (Galle) to Alexander Bannerman (Aberdeen), 7 July 1840, Papers of the Mackenzie family, National Records of Scotland (NRS), GD46/9/6, no. 11.

70. James Alexander Stewart Mackenzie (Colombo) to James McAdam (London), 28 March 1838, Papers of the Mackenzie family, NRS, GD46/9/6, no. 99.

71. John Ferguson, *Ceylon in 1893* (London: John Haddon and Co., 1893), p. 230.

72. Arthur Sinclair, *Tropical Lands Recent Travels to the Sources of the Amazon, the West Indian Islands, and Ceylon* (Aberdeen: D. Wylie & Son, 1895), p. 160.

73. Angela McCarthy (ed.), *A Global Clan: Scottish Migrant Networks and Identities since the Eighteenth Century* (London and New York: Tauris Academic Studies, 2006).

74. Barron, 'Sir James Emerson Tennent', p. 13.

75. T. M. Devine, *The Tobacco Lords, A Study of the Tobacco Merchants of Glasgow and their Trading Activities, c.1740–9* (Edinburgh: John Donald, 1975), p. 3.

76. Douglas J. Hamilton, *Scotland, the Caribbean and the Atlantic World, 1750–1820* (Manchester: Manchester University Press, 2005), p. 55.

77. Ibid. pp. 4, 18.

78. *Aberdeen Journal*, 15 September 1875.

79. The description of Taylor is from veteran planter A. Morrison. See 'Pioneers of the planting enterprise in Ceylon', p. 2. For employment with the Haddens see letters from James Taylor (London) to his father Michael Taylor (Mosspark), 16 October 1851 and 18 October 1851, Taylor papers, NLS.

80. James Taylor (Loolecondera) to his father Michael Taylor (Mosspark), 18 March 1872, Taylor papers, NLS. Blacklaw's quote is cited in Forrest, *A Hundred Years of Ceylon Tea*, p. 61. Some accounts refer to Moir as Taylor's cousin but that he was a cousin to Taylor's mother is evident from my reconstruction of the family tree. Another account from 1895, presumably by Blacklaw also, further notes the Laurencekirk contingent: 'Peter Moir led the way, and 13 of us followed – Jamie Moir, David Moir, Charlie Moir, H. and W. Stiven, Jamie Taylor, Sandy Robertson, J. Oliphant, five Blacklaws, and the Bissets from close by.' See *Overland Ceylon Observer*, South Asian newspapers online, digital edition dated 1 August 1895, p. 11.
81. James Taylor (Loolecondera) to unidentified recipient, 21 February 1859, Taylor papers, NLS.
82. FEFP [Fanny Emily Farr Penny], *Fickle Fortune in Ceylon* (Madras: Addison and Co., 1887), p. 12.
83. *Fickle Fortune*, p. 36. Also cited in Barron, 'Science and the nineteenth-century Ceylon coffee planters', p. 17.
84. Sir Thomas L. Villiers, *Some Pioneers of the Tea Industry* (Colombo: The Colombo Apothecaries' Co. Ltd, 1951), pp. 6–7.
85. Forrest, *A Hundred Years*, p. 105.
86. Helga Nowotny, 'Women in public life in Australia', in C. Fuchs Epstein and R. L. Coser (eds), *Access to Power: Cross National Studies of Women and Elites* (London: George Allen & Unwin, 1981), p. 148.
87. 'Pioneers of the planting enterprise in Ceylon', p. 4.
88. *Overland Ceylon Observer*, South Asian newspapers online edition dated 12 May 1892, p. 8, and 2 July 1890, p. 17; 'The tea industry of Ceylon', *Tropical Agriculturalist*, 1 March 1888, p. 601.
89. For an overview of colonial knowledge see Tony Ballantyne, 'Colonial knowledge', in Sarah Stockwell (ed.), *The British Empire: Themes and Perspectives* (Oxford: Blackwell, 2008), pp. 177–97.
90. *Overland Ceylon Observer*, online edition dated 12 May 1892, p. 8; Anon., 'The Late Mr James Taylor of Loolecondera', 4 May 1892, Taylor papers, NLS.
91. *Tropical Agriculturalist*, 1 November 1892, p. 337.
92. *Overland Ceylon Observer*, 10 June 1872, p. 233, digitised version dated 28 May 1872, p. 44.
93. *Tropical Agriculturalist*, 1 August 1890, p. 79.
94. Belich, *Replenishing the Earth*.
95. Sarah Rose, *For All the Tea in China: Espionage, Empire and the Secret Formula for the World's Favourite Drink* (London: Hutchinson, 2009), p. 41.
96. James McCarthy, *Monkey Puzzle Man: Archibald Menzies, Plant Hunter* (Dunbeath: Whittles, 2008).
97. Antrobus, *A History of the Assam Company*, pp. 17–28, 65, 270.

8

'Our Old World Diff'rences are Dead': The Scottish Migrant Military Tradition in the British Dominions during the First World War

Stuart Allan and David Forsyth

Our old world diff'rences are dead,
Like weeds beneath the plough,
For English, Scotch and Irish-bred
They're all Australians now!

T HE AUSTRALIAN NATIONALIST SENTIMENT conveyed by celebrated bush balladeer A. B. 'Banjo' Paterson's 1915 poem 'We're All Australians Now' represents a development which is widely recognised to have been common to the experience of the British dominions during and after the First World War.[1] In these countries, the war came to be regarded as a milestone on the journey from colonial status to independent nationhood. Their war efforts may have been articulated in terms of the loyal defence of the British Empire and of the values ascribed to it, but the share taken by the dominions in mobilisation, sacrifice and ultimate victory was understood, as Paterson asserted of his own country, to make Australians feel more Australian in consequence. 'We're All Australians Now' was written at home in the summer of 1915 during a brief hiatus in Paterson's war service, which would shortly take him to Egypt as an officer of the Remount Service of the Australian Imperial Force.[2] He was Australian born, the son of a Scotsman who had emigrated to New South Wales in the early 1850s but, with more socially elevated English and Irish forbears on his mother's side, he never traded on the Scottish end of his ancestry.[3] He identified more readily with the country of his birth, which he had seen federated as a nation in 1901, and his literary work, especially 'The Man from Snowy River' and 'Waltzing Matilda', was already influential in formulating the romantic figure of the bushman as a leading character in the foundation myth of Australian identity. By the end of the First World War, the classic image of the Australian soldier, the strapping, scruffy, unflappable veteran of Gallipoli, Pozières and Romani, had been melded with Paterson's bushman, principally through the influence of war correspondent, official historian and propagandist C. E. W. Bean, to ingrain the archetype of the ideal Australian in popular consciousness.[4]

If, by 1918, to be an Australian soldier was to be a true Australian, much the same might be said for the war's impact on national consciousness in New Zealand, South Africa, Canada and, though with a different long-term outcome, in Newfoundland.[5] The extent to which dominion nationalism at this period both complemented and challenged popular identification with membership of the British Empire has since become a subject of debate.[6] But into the mix of wartime and post-war propagandist writing, monument building and commemorative ritual promoting narratives of dominion war efforts in terms of national unity, a further ingredient might be added from the perspective of Scottish history. Generations of migration from Scotland to the colonies of settlement had brought with it cultural traits by which Scots identified themselves and identified with one another. None was more outwardly manifest than the traditions of war and military service by which, in particular, the Scottish regiments of the British army were instantly recognised and widely respected throughout and beyond the British Empire.

In a centenary exhibition at the National Museum of Scotland in 2014, the interaction between Scottish military traditions, British imperial identities and dominion nationalism during the First World War was explored through the symbolic and personal associations of material culture.[7] While the phenomenon of migrant Scottish regiments, of the kilt wearing, bagpipe playing soldiers of Canada or South Africa, was already well known as an aspect of the military histories of the countries concerned, the exhibition employed a comparative and contextual approach which took the subject into the field of diaspora studies.[8] An essential question which emerged shapes this chapter: the need to explain an apparent paradox over how Scottish identity came to be so prominently represented in the military culture of the expeditionary forces and propaganda imagery of Canada and South Africa but was, in contrast, subdued and sublimated in those of Australia and New Zealand.

OVERSEAS EXPEDITIONARY FORCES

Of the sixty-nine infantry battalions which existed in the course of the war as part of the operational Canadian Corps on overseas service, eleven had Scottish titles and identities. The South African Brigade of white volunteers assembled for service beyond Africa four infantry battalions strong, and one of these, the 4th South African Infantry, was the kilt wearing 'South African Scottish'.[9] The battlefield performance and inherited traditions of these battalions gave them an honoured place in the memory of the war in each of these countries, a prominence arguably greater than their proportional contributions. This was already apparent before the end of the war. The application of the colourful Highland military image to recruitment and propaganda in South Africa and Canada transcended the requirements of recruiting the Scottish infantry battalions. An official recruiting poster of 1918 for the South African Brigade (Figure 8.1) represented the whole Brigade, already revered for its performance and sacrifice on the Western Front, with the figure of a single, kilted Scottish soldier.[10] A 1918 propaganda poster published in London, entitled 'The British Commonwealth in Arms' (Figure 8.2), similarly represented national contributions by employing figures of individual soldiers, based on the self-defining dress distinctions of the contributing parts of the empire. For the British themselves, the figure was an infantryman in standard British service dress, likewise for Newfoundland. For Australia, the figure displayed the distinction of the 'slouch hat' by which Australian soldiers had come to be identified. For New Zealand, the same function was served with depiction of the New Zealanders' alternatively folded 'lemon squeezer' uniform hat. But for Canada and for South Africa, national military identity was represented by figures of kilted and bonneted Scottish infantrymen. It must be allowed that the Scottish imagery provided some colour and shape to this poster from a graphic design point of view, but it was published for the eyes of the whole empire, suggesting that the correlation between Scottish military traditions and the wartime identities of Canada and South Africa was accepted as a norm.[11] No such Scottish units took the field in the name of Australia or New Zealand. And yet each of these destination countries had shared a similar experience of Scottish immigration, Scottish associational culture, and the proliferation of 'Scottish' military units in pre-war volunteer forces which were maintained in peacetime for the purposes of home defence. Could it have been that sentimental ties to the Scottish homeland were somehow weaker in Britain's Pacific dominions?

Empirical information about the make-up of the overseas expeditionary forces dispatched to the war might be expected to go some way towards providing an answer. There is little by way of statistical evidence to delineate the proportion of these soldiers who were Scottish born, or who identified themselves as Scottish, since this was not a matter of practical concern worth recording by the administrations which sent them. But we may at least refer to broad assessments of the

Figure 8.1 South African Brigade recruiting poster, 1918. (© Imperial War Museum, art.IWM PST 12316)

proportion of home-born, as opposed to overseas-born and therefore immigrant recruits who made up the respective dominion expeditionary forces. While the figures are not robust in each case, there is a note-worthy discrepancy. For Australia, men of British birth are estimated to have represented 27 per cent of the first contingent of the Australian Imperial Force which sailed for Egypt in 1914 and then on to Gallipoli. For the New Zealand Expeditionary Force, bound for the same des-tinations, some 22 per cent were British born. In contrast, although a smaller proportion of the Canadian population overall was born in Britain than was the equivalent for Australia or New Zealand, 64 per cent of the first contingent of the Canadian Expeditionary Force bound first for England in the autumn of 1914, and then for the Western Front,

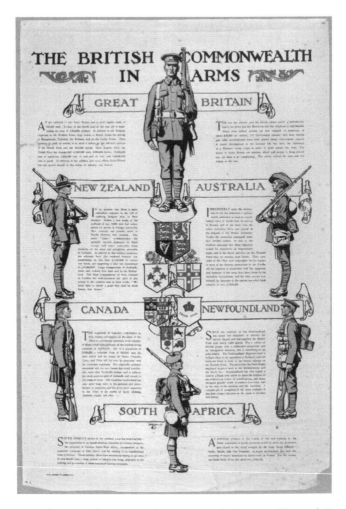

Figure 8.2 British imperial propaganda poster, with the war efforts of Canada and South Africa represented by kilted soldiers, 1918. (© Canadian War Museum, CWM 19900348-004)

was British by birth.[12] Equivalent figures are not available for the profile of the South African Brigade on the Western Front, but official historian John Buchan examined the Brigade's Scottish 4th Battalion on a similar basis, finding that of 1,282 of all ranks, 337 were Scottish born, 258 English, thirty Irish, thirteen Welsh, 595 South African and forty-nine of other origin. The British born therefore constituted 50 per cent of the total which, the greater preponderance of Scots aside, Buchan suggested was typical of the Brigade as a whole.[13]

It does not necessarily follow, however, that the expeditionary forces of Canada and South Africa, carrying greater concentrations of first generation immigrants, were more likely to adopt elements of military identity looking back to the old country. At an individual level, place of birth might not have been significant. As James Wood pointed out in the context of the Canadian experience, 'British born' might in many cases mean the immigrant arrived in Canada at an early age, and had grown up there, which raises the question of whether the pull of loyalty to Britain was inevitably stronger than it would have been for those men of military service age born in Canada itself.[14] Wood also noted that recent migrants were more likely to be found in urban occupations with fewer economic and family ties locally, and therefore were less inhibited from volunteering for service overseas. The relatively low proportion of Canadian-born recruits in the first Canadian Expeditionary Force was a subject of disquiet within the political and military establishment, where there was awareness that farmers and French-Canadians at first seemed reluctant to volunteer.[15] This need not have been an identity issue, however, as initial mobilisation arrangements in New Zealand and Australia may have been more effective in reaching and recruiting a wider spread of the eligible population than was achieved at first in Canada.

Furthermore, as the South African figures compiled by John Buchan appear to demonstrate, overseas service in a Scottish unit did not necessarily entail a direct connection to Scotland. It is unclear how many volunteers joining a battalion such as this previously identified themselves as Scottish, whether dominion born or born in other parts of the British Isles. Conversely, a cursory glance at the histories of the expeditionary force units of Canada or South Africa will reveal an abundance of Scottish names in units which did not display Scottish identities. Perhaps the most celebrated 'Scot' of the Canadian Expeditionary Force, the poet John McCrae of 'In Flanders Fields' fame, was born in Canada to Canadian-born parents and served not in a Scottish unit but in the Canadian Field Artillery.[16] In this, he was by no means unusual. So complex were the factors of birth, mobility, class, local and individual circumstance affecting enlistment, it is not possible to relate convincingly the existence, absence or prominence of dominion Scottish units in the First World War directly to the overall recruiting profiles of the countries concerned. The answer to the discrepancy between the Scottish traditions of the Canadians and South Africans on the one hand, and the more nationally conforming military identities of the forces of the Pacific dominions on the other, lies instead amidst the imperial politics of pre-war military administration, the manner in which mobilisation for a major war was organised and the local circumstances in which it was carried out.

VOLUNTEERING AS ASSOCIATIONAL CULTURE

The burgeoning of diaspora Scottish corps which functioned prior to 1914 owed much to the revival of the volunteer movement in Great Britain a half-century earlier, predicated on the idea that responsible, respectable members of civil society should, by right, play some part in the defence of the realm. The volunteer ethos attracted adherents across the domestic political spectrum who shared media-fuelled concerns that the political and military establishment was leaving Britain exposed to the threat of a resurgent and potentially bellicose France. From 1859, substantial numbers of British middle-class men, in concert with similarly motivated men of the skilled and respectable working class, signed up for new locally organised volunteer infantry units, founded by prominent citizens, to practice drill and rifle-shooting, or to learn gunnery in artillery units around the coast.[17] The volunteering culture was, in part at least, an implicit criticism of stagnation in professional military standards and conventions, an attempt to pressurise government, by power of example, into modernisation and reform in military affairs. But in Scotland, there was a distinctive factor. The reputation of the professionals, the regular Scottish regiments of the British army, stood high in popular esteem, since, with their instantly recognisable garniture of tartan, bonnet, broadsword and bagpiping, they were widely held up as representative of Scottish difference and Scottish dignity as a culturally autonomous partner in the British imperial state. Their recent prominence in positive representation of the otherwise unsettling military campaigns in the Crimean War and 'Indian Mutiny' had further heightened their prestige. Scottish rifle volunteer units might have shared the citizen soldier ethos of their wider British counterparts but they were not slow to emulate the Scottish regiments, sporting Highland flourishes to their sober grey or buff uniforms more characteristic of wider volunteer culture, or to form Highland companies sporting the kilt.

Scottish migrants carried this ready identification with the lore of the Scottish regiments to their new lives overseas. As a result, it was almost a matter of course that Scottish military traditions should have appeared amidst the volunteer military units and local militias which were emerging in the colonies of settlement as a supplement to the overstretched professional imperial forces garrisoning the empire.[18] Among the earliest was a Highland company of the 5th Battalion Volunteer

Militia Rifles of Montreal which, formed in 1862, was mustered at the very inception of the re-born volunteer movement empire-wide. By the 1890s, Highland companies and Scottish battalions were ubiquitous wherever Scottish settlement and auxiliary military activity was to be found. Even Newfoundland, with its tiny population, and no auxiliary forces before 1914 other than a small naval reserve, was not immune. An array of military cadet units, most connected to churches, included the Newfoundland Highlanders established in 1907 by the Presbyterian Church as St John's.[19]

Although these corps were constituted as authorised military forces serving the colonial state, it is useful to recognise that they were also, in a large part of their essence, private patriotic clubs. For those which emulated the Scottish regiments of the British army in appearance and tradition – and several took emulation to the length of wearing versions of the same uniform and establishing affiliations – there was usually a close correspondence between part-time auxiliary military activity and the sponsorship or co-membership of local Caledonian, Scottish or St Andrew's societies. Such societies were widely found through areas of British imperial settlement receiving Scottish migrants, and in centres of imperial commerce outside formal empire. They are recognised to have extended their functions beyond their outward purposes of friendly association, recreation and charitable function into more subliminal influence in the exercise of power through patronage, business networking, exclusivity and the reinforcement of social hierarchies.[20] Much the same may be said for the volunteer regiments which grew out of and reinforced these networks, and whose distinctive appearance, music and ceremonial earned them a prominent place in the formalities of public life in their local spheres of influence.[21]

DOMINION NATIONALISM AND IMPERIAL DEFENCE

For the dominion governments which recognised these quasi-Scottish military corps, the overtones of an ethnically specific and old country military culture were not initially a matter of great concern. Scottish, and indeed Irish, volunteer units proliferated without government interference for as long as they were viewed to be beneficial to recruitment, were not seen to inhibit military efficiency and were accepted as customary. In Canada, the various Scottish corps could claim precedents dating back to the American War of Independence, and volunteering arrangements established in Canada offered in turn a precedent which was observed in South Africa, Australia and New Zealand. However, like all the military corps in the dominions, the Scottish units existed in a delicate political context. Military organisation and expenditure was a contested element in the dealings of dominion governments with the imperial centre. From the 1890s, the requirements of imperial defence as viewed from London sat uneasily with the interests of dominion politicians who increasingly concerned themselves with questions over the cost of defence, where it should be borne, and to whom, in consequence, defence forces should be accountable. These were matters that went to the heart of responsible self-government and ones over which dominion electorates held views.

The overall trend was for British governments to seek greater budgetary contribution from their colonial and dominion partners without conceding that this gave the contributors a right to exercise greater control over their own defence arrangements. Imperial defence policy rested on the global supremacy of the Royal Navy, and the deduction that military forces in the dominions and colonies could be maintained and organised at the modest levels which this strategic reality implied. More controversial was the well-founded perception that Britain was less interested in the capacity of countries of the empire to defend themselves, and more interested in the prospect of a reserve of manpower which the architects of imperial policy could harness for overseas service as an integral part of a greater imperial army. This idea was not without support among imperial patriots in the countries concerned, but efforts of British military planners to move in this direction never received the full endorsement of colonial and dominion governments.[22]

The notion of a truly imperial British army came to the fore at the end of the century when British regular forces suffered a string of reversals at the hands of the Boer Republics in the early stages of the South African War. In response to these defeats of 'Black Week' in December 1899, the volunteer movement at home and in the dominions organised and dispatched contingents of overseas service volunteers to support the regulars in the field. In this arena, Scottish imperial volunteer units took the field in the shape of the Cape Town Highlanders, 'the oldest kilted regiment in the Southern Hemisphere', which had been formed as a volunteer corps in the Cape Colony in 1885, and a new mounted corps, the Scottish Horse, which was raised from among the Scottish community in the South African colonies and bulked out by contingents of amateur soldiers from Scotland and an influx of volunteers from Australia.[23] The idea was thereby established of an empire-wide community of Scottish citizen soldiers which could be called upon in an imperial emergency by appeals to Scottish identity and military traditions. But although the bearing of arms in South Africa by Canadians, Australians, New Zealanders and South Africans represented an affirmation of the political maturity of the dominions as imperial nations, the fact remained that the status of volunteers for overseas service in South Africa was carefully defined. Whether they were already part-time soldiers or not, volunteers who offered their services as individuals in this emergency situation were sent with the agreement of their governments for that purpose alone, and departed as part of specially formed contingents with no formal connection to the existing structures of home defence. The established corps of part-time soldiers defending the dominions remained where they were, even if some of their members departed for South Africa. It was a distinction which dominion governments were keen to maintain. It neatly resolved the tension between their wish to demonstrate imperial loyalty, responsibility and military value, while simultaneously maintaining the integrity of self-government in defence matters.

The dominion contribution to eventual British victory in South Africa encouraged the British government's drive to centralise. In 1902 a Committee of Imperial Defence was instituted to advise the government on strategic matters. In 1904 the commander of the British army's new integrated staff of senior officers was designated Chief of the *Imperial* General Staff, a move with self-evident implications for the command relationship between the War Office and dominion military establishments. The introduction of the Territorial Force system in Britain in 1907 created a uniformly organised volunteer reserve fully integrated with general staff planning, and this approach was seen to have empire-wide application. At the London Imperial Conferences of 1907 and 1909, dominion governments resisted pressure to agree contributions to an all-purpose integrated imperial army, but accepted that standardisation in training and equipment, and full co-operation with a British-dominated general staff system, was sensible. The question of what would happen in the event of a major war was left open; the tacit understanding remained that, in a greater projection of recent experience in South Africa, the dominions would contribute expeditionary forces raised at short notice through voluntary recruitment.[24]

The prospect of a future imperial emergency was meanwhile coming into focus. The dreadnought crisis of 1909 saw doubts expressed in parliament about Britain's ability to maintain naval supremacy over the fast-expanding German imperial navy. The implied threat to imperial communications and defence was picked up by press and public far beyond Britain itself and acted to dilute earlier resistance among dominion politicians to the prospect of ceding military control of their forces to the British centre. For Australia and New Zealand, the German colonial presence in the Pacific brought the perceived danger close to hand, and compounded existing unease over the growing naval power of Japan. Official responses in the respective dominions were directed principally towards naval measures. But in the atmosphere of impending crisis changes were made to local military arrangements, with consequences affecting the Scottish part-time units in Australia and New Zealand especially.

COMPULSORY MILITARY SERVICE

A significant development in which the dominions diverged in their military defence arrangements prior to 1914 was that some opted to introduce an element of compulsion. Universal military training, or part-time national service, as an obligation on young men, was not seen necessarily to contradict the ethos of citizen soldiering. Although in Canada and in Britain itself the idea had its proponents, the voluntary principle held sway there. The adoption of forms of compulsion in the Pacific dominions and South Africa can be seen in terms of these governments asserting their local control of defence. Introduced by legislation in Australia in 1909 and 1911, and in New Zealand in 1912, compulsory military training heralded a restructuring of local defence forces in which the old volunteer units, including those with Scottish identities, were effectively nationalised. So, for example, the Victorian Scottish Regiment, formed in the Australian colony of Victoria in 1898 as a volunteer corps, found itself absorbed into a new unit, the 52nd (Hobson's Bay) Infantry of the Citizen Force, part of a national militia which retained a quota of officers and non-commissioned officers from the old volunteers who wished to stay on, but whose unit strength was predicated on trained cadets conscripted and organised on national lines. The original volunteers preserved the Scottish aspect of the regiment's heritage as best they could and, unlike the conscripts, continued to wear Scottish dress, but officially the unit was Scottish no longer.[25]

Overall, opposition to the Australian reforms was muted, but it was in the 'national' volunteer corps that the loss was keenly felt. Support came from the British army's inspector general of Australia's military forces, Major-General George Kirkpatrick, who in 1913 moved that two Scottish regiments, an Irish regiment and an English regiment should be retained outside the compulsory system to form a brigade of volunteers for expeditionary service if required, a proposal reflecting the stipulation that the trained conscripts of the Citizen Force were not liable for service outside Australia. Labor Defence Minister George Pearce dismissed Kirkpatrick's idea in the Senate, alluding to the extra expense of clothing and equipping the Scottish and other 'national' units, and concluding that Australian men were wanted to fight for Australia, not to identify with the old country, a nationalist view that had informed Pearce's oversight of the original reforms.[26] New Zealand took the principle of universal military training further still. The various Scottish corps were removed from the defence establishment along with the other old volunteer units as, from 1909, New Zealand centralised and organised its new Territorial Force by province and based it on compulsory service. Unlike in Australia, the new system openly encompassed a plan to provide an expeditionary force for overseas service in the event of imperial emergency, which would be manned by volunteers from among those already serving in the Territorial Force. This expeditionary force was also to be organised on a national and provincial basis, and was predicated on realistic calculations of how many men New Zealand could offer, and on far-sighted assessment of the size of force which could be adequately reinforced in the event of a long war.[27] There would be no place for units with Scottish identities in this carefully planned and tightly controlled national system.

Scottish units fared better in the new Union Defence Force of South Africa. By the Defence Act of 1912, South Africa introduced compulsory military training for males of European descent and military age, with liability for active service in wartime. Faced with the delicate task of reconciling British and Afrikaner military traditions, the Union government had an eye to flexibility in creating a white national army around a small permanent professional core. Part-time service in existing Citizen Force units was one of the options available to men eligible for service, and the pre-1912 volunteer infantry regiments endured, manned by a mix of conscripts and volunteers. Among them were the Cape Town Highlanders and a further Scottish corps, the Transvaal Scottish, which had been raised as a volunteer infantry regiment in Johannesburg in 1903 to follow up the recruiting success of the Scottish Horse during the South African War. The Union Defence Force was intended to maintain the imperial state in South Africa against internal threats implied by Afrikaner and African alienation to British rule, and from external threat including the German colonial presence in neighbouring South-West Africa (Namibia). As in Australia, no detailed provision was made for the raising of an overseas expeditionary force to support British forces further afield should a European or global emergency arise.[28]

In retaining the voluntary militia basis of its defence system, and therefore retaining existing Scottish regiments on its part-time militia establishment, the Canadian government did, however, apply some contingency planning to the question of raising an expeditionary force for a European war. But as late as 1914, the emergency procedure was still far from clear. The foremost plan, favoured by director of mobilisation Colonel G. C. W. Gordon-Hall, entailed making a selection from existing militia units to build a Canadian division for overseas service. An earlier plan drawn up by his predecessor Major-General Willoughby Gwatkin was closer in its approach to the New Zealand system, with volunteer battalions to be raised from regions of the country according to population density, which were to be assembled, equipped and trained locally before mustering for embarkation at division strength. Existing militia units would meanwhile continue in their established home defence role.[29] These two incompatible scenarios both remained on the books when war broke out in August 1914. In the event, neither plan reckoned with the preferences of the Minister of Militia and Defence, Colonel Sam Hughes. When theory turned to reality, Hughes chose to proceed otherwise.

MOBILISATION

The dominions were entered into the war against Germany and her allies de facto in consequence of the declaration of war by the British government on 4 August 1914.[30] Popular war enthusiasm was manifested in each country, and if loyalty to the empire and commitment to its cause was not unanimous, outside the boundaries of an Afrikaner or French Canadian world view there was no more scepticism or open dissent than in the old country. There was never any doubt that each dominion would mobilise expeditionary forces for overseas service, and the work began immediately. In Canada, Hughes took the initiative. In a move which has been taken to reflect his distrust of the senior commanders and staff officers of the Canadian permanent force and militia, Hughes bypassed existing mobilisation plans on the grounds that these organisations were too cumbersome to respond to the emergency with sufficient speed. Instead, he sent telegrams to the commanding officers of every militia battalion in the country inviting them to recruit as many volunteers as possible, form them into one or two companies locally and bring them to a mass camp at Valcartier, Quebec, where they would be assembled into an expeditionary force for training and deployment in Europe.[31] Speaking in the Canadian parliament two years later, Hughes acknowledged that his plan had been improvised in order to tap into the crusading enthusiasm of the earliest volunteers without delay. He described his scheme as 'really a call to arms, like the fiery cross passing through the Highlands of Scotland, or the mountains of Ireland in former days'.[32] Significantly more men than the numbers required arrived at Valcartier, all expecting to serve in the scratch battalions they had formed locally, and with the officers expecting to be maintained in the ranks they had attained in this plethora of newly formed local units. Substantial reorganisation was required before meaningful training and deployment could progress, and many found their expectations frustrated.

In this first rush to the colours, and again in the subsequent expansion of the force to provide the first two contingents of the Canadian Expeditionary Force, Hughes's mobilisation plan gave freedom to local militia battalion commanders and prominent private citizens to raise new battalions at their own behest. It was this local freedom of action which brought forth fully formed, fully staffed infantry battalions with titles, insignia and uniforms of their own choosing. Unsurprisingly, given the migrant profile of Canada, a proportion of expeditionary force battalions were formed in circumstances where there was a direct link to existing Scottish militia regiments, from areas of especially strong Scottish settlement, or where commanding officers or local notables had a personal affinity for things Scottish. There was nothing to stop them from adopting traditional Scottish military identities.

Like many of the other new battalions raised for overseas service, relatively few of these Scottish infantry battalions ultimately departed Canada under the original title and organisational composition with which they had arrived at Valcartier. Their personnel were instead drafted into other units or became reserve battalions in England feeding recruits to front line units. Nevertheless, a sufficient number of the Valcartier units remained intact through the reorganisation process to constitute a strong Scottish presence in the Canadian Corps on the Western Front which, in the last two years of the war, made a considerable reputation for itself as a highly capable fighting formation.

Despite South Africa's introduction of compulsory military training in 1912, the South Africans who arrived on the Western Front in 1916 were organised entirely separately from the pre-war system of defence operating at home. In the early months of the war, existing Union Defence Force units, including the migrant Scots of the Cape Town Highlanders and the Transvaal Scottish, participated in the conquest of German South-West Africa. But this deployment, and the subsequent contribution of volunteers to the campaign in East Africa, was as far as the Union government felt able to go in deploying Union forces outside

South Africa. To send troops to fight in Europe was a delicate matter. The Union government was aware that its wish to assert South Africa's place in the imperial family of nations by contributing to the fight in Europe was not shared by a substantial minority of the white electorate. Caution was required in the face of the war, scepticism of the opposition National Party representing a significant proportion of Afrikaner public opinion. Those volunteers who came forward to join the Overseas Expeditionary Force, which first assembled at Potchefstroom in 1915, saw things differently, and although this new South African Brigade was prominently urban middle-class and of British descent in its recruitment profile, it included many Afrikaners. Nevertheless, the government felt compelled to define these volunteers as British imperial troops, and specifically not as part of the constituted forces of the Union of South Africa. Unfortunately, this neat accommodation meant that the overseas volunteers received British rates of daily pay substantially less than the equivalent paid to South Africa's own Union troops in German South-West and East Africa. The discrepancy was to rankle with the volunteers for years, especially when they came into contact with other dominion troops on the Western Front and discovered the extent of their own relative poverty.[33]

Much as had been the experience in Canada, it was the element of improvisation in the hasty recruitment and organisation of these volunteers that allowed scope for pre-existing military traditions to find expression. As the result of lobbying by the Scottish-born mining magnate Sir William Dalrymple, and with many recruits drawn from the Cape Town Highlanders and Dalrymple's own Transvaal Scottish Regiment, the new 4th South African Infantry Battalion was granted permission to identify itself as Scottish. When the South African Brigade disembarked at Marseilles in April 1916, following a period of active service in North Africa, the men of the 4th Battalion had swapped their tropical helmets for the khaki 'Tam o' Shanter' bonnets worn by Scottish infantrymen, and were sporting the Murray of Atholl tartan kilts with which they had been issued at Bordon Camp in Hampshire in November 1915 through the agency of the Scottish aristocrat the Marquis of Tullibardine. They were led through the crowd-filled Marseilles streets by the regimental pipes and drums, playing instruments received as a gift from a patriotic Scottish well-wisher in Johannesburg.[34] The rest of the Brigade wore the uniform of conventional British infantry, and yet the extent to which Scottish military identity transcended the 4th Battalion and attached itself to the Brigade as a whole is a phenomenon which has attracted the comment of South African historians.[35] The effect was enhanced by the

Brigade's deployment for operational service on the Western Front as one of the constituent brigades of the 9th (Scottish) Division, an administrative decision determined by the need to reinforce British divisions and which owed nothing to pan-Caledonian sentiment.

In contrast, there was no place for Scottish units, or for scratch volunteer units of any description, among the carefully marshalled conscription system which created and reinforced the New Zealand Expeditionary Force according to the government's pre-war plan. And although the Australian Imperial Force was voluntarily recruited as a separate entity from the part compulsory home-based Citizen Force, it was similarly organised by province and population quota. There was no administrative hiatus equivalent to the situation in Canada in 1914, or in South Africa in 1915, in which the proponents of Scottish military traditions could find opportunity to impose themselves into the system. Nevertheless, the 5th Battalion of the Australian Imperial Force contrived to maintain some sense of a Scottish identity, proceeding from shared membership of some of its recruits with the aforementioned 52nd Infantry of the pre-war Citizen Force and its antecedent 'Victorian Scottish' traditions.[36] This was most apparent in the regimental pipes and drums it put together and maintained on the Western Front. Photographs taken at Sailly-le-Sec in April 1918 show a complement of ten pipers and five drummers (Figure 8.3).[37] The tenacity of the military bagpiping tradition was an indication that neither dominion nationalism, nor the organisational imperatives of a major war, could entirely prevent Scottish military identity from having some place in the culture of what became the famous 'ANZAC' forces of Australia and New Zealand. A pipes and drums, with instruments supplied by the Caledonian Society of Otago, was provided for the new Otago Infantry Battalion of the New Zealand Expeditionary Force in October 1914, albeit that the battalion otherwise acknowledged no Scottish identifying traits.[38] There is further photographic evidence of pipe bands with New Zealanders on the Western Front attached to the Waikato companies of the Auckland Regiment (Figure 8.4), and even with the Machine Gun Section of the 4th Australian Division in 1918, an entirely new unit formed in the field with no territorial basis for recruitment which could have connected it to any Scottish population or affinities at home.[39]

Military pipes and drums were valued officially for the purposes of ceremony and morale but, as for military musicians more generally, they were an inessential adjunct to wartime military establishments which individual units could choose to sustain if they so wished, but for which

Figure 8.3 Pipes and drums of the 5th Infantry Battalion, Australian Imperial Force, France, 1918. (Australian War Memorial, E02261)

Figure 8.4 Pipes and drums of a Waikato company of the Auckland Regiment, France, 1918. (Royal New Zealand Returned Services' Collection, Alexander Turnbull Library, Wellington, New Zealand, G-13177-1/2)

little or no official financial provision was made. The same status might be ascribed more generally to Scottish military traditions in the expeditionary forces of the British dominions. These traditions were a subculture of British military culture and practice inherited from the imperial centre by the former colonies. They were welcomed and tolerated in as far as they did not detract from the greater message that dominion governments wished to convey even as they loyally came to the aid of the mother country: that these were new armies raised by new imperial nations. The varying extent to which Scottish forms pervaded dominion forces in the First World War was more a circumstance of the politics of pre-war defence policy, and of the state of preparation for war, than it was a reflection of differing local attitudes to old country traditions. In this light, while heralding the death of old world differences in 'We're All Australians Now', Banjo Paterson might have been just a little premature. The martial traditions of Scotland, at very least in their musical expression, might have had to give way to other loyalties, but they were not regarded as wholly incompatible with the new sense of nationhood which service and sacrifice in a world war was seen to have brought to the British dominions.

NOTES

1. A. B. Paterson, 'We're all Australians now', published as an open letter to the troops, 1915.
2. Derek Parker, *Banjo Paterson, The Man Who Wrote Waltzing Matilda, His Life and Poetry* (Warriewood: Woodstane Press, 2012), pp. 115–18.
3. Colin Roderick, *Banjo Paterson. Poet by Accident* (St Leonards, NSW: Allen & Unwin, 1993), pp. 19–20.
4. E. M. Andrews, *The ANZAC Illusion: Anglo-Australian Relations During World War I* (Cambridge: Cambridge University Press, 1993), pp. 56–7.
5. The memory of its First World War contribution remained a marker for Newfoundland identity as it approached confederation with Canada in 1949. See David Mackenzie, 'Maritime Canada and Newfoundland', in David Mackenzie (ed.), *Canada and the First World War: Essays in Honour of Robert Craig Brown* (Toronto: Toronto University Press, 2005), pp. 350–76.
6. Jeff Keshen, 'The Great War soldier as nation builder in Canada and Australia', in Briton C. Busch (ed.), *Canada and the Great War* (Montreal: McGill-Queen's University Press, 2003), pp. 3–26.
7. The role of objects in articulating Scottish and dominion military identities, loss and commemoration was elaborated in a book accompanying the

exhibition of the same name: Stuart Allan and David Forsyth, *Common Cause: Commonwealth Scots and the Great War* (Edinburgh: National Museums Scotland, 2014).

8. A lead was given here by Wendy Ugolini, 'Commonwealth Scottish regiments', in Edward M. Spiers, Jeremy Crang and Matthew Strickland (eds), *A Military History of Scotland* (Edinburgh: Edinburgh University Press, 2012), pp. 485–505.

9. South Africa's manpower contribution on the Western Front extended to the black African and mixed race non-combatant auxiliaries of the South African Native Labour Corps and the Cape Coloured Labour Battalion, organised and deployed separately.

10. 'Carry on the fight where your comrade fell', Imperial War Museum, Art. IWM PST 12316.

11. 'The British Commonwealth in arms', Canadian War Museum, CWM 19900348-004.

12. Timothy C. Winegard, *Indigenous Peoples of the British Dominions and the First World War* (Cambridge: Cambridge University Press, 2011), p. 71.

13. John Buchan, *The History of the South African Forces in France* (London: Thomas Nelson & Sons, 1920), p. 17.

14. James Wood, *Militia Myths: Ideas of the Canadian Citizen Soldier, 1896–1921* (Vancouver: UBC Press, c.2011), p. 213.

15. Ibid. p. 220.

16. Dianne Graves, *A Crown of Life: The World of John McCrae* (Staplehurst: Spellmount, 1997), pp. 1–7.

17. Ian F. W. Beckett, *The Amateur Military Tradition, 1558–1945* (Manchester: Manchester University Press, 1991), pp. 164–95.

16. Ian F. W. Beckett, 'Introduction', in Ian F. W. Beckett (ed.), *Citizen Soldiers and the British Empire 1837–1902* (London: Pickering & Chatto, 2012), pp. 1–21.

19. Colonel G. W. L. Nicholson, *The Fighting Newfoundlander: A History of the Royal Newfoundland Regiment* (St John's: Government of Newfoundland, n.d. [1964]), pp. 91–6.

20. See Tanja Bueltmann, Andrew Hinson and Graeme Morton (eds), *Ties of Bluid, Kin and Countrie: Scottish Associationalism in the Diaspora* (Guelph: University of Guelph, 2009).

21. The relationship between regiments and associational culture in Canada is tested in Patrick Watt, 'Militia chieftains: profiling the founders of Canada's Scottish militia regiments', *International Review of Scottish Studies*, 39 (2014), pp. 27–54.

22. On the progress of this debate in the dominions see John Mordike, *An Army for a Nation: A History of Australian Military Developments, 1880–1914* (Sydney: Allen & Unwin, 1992); Stephen J. Harris, *Canadian Brass: The Making of a Professional Army, 1860–1930* (Toronto: University of Toronto

Press, 1988), pp. 43–100; Christopher Pugsley, *The Anzac Experience: New Zealand, Australia and Empire in the First World War* (Auckland: Reed, 2004), pp. 51–70; Timothy J. Stapleton, *A Military History of South Africa: From the Dutch-Khoi Wars to the End of Apartheid* (Santa Barbara: Praeger, 2010), pp. 113–16.

23. Neil Orpen, *The Cape Town Highlanders, 1885–1995* (Cape Town: Cape Town Highlanders History Committee, 1986), p. 1; John M. MacKenzie with Nigel R. Dalziel, *The Scots in South Africa: Ethnicity, Identity, Gender and Race, 1772–1914* (Manchester: Manchester University Press, 2007), pp. 255–6.

24. Craig Wilcox, 'Edwardian transformation', in Craig Stockings and John Connor (eds), *Before the Anzac Dawn: A Military History of Australia to 1915* (Sydney: NewSouth Publishing, 2013), p. 264. See also Wood, *Militia Myths*, pp. 187–8.

25. Brigadier F. W. Speed, *Esprit de Corps: The History of the Victorian Scottish Regiment and the 5th Infantry Battalion* (Sydney: Allen & Unwin, 1988), pp. 15–17.

26. John Connor, *Anzac and Empire: George Foster Pearce and the Foundations of Australian Defence* (Cambridge: Cambridge University Press, 2011), pp. 35–6; Ben Wilkie, 'Warriors of empire: popular imperialism and the Victorian Scottish Regiment, 1898–1938', *Victorian Historical Journal*, 85, 1 (2014), pp. 73–96.

27. Pugsley, *The Anzac Experience*, pp. 51–70.

28. Bill Nasson, *Springboks on the Somme: South Africa in the Great War, 1914–1918* (Johannesburg: Penguin, 2007), pp. 2–4.

29. Harris, *Canadian Brass*, pp. 94–109.

30. Canada's declaration of war on Germany the following day was, effectively, not required.

31. Harris, *Canadian Brass*, pp. 94–109. The organisational problems associated with Hughes's decisions were acknowledged in the official history: Gerald W. L. Nicholson, *The Canadian Expeditionary Force, 1914–19* (Ottawa: Queen's Printer, 1962), pp. 14–62.

32. Quoted in Ronald Haycock, *Sam Hughes: The Public Career of a Controversial Canadian, 1885–1916* (Waterloo: Wilfrid Laurier University Press, 1986), p. 181.

33. Nasson, *Springboks on the Somme*, pp. 95, 126.

34. Peter K. Digby, *Pyramids and Poppies: The 1st SA Infantry Brigade in Libya, France and Flanders* (Rivonia: Ashanti, 1993), pp. 82–8.

35. Bill Nasson, 'Delville Wood and South African Great War commemoration', *English Historical Review*, 119, 480 (2004), pp. 57–86. See also Jonathan Hyslop, 'Cape Town Highlanders, Transvaal Scottish: "military Scottishness" and social power in nineteenth and twentieth century South Africa', *South African Historical Journal*, 47:1 (2002), pp. 96–114.

36. The 27th and 30th Battalions similarly assumed informal kinship with

former Scottish volunteer units in South Australia and New South Wales respectively.

37. Australian War Memorial, E02261.
38. *Otago Daily Times*, 12 October 1914, p. 8.
39. Alexander Turnbull Library, G-13177-1/2; Australian War Memorial, E03269.

9

'Part of my Heritage': Ladies' Pipe Bands, Associational Culture and 'Homeland' Identities in the Scottish Diaspora

Erin C. M. Grant

INTRODUCTION

THROUGHOUT THE IMPERIAL AND non-imperial destinations to which Scots gravitated, they expressed their ethnic identities in various ways, including the founding of Caledonian societies, the building of memorials and statues, and the organisation of festivals such as Highland Games and pipe band competitions.[1] Angela McCarthy explains that although scholars are alert to these components, they have generally focused either on one particular aspect, such as ethnic societies, or fleetingly mentioned such elements without sustained analysis.[2] For many ladies' pipe band members, and indeed other members of Scottish groups, their association was linked – to varying degrees – to a sense of Scottish ethnicity.[3] This chapter will extend this scholarship by surveying Scottish ethnic identities through two approaches: public group expressions of Scottishness, as revealed by ladies' pipe bands and their various connections to other forms of Scottish associational culture; and personal expressions of individual band members. It therefore engages with established research on associational culture, but also emphasises personal articulations of Scottishness. This central objective is important, for, while

> Scottish associational culture was critical for some, it alone cannot shape our understanding of ethnic identities, Scottish or otherwise. Indeed, given that most Scottish migrants did not join a Scottish association, it was their personal sense of Scottishness which overshadowed their ethnic affiliations.[4]

As sociologist David McCrone puts it, 'Perhaps too much attention is paid to the identity labels that people are "forced" to wear, and not enough on how they select and actively present themselves to others.'[5]

This chapter draws on a larger study which examined ten ladies' pipe bands across Scotland and its diaspora (Australia, Canada, England and

New Zealand) between 1918 and 2012. It uses as evidence interviews conducted both in person, and where necessary, by email. The ages of the interview subjects vary, with most of these women beginning their piping hobbies as teenagers (mostly around twelve to eighteen years old) in the late 1940s and throughout the 1950s and 1960s. Their current ages therefore range between fifty-six and ninety-two, reflecting a sampling of musicians in age and association to a Scottish descent group. All these interviewees were recruited through social networking. In Australia, no former members could be located, and in England, no interest could be summoned. Despite the unavailability of interviews for some bands, written documents and transcriptions of memories help rectify these inconsistencies.

In this context, this chapter will argue that although ladies' pipe bands can be placed within the broader framework of Scottish associational culture, displaying similar group expressions of Scottishness across the diaspora, personal sentiments of Scottish ethnicity held by individual members of ladies' pipe bands transcend group expressions of Scottishness created and perpetuated by the bands, their music and their performances throughout the twentieth century and continuing into the twenty-first century. Rather, these public expressions appear to hold greater meaning for their audiences who were seeking their own personal sense of Scottish ethnicity. This chapter will also add to a new emphasis on personal articulations of Scottishness by beginning to fill the gap in research on multigenerational conceptions of Scottish identity in the diaspora. Lastly, an examination of connections to Scotland, with a particular focus on homeland pilgrimages undertaken by ladies' pipe bands as bands and as individual members, will determine the role that Scotland itself played in fostering Scottish ethnicity for band members in the diaspora.

LADIES' PIPE BANDS AND SCOTTISH ASSOCIATIONAL CULTURE

Scholarship about the history of the pipes has, over the last few decades, focused on the origins and evolution of the instrument, the types of music it produces and the military role it has played historically by high profile pipers.[6] However, this discipline is still in its genesis in terms of academic study. Further, existing musical scholarship on the pipes gives minimal attention to women's involvement with this instrument. Although many female pipers existed, both as individuals from the nineteenth century and earlier, and as soloists and bands throughout the twentieth century, historians and pipers have overlooked this part of piping history for various reasons that fall outside the scope of this chapter.[7] As this chapter aims to normalise female pipers within the historical context of both piping and Scottish history, especially as their participation increased throughout the twentieth century, it does not focus on a gender discussion, but on the personal identities of band members who are descendants of Scottish migrants.

A recent claim has been made that pipe bands do not fit easily into the framework for understanding Scottish associational culture.[8] Yet current research demonstrates that the foundations of pipe bands should be seen as an important part of Scottish associational culture through their formation, hierarchy and purpose.[9] Ladies' pipe bands, as with male pipe bands, are clubs with membership often continuing for generations with common goals to actively participate in the art of perpetuating one of Scotland's most prominent cultural icons (the pipes), as well as to share in that experience with other members through performance, competition and discussion, both in Scotland and across the diaspora. Although an insider perspective is useful in order to understand the nuances of piping culture, it is important to emphasise that a framework for understanding Scottish associational culture in the twentieth and twenty-first centuries which does not include pipe bands and piping societies is flawed.

Ladies' pipe bands across the Scottish diaspora, including Australia, Canada and New Zealand, have often fostered relationships with other Scottish cultural groups, demonstrating a strong sense of community among them within their various locations. In Dunedin, New Zealand, the Dunedin Ladies' Scottish Pipe Band and the Dunedin Ladies' Highland Pipe Band, both established in 1947, were individually connected to Scottish affiliations through institutional, financial and moral support. For example, both bands, including local men's pipe bands in Dunedin, belonged to a Council of Scottish Societies, which represented all like societies in Otago from 1925. Former band member of the Dunedin Ladies' Scottish, Trudy, explains that the band also had ties to the Dunedin St Andrew's Society:

> This has gone on for many many years, played for St Andrew's Society for their November dance, we did that every year, there were things that you do every year and some things that come up that you've never done before.[10]

All of the Scottish societies in Dunedin – the Burns Club, the St Andrew's Society, the Caledonian Society and the Gaelic Society – scrambled to get pipers to play at their various monthly meetings to add to the sense of occasion and Scottishness of these gatherings. Regardless of personal identities, then, the pipers and pipe bands and their group identities were closely connected with a broader Scottish associational community outside of their own band practices and performances.

For comparison in New Zealand, in terms of a connection to other Scottish societies or a broader Auckland Scottish network, former Auckland Ladies' Pipe Band member Barbara Upfold explains, 'The only non-Scottish community contact we had was when the band played in public when people asked us to play'.[11] The majority of their performances were linked to other Scottish associations, suggesting a close connection to an Auckland Scottish community. For example, the band's first engagement was to play at the Onehunga Caledonian Society's social in 1949, and they reportedly played at most Caledonian evenings thereafter.[12]

In Australia, the earliest ladies' pipe band, the Australian Ladies' Scottish Pipe Band, established in 1918, was similarly linked to broader Scottish associational culture. While some of the larger events performed were run by non-ethnic organisations, the majority of smaller local events were coordinated by Scottish associations. Sports days in Melbourne, for example, often held at Bunyip Park, took place under the auspices of the local Caledonian society.[13] In addition, the Scottish Thistle Society played an active role, holding many events such as concerts and socials, including one in December 1922, where a collection of Scottish songs, dances and pipe tunes were performed by the Australian Ladies'.[14] The Scottish Thistle Society was likewise mentioned in combination with the Australian Ladies' in numerous newspaper records of band performances.[15] In terms of comparison over time, the 1940s and 1950s saw continued mutual support between Scottish associations and ladies' pipe bands in Australia, demonstrating little disruption in the strong backing received in the two previous decades. The Fremantle Ladies' Highland Pipe Band, established towards the end of 1946, for example, was associated with its local Scottish community and connected to the Fremantle Caledonian Society, which held regular dances where many of the first members of the band were introduced to the pipes and drums. Most of the ladies' pipe band members were friends or relatives of people involved in the men's Fremantle Highland Pipe Band or the Caledonian Society.[16] This connection with Scottish associations was a long-standing one and bands like the Fremantle Ladies' played for Scottish galas and balls until the 1960s.[17]

In Canada, the Vancouver Ladies' Pipe Band, established in 1927, similarly reported heavy involvement with Scottish clubs and societies in the role of entertainers, playing at Highland Games, festivals, Burns

Suppers, parades and a variety of other functions. The Vancouver Ladies' also held, since the late 1920s, an annual competition and festival which contributed greatly to the Scottish scene in the Vancouver area.[18] Like ladies' bands in Dunedin, the Vancouver Ladies' had connections to their own local Burns Club and began sponsoring a Burns Supper in 1951 as a fundraising event, which grew to be one of the largest and most successful in the city.[19] Similarly, the Winnipeg Heather-Belle Ladies' Pipe Band in Manitoba demonstrates several connections to Scottish societies. The formation of this band, in 1951, is owed to the Sons of Scotland Benevolent Association, which aimed to promote Scottish heritage and culture by sponsoring dancing, piping classes, competitions and concerts. According to band records, the pipes were integral to the society's monthly meetings and to their many social events.[20] The band history shows that in addition to the pipe band, the girls who joined initially had parents who were members of the Sons of Scotland, or were members themselves. Indeed, 'most of the girls were in their mid-teens and already immersed in a world of Scottish culture, music and Highland dance'.[21] The band also had connections to a number of other local Scottish and piping societies. For example, the band belonged to the Manitoba Pipers and Drummers Association, as did all other bands from this region, and in 1958 three members of the Winnipeg Heather-Belles, Margaret Newton, Helen Butler and Jean Marr, became the first women to be elected to the executive.[22]

From this evidence, it is clear that in New Zealand, Australia and Canada, ladies' pipe bands maintained similar active relationships with their local Scottish associational communities. In England, by contrast, there is little mention of ladies' pipe band involvement with other Scottish associations, although the Dagenham Girl Pipers, established in 1930, performed for events held by the Dagenham Caledonian Society, such as their Burns night held in 1935.[23] Within the framework of comparative and transnational approaches to diaspora,[24] research on ladies' pipe bands does not reveal any reciprocal transnational interactions and sensibilities nurtured among these globally scattered communities. The cross-national dimension, however, shows that the involvement between ladies' pipe bands and other Scottish associations is consistent in the experiences of similar multigenerational descent groups in different nations and regions. Yet, as McCarthy points out, in examining conceptions of identity within multigenerational descent groups, the extent to which individual members articulated and reinvented ethnic identities has been identified as a gap in scholarship.[25]

'PART OF MY HERITAGE': PERSONAL ETHNIC IDENTITIES

Personal connections

Ladies' pipe bands across the Scottish diaspora boasted strong ties to local Scottish community networks. It is important to ask, however, if the members themselves felt a personal connection to either Scotland or to a sense of Scottish identity through their participation in Scottish associational culture, or if their sense of identity was derived from a more personal connectedness. In many cases, because band members had family connections to Scotland through multigenerational descent groups, their sense of ethnicity was often multi-faceted. In New Zealand, when asked if playing in the ladies' band made her feel connected to her Scottish heritage, former member of the Dunedin Ladies' Highland Pipe Band Erleen Woodhouse explained:

> Yes, totally, because New Zealand was founded by Scotsmen, and all our, most of our relations were from Scotland. I suppose in a way when we were growing up we really sort of felt Scottish because we were surrounded by it. And you know, growing up with all the bands. There were so many Scottish characters back then that there isn't today . . . My grandparents spoke Gaelic . . . Not one person [in the family] learnt it, isn't that sad?[26]

Although Woodhouse does not base her sentiments about Scottish migration to New Zealand on factual record, for her, it was not just the band, but also the combination of playing pipes and her family connections that tied her directly to Scotland. Further, her note about the Gaelic language is significant because it was not passed down through subsequent generations. Since the playing of pipes in this family began with Woodhouse, this demonstrates an adaptation of intergenerational Scottish identities resulting from the motivations of first and second generation New Zealanders, rather than those from Scotland directly.

Similar sentiments can be found from band members elsewhere in New Zealand, as well as in Canada. In Auckland, former member of the Auckland Ladies' Barbara Upfold explains:

> I think that pipe bands here still typify the Scottish theme and the bagpipes will always be recognised as a Scottish instrument . . . Yes, I did feel connected to Scottish history but I joined because I enjoyed Scottish music and had the opportunity to learn about it.[27]

As with opinions from Dunedin pipers, Upfold points to an inherent belief that piping and drumming is Scottish and connects its players to the 'homeland', both physically and emotionally. Another former member of the Auckland Ladies', Jeanette McFarland, responds, 'I definitely felt connected to my Scottish heritage through the band as my parents didn't show any interest themselves until I became involved and showed interest'.[28] So not only did McFarland feel that she was connecting with a part of her heritage, but she was able to encourage her own parents to participate in the cultivation of this identity, adding a twist to the process of multigenerational descent groups and how they articulated and reinvented their ethnic identities.

In Canada, when asked about her feelings of identity, former member and piper Carol McPhaden describes her personal sense of identity and how it was connected to the band:

> Yes I was feeling more Scottish and also more proud of my roots. The ripple effect was that I was more proud to be a woman and in a women's pipe band. The fact that we were Canadian women of Scottish heritage was a continuing sense of pride. That never decreased . . . Coming from an abusive marriage, my sense of self-worth greatly increased. I have been strong and whole ever since.[29]

There are many other similar expressions from former members who felt a number of layers of pride and identity, which is indicative of the experiences of many people who are active in diaspora communities across the world. That a band member can have a sense of Scottish identity does not necessarily detract from their sense of Canadian identity or their sense of self as a piper or a woman.

In a recent publication, Tanja Bueltmann argues that connections to Scottish ethnicity through membership of Scottish associations ensured both enduring and diverse ways in which multigenerational Scots actively maintained and experienced the Scottish diaspora.[30] McCarthy discusses the significance of such connections and notes that further research is required to determine the continuation (or not) of these elements down through the generations.[31] She points to a gap in evidence in New Zealand of hyphenated identities, but the examples of ladies' pipe bands can be used as evidence that multigenerational descent groups can be seen as holding multiple identities not only in New Zealand, but the rest of the diaspora as well.

While many members of ladies' pipe bands felt connected to a sense of Scottish identity through their participation in associational culture, other examples demonstrate that this is not always the case. Trudy, former member of the Dunedin Ladies' Scottish, explains her thoughts on identity which deviate slightly from the two other Dunedin pipers interviewed: 'I am a Kiwi but going back on my father's side we are

Scottish back in the ancestries'.[32] However, when asked if playing the pipes made her feel closer to her Scottish heritage, she answered:

> No, no, I just heard them and thought I want to try that. No it didn't make me feel any more Scottish. I always wanted to go to the [Edinburgh Military] Tattoo, it was a dream. It was coming up three years ago we went. My daughter was overseas for a year and it was major.[33]

From these comments, it is possible to conclude that Scottish identity in connection with the pipes may be taken for granted and although many ladies' pipe band members were connected to Scotland by family heritage, it was not always a significant factor in learning to play the pipes. According to musicologist Jennifer Post, homeland and its significance as a basis for group identification and social action, and especially how it is connected to geographic place and a sense of belonging, are key issues for musicians and singers.[34] While not all pipers and drummers identified with Scotland or with being Scottish, it played a significant role in what they consider to be their musical identity, which should be seen as separate from their personal ethnic identities.

Barbara Smith, former member of the Dunedin Ladies' Scottish, explains that it was not actually a Scottish connection where she first learnt that she could try to play the pipes:

> My father used to get newspapers sent out from Britain and there was a day that had a yellow cover on it . . . and it had the Dagenham Girls pipe band on it, so I knew then, that girls played in the pipe bands. [Then] my cousin told me that you could go and learn to play the pipes, then, cos I think I just started secondary school, that suited me. That was good. I do remember the Dagenham Girls pipe band, have you heard of them? That was my first inkling that women could play in the band so that's kind of where it came from.[35]

In this case, the playing of pipes was not connected to Smith's sense of Scottish identity, but more related to her love of the music. The Dagenham Girls, from Dagenham, England, demonstrated to Smith that it was possible to play in a pipe band and be a non-Scottish woman. However, growing up in Dunedin, with its strong sense of Scottish association, the geographic place (providing opportunity) and an inherent sense of belonging would also have contributed to her decision to play the pipes.

There were also members in the Winnipeg Heather-Belles without Scottish descent which helps to demonstrate what kind of meaning ladies' pipe bands might have had for them. For example, Sheila Phillips, who played in the band from 1957 to 1969, explains:

Despite not having a Scottish background, I'd always enjoyed Scottish music and dance. A lot of my friends were Scottish . . . Working and performing as a group is a great discipline. I feel it kept me young – there were always players who were younger and their enthusiasm was infectious.[36]

So while not directly connected to Scotland through family lineage, this excerpt explains how non-Scots, what David Hesse terms 'affinity Scots', could still be connected to a Scottish identity through friends and fellow band members to help achieve the goals of the Winnipeg Heather-Belles by encouraging the further growth of the culture in Canada.

Given scholars have neglected the topic of women's expressions of ethnic identity in the Scottish diaspora, this chapter can be seen as a much needed beginning to this investigation. Kim Sullivan found in her comparative study of Scottish societies in Otago, Toronto and Melbourne that distinctive characteristics developed across the diaspora, separating each of these societies despite their common goals and purposes. She concludes that there were differences in the shape they took, and that the expressions of ethnic identity they projected differed significantly from one case to the next.[37] Contrary to these findings, case studies of ladies' pipe bands in New Zealand, Australia and Canada indicate that despite some small differences, the majority of band members demonstrated similar expressions of personal ethnic identity and connections to Scotland. The reasons for this are not clear, but it does suggest a piping diaspora.

T. M. Devine observes that it is more than likely that Scottish societies, despite their visibility, attracted no more than a minority even of first generation migrants, leading to a notable collapse in Scottish associational affinity – at least in the United States.[38] Pipe bands, however, which can be seen and heard in public, provided and continue to provide affinity and nostalgia for all Scots across the diaspora, regardless of their connection to Scotland. Devine also speculates that second and third generations of Scots' memories of the old country at the institutional level, if not in personal and family recollections, seem destined to fade.[39] Yet pipe bands, in both their membership and performances, continue to rouse feelings in both Scots and non-Scots alike, and will likely continue to do so for generations to come.

CONNECTIONS TO THE 'HOMELAND'

The first two sections of this chapter demonstrate similarities and linkages between ladies' pipe bands and Scottish associations more broadly in the diaspora, and establish the extent to which members of ladies' pipe bands identified themselves with a Scottish heritage. However, an investigation of Scottish diaspora identities must also ask whether these connections translate to strong ties to the homeland. The final section of this chapter therefore examines connections to Scotland as a homeland, with a particular focus on travel to Scotland undertaken by female pipers, both in bands and as individual members, in order to determine the role that Scotland played in fostering Scottish ethnicity in the diaspora. While there are tangible links between Scotland and ladies' pipe bands through equipment, uniform purchases and transfer of knowledge, linkages found through individual identities and travel can be seen as more meaningful to personal identities and a sense of homeland.

Group travel to the homeland

A developing interest in the historiography of Scotland and its diaspora is the experience of returned migrants.[40] The desire for travel, especially to Scotland, can be seen as part of the beginning of roots tourism, whereby émigré Scots and their descendants return to the homeland to explore their ancestral history and culture. According to Devine,

> When the immigrants of Victorian times left Scotland, many took with them these mythical symbols of tartans, kilts, pipes and drums, Highland Games and other traditions. These were embellished in the New World by subsequent generations of the Scottish diaspora.[41]

The perpetuation of these symbols through local and national community involvement left an intrinsic desire to regard Scotland as an imagined homeland and with it, the impulse to return.

There are several examples of ladies' pipe bands making homeland pilgrimages to Scotland. In Australia, Scottish family connections of Australian Ladies' band members were linked in newspapers to their 1926 world tour: 'And so the Scottish part of their tour ... holds a peculiar interest for them'.[42] This excerpt suggests that a person with a Scottish heritage is assumed, by mass culture and media, to have an interest in the homeland. Among the tourist activities in which the Australian Ladies' took part were 'a tour of the capital, cheering loudly as soon as the train crossed the border, gathering heather, visiting the other cities and principal towns as well as participating in various Highland gatherings, such as Braemar'.[43] The band's visit to Scotland in August 1926 was captured in a silent film when the band performed with the massed bands and on their own at the Cowal Gathering in Dunoon.[44] During their visit, the Australian Ladies' were also well received with large audiences noted specifically at Edinburgh and Glasgow.

In Canada, examples of homeland pilgrimage to Scotland can likewise be found. In the Vancouver Ladies', Aileen MacLeod discusses her band's journey to Scotland in 1980:

> Winning at the Worlds in Glasgow was pretty surreal. The other bands on the field crowded right in and almost squished us . . . it was a lot like being celebrities. One young fellow from Skye asked my Dad if we were all movie stars?! Funny. It was a great time of life.[45]

The Winnipeg Heather-Belles also travelled to Scotland. They began planning their trip to Scotland in 1961 and according to band records, this was the main priority until in 1968 it became a reality. The band competed in the Cowal and Dunoon Highland Games, and at Rothesay, Airdrie and Edinburgh. The band travelled to Scotland again in 1985 where it competed in multiple competitions including in the World Pipe Band Championships. They also toured St Andrews, Loch Lomond and the Trossachs and attended the Edinburgh Military Tattoo.[46] Many band members recall the trips made, with Scotland being at the top of their list of highlights. Kerry Ducharme, who played in the band from 1982 to 1986, exclaims, 'The friends and the travelling! I made life-long friends and the two trips to Scotland were amazing.'[47] Competition might have been a significant motivation for travel to Scotland, but travel and touring also appeared to be important to band members. Like many other ladies' pipe bands that travelled, other tourist activities were planned in conjunction with trips to Scotland. On their 1982 visit, the whole band also took a five-day side trip to London for a break from competing and performing.[48] As such, band trips to Scotland can be seen as important for competition and, in some cases, connected to roots tourism. Yet other types of tourism experiences were important, demonstrating more than one reason for travel aside from visiting the 'homeland'.

Individual pilgrimages

One of the key observations for New Zealand ladies' pipe bands was that none collectively participated in what academics have defined as the 'homeland pilgrimage', but individual members of ladies' pipe bands did. Dunedin Ladies' Scottish former member Barbara Smith, who previously identified Scotland as 'back home', even though she was born in Dunedin, New Zealand, explains how she felt travelling to Scotland later on in life:

When I went home there and I was getting on, you know it wasn't that long ago, yeah it was quite touching actually. When my father left from the docks because in those days it wasn't planes it was all by boat, and yes I kind of think, I'm not saying for everybody but for me it was, it felt like me going back home, like it was somewhere that part of me was related to. Even though I'm born and bred here [in New Zealand] it's you know, it was quite touching so this year maybe I hope to go to where my father was born, which was up in North Uist, right up in the islands and yeah he came over when he was about 4 to the mainland with his family.[49]

Local Dunedin piping authority Warwick Johnson explains that in New Zealand, referring to Britain or Scotland as 'back home' was standard.[50] In Auckland, McFarland also discusses the idea of visiting Scotland, although this was not with a band, but due to her own family connections, which coincidentally came from the same area as Smith's relatives:

Yes, it did feel like a pilgrimage going back to trace my grandfather's people. When I arrived in North Uist I was surprised how emotional and sad I felt, as the circumstances regarding my great grandmother leaving were very sad, but that's another story. I felt much happier when I returned again three years later.[51]

Trudy of the Dunedin Ladies' Scottish also embarked on her own individual pilgrimage, although unlike Smith and McFarland, she claimed that she just wanted to see the Edinburgh Tattoo in order to fulfil a lifelong dream that was unconnected to a Scottish identity.[52] Other individual pilgrimages were made by members of ladies' pipe bands, all with comparable stories, which points to a similar shared experience across the diaspora and throughout several generations of Scots descendants. Johnson explains that since the 1960s, most New Zealanders have aimed to go overseas for their 'OE' (overseas experience) and that the United Kingdom was almost always the first destination.[53] Conversely, in her stories of band travels to Scotland, Aileen MacLeod focused her discussion on competition, rather than family connection to the homeland. She explains,

We emigrated from Scotland when I was a year old. We ended up being more Scottish here than we would have been if we'd stayed there. For instance, none of my cousins over there played the bagpipes or did Highland dancing![54]

Bueltmann considers Scotland a popular destination for émigré Scots from the late nineteenth century for multiple reasons. These include the desire to tour historical sites, promote emigration to the new world, and explore ancestral roots, hence the idea of pilgrimage.[55] Marjory Harper and Stephen Constantine have similarly discussed this movement, explaining that heritage tourism demonstrates the importance of identity – even invented identity – to what they describe as 'rootless or restless migrants'.[56] Although these historians identify a trend that can be found as early as the nineteenth century and carried on throughout the twentieth century, their focus is mainly Scottish-born migrants, rather than those of subsequent generations. However, Harper and Constantine note that roots tourism allows both migrants and their descendants who 'feel the shallowness of their roots in the new world to claim an ancestral landscape and identity, however artificial, in what has been called [by Paul Basu] "homecomings for homeless minds"'.[57]

Although a description of shallowness and homelessness may be used to describe the tourists of these previous studies, the oral history of ladies' pipe band members does not reflect this attitude. Thus far, ladies' pipe band members in New Zealand and Canada, though generations removed from Scotland, express pride as New Zealanders and as Canadians, but also relish their Scottish heritage, hence their personal pilgrimages. There is no sense of feeling lost in their new land, only a sense of curiosity regarding their pasts. Further, the individual nature of these examples of pilgrimage provides additional evidence that for ladies' pipe band members of multigenerational Scottish descent, expressions of Scottish ethnicity were derived more from personal or family identities than from connections to Scottish associational culture (the pipe band).

What this chapter highlights is that homeland pilgrimages undertaken by ladies' pipe bands as individual members and as groups fulfilled a desire to connect to their Scottish roots. Contrary to academic opinion, however, this was not an attempt to fill a gap in an otherwise empty identity, as may have been the case for many Scottish born migrants. Instead, travel was undertaken to achieve personal competition and performance goals as well as out of interest. In the case of some individual members, travel augmented an already strong sense of self as second, third and fourth generational 'Scots' in the diaspora.[58] According to Bueltmann, the majority of significant interactions and active connections to the homeland that existed in the diaspora through roots tourism during the early nineteenth and twentieth centuries occurred through institutional Scottish associations.[59] The homeland connections of ladies' pipe bands follow this trend, but individual pilgrimages to Scotland based on family or personal relationships are just as meaningful, if not more so, especially to subsequent generations of descendants of Scots who migrated throughout the diaspora.

CONCLUSION

Australian, Canadian and New Zealand ladies' pipe bands maintained similar active relationships with their local Scottish associational communities. Although the present research on ladies' pipe bands did not reveal any reciprocal transnational interactions and sensibilities nurtured among these globally scattered communities, the cross-national dimension of the research did reveal that the involvement between ladies' pipe bands and other Scottish associations within one country is consistent in the experiences of similar multigenerational descent groups in different nations and regions.[60] In this context, ladies' pipe bands, as with all pipe bands and bagpipe performances, fit neatly as an important subcategory within the broad network of Scottish associational culture. Because of this, they can be seen as a collection of previously unknown examples of women's participation within a network that previously saw female members as exceptions to the norm.

Further, most ladies' pipe band members in the Scottish diaspora were descendants of Scots (rather than Scottish-born migrants themselves) which sheds light on a glaring gap in scholarship regarding ethnic identities: the sense of identity held by multigenerational descent groups, as well as the extent to which these were articulated and reinvented.[61] Those who are not offer another perspective. Although members of ladies' pipe bands in Scotland were, of course, Scottish, all of the interviewees for this chapter in the diaspora belong to subsequent generations – with some related to Scots ancestors, and some not connected at all. This chapter therefore reveals similar connections to Scottish ethnicity across the diaspora within the membership of ladies' pipe bands. Although some personal expressions of Scottishness can be understood in connection to band membership, more often than not in these multigenerational descent groups, Scottish ethnicity is derived from personal or family identities and not in connection to Scottish associational culture.

Unlike existing studies of tartan tourism, ladies' pipe band members in the diaspora appear to be equally connected to both their real home, and to a perceived 'homeland' in Scotland that is fuelled by a curiosity to connect with their roots, but is not seen as filling a gap in a 'homeless mind'. All of the case studies for this chapter demonstrate a strong connection to other, often larger, societies. This not only adds to the sense of Scottish ethnicity that these bands demonstrated, but also to their own sense of personal identities, which are equally, if not more, important as institutional methods for preserving ethnicity continue to decline. Scotland itself has also played a role in cultivating Scottish ethnicity among members of ladies' pipe bands in the diaspora through visits to the homeland and providing supportive audiences. While a discussion of audiences in Scotland and their perception of ladies' pipe bands falls outside the scope of this chapter, it is significant to note that there were millions of spectators who witnessed performances of these bands across Scotland and its diaspora. Although the meanings that these performances had to audience and band members alike were varied, they both ably demonstrate the complexity of intergenerational Scots and their identities in the diaspora.

In conclusion, the identities of the women who played in ladies' pipe bands as part of the wider archive of associational culture has proven to be a useful tool in the task of enhancing and augmenting current understandings of women's participation and contributions within the Scottish diaspora. This chapter can also be used to help fill the gender gap in studies on Scottish associational culture and as an educational tool for piping society. That is not to say that these bands are, or ever have been, universally representative of Scottish diasporic conscious-ness, but the collection of memories reflected in this chapter are invalu-able for examining how Scottish ethnicity has been understood by the cultural participants themselves and how their personal identities have been reflected, demonstrated and understood by subsequent generations.

NOTES

1. John M. MacKenzie, 'Essay and reflection: on Scotland and the empire', *International History Review*, 15:4 (1993), p. 737; Angela McCarthy, 'Scottish migrant ethnic identities in the British Empire since the nineteenth century', in John M. MacKenzie and T. M. Devine (eds), *Scotland and the British Empire* (Oxford and New York: Oxford University Press, 2011), pp. 121–2; T. M. Devine, *To the Ends of the Earth: Scotland's Global Diaspora, 1750–2010* (Washington: Smithsonian Books, 2011), p. 170. As a symbol of Scotland and its identity, this idea is substantiated by common belief within both the piping community and Scottish communities more broadly. Scholarship on Scotland that provides mention of the pipes con-sistently recognises the pipes as a pillar of Scottish culture.

2. McCarthy, 'Scottish migrant ethnic identities', p. 122. Exceptions include Angela McCarthy, *Scottishness and Irishness in New Zealand since 1840* (Manchester: Manchester University Press, 2011), and Leigh S. L. Straw, *A Semblance of Scotland: Scottish Identity in Colonial Western Australia* (Glasgow: Grimsay Press, 2006).

3. Anthony D. Smith, *National Identity* (London and New York: Penguin

Books, 1991), pp. 21, 9, 14. Six key aspects constitute an ethnic identity: a collective proper name; myth of common ancestry; shared historical memories; one or more elements of a common culture; an association with a specific homeland; and a sense of solidarity.

4. McCarthy, 'Scottish migrant ethnic identities', p. 122.
5. David McCrone, 'Who do you say you are? Making sense of national identities in modern Britain', *Ethnicities* 2:3 (2002), p. 216.
6. Significant historical texts on the history of the Great Highland Bagpipes include Joshua Dickson, *When Piping was Strong: Tradition, Change and the Bagpipe in South Uist* (Edinburgh: John Donald, 2006); William Donaldson, *Pipers: A Guide to the Players and Music of the Highland Bagpipe* (Edinburgh: Birlinn, 2005); Bridget MacKenzie, *Piping Traditions of Argyll (c.1800–2000)* (Glasgow: College of Piping, 2004); and Roderick Cannon, *The Highland Bagpipe and its Music* (Edinburgh: John Donald Publishers, 1988, 2002).
7. For a complete and in depth analysis of gender in the history of the Great Highland Bagpipes, see Erin C. M. Grant, 'The Ladies' Pipe Band diaspora: bands, bonnie lassies and Scottish associational culture, 1918–2012', unpublished PhD thesis, University of Otago, 2013.
8. Tanja Bueltmann, *Clubbing Together: Ethnicity, Civility and Formal Sociability in the Scottish Diaspora to 1930* (Liverpool: Liverpool University Press, 2015), p. 105.
9. Grant, 'The Ladies' Pipe Band diaspora'.
10. Anon. ('Trudy'), interview by the author, Dunedin, New Zealand, January 2011. This band member was renamed for her privacy.
11. Barbara Upfold, interview by the author, Auckland, New Zealand, June 2010.
12. Barbara Upfold, *Auckland Ladies' Highland Pipe Band Inc.: Silver Jubilee* (Auckland: 1973), p. 5.
13. 'Items of interest', *South Bourke and Mornington Journal*, 15 January 1920, p. 2. National Library of Australia: Trove Newspaper Archive, available at <http://trove.nla.gov.au/newspaper/> (last accessed October 2015).
14. 'Scottish Thistle Society: concert and social', *Williamstown Chronicle*, p. 9, December 1922, p. 2. National Library of Australia: Trove Newspaper Archive, available at <http://trove.nla.gov.au/newspaper/> (last accessed October 2015).
15. Various, National Library of Australia: Trove Newspaper Archive, available at <http://trove.nla.gov.au/newspaper/> (last accessed October 2015).
16. Lynne Cairns, *A Hundred Pipers and O'er and O'er: The Story of the Fremantle Ladies' Highland Pipe Band, 1947–1993* (Perth, WA: L. Cairns, 1998), p. 5.
17. Ibid. p. 44.
18. Carl Ian Walker, *Pipe Bands in British Columbia* (Squamish: Western Academy of Pipe Music, 1992), p. 217.

19. Ibid. p. 214.
20. Mona Donald, Ethel Hook, Velma Davis and Carol McPhaden, *The Story of the Heather Belles* (Winnipeg, Manitoba: Hignell Book Printing, 2010), p. 5.
21. Ibid. p. 5.
22. Ibid. p. 27.
23. Linda Rhodes, *The Dagenham Girl Pipers* (Dagenham: Heathway Press, 2011), p. 25.
24. Kevin Kenny, 'Diaspora and comparison: the global Irish as a case study', *Journal of American History*, 90:1 (2003), p. 135.
25. McCarthy, 'Scottish migrant ethnic identities', p. 142.
26. Erleen Woodhouse, interview by the author, Dunedin, New Zealand, 18 January 2011.
27. Elizabeth Hindmarsh and Barbara Upfold, joint interview by the author, Auckland, New Zealand, June 2010.
28. Jeanette McFarland, interview by the author, Auckland, New Zealand, June 2010.
29. Carol McPhaden, interview by the author, Winnipeg, Manitoba, December 2012.
30. Tanja Bueltmann, *Scottish Ethnicity and the Making of New Zealand Society* (Edinburgh: Edinburgh University Press, 2011), pp. 200–1.
31. McCarthy, 'Scottish migrant ethnic identities', p. 56.
32. 'Trudy', interview.
33. Ibid.
34. Jennifer C. Post, '"I take my *Dombra* and sing to remember my homeland": identity, landscape and music in Kazakh communities of western Mongolia', in Tina K. Ramnarine (ed.), *Musical Performance in the Diaspora* (London and New York: Routledge, 2007), p. 49.
35. Barbara Smith, interview by the author, Dunedin, New Zealand, 31 January 2011.
36. Donald et al., *The Story of the Heather Belles*, p. 116.
37. Kim Sullivan, 'Scots by association: Scottish diasporic identities and ethnic associationism in the nineteenth-early twentieth centuries and present day', unpublished PhD thesis, University of Otago, 2010, p. 73.
38. Devine, *To the Ends of the Earth*, p. 276.
39. Ibid. pp. 275–6.
40. T. M. Devine, *The Scottish Nation, 1700–2000* (London: Penguin Books, 2006), pp. 249–72; T. M. Devine, *Scotland's Empire, 1600–1815: Scotland's Empire and the Shaping of the Americas* (Washington: Smithsonian Books, 2004), pp. 171–3. Separate studies by R. H. Campbell and Richard J. Finlay discuss the psychological impact of the well-publicised exploits of Scots in the colonies, resulting in a growing sense among homeland community that Scots were natural born colonisers, encouraging larger numbers of further emigration. See R. H. Campbell, 'Scotland', in R. A.

Cage (ed.), *The Scots Abroad: Labour, Capital, Enterprise, 1750–1914* (Sydney: Croom Helm, 1985), p. 23; Richard J. Finlay, 'The rise and fall of popular imperialism in Scotland, 1850–1950', *Scottish Geographical Magazine*, 113:1 (1997), p. 17; Sullivan, 'Scots by association', p. 19; Mario Varricchio (ed.), *Back to Caledonia: Scottish Homecomings from the Seventeenth Century to the Present* (Edinburgh: John Donald, 2012); Marjory Harper (ed.), *Emigrant Homecomings: The Return Movement of Emigrants, 1600-2000* (Manchester: Manchester University Press, 2005).

41. Devine, *To the Ends of the Earth*, p. 281.
42. 'Lady pipers in Scotland to compete at Braemar', *Scotsman*, 27 August 1926.
43. Ibid.
44. The Cowal Games, Pathe, <http://pathedev.bigeyedeers.co.uk/video/the-cowal-games-on-sleeve-as-thecowel-games>.
45. Aileen MacLeod, interview by the author, Vancouver, Canada, September 2011.
46. Ibid. p. 82.
47. Ibid. p. 116.
48. Ibid. p. 78.
49. Smith, interview.
50. Warwick Johnson, interview by the author, Dunedin, New Zealand, 18 March 2013.
51. McFarland, interview.
52. 'Trudy', interview.
53. Johnson, interview.
54. MacLeod, interview.
55. Tanja Bueltmann, 'Through the fair land of Scotia: émigré Scots touring the homeland', *History Scotland*, 11:3 (2011), p. 23.
56. Marjory Harper and Stephen Constantine, *Migration and Empire* (Oxford: Oxford University Press, 2010), pp. 334–5; Harper (ed.), *Emigrant Homecomings*.
57. Ibid. p. 335; Paul Basu, *Highland Homecomings: Genealogy and Heritage Tourism in the Scottish Diaspora* (Oxford: Routledge, 2007).
58. Also as pipers, knowledge of Scotland is already strong and with piqued interest, curiosity leading to travel further develops this knowledge.
59. Tanja Bueltmann, '"Gentlemen, I am going to the old country": Scottish root-tourists in the late nineteenth century and early twentieth centuries', in Varricchio (ed.), *Back to Caledonia*, p. 163.
60. Kenny, 'Diaspora and comparison', p. 135.
61. McCarthy, 'Scottish migrant ethnic identities', p. 142.

10

Understanding Scottishness among Sojourners, Settlers and Descendants in Hong Kong and New Zealand

Iain Watson

INTRODUCTION

IDENTITIES AND THEIR CONSTRUCTION are often complex processes for migrants who in an increasingly globalised and transnational world may have a number of identities upon which to draw. Mary Waters, researching white ethnic identity among multigenerational groups in suburban California, describes the choice as 'a social process that is in flux ... a dynamic and complex phenomenon'.[1] Additionally, it is a process that can change dependent on age, time and environment. Nor is it based on a set of rules structured along primordial ancestral lines. This chapter seeks to evaluate identity selection and the use of Scottish identity or 'Scottishness' among Scottish migrants to New Zealand (labelled 'settlers') and Hong Kong ('sojourners') and the multigenerational descent group in New Zealand. It does so by deploying the responses generated by a small sample of 145 respondents who answered a complex questionnaire, circulated through the New Zealand Society of Genealogists Scottish Interest Group and the Hong Kong St Andrew's Society, designed to identify potential oral history interviewees. These responses are supported by in-depth, semi-structured life-story oral history interviews.

Of the Hong Kong migrants who completed questionnaires, twenty-four were born in Scotland, four in England and six elsewhere, while of the New Zealand migrant cohort twenty-one were born in Scotland, five in England, and one in Europe. Most of the latter cohort arrived in New Zealand before the 1980s. For the multigenerational descent group eighty-three were born in New Zealand and one in Australasia (location undefined but of Scottish descent). The age and gender demographics of the sample is shown in Table 10.1, and highlights that those most likely to engage with the project are middle-aged or retired; for the purposes of life-story interviews this is a preference. The most significant drawback,

Table 10.1 Survey demographics by gender and age

Gender	Scots migrants to Hong Kong				Scots migrants to New Zealand post-1950				Multi-generational descent group in New Zealand				Totals			
	M		F		M		F		M		F		M		F	
Age																
18–30	1	4%	0	0%	0	0%	1	8%	0	0%	0	0%	1	1%	1	1%
31–45	2	7%	3	50%	1	7%	0	0%	0	0%	0	0%	3	4%	3	4%
45–65	20	71%	3	50%	6	40%	4	33%	11	33%	17	33%	37	49%	24	35%
65+	5	18%	0	0%	8	53%	7	58%	22	67%	34	67%	35	46%	41	59%
Totals	28	19%	6	4%	15	10%	12	8%	33	23%	51	35%	76	52%	69	48%

Sources: Scottish Migration to New Zealand, Bristol Online Surveys, closed 31 July 2014, https://www.survey.ed.ac.uk/scotsinnz; Scottish Migration to Hong Kong, Bristol Online Surveys, closed 31 July 2014, https://www.survey.ed.ac.uk/scotsinhk

however, is that the respondent pool is likely to be strongly connected to their Scottish identity and such surveys unfortunately overlook those who may be less engaged.

Interviewees were primarily selected on the basis of a post-1950s migration date but included multigenerational descendants for comparative purposes. Fifty-two settlers and sojourners have been interviewed (see Table 10.2 for age group and gender distribution). Thirty-four were identified from survey responses while the balance were identified using the 'snowball' method, where interviewees were asked to identify others who might consider being interviewed.

None of the settlers or sojourners who completed questionnaires or interviews are unskilled. For those who migrated to New Zealand this reflects post-war immigration policies, which saw the Dominion Population Committee recommending 'a carefully focused policy designed to fill labor shortages in expanding secondary and tertiary industries',[2] while the 'Pacific provided a valuable source of unskilled labor'.[3] The limited assisted migration schemes deployed until the mid-1970s were primarily targeted at British migrants and 'sought to recruit working age migrants for contracted employment in essential industries'.[4] When the post-war average unemployment rate of 1.1 per cent doubled to 2.1 per cent in 1976 policies changed and immigration curtailed as unemployment continued to rise peaking at 11.6 per cent in 1991.[5]

Hong Kong in 1945 was a colonial backwater. Its population had fallen to approximately 600,000 from a 1941 estimate of 1,640,000, owing to food shortages and deportations.[6] Its growth, originally as a regional manufacturing and entrepôt centre and subsequently as a regional financial hub, was as a direct consequence of events in China. As refugees from mainland China provided the unskilled labour the colony needed to effect this transformation, there was no need to source unskilled labour elsewhere. However, the inflow of migrants brought problematic education levels, as at the first full post-war census in 1961 of the 1,852,613 individuals aged fifteen and over, 34.8 per cent had no formal education, 39 per cent had attained primary level, 22.5 per cent secondary level, 1.3 per cent a post-secondary qualification and just 2.4 per cent held a degree or were in university.[7] As a result sojourning opportunities were available in managerial and professional roles to cope with the colony's administration, infrastructure and services needs.

In contrast, the 2011 census shows that of the 6,248,016 individuals aged over fifteen, only 6.3 per cent had no formal education, 16.4 per cent had attained primary level, 50 per cent secondary level, 9.3 per

Table 10.2 Interviewee demographics

Gender	Migrants to Hong Kong		Returnee migrants to Hong Kong		Migrants to New Zealand post-1950		Multi-generational descent group in New Zealand		Totals			
	M	F	M	F	M	F	M	F	M		F	
Age												
18–30	0	0	0	0	0	0	0	1	0	0.0%	1	1.9%
31–45	1	1	0	0	0	0	0	1	1	1.9%	2	3.8%
45–65	7	1	1	4	4	2	0	2	12	23.1%	9	17.3%
65+	2	0	4	1	6	6	3	5	15	28.8%	12	23.1%
Totals	10	2	5	5	10	8	3	9	28	53.8%	24	46.2%

cent hold post-secondary qualifications and 18 per cent a university education.[8] Despite the change in educational attainment, the numbers of British citizens have changed little, rising from 29,000 in 1971[9] to 33,733 by 2011,[10] although as a percentage of the total population this represents a decline from 0.74 per cent in 1971 to 0.48 per cent in 2011. More importantly the change in Hong Kong's educational profile has facilitated its establishment as a regional financial centre.

Addressing Scottish migration after 1950 pushes history into the realm of sociology, where American sociologists such as Mary Waters, Richard Alba, Stanley Lieberson and Rogers Brubaker have researched ethnic identities and assimilation in the United States.[11] Marjory Harper and Angela McCarthy have both used oral history and written sources to evaluate Scottish migration to New Zealand in the twentieth century while Megan Hutching's oral histories of UK migrants have added to this work.[12] This project is intended to add to that research and take those studies on to the twenty-first century.

While there has been extensive research into twentieth-century migrations, there is a gap in the study of sojourning migrants and their transnational impact. Nor has there been much other than corporate hagiographies written about the Scottish role in Hong Kong. This study looks to begin the process of addressing this omission.

MIGRANT PERCEPTIONS

When asked 'What do you believe are the distinctive features of Scottish culture?' (Table 10.3), respondents could answer in free-form. In other words, no choices were provided for respondents to draw on and respondents may have mentioned one or more of the markers tabulated, with the numbers indicating the percentage of migrants who mention certain traits. To borrow from the marketing industry, the responses highlight 'Front-of-mind' awareness among respondents. Additionally, shaded cells indicate significant divergence (>9 per cent) between respondents in Hong Kong and New Zealand when the identity marker was mentioned by more than 20 per cent of respondents in any group.

The responses show that Scottish sojourners in Hong Kong identify with the homeland in terms of its physical environment and food and drink, arguably a reaction to the alien environment of Hong Kong. Scots in New Zealand, by contrast, are less taxed by their new environment. The more familiar landscapes and foods of New Zealand account for this disparity. Ian Johnstone, raised in the Cumbrian borderlands, and finding himself in rural South Canterbury in 1961, comments:

Table 10.3 Markers of Scottish culture

What do you believe are the distinctive features of Scottish culture?	Scots migrants to Hong Kong	Scots migrants to New Zealand post-1950	Multi-generational descent groups in New Zealand
Physical culture			
Bagpipes, music and dancing	44%	36%	43%
Physical environment (mountains, lochs, hills and glens)	21%	8%	5%
Tartanry	18%	8%	11%
Food and drink	21%	4%	10%
Scottish associations and Highland games	9%	0%	15%
Non-physical culture			
History, tradition and customs	24%	32%	20%
Education	24%	16%	10%
Art and literature	15%	16%	7%
Language and dialect	12%	16%	3%
Law and civil governance	12%	0%	0%
Church and religion	6%	0%	3%
Character traits			
Family, hospitality and humour	12%	28%	10%
Anglophobia, nationalism and patriotism	12%	4%	2%
Integrity, fairness and loyalty	9%	4%	11%
Pride, passion and perseverance	9%	4%	3%
Industriousness and entrepreneurialism	6%	4%	8%
Inventiveness, science and enlightened thought	3%	12%	5%
Individuality, independence and self-reliance	3%	8%	5%

Sources: Scottish Migration to New Zealand, Bristol Online Surveys, closed 31 July 2014, https://www.survey.ed.ac.uk/scotsinnz, Question 46a; Scottish Migration to Hong Kong, Bristol Online Surveys, closed 31 July 2014, https://www.survey.ed.ac.uk/scotsinhk, Question 46a

'It's a factor in my whole sense of identity, South Canterbury . . . the countryside is kind of Border country . . . it's like the Borders . . . the ocean is bigger and nearer but it's rolling hill country.'[13]

Additionally, Scottish migrants to New Zealand often cite family, friends, humour and hospitality as identity markers, and this points to a sense of dislocation from Scotland and familial and friendship ties. Anne Bowden, a librarian from Dunfermline married to a Royal New

Zealand Navy serviceman and who migrated to New Zealand in 1963, recalled, 'I was homesick the first year, I cried every night I think . . . but I wasn't homesick for the place, it was the people.'[14] Jean Hanna, who migrated in 1958, suffered similarly and commented that her husband John would return home at lunchtime to see her. She coped with her first Hogmanay, in the height of the New Zealand summer, by being determined that

> it was going to be traditional, as John was in the pipe band. I made steak pie, potatoes and peas . . . I lit the fire, you always had a lovely fire when you had New Year at home and I made a pudding, a jelly and it was so hot the jelly wouldnae set![15]

Other than the homesickness marker, there are few differences in identity markers between the multigenerational descent group and settlers in New Zealand. Table 10.3 supports the position that the 'common stereotype of Scots in New Zealand still tends to be the "traditional" Highland image of bagpipes and Highland flings, tartans, and claymore-wielding clansmen';[16] interestingly, the same can be said for Hong Kong migrants. This reflects the pervasiveness of this image globally, from the 'hallucination'[17] of 'Sir Walter [Scott]'s Celtified pageantry'[18] for George IV's 1822 visit through to the unabashed use of tartanry and Scotland's Highland vistas by today's tourist industry. These create what David McCrone describes as a 'landscape of the mind'[19] and what Paul Basu maintains represents a 'Scotland as existing outside time'.[20]

However, migrants and the multigenerational descent group in both New Zealand and Hong Kong see this iconography as hackneyed and removed from reality. Patsy Montgomery, the manager of the Waipu Museum in New Zealand, highlights this:

> Although . . . the symbolic representations of what it is to be Scottish are incredibly clichéd and probably more a modern invention in many respects, they are something that's powerfully universal and you are able to instantly hang your hat on some element of Scottishness.[21]

Gordon Watson, a sojourner in Asia, the West Indies and West Africa and a National Serviceman in Hong Kong in 1949 and 1950, notes, 'It doesn't matter if you were a Highlander or a Lowlander, the kilt was your dress, because it represents being Scottish'.[22]

Table 10.3 also demonstrates how migrant perceptions can be fixed at the time of departure. All groups identify Scottish history as being an important identity marker, ranking it the second most referenced cultural marker after bagpipes, music and dancing, with an average of a quarter of respondents locating Scottish history as a 'Front-of-mind' marker.

A closer examination of Scottish history's role in defining identity is tabulated in Table 10.4. Again, the responses are a 'Front-of-mind' assessment, with no choices provided, thereby allowing respondents to mention any number of events from Scotland's history. The numbers indicate the percentage of migrants who mention a particular event while the shaded areas show where there is a significant divergence (>9 per cent) between respondents in Hong Kong and New Zealand and the historical reference was 'Front-of-mind' for more than 20 per cent of respondents in any group.

The significant disparity between the multigenerational group in New Zealand and migrants in New Zealand and Hong Kong is the Clearances.[23] For the multigenerational group it is their most referenced historical marker, whereas both migrant groups evidence similar evaluations of the event. The fact that the Clearances are not as relevant to newer migrants indicates historical perception in relation to time of departure.

The significance of the Clearances marker suggests the construction of a victim diaspora narrative. Rosalind McClean, however, has shown that less than 5 per cent of Scottish migrants to Australasia in 1840–80 were from the 'extreme peasant fringe',[24] and that the origins of those migrants mirrored the distribution of the Scottish population of the time. Building on McClean's study and utilising data gathered by the New Zealand Society of Genealogists, it has since been determined 'that 70.03 per cent of Scots arriving in New Zealand between 1840 and 1920 were born in the Eastern or Western Lowlands or a Border county'.[25]

Clearly the migration was not a victim diaspora, nor does such a narrative sit easily with the promotion of Scottish migration as having been integral to the evolution of the New Zealand nation state. Of the New Zealand groups surveyed, 85 per cent agree to some extent that the Scots have had a cultural impact on New Zealand society.[26] Yet it remains difficult to explain why the Clearances are so important to the multigenerational group. Even the on-line *Te Ara: The Encyclopedia of New Zealand*, categorically states that 'Few Scots emigrated as refugees of the infamous Highland Clearances'.[27] This perception of history seems to be representative of the Highlandism referred to above, which goes together with the multigenerational group's identification with Jacobitism, drawing on a hardship narrative akin to that experienced by the early pioneers. Such an explanation lends weight to Eric Richards's argument that the 'exceptionalism of the Highlands has been over-rated

Table 10.4 Scottish history identity markers

What historical events do you believe define Scotland and the Scottish migrants?	Scots migrants to Hong Kong	Scots migrants to New Zealand post-1950	Multi-generational descent groups in New Zealand	All New Zealand groups
Bruce, Wallace, the Wars of Independence, Flodden	41%	55%	25%	31%
The Clearances	35%	36%	70%	63%
The Union of Crowns and Parliaments	32%	55%	6%	15%
Jacobite Risings and Culloden	29%	45%	38%	40%
Industrial Revolution, engineering, inventions and exploration	18%	18%	11%	13%
The Scottish Enlightenment	15%	5%	0%	1%
Participation in the British Empire	12%	5%	7%	6%
Highland regiments and Scottish military prowess	9%	5%	7%	6%
Darien	9%	5%	1%	2%
Migration	6%	0%	4%	4%
Scottish parliament and nationalism	6%	5%	0%	1%
Twentieth century industrial decline	3%	23%	2%	6%
Reformation/ Church of Scotland	3%	5%	6%	5%
Participation in the slave trade	3%	5%	0%	1%
Education	3%	5%	0%	1%
Radical politics, the Labour Party and Red Clydeside	0%	9%	1%	3%

Sources: Scottish Migration to New Zealand survey, Question 40; Scottish Migration to Hong Kong survey, Question 40.

at the expense of the significance of the Clearances as a well-documented exemplar of the perils facing a poor society on the edge of industrialisation'.[28]

The point Richards makes here hints at another reason why the Clearances hold a particular relevance for the multigenerational group. The escape of the rural poor from a society in which they are oppressed by governing elites has become an allegory for the idea that New Zealand's egalitarianism was fostered by Scottish migrants. Patsy Montgomery, a New Zealander of Scots multigenerational descent, highlights this in her definitive statements that she can

> quite clearly trace New Zealand's egalitarianism back to Scots migrants. It's estimated that up to 50 per cent of New Zealanders can claim Scottish ancestry and all the significant reforms that were made in the first part of the 20th century in New Zealand were brought about by Scots immigrants.[29]

This perception has significant traction in New Zealand, earning itself a mention in *Te Ara*, which states that 'the egalitarian spirit of Scottish culture helped make New Zealand a nation of rough equality, compared with the class system of England'.[30] Furthermore, James Belich, styling New Zealand as '*the* neo-Scotland',[31] describes the 'Scottish values of Otago [as] being egalitarian and down-to-earth'.[32]

Table 10.4 highlights two other points demonstrating how contemporary historical contexts can influence migrant identity. First, given the proximity of the survey to the 2014 Independence Referendum, Scottish migrants to Hong Kong and New Zealand identify more with the Union of the Crowns and/or Parliaments and the Wars of Independence than the Clearances. In this respect it would be interesting to evaluate whether these responses have a mid- to long-term relevance in five to ten years' time. Secondly, 23 per cent of post-1950 migrants to New Zealand highlight twentieth-century industrial decline as an issue. Indeed Scotland's industrial decline has been reiterated in a number of the New Zealand interviews conducted, as John Hanna, apprenticed as a marine engineer on the Clyde from 1951 to 1956, outlines in his decision to emigrate:

> the work on the Clyde started to go down and that had an incredible effect . . . there was a lot of industrial action on the Clyde . . . Some of them were quite silly, but what that meant was that customers could never depend on having their ship finished in time. So you put that together with the general decline and the amount of work that was available and things didn't look very good on the career front.[33]

Markedly, such narratives are largely absent from interviews with Hong

Table 10.5 Authors of histories read by respondents

Authors	All groups	Scots migrants to Hong Kong	Scots migrants to New Zealand post-1950	Multi-generational descent groups in New Zealand	All New Zealand groups
Sir Walter Scott	38%	26%	54%	38%	41%
Nigel Tranter	32%	35%	54%	24%	32%
John Prebble	28%	41%	35%	20%	23%
Magnus Magnusson	18%	26%	31%	11%	15%
Neil Oliver	16%	12%	38%	11%	17%
T. M. Devine	13%	26%	15%	7%	9%
T. C. Smout	8%	6%	23%	4%	8%
Hugh Trevor-Roper	8%	6%	12%	8%	9%
Michael Fry	4%	15%	0%	1%	1%
Rosalind Mitchison	3%	3%	12%	1%	4%
J. D. Mackie	3%	12%	0%	0%	0%

Sources: Scottish Migration to New Zealand survey, Question 39; Scottish Migration to Hong Kong survey, Question 39.

Kong sojourners, other than as a peripheral comment. This reflects the predominance of professions such as lawyers, accountants, bankers and civil engineers among those migrants.

These perceptions are fuelled by contact with Scotland, its histories and media. Table 10.5 shows whose histories respondents favour. Again, the numbers indicate the percentage of each group who identify individual historians, without limiting the number they can name, although this time a 'tick-list' was provided with room for respondents to identify additional historians.

Table 10.5 highlights the preference of all groups for the historical novels of Sir Walter Scott and Nigel Tranter in addition to the popular histories of John Prebble, Magnus Magnusson and T. M. Devine. Neil Oliver's *A History of Scotland* is well read among migrants to New Zealand and its prominence is presumably attributable to the success of the BBC Scotland Television documentary of the same name, which Oliver presented and which was aired in New Zealand in late 2010.

The table also indicates that migrants would appear to be more engaged with Scotland's histories than those of multigenerational descent. This is especially true for migrants to New Zealand. This highlights a preference for continued contact with the homeland and can be a long-term position, sometimes synonymous with a desire to return for more than just heritage tourism. John and Jean Hanna had still not taken out

Table 10.6 How well informed about Scotland do respondents believe themselves
to be?

How well informed do you believe yourself to be about Scotland and Scottish affairs?	All groups	Multi-generational descent groups in New Zealand	Scots migrants to New Zealand post-1950	Scots migrants to Hong Kong
Well informed	6%	4%	9%	12%
Relatively well informed	44%	38%	41%	64%
Neither well or poorly informed	29%	32%	27%	20%
Relatively uninformed	14%	16%	18%	4%
Not very informed	7%	10%	5%	0%

Sources: Scottish Migration to New Zealand survey, Question 45; Scottish
Migration to Hong Kong survey, Question 45.

New Zealand citizenship twenty years after migrating in 1958, nor had
they seen any need to do so until the lead up to the 1981 New Zealand
general election, as Jean indicates:

> John had ideas that maybe we would go back for a term to Scotland and we
> could teach over there. But at this time, Muldoon, who was Prime Minister
> was very much against redneck Clydesiders as he called them and we thought
> if we go over there and we don't have New Zealand citizenship, we might
> not get back . . . So we sent away for papers to get the ball rolling for New
> Zealand citizenship.[34]

Hong Kong sojourners, with their expectation of return, while still
engaged with history, have their connections with Scotland refuelled
by return visits 'home', and need less reaffirmation of their Scottish
ties than settler migrants. Unsurprisingly, as Table 10.6 shows, they
consider themselves relatively well informed about Scottish affairs. In
contrast, Scottish migrants to New Zealand only perceive themselves to
be marginally better informed than the multigenerational descent group,
almost as if the act of migrating to settle and integrate necessitates the
downgrading of the settlers' ties to the homeland. John Hanna remarks
on how he had to initially behave around New Zealanders:

> they were very interested in immigrants and hence asked the question 'How do
> you like New Zealand?' And it was hard to be frank because some people were
> a bit defensive and so we kind of learned that, that New Zealand was fine.[35]

Despite Scottish migrants to New Zealand believing they are no
better informed than the multigenerational cohort, their information
sources and networks are similar to those of Scots in Hong Kong (see

Table 10.7). John Hanna's insight suggests a possible reason in the form of competing loyalties to Scotland and the new homeland. This is something that Scots in Hong Kong, with their expectation of return and limited integration, are less taxed by. Yet despite these divided loyalties, when Scots settlers in New Zealand were given five choices (New Zealander, Scottish, British, hyphenated-Scot or other) to identify their ethnicity, 59 per cent still see themselves as Scottish and only 14 per cent as New Zealanders with the balance bar one, who answered British, considering themselves a hyphenated-Scot (i.e. Scottish-New Zealander).[36] In contrast, 76 per cent of the New Zealand born identify as New Zealanders and 22 per cent as hyphenated-Scots, with just one second generation settler identifying as Scottish. This speaks to a rapid rate of Scottish assimilation in New Zealand.

Table 10.7 identifies the media sources which keep individuals informed about Scotland. The numbers indicate the percentage of each group who selected from a 'tick-list', without any limit to the number available for selection. The shading indicates where the other groups deviate in excess of 10 percentage points from the multigenerational descent group.

Family and friends in the United Kingdom are cited as one of the most significant sources of information for Scottish migrants. In Hong Kong, where the majority of local media is in a foreign language, sojourners also rely heavily on cable/satellite TV, radio, the Internet and British print media for information outside their friends and family networks. While the same dynamic does not affect New Zealand migrants, they are still less reliant on local media sources than the multigenerational descent group.

Significantly, Table 10.7 identifies that Scots in Hong Kong are active users of local Scottish networks and associations. This contrasts with the activity of migrant Scots in New Zealand, who appear to be less engaged with New Zealand's Scottish associations than those of the multigenerational descent group and significantly less inclined to use Scottish networks within New Zealand. Cultural familiarity renders the need for Scottish networks in New Zealand less pressing. In contrast Hong Kong sojourners find themselves in a particularly alien environment where in mid 2011 the British resident population accounted for just 0.48 per cent of Hong Kong's population.[37]

This reliance on Scottish and expatriate networks suggests a level of ghettoisation, albeit a somewhat privileged bourgeois ghetto. Yet whatever the comforts of expatriate life, migrants find themselves in an environment in which most are ethnically, culturally and linguistically

Table 10.7 How do respondents keep informed about Scotland?

How do you normally keep yourself informed about Scotland?	Multi-generational descent groups in New Zealand	Scots migrants to New Zealand post-1950	Scots migrants to Hong Kong
Internet and electronic media			
UK Internet websites	33%	45%	76%
Local television and radio	47%	32%	20%
Cable/satellite television and radio	23%	32%	52%
Local Internet websites	17%	14%	8%
Non-family Scottish networks			
Scottish friends and contacts in the UK	31%	59%	64%
Scottish societies and associations	46%	32%	44%
Scottish friends and contacts locally	27%	32%	72%
Scottish friends and contacts elsewhere	7%	14%	16%
Non-family, non-Scottish networks			
Other friends and contacts in the UK	3%	5%	20%
Other friends and contacts locally	4%	0%	8%
Other friends and contacts elsewhere	4%	5%	8%
Family networks			
Family in the UK	21%	73%	64%
Family locally	19%	5%	12%
Family elsewhere	0%	14%	8%
Traditional print media			
UK print media (newspapers and magazines)	21%	32%	84%
Local print media (newspapers and magazines)	37%	23%	20%
Global print media	6%	5%	12%
Not ordinarily informed			
Don't ordinarily keep myself informed	7%	5%	0%

Sources: Scottish Migration to New Zealand survey, Question 45a; Scottish Migration to Hong Kong survey, Question 45a.

excluded from the majority. This holds true for those who choose to be more closely involved with local society. Michelle McEwan, the only European teacher in the Po Leung Kuk (a leading Hong Kong charitable organisation) and a single mother, found herself isolated after her partner's return to Scotland in 2011, commenting, 'I had very few friends, really. I had no friends really outside of my work'.[38] After living within a Chinese environment for her first six years in Hong Kong, she then developed a partially but not exclusively Scottish network. This came about through a friend whose networking activities she engaged in:

> she's English, her parents are Scottish. So when she came here as a single woman with no children and no employment and no ties, she joined everything. Now, she joined the American Women's Association, the Australian Women's Association. She had joined the St Andrew's Society . . . the Hong Kong Highlanders . . . she joined everything . . . I started to get drawn into these different things. The American Women's Association has a bazaar at Christmas time, so I went with Christine once to the bazaar. The St Andrew's Society have the Chieftain's Bottle once a month so a few times I went to the Chieftain's bottle.[39]

USING IDENTITY

Environment and time from departure appear to play a role in migrant identity perceptions. Physical environments such as the alien landscape of Hong Kong promote an identity informed by idyllic memories of Scotland's physical landscapes and iconography. Yet those same imagined landscapes can also be used to facilitate integration as they did for Ian Johnstone, newly arrived in South Canterbury. Additionally, a more permanent dislocation from the homeland heightens among Scottish migrants in New Zealand a sense of Scottish identity located in family, friends, hospitality and humour.

Over this sits the globally recognisable Highland identity of tartanry, bagpipes, clansmen and Jacobite romances. For migrants these identities are perpetuated by the romanticised histories of Scott and Tranter, together with the populist historical narrative of Prebble. Yet despite this iconography's currency within the migrant community, Scottish migrants in both New Zealand and Hong Kong appear to be well aware of their mythic nature.

It is difficult to pin a formulaic Scottish identity on migrants as they can use different ethno-cultural markers from a buffet of what they believe to be intrinsically Scottish characteristics. They are selective about what aspects of their Scottish identity they use and this is flexible over time and environment, not to mention individual circumstance.

Patsy Montgomery, the manager of the Waipu Museum, whose grandfather migrated in the early twentieth century from Carluke in Lanarkshire, comments on her Scottish identity as follows:

> as a child I became absolutely fascinated with my father's family who ... were Scots and they were a family that warranted being fascinated with because they were very clever gifted people and had valued education for women. I had seven great-aunts only one of them had married and they were educated Edwardian women ... That's where New Zealand, we believe, developed its very egalitarian education system and the focus of education for women comes directly from the Scottish immigrants and my father's family were kind of typical of Scottish, educated Scottish immigrant families. So one of my great-aunts became one of the first New Zealand women to become a doctor but she was never noted within her home country because they sent her back to Scotland to graduate in medicine and she actually never came home. She did amazing things like go to the Spanish Civil War and then she became a public health doctor in London ... So I had these kind of fascinating people in the family, which made me focus more on ... the sense of Scottish descent than on any other family.[40]

Patsy chooses to identify her Scottishness with education, and particularly the education of women, together with egalitarianism. As Patsy trained as a teacher this is perhaps unsurprising, while the values of egalitarianism and community are core to her reasons for leaving Auckland and the values she attributes to the Waipu community founded by West Highlanders from Nova Scotia in the nineteenth century: 'I found that what I had discovered was a well-organised community, a community with great leadership, a community that was essentially egalitarian and was very joyful and playful and had lots of fun together, so I just stayed.'[41]

Here, perceived Scottish identity markers or traits are used to site Patsy within her environment and the choice of which identities to use are set by her. In addition, Scottish identities can be used by both sojourner and settler migrants to create networks that similarly site individuals. However, the intensity with which Scottish identity is used to facilitate networking can be diminished if other networks are available to the migrant. David Hamilton, a retired banker and returned sojourner whose career took him across the globe to Libya, Kuwait, the Lebanon, Jordan, Hong Kong, the United States and Armenia, says of his networking in Hong Kong where he had other professional networks available:

in Hong Kong, I never used Scottishness . . . Going back, you know, the little fish in the big pool thing. I never networked because I was never, as were some people in Hong Kong, a big fish in a little pond because of the way their companies were structured. I was in this goliath, Hongkong Bank. I did meet other people who networked all the time, Lindsay's [David's partner] boss networked all the time his, his Scottishness . . . but I didn't have a need, I don't think we did in the Hongkong Bank, other than it had been full of Scots and Irishmen at one stage or another.[42]

This does not mean that David eschewed Scottish networks altogether. Indeed, in countries where the Hongkong Bank was a minor player, his Scottish networking was more pronounced and even in Hong Kong he was and remains a keen Scottish country dancer and still wears his kilt for formal occasions but with a certain circumspection since his return to Scotland.

There is a gendered response to migration with female narratives located in relation to the lives of others, particularly family, and appearing to experience family dislocation more keenly than males. This is not to say that males do not feel the same sense of loss; rather, their narrative tends to emphasise the risk taken in migrating. This phenomenon is not new to oral historians nor is it exclusive to Scottish migrants. Across the world's migrant groups 'women's recollections are filled by family members, joint decisions and the contexts for migration'.[43] Nor is this narrative exclusive to settler migrants, as Lindsay Hamilton's concern regarding her son's ethnicity reflects:

We were always going to come back home . . . Our son [Gavin] was born in Hong Kong and then when he was two and a half we moved to New York and we lived in New York until he was six and then came back to Scotland for just under two years while David went to Armenia and Gavin asked me, 'Why did we come to Scotland?' and I said, 'Because Dad got a job in Armenia and it wasn't going to be so easy for us to go' and he said, 'No, no, why did we come to Scotland?'
'Because Dad got a job in Armenia and', 'No. Why Scotland?' And it dawned on me, he didn't realise he was Scottish, he was six years old and he didn't know. So that was a bit of a shock that he didn't know, but then why would he?[44]

This chapter has attempted to demonstrate throughout that identity is both fluid and changing as much for a six-year-old as it is for an adult and is ultimately the individual's choice. Nor is it a simple choice as Alex Loggie, from Northumberland, where he and his brother were born and raised by Scots-born parents, attests:

I've never identified myself as anything other than Scottish. Sometimes, I'm reluctant to say, 'Yes, I'm an anglicised Scot.' I remember having an argument with my older brother, who was a pro-footballer, about 'If you were selected to play nationally, who would you play for: Scotland or England?' and he said, 'England.'[45]

Scottish identities are shaped and formed by an individual's environment and perceptions, such that no individual's interpretation of their Scottish identity is likely to be the same. The use of these constructed identities is also conditioned by individual environment and challenge. Fortuitously, the multiplicity of the components attributable to being Scottish allows for a wide range of identity permutations. Yet despite these possible Scottish identities, the recognisable Highland iconography is used by Scottish migrants, well aware of its invented origins, to identify themselves as Scottish to other nationalities and ethnicities and to establish a common bond and facilitate networking with other Scots or affinity Scots (those who identify with Scotland without possessing Scottish ancestry).

Return to Scotland, however, holds challenges of its own and the Scottish identity that has been created and used overseas may need realigning to the reality of Scotland upon return. After more than 30 years away from Scotland and despite regular return visits 'home' during that time, David Hamilton reflects on his Scottishness at home and abroad:

Being Scottish abroad was fun and we had an identity . . . When we first came back we went to a couple of formal Scottish nights . . . overseas most people don't really know how the dances go and they just enjoy it. Whereas here . . . you get people who take it terribly seriously and if you're not doing it correctly they get very upset etcetera . . . Scottishness overseas is a different kind of Scottishness.[46]

The longer the migrant is a sojourner the more difficult the homecoming adjustment is likely to be to the extent that many long-term sojourners find themselves more comfortable in the company of other returned sojourners than that of the wider Scottish population. Ironically, their life-cycle repeats itself and once again they find themselves in a minority, but this time within a motherland that is no longer as familiar to them as they had thought it would be.

CONCLUSION

There are two clear points to be drawn from the survey and oral testimony deployed in this chapter. First, the reasons for and the processes through which migrants chose their Scottish identity are based on a fluid and wide range of ethno-cultural markers, making their Scottish identities more of a convenience than a reality. This manufactured identity serves as a tool to facilitate social integration within both sojourner and settler environments and explains both where migrants come from and their otherness in a new social milieu.

Second, they are often individual constructs derived from a personal selection of cultural markers. Intriguingly, this highly individual construction also works on a private level as well and can be used to explain themselves and their value systems in a more intimate sphere. Claude Lévi-Strauss describes this 'identity as a sort of *foyer virtuel* [virtual home] to which we must refer to explain a certain number of things, but without it really existing.'[47]

The evidence is that the identities of recent Scottish migrants, whether they be settlers or sojourners, are individually manufactured, plural and fluid, subject to change, dependent on environment and needs at any given moment. The same is also true of multigenerational descent groups, although time and distance alters their perception of a Scottish identity to a more romanticised one, but still one that can be reinvented and used to site them in their environment. Nor is there any Scottish exceptionalism here as the conclusions support Waters's research into Californian multigenerational white ethnics who also 'choose how much and which parts of their ethnicity to make a part of their lives'.[48] If anything surprising can be drawn from the comparison, it is how, despite an expectation of return, sojourners behave in similar ways to settlers.

NOTES

1. Mary C. Waters, *Ethnic Options; Choosing Identities in America* (Berkeley: University of California Press, 1990), p. 16.
2. Patrick Ongley and David Pearson, 'Post-1945 international migration: New Zealand, Australia and Canada compared', *International Migration Review*, 29:3 (1995), p. 767.
3. Ibid. p. 774.
4. Ibid. p. 773.
5. Statistics New Zealand, quoted in Brian Easton, 'Economic history – Government and market liberalisation', *Te Ara - the Encyclopedia of New Zealand*, updated 3 February 2015, available at <http://www.TeAra.govt.nz/en/graph/24362/unemployment-1896-2006>.
6. Fan Shuh Ching, *The Population of Hong Kong* (Hong Kong: Committee for International Coordination of National Research in Demography,

1974), p. 2.

7. Hong Kong Census and Statistics Department, *Hong Kong Statistics, 1947–1967* (Hong Kong; Census and Statistics Department, 1969), pp. 13, 189.

8. Census and Statistics Department, the Government of the Hong Kong Special Administrative Region, *2011 Population Census Summary Results* (Hong Kong: Census and Statistics Department), pp. 5, 42.

9. Fan, *The Population of Hong Kong*, p. 18.

10. Hong Kong Census and Statistics Department, *2011 Population Census, Summary Results,* pp. 5, 36.

11. See Waters, *Ethnic Options*; Richard D. Alba and Victor Nee, *Remaking the American Mainstream: Assimilation and Contemporary Immigration* (Cambridge, MA: Harvard University Press, 2005); Stanley Lieberson and Mary C. Waters, *From Many Strands: Ethnic and Racial Groups in Contemporary America* (New York: Russell Sage Foundation, 1990); Rogers Brubaker, *Ethnicity without Groups* (Cambridge, MA: Harvard University Press, 2004).

12. See Marjory Harper, *Scotland No More: The Scots who left Scotland in the Twentieth Century* (Edinburgh: Luath Press, 2012); Angela McCarthy, *Personal Narratives of Irish and Scottish Migration, 1921–65: 'For Spirit and Adventure'* (Manchester: Manchester University Press, 2007); Megan Hutching, *Long Journey for Sevenpence: Assisted Immigration to New Zealand from the United Kingdom, 1947–1975* (Wellington: Victoria University Press, 1999).

13. Ian Johnstone, interviewed by Iain Watson, 15 July 2014, Wellington, New Zealand, held at the School of Scottish Studies Sound Archive, University of Edinburgh.

14. Ann Bowden, interviewed by Iain Watson, 28 July 2014, Auckland, New Zealand, held at the School of Scottish Studies Sound Archive, University of Edinburgh.

15. John and Jean Hanna, interviewed by Iain Watson, 18 July 2014, Wanganui, New Zealand, held at the School of Scottish Studies Sound Archive, University of Edinburgh.

16. Brad Patterson, Tom Brooking and Jim McAloon with Rebecca Lenihan and Tanja Bueltmann, *Unpacking the Kists: The Scots in New Zealand* (Montreal and Kingston: McGill-Queen's University Press, 2013), p. 54.

17. J. G. Lockhart, *The Life of Sir Walter Scott, Bart: Volume V* (Philadelphia: Carey, Lea and Blanchard, 1837), p. 161.

18. Ibid. p. 159.

19. David McCrone, *Understanding Scotland: The Sociology of a Stateless Nation* (London: Routledge, 1993 [1992]), p. 16.

20. Paul Basu, *Highland Homecomings; Genealogy and Heritage Tourism in the Scottish Diaspora* (London: Routledge, 2007), p. 69.

21. Patsy Montgomery, interviewed by Iain Watson, 11 January 2013, Waipu,

New Zealand, held at the School of Scottish Studies Sound Archive, University of Edinburgh.

22. Gordon Watson, interviewed by Iain Watson, 13 November 2012, Blainslie, Scotland, held at the School of Scottish Studies Sound Archive, University of Edinburgh.

23. The responses were predominantly 'Clearances' and/or Highland Clearances. Two respondents used the phrase Highland and Lowland Clearances and were both Hong Kong migrants.

24. Rosalind McClean, 'Scottish emigrants to New Zealand, 1840–1880: motives, means and background', unpublished PhD thesis, University of Edinburgh, 1990, p. 161.

25. Patterson et al., *Unpacking the Kists*, p. 25.

26. Scottish Migration to New Zealand, Bristol Online Surveys, closed 31Jul2014, https://www.survey.ed.ac.uk/scotsinnz, Questions 41g and 42.

27. John Wilson, 'Scots – 1840–1852: organised settlement', *Te Ara – the Encyclopedia of New Zealand*, updated 13 July 2012, <http://www.TeAra.govt.nz/en/scots/page-2>, p. 2.

28. Eric Richards, *The Highland Clearances* (Edinburgh: Birlinn, 2000), p. 328.

29. Interview with Patsy Montgomery, 2013.

30. John Wilson, 'Scots – Scots in public life', *Te Ara - the Encyclopedia of New Zealand*, updated 13 July 2012, <http://www.TeAra.govt.nz/en/scots/page-10>, p. 10.

31. James Belich, *Paradise Reforged: A History of the New Zealanders From the 1880s to the Year 2000* (Auckland: Penguin Books (NZ) Ltd, 2001), p. 221.

32. Ibid. p. 221.

33. Interview with John and Jean Hanna, 2014.

34. Ibid.

35. Ibid.

36. New Zealand survey, Question 3.

37. Hong Kong Census and Statistics Department, *2011 Population Census, Summary Results*, pp. 5, 36.

38. Michelle McEwan, interviewed by Iain Watson, 5 August 2014, Hong Kong, held at the School of Scottish Studies Sound Archive, University of Edinburgh.

39. Ibid.

40. Interview with Patsy Montgomery, 2013.

41. Ibid.

42. David Hamilton, interviewed by Iain Watson, 9 April 2014, Edinburgh, Scotland, held at the School of Scottish Studies Sound Archive, University of Edinburgh.

43. Graham Smith, *Oral History* (Coventry: University of Warwick, 2010) p.

12.

44. Lindsay Hamilton, interviewed by Iain Watson, 29 April 2014, Edinburgh, Scotland, held at the School of Scottish Studies Sound Archive, University of Edinburgh.
45. Alex Loggie, interviewed by Iain Watson, 17 July 2014, Wanganui, New Zealand, held at the School of Scottish Studies Sound Archive, University of Edinburgh.
46. Interview with David Hamilton, 2014.
47. Claude Lévi-Strauss (ed.), *L'Identité* (Paris: Presses Universitaires de France, 1977), p. 332 [author's translation].
48. Waters, *Ethnic Options*, p. 16.

11

Encountering an Imaginary Heritage: Roots Tourism and the Scottish Diaspora

Tawny Paul

The poetry of history lies in the quasi-miraculous fact that once, on this earth, on this familiar spot of ground, walked other men and women, as actual as we are today, thinking their own thoughts, swayed by their own passions, but now all gone, one generation vanishing into another[.][1]

AROUND THE WORLD, SOME 40 million people claim Scottish ancestry. Every year thousands of members of the Scottish diaspora travel to their imagined homeland. They come to Scotland to experience the culture of their ancestors and to walk in the places where their forebears walked. They come to Scotland because, like many diasporic populations around the globe, they imagine that their home is somewhere other than in the place they reside, and they travel in order to connect with their roots. Scotland is, of course, not the only country with a strong tradition of roots tourism. Cultural heritage trips, in which participants seek out an embodied experience of culture and connection, are part of a growing global fascination with heritage and genealogy. Nations with significant migration histories, including Israel and China, have, like Scotland, recognised the power inherent in their global communities and actively promote heritage tourism programmes.[2]

Coming from distinctive ethnic traditions and migration histories, roots tourists in these different national contexts are united by their identity relationship to the homeland as a place. According to Paul Basu, the homeland is 'situated at the centre of diasporic consciousness, anchoring it spatially and temporally'.[3] Unlike some diasporic populations, most global Scots are several generations removed from the migration process (if they have any tangible genealogical connection at all), so they have no first-hand experience of place. They therefore imaginatively construct Scotland through family traditions, material culture and society and clan gatherings.[4] Scotland is nostalgically imagined as a place of living history and a land lost in time, or in the words of G. M. Trevelyan, a 'familiar spot of ground' connecting them to past generations. The imagined Scotland is dominated by a romanticised Highland landscape punctuated by images of clans, castles, tartan and bagpipes.[5] The individual's own relationship to that space is conceptualised through narratives of Clearance that may have very little basis in academic historical understandings of Scotland's past.[6] Though there are many definitions of 'diaspora' (a term that has come under recent criticism for its diffuse meanings as both a condition, a process and a collectivity), diaspora Scots tend to privilege narratives of exile.[7] Roots tourists express very little sense of connection with the history of Scotland's global mercantile networks, or with Scottish ancestral engagement in imperial ventures.

In travelling to Scotland, roots tourists expect to come in contact with a place constructed in these imaginary terms. Materialised through place, they see the past as literally 'visitable', making the journey to the homeland both a physical journey and a journey through time.[8] In reality, however, Scotland is a much less romantic place than the homeland imagined by its diaspora. Scotland the myth and Scotland the place do not look much alike. The majority of the population resides not in the Highlands, but in the urbanised and post-industrial landscapes of the Central Belt. Just like any nation, Scotland faces modern social problems. It is not shielded from modernity, but rather embedded in a world of movement. The social, political and physical realities of Scotland as a place mean that homeland journeys can expose issues of congruency, involving an encounter between an imaginary heritage and real place. This chapter explores the nature of that encounter. It considers how individuals deal with their 'imaginary' once they experience the real place, and how the encounter affects their perceived relationship to the homeland.

The nature of the encounter is examined through a case study of the experiences of young adults, an age group relatively neglected in diaspora heritage literature, which tends to conceptualise roots tourism as a form of travel undertaken by people at mid life or post-retirement. The study involved thirty-five young people (aged eighteen to twenty-one) who came to Scotland in 2013 as visiting international students at the University of Edinburgh. The student experience, which differs from the average heritage tour both in quality and duration, can provide only partial insight into roots tourism. Students are, however, an excellent demographic in which to examine heritage encounter. Unlike roots tourists, whose short visits enable them to choose spaces where they might project their heritage imaginaries, students' extended period of engagement with Scotland as a space for everyday living compels a more thorough encounter between imaginary and real, and provides an alternative picture of engagement. Previous studies suggest that the Scottish heritage most frequently embraced is Highland heritage, and that heritage tourists tend to map Scotland not by current economic or population centres, but by places of historical relevance to heritage, with a predominantly Highland focus.[9] Many visitors, however, experience Scotland through its cities.[10] For young visitors, Scotland is mapped by the availability of public transportation, naturally shifting their geographic focus to population centres. The process of seeing Scotland through urban places can force a more direct confrontation between the 'imagineered' Scotland as a land lost in time and Scotland as a modern, physical, reality.

Participants in this study resided in Scotland for one semester (four months). They were recruited by email through the University of Edinburgh's International Office prior to arrival, and were selected because they self-identified as having a 'deep Scottish connection', though the nature of that connection was left deliberately open-ended. This allowed participants to define their own sense of Scottishness and facilitated the participation of 'affinity Scots' with no genealogical connection (a term outlined by David Hesse in this volume). Participants came from ten home countries, representing a tapestry of Scotland's global community (Figure 11.1), and 90 per cent of participants were female. The majority of students came from North America and claimed ancestry as their primary means of connection. For a significant European and Asian minority, however, Scotland provided the 'ersatz ancestry' described by Hesse. For these individuals, Scottish traits provided a sense of affinity and visiting Scotland was a means of tapping into their own lost histories.[11] For example, one student from northern Greece felt a connection to Scotland based upon a sense of northern affinity. Manifested in atmosphere, weather, and architecture, she felt that experiencing such scenery provided insights into common culture and history: 'You can understand how the personalities were, how the culture affects people and their thinking'.[12] For a student from Hong Kong, visiting Scotland was about tapping into a deeper history than she was able to experience at home:

> I don't have blood connections at all with Scotland ... Living where I'm from is quite different from Scotland. Scotland is a country that is full of history. But the place I'm from only became the colony of Britain around 200 years ago, so its history is only just around 200 years old. It's a very new place, and living there is sort of like the opposite to Scotland.[13]

Students' sense of affinity, however diverse, was crucial to their decisions to study in Scotland. When asked why they chose Edinburgh, the

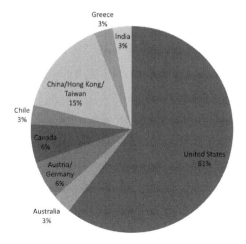

Figure 11.1 Home countries of study participants.

majority of students cited both heritage connections and Edinburgh's status as a top-ranking university as central to their decision.[14] Though visiting students are far less numerous than heritage tourists, it is possible that heritage students provide a large segment of the some 12,000 international students welcomed in Scotland every year.[15]

Over the four-month period, the process of encounter was traced in written, oral and visual forms. Students completed a written pre-arrival survey and participated in a post-arrival focus group where they were asked about their connections to Scotland and their sense of heritage. Their 'discovery' of Scotland and encounter with place was then recorded through site visits, using a photo-elicitation methodology. Students were asked to take pictures of places and things that seemed authentically 'Scottish' and places where they found a sense of personal connection, and to reflect upon their experiences immediately after their visits by recording short voice memos. Because the camera is a 'tool that encourages and even requires active performances related to self-identity', the photographs capture moments of encounter with heritage, providing points of entry into the process meaning-making.[16] Fuller reflections on the experience of encounter were traced through individual interviews at the end of the four months, using the photographs taken as a basis for discussion.[17] By collecting data across the duration of their stay and in several forms, the study intended to capture a multifaceted account of the individual experience of encounter.

THE SCOTTISH IMAGINARY

Members of the Scottish diaspora celebrate a heritage that is couched in imaginary terms. Though individuals view their heritage as fixed, based on clear genealogical links and the 'facts' of their family histories, numerous studies have demonstrated that heritage is not an already existing object, but is rather something constructed, produced and constantly evolving.[18] As a product of ideology, heritage is based on the needs of the present, a product of the new that 'has recourse to the past'.[19] Heritage is how we make sense of the past and how we give that past meaning.

To suggest that the heritage of diaspora Scots is 'imaginary' is not to suggest that it is fake. The 'imaginary' as it is used in anthropological theory is a concept with more subtle meanings, referring to a society's shared values and unifying core beliefs. As defined by Charles Taylor, the 'social imaginary' is a widely shared, implicit cognitive schema, or 'that common understanding that makes possible common practices and a widely shared sense of legitimacy', and it is central to the formation of group identity and shared understanding.[20] Around the world, the Scottish diaspora is bound together by a shared imagining of its lost homeland.[21] Diaspora communities privilege narratives of exile and gaze upon Scotland with a sense of nostalgia. Learning the appropriate symbols of Scottishness is a key component of belonging, providing a point of identification when individuals meet at Highland Games or community gatherings. The imagining of Scotland provides a coherent sense of Scottishness across disparate heritage communities.

Prior to arriving in Scotland, young roots tourists conceptualise their relationship with Scotland through a heritage imaginary grounded in stories and celebrations. Most participants described having grown up with a tradition of Scottishness, and being familiar with Scotland through family or group commemoration. One young American described how 'My grandmother likes to cook her mother's traditional Scottish recipes, so I sometimes help her with that.'[22] Another told of how her mother was very active in genealogical research while she was growing up: 'I grew up listening to many stories about my Scottish ancestors . . . Mom definitely romanticised Scotland for me.'[23] Sometimes, through the family, Scottish heritage was celebrated with larger Scottish communities, clubs, or societies. As these examples suggest, group commemoration activities often had gendered dimensions and were carried on especially by women. While the Scottish dreamscape has been noted for celebrating a very traditional form of masculinity, leaving little room for women other than as passive observers, female family members play crucial roles in the creation and maintenance of memory through storytelling.[24]

But while common experience is central to diaspora identity, for young people, claiming Scottishness can be as much about forging a unique identity within a multicultural society as it is about group membership. As one student commented, 'you get these really emotionally charged stories about your ancestors, and it sets you apart. It sets you apart from the other Swedish and Norwegian kids at school.'[25] Shared imaginaries thus not only cement the Scottish diaspora community, but they provide a point of difference, and 'the means by which individuals understand their identities and their place in the world'.[26]

Within the diaspora, common narratives of the lost homeland and imaginings of Scotland's place identity are made tangible in a material culture, in which objects become 'sites of memory'.[27] Links to Scotland's past are deep and imagined, but individuals experience them as being real and concrete. Familiar symbols of Scotland, including kilts, bagpipes, Scottish music, and food and drink including whisky, shortbread and haggis are strategically consumed, and the diaspora has a particularly strong enthusiasm for the invented traditions of tartanry. Following this tradition, participants described their Scottishness through reference to their families' Scottish 'things'. One participant remembered his grandfather's house:

> There would be a MacLeod tartan – my grandfather had that over the sofa. He had all these different Scottish things or clan things that had been passed down to him, or he visited Scotland and had picked up – like a chanter for a bagpipe.[28]

Another described how her father set up a 'Scotland wall' in their house, where the Declaration of Arbroath, a picture of the family's clan castle and other memorabilia hung.[29] Thus through material cultural, the diasporic imaginary heritage is grounded in tangible things, 'carried in images, stories and legends'.[30]

The communal or family practices of Scottishness mean that for young diaspora travellers, coming to Scotland often has as much to do with affirming their place in a diaspora community as it does with establishing connections with the physical place. Coming to Scotland to acquire 'authentic' local knowledge provides social capital within diaspora communities. Within these communities, travel is a means by which individuals can make themselves distinctive, and through which sub-diasporic social identities are 'defined and asserted through difference'.[31] Some participants actively described their trips as fulfilling a desire to carry on family tradition and to contribute to the family's cultural 'maintenance'. One young woman described her expectations around planning a trip to visit the family's ancestral clan space: 'My Dad especially has talked about it for so long and I've grown up with the idea of getting to finally go back and see it.'[32] For others, travel to Scotland to acquire cultural knowledge was conceptualised as a responsibility. With grandparents growing old, participants feared the loss of family knowledge and felt a duty to maintain the family's heritage: 'As I get older and older, we lose generations of people, so the people who would know are gone.'[33] For Scots, like homeland tourists in other nations, the heritage tour is about making a commitment to the obligations of ethnic belonging. While Filipino and Israeli tours emphasise political commit-ment, however, in the Scottish case obligation is more about committing to the maintenance of family and the diasporic community.[34]

Taking their cues from family, young ancestral visitors embark on their travels with clear ideas about what being Scottish means. For these young travellers, Scotland is imagined not merely as a physical place, but as idea and an ideal.[35] One participant told of how she associated Scottishness with idealised character traits, having grown up with stories of Scottish ancestors, which her mother used 'like allegories for how I should behave – like with honour and pride'.[36] Students grew up around Scottish heroes who exemplified honour, bravery and honesty. They expected to meet people with 'timeless values' and 'traditional' Scottish character, for example a loyalty to clan, and the 'perseverance that you see with sometimes having to take the backseat but still always staying strong'.[37] Through character, modern people can contribute to the sense of a land grounded in the past, as 'characteristics' are seen as having been inherited from ancestors.

Notions of 'timeless values' are part of the project of imagining Scotland as a land lost in time, and diasporic Scots gaze upon the homeland with a sense of nostalgia.[38] As a place, Scotland is seen to provide a direct connection with an ancestral past. The whole of Scotland becomes clan lands, or spaces linked to clan names and histo-ries.[39] Travel to Scotland is about visiting the past rather than another country. Heritage tourists are less interested in experiencing the Scottish culture of today, and more focused on the (perceived) culture of their ancestors.[40] Scotland is identified with the Highlands, which are seen as a traditional, untouched landscape.[41] Indeed, in venturing to these spaces, roots tourists conceptualise their journeys as a form of time travel, and Scotland is imagined as a place where history can literally be experienced.

This diasporic Scottish imaginary is combined with and reinforced by media representations and a tourism imaginary, a collection of 'stories, images, and desires, running the gamut from essentialized, mythologized, and exoticized imaginaries of otherness to more realistic frames of reference that set the tourism machinery in motion'.[42] Movies, including *Braveheart* and more recently, Pixar's *Brave*, reproduce Scottish place myths. The tourism and heritage sectors draw on Scotland's globally familiar brand, marketing romantic and majestic images of the country both abroad and at home that focus on landscapes, kilts and castles. The imaginary Scotland is then projected onto the physical place. Heritage spaces are constructed as 'objects for the tourist gaze', and tourism imaginaries become tangible and real as archaeological sites, museums, and monuments.[43] Diaspora audiences draw from these tourism imaginaries, incorporating them into their sense of homeland. The production and consumption of a Scottish imaginary thus becomes a joint endeavour between diaspora and homeland. Far from being a passive gaze, the imaginary is a process of active production and consumption, in which symbols, stories and images are appropriated according to the cultural needs of individuals and communities.

THE ENCOUNTER

The imaginary frames individual travellers' motivations and expectations, and it is central to how visitors encounter and construct places. Indeed, as Salazar has suggested, 'it is hard to think of tourism without imaginaries or "fantasies"', and these imaginaries contribute to 'global place myths'.[44] Studies of diasporic encounters in other places suggest that the nature of that encounter can have as much to do with the culture of origins of visitors as being in the homeland itself.[45] Having learned from their families to imagine Scotland as a homeland lost in time, one might expect that the experience of encountering a modern nation would be difficult and perhaps unwelcomed. However, pre-arrival surveys suggest that among young Scots, this encounter is anticipated and at times even actively sought. Participants expressed a reflexive understanding that the Scotland they grew up with might be a myth, and the decision to study abroad was expressed as a desire to find the 'real', 'authentic' place. As one participant commented, 'I hope to dive into the true culture of Scotland while studying there'.[46]

Authenticity is contested and perceived in various ways, and the search for authenticity amongst visitors is not particularly unique. Indeed, finding authenticity has been identified as one of the prime motivators for tourism and historic site visits, though this term is highly ambiguous.[47] But while authenticity has often been defined as unspoiled, untouched or traditional, young diasporic Scots seem to define authentic Scotland as the modern, living place rather than the imagined past. As one participant commented, 'coming here, I really think I'm trying to get stronger connections, and kind of to see modern Scotland as well, to tie into the idea that I had of the past from my family.'[48] For young diasporic Scots, life stage seemed particularly important in framing the desire for an authentic encounter. Developing a sense of ethnic heritage and belonging can be central to identity formation, which is one of the fundamental psychosocial tasks for young people in the transition to adulthood. As Mary Waters suggests, individuals tend to choose an ethnicity between the ages of seventeen and twenty-one.[49] Yet, although carrying on a family tradition was a clear impetus for travel to Scotland, doing so on their own terms was crucial. The language used by participants strongly reflected a desire for personal independence, one of the central features of emerging adulthood.[50] Participants expressed a desire to get to know their roots, but discovering Scotland independently from their families and claiming a 'different' Scotland than the one they inherited was important.

Despite intentions, in the process of encounter, imaginaries provide a clear starting point. Participants adhered to a kind of tourist 'habitus', in which encounters with place affirmed imaginaries. Diaspora Scots, like other ethnic groups, tend to privilege experiences that confirm 'mythic' or traditional pasts. Shaul Kelner and colleagues, for example, find that Jewish homeland tourists find the encounter with 'heavenly' Israel to be more meaningful in building a sense of community identity than encounters with the 'earthly' Israel of Bauhaus architecture and everyday life.[51] Similarly, roots tourists in China seem uninterested in embracing narratives of homeland progress and success, identifying instead with traditional or 'difficult' pasts.[52] Adhering more or less to the idea that a visit to Scotland provides an experience of the ancestral past, participants initially sought out spaces perceived as old, seeking out a past materialised in buildings, things and places. Experiencing the historicity of the city allowed one participant to 'see into the past that my ancestors would have experienced'.[53] Others described enjoying places where 'you can get lost and feel like you're from another time'. With these comments, students spoke to the central, affective nature of heritage, making the past 'visitable'. Embodied in places and buildings, the presence of the past can literally be 'felt'.[54] For these travellers, old spaces provided a direct, imagined link to heritage. As David Lowenthal wrote, 'the locus of memory lies more readily in place than in time'. Temporal ambiguity plays a major role in tourist activity, which is directed at 'experiencing' the past.[55]

Many roots tourists describe a general sense of 'feeling' Scotland's past. Others, however, project more specific facets of heritage onto particular spaces. Though the sense of 'homeland' can encompass different spaces, from nation to county to domestic space, the more specific the site of memory, the more specific the sense of connection.[56] For one student, being in the same place as a childhood hero, the athlete Eric Liddell, was a point of connection. After discovering that he attended the University of Edinburgh, she developed a daily ritual of walking through the university gates where she imagined that he too would have walked: 'I walked in the same place he did. I guess it establishes that place. It sort of gives that connection. Knowing that he was here is pretty cool.'[57] In this example, the heritage imaginary is projected onto a landscape, and becomes 'emplaced'. The lived landscape becomes a heritage landscape, fortifying a sense of connection.[58] The encounter between the imaginary and real or tangible landscape is thus one of affirmation and reproduction, wherein photographs 'certify' experience.[59] In a process described by Pierre Bourdieu as 'incorporation and objectification', the imagined past is objectified in a site of memory, and the site then reflects the sense of heritage back onto the visitor, enhancing its emotive appeal.[60] The imaginary and the real become blurred in the project of place making.

The act of affirming and projecting an imaginary on to the landscape can be sealed by the act of taking photographs. In taking photographs that represented their 'authentic' Scotland, students participated in a representational loop or 'hermeneutic circle'. Having seen images either in diasporic material culture, promotional material or other media sources, they searched for these pictures in the experience of travel itself. In taking photographs, they sealed or reproduced these same image types, becoming 'players in the game of directed viewing' by anticipating photographic views.[61] This process of imaginative reproduction occurred as students sought photographs that represented their inherited sense of 'historic Scottishness'. Photographs of Edinburgh represented the city as old, depicting historic buildings and ruins. One student, who presented an image of the Old Town (Figure 11.2) as 'authentic', described the photograph's ability to connect past with present and to seal a sensory or emotive moment: 'You get the ruin in the picture and you see the history. You can feel like you're back in another time.'[62] Taken from Calton Hill, this image was deliberately framed so as to

Figure 11.2 The Old Town, Edinburgh, from Calton Hill, March 2013.
(© Tawny Paul)

leave out the modern train station, portraying Edinburgh as a landscape dominated by history.

The Scottish heritage most often celebrated by the diaspora is Highland heritage. This posed a problem for students who spent the majority of their time in Edinburgh. Some sought to affirm their associations between Scotland and Highlandism by seeking out rural landscapes within the urban setting. Several photographed Arthur's Seat (Figure 11.3), an extensive park and volcano set in the city centre, which was imagined as Highland-esque and described as seeming remote, ancient and untouched. When these photographic views could not be sourced, Scotland's capital city was initially interpreted as being 'not Scottish'. According to one student, the places that represented Scotland were the 'more rural, more Highland areas, rather than working industry areas'.[63] Taken back to their country of residence as souvenirs, images of the historic nation would reinforce the diaspora's imagined Scottish landscape. They would also affirm the participants' own roles within their diasporic communities as imaginative participants in the link to homeland, providing 'a visual record of extant social roles and relations'.[64]

Figure 11.3 Arthur's Seat, Edinburgh, February 2013. (© Tawny Paul)

Imaginaries can only partly be confirmed by a physical landscape. Interactions with people and reception by locals are crucial to the encounter between imaginary and real. Studies of homeland tourism in China and the Philippines suggest that roots tourists expect to fit in and to be received as members of the national community. As Marco Garrido suggests, Filipino-Americans participate in 'authenticity games', which involve both passing as local and criticising locals for not being Filipino enough.[65] Similarly, Scottish students arrived with expectations of belonging and acceptance. As one student described:

> I always had in the back of my mind, that's heritage, that's where I want to be . . . I wanted to be in this country and in this city, just for no valid, logical reason. Just for a gut feeling of oh, yeah, that's where I belong.[66]

Another described his intention to 'feel like a resident rather than a visitor'.[67] Others expected their Scottish identity, which created difference at home, to form the basis of belonging in Scotland. Participants who successfully 'passed' as Scottish described feeling an overwhelming sense of joy. One student recounted the feeling of fitting in: 'That feeling of a real sense of, I can kind of blend in here. I enjoyed that'.[68]

Though roots tourists often have ambitions to fit in, locals do not necessarily see them as sharing a common identity. Andrea Louie's work on Chinese homeland tourism suggests that mainland Chinese question whether those overseas remain culturally Chinese, given their different habits and language.[69] Though Scottish roots tourists consider Scotland to be a homeland, they visit the nation as foreign nationals. Upon openly claiming Scottish heritage, many experienced ambivalent or negative reactions. Looking like the imaginary Scot turned out not to be enough. One student described how 'You say I'm of Scottish heritage in America and people say "oh yeah, red hair, of course". But you say it here and people are more surprised'.[70] Another recounted being mocked or laughed at by other students. In light of these responses, she stopped being so open about her claims of belonging: 'I don't tell people anymore. When they ask me why I came, I pretty much leave out the heritage part. People roll their eyes.'[71]

This sense of rejection or 'displacement' can be shocking and difficult, but over time may lead to a complex exploration of inheritance and belonging. For some students, it provided the impetus for a changing sense of their own place within Scotland. The reality of 'multiple rootedness and multiple otherness' required a new Scottish imaginary and a new way of placing themselves within it, as a more complex exploration of inheritance and belonging. Most participants described neither an eagerness to have their myths shattered, nor a refusal to incorporate the reality of Scotland into their imaginaries, but rather a willingness to build upon preconceived notions of place identity in a way that allowed a 'safe' shifting of their own sense of belonging over time. In Edinburgh, an inherited sense of place could be combined with new experiences.

For participants, interactions with the urban landscape provided the opportunity to re-imagine Scotland as a complex hybrid of land lost in time and place embedded in present time. Students recounted enjoying the experience of 'feeling' the past, but they did not reject contemporary Scotland. Instead they were surprised and fascinated by the juxtaposition of old and new and the way in which historic architecture was integrated into a modern city. The spaces identified by participants at the end of the project as the most authentic and 'real' effectively blended the sense of old and new in Edinburgh, combining past and present. For these young visitors, the integration of past and present became one of the central features of Edinburgh's sense of place. Showing a picture of Arthur's Seat, one participant described the image as authentic because it combined 'the past and the history of the landscape with modernity'.[72] Another commented on the presence of the cranes over the Old Town (Figure 11.4), commenting that it showed 'not just the picturesque city.

Figure 11.4 Salisbury Crags and city of Edinburgh, March 2013. (© Tawny Paul)

It's still in the process of rebuilding and reconstructing over the old. It keeps it linked to the present.'[73] The city is a landscape composed of layers of memory.

This integration of old and new allowed for a subtle shifting of space-time. Rather than seeing Scotland as a place lost in time, and with a sense of nostalgia that sharply divides then and now, it can be conceptualised as anchoring past, present and future.[74] As one student explained, 'I like the idea that there are so many years of other things happening here, that are still present even though we're in the future.'[75] By integrating the old and the new, place fulfils the need to connect the present to the past in an unbroken trajectory.[76]

Incorporation of the modern landscape into the Scottish imaginary paralleled the conceptualisation of Scotland as a place with modern attributes. Some came to imagine Scotland as a forward thinker. At the end of their stay, when asked to select their photographs that best represented Scotland, students chose images that portrayed the nation's identity as a forward thinker and as an innovator. They discovered this aspect of Scotland's identity in diverse sites throughout the city. One student chose an image from the National War Museum, noting the contributions that Scotland has made to the medical field in terms of education and prosthetics development. Another found Scottish identity in the Royal Botanic Gardens, pointing out the country's efforts to preserve plant diversity. One student commented that becoming aware of Scotland's modern inventions in the National Museum changed her perceptions of the place: 'Learning of Scottish things like the TV makes you less tempted to consign it to an older past. This is an ancient romanticised city, but it contributes to technology, and things like that. It ties it into modern ideas.'[77]

Other students found it helpful to shift their imaginaries away from Scotland as a static place, embodying a sense of history that, in the words of Robert Hewison, is 'past, dead and safe', to think of it more as a modern place embedded in a world of movement.[78] Most students came expecting to find a homogenous population composed of individuals who looked like the archetypal 'imaginary' Scot: 'You think Scotland and it's an island, so you think there isn't much diversity.'[79] Instead, participants were surprised by the discovery of social and cultural diversity. As one explained, 'I've met so many different people . . . that has been cool too to break down your ideas of a place – is the people that you meet.'[80]

Finding a different, new Scotland and making it 'their own' brought a very personal connection, one that accorded with a sense of independence and emerging adulthood. Building upon inherited family narratives in ways that challenged them was central to the process of identifying with Scotland. This involved, in part, coming to terms with the initial feelings of dislocation from ancestry that many described, resulting ultimately in a stronger sense of connection. One woman described how her sense of personal heritage had changed:

> Edinburgh stands on its own now. It doesn't have to be backed up by me having these reasons because of my ancestry. It's just cool on its own. And it's not about me. I think that's what's changed. I have a real respect for the place now having experienced it.[81]

As this example suggests, the process of encounter, whether or not anticipated as 'authentic', was interpreted as one of the most enriching and important aspects of travel to Scotland and central to forming a sense of long-term connection to place.

CONCLUSION: ENCOUNTER, IMAGINARY AND BELONGING

For members of the Scottish diaspora, the experience of travelling to the homeland is often defined by a process of encounter. This process is about much more than the relationship between expectation and experience. It is central to shaping individual perceptions of heritage, place and belonging, and it has implications for Scotland's relationship with its modern diaspora. As this chapter has shown, the nature of the encounter between imaginary and place is complex and multifaceted. It involves something more complicated than an outright rejection of the imaginary, or a refusal to incorporate the real into a sense of place.

This study suggests that young diaspora Scots, whose experiences of Scotland are focused predominantly in the urban Central Belt rather than travel to the Highlands, have a slightly different experience of encounter than their older counterparts. While Basu's study of roots tourists describes a process of 'projection' on to the Scottish landscape, this study suggests more a process of incorporation, adjustment, and a shifting sense of place identity. While more quantitative research is necessary to draw conclusions based upon age, this qualitative study provides a starting point for establishing a more multifaceted under-standing of the diaspora's experiences of the Scottish homeland. A complex understanding is necessary because as heritage theory has long made clear, there are always multiple ways of reading the same heritage, and places are nearly always contested. There are many Scotlands, and the homeland journey can involve the affirmation, the rejection and the re-evaluation of pre-conceived imaginaries.

For young travellers, the encounter involves a subtle process of negotiation fostered by the condition of 'multiple rootedness'. In other words, a shifting sense of Scotland and its place identity was possible for many and felt 'safe' because students described themselves as belonging to two Scotlands: Scotland itself, and the diasporic community located in their normal place of residence. Therefore, Scottish place identity could change quite dramatically, while a sense of diaspora heritage could remain stable. Some participants' comments suggested that their emotional connection to 'Scotland' was in reality more of a connection to a Scottish community at home. Therefore, student engagement with Scotland could involve quite a dramatic transformation in individual understandings of place because their sense of identity and community back at home, often referred to as a 'family', would not be disrupted. Acknowledging the very real possibility that genealogical research would not affirm her ties to Scotland, one participant felt strongly that:

> even if we found out that we weren't Buchanan, we've created such a con-nection with the people at the Games that it still feels like home, it's still our family even if we're not blood-tied anymore. I think it would be important to explore what our true heritage was, of course, but the connection would never ever be lost completely.[82]

One participant found herself embracing the modern, global Scotland, but maintained a sense of belonging to the global Scottish community, commenting that 'Scottish people have gone all over the world. They have lived everywhere and settled everywhere, and I'm part of that. I'm part of that tradition of moving around.'[83]

The young people involved in this study experienced a subtle shift from a Scottish imaginary and a sense of affinity based on ethnicity, to an affinity based on values. This shift meant that their affinity was not based only on a sense of genealogy and family connection to the past, but also on their own experiences and their sense of Scotland's ambitions as a nation grounded in present time. One of the most important features of the Scottish imaginary is that it is not fixed, but rather highly flexible, and this flexibility provides for its maintenance. The imaginary can incorporate both the mythical and real, providing a buttress against a sense of dislocation. As one student explained, what made Scotland special was that despite being a modern, innovative and global player with ties to the world, it maintained a sense of local identity. This sense of flexibility offers possibilities. For the diaspora, Scotland has long been the nostalgic land of ancestors, divorced from the modern nation state. Ties to Scotland exist in the imagination, while ties to physical home, whether that be in the United States, Canada or New Zealand, are in everyday living. As Scotland seeks to reach out to and engage with its global community, the experiences of young people offer possibilities. The nature of the transnational experience means that there are multiple ways of imagining, inhabiting, and belonging to this homeland.

NOTES

1. G. M. Trevelyan, 'Autobiography of an historian', in G. M. Trevelyan, *An Autobiography and Other Essays* (London: Longman, 1949), p. 13.
2. Shaul Kelner, *Tours That Bind: Diaspora, Pilgrimage and Israeli Birthright Tourism* (New York: New York University Press, 2010); Marco Garrido, 'Home is another country: ethnic identification in Philippine homeland tours', *Qualitative Sociology*, 34:1 (2010), pp. 177–99; Andrea Louie, *Chineseness Across Borders: Renegotiating Chinese Identities in China and in the US* (Durham, NC: Duke University Press, 2010); Gary McCain and Nina M. Ray, 'Legacy tourism: the search for personal meaning in heritage travel', *Tourism Management*, 24:6 (2010), pp. 713–17.
3. Paul Basu, *Highland Homecomings: Genealogy and Heritage Tourism in the Scottish Diaspora* (London: Routledge, 2006), p. 66.
4. Celeste Ray, *Highland Heritage: Scottish Americans in the American South* (Chapel Hill: University of North Carolina Press, 2001).

5. David McCrone, *Scotland the Brand: The Making of Scottish Heritage* (Edinburgh: Edinburgh University Press, 1995).

6. Laurence Gourievidis, *The Dynamics of Heritage: History, Memory and the Highland Clearances* (Farnham: Ashgate, 2010), p. 43; Eric Richards, *Debating the Highland Clearances* (Edinburgh: Edinburgh University Press, 2007).

7. Rogers Brubaker, 'The "diaspora" diaspora', *Ethnic and Racial Studies*, 28 (2005), p. 4.

8. Basu, *Highland Homecomings*, p. 289.

9. Ray, *Highland Heritage*, p. 128.

10. VisitScotland, 'Summary of ancestral research' (2012), p. 17; VisitScotland, 'Scotland visitor survey 2011, regional results: Edinburgh City', pp. 1–2.

11. David Hesse, *Warrior Dreams: Playing Scotsmen in Mainland Europe* (Manchester: Manchester University Press, 2014), pp. 194–5.

12. Participant interview, 27 March, 2013.

13. Focus Group, 6 February 2013.

14. Pre-arrival written survey, December 2012.

15. HESA International Students Report, 7 July 2014.

16. Theopisti Stylianou-Lambert, 'Tourists with cameras: reproducing or producing?', *Annals of Tourism Research*, 39:4 (2012), p. 1822.

17. Douglas Harper, 'Talking about pictures: a case for photo elicitation', *Visual Studies*, 17:1 (2002), pp. 13–26.

18. See for example, Sharon MacDonald, *Memorylands: Heritage and Identity in Europe Today* (London: Routledge, 2013); Laurajane Smith, *Uses of Heritage* (London: Routledge, 2006).

19. Barbara Kirschenblatt-Gimlett, 'Theorizing heritage', *Ethnomusicology*, 39:3 (1995), p. 369.

20. Charles Taylor, 'Modern social imaginaries', *Public Culture*, 14 (2002), pp. 106–7.

21. Basu, *Highland Homecomings*, p. 93

22. Participant interview, 25 April 2013.

23. Participant interview, 25 April 2013.

24. Hesse, p. 206; Celeste Ray, 'Bravehearts and patriarchs: masculinity on the pedestal in southern Scottish heritage celebration', in Ray (ed.), *Transatlantic Scots*, p. 237.

25. Participant interview, 25 April 2013.

26. Dilip Parameshwar Gaonkar, 'Toward new imaginaries: an introduction', *Public Culture*, 14:1 (2002), p. 4.

27. Pierre Nora, 'Between memory and history: les lieux de memoire', *Representations*, 26 (1989), pp. 7–25.

28. Focus group, 6 February 2013.

29. Focus group, 20 February 2013.

30. Taylor, 'Modern social imaginaries', p. 107.

31. Basu, *Highland Homecomings*, p. 93.

32. Focus group 20 February 2013.
33. Focus group, 2 February 2013.
34. Taylor et al., 'Homeland tourism', pp. 82–3; Garrido, 'Home is another country', pp. 190–6.
35. Basu, *Homeland Tourism*, p. 47.
36. Participant interview, 25 April 2013.
37. Participant interview, 23 April 2013.
38. Basu, *Highland Homecomings*, p. 47.
39. Celeste Ray 'Ancestral clanscapes and transatlantic tartaneers', in Mario Varricchio (ed.), *Back to Caledonia, Scottish Homecomings from the Seventeenth-Century to the Present* (Edinburgh: John Donald, 2012), pp. 178–9.
40. Ray, *Highland Heritage*, p. 132.
41. Basu, *Highland Homecomings*, p. 91.
42. Noel B. Salazar 'Tourism imaginaries: a conceptual approach', *Annals of Tourism Research*, 39:2 (2012), p. 866.
43. John Urry, *Consuming Places* (London: Routledge, 1995), p. 164.
44. Salazar, 'Tourism imaginaries', p. 865.
45. Duncan Light, 'Taking Dracula on holiday: the presence of "home" in the tourist encounter', in Laurajane Smith, Emma Waterton and Steve Watson (eds), *The Cultural Moment in Tourism* (London: Routledge, 2012), pp. 59–60.
46. Pre-arrival written survey, December 2012.
47. Ning Wang, 'Rethinking authenticity in the tourism experience', *Annals of Tourism Research*, 26:2 (1999), pp. 349–70.
48. Focus group, 6 February 2013.
49. J. Arnett, 'Emerging adulthood: what is it, and what is it good for?', *Child Development Perspectives*, 1 (2007), pp. 68–73; Mary Waters, *Ethnic Options: Choosing Identities in America* (Berkeley: University of California Press, 1990), p. 43.
50. Moin Syed and Lauren Mitchell, 'Race, ethnicity and emerging adulthood: retrospect and prospects', *Emerging Adulthood*, 1:2 (2013), p. 84.
51. Shaul Kelner, Leonard Saxe, Charles Kadushin et al., *Making Meaning: Participants' Experience of Birthright Israel*, Birthright Israel Research Report 2 (Waltham, MA: Maurice and Marilyn Cohen Center for Modern Jewish Studies, Brandeis University, 2000), p. 29.
52. Louie, *Chineseness Across Borders*.
53. Participant interview, 14 April 2013.
54. MacDonald, *Memorylands*, p. 18.
55. David Lowenthal, 'European landscape transformations: the rural residue', P. Groth and T. W. Bressi (eds), *Understanding Ordinary Landscapes* (New Haven: Yale University Press, 1997), p. 180.
56. MacDonald, *Memorylands*, p. 97.
57. Participant interview, 3 April 2013.

58. Nora, 'Between memory and history', p.12.
59. Susan Sontag, *On Photography* (London: Penguin Books, 2002), p. 9.
60. Pierre Bourdieu, *Outline of a Theory of Practice* (Cambridge: Cambridge University Press, 1977), p. 72; Basu, *Highland Homecomings*, p. 156.
61. Lambert, 'Tourists with cameras', p. 1820.
62. Participant interview, 23 April 2013.
63. Participant interview, 3 April 2013.
64. Pierre Bourdieu and Marie-Claire Bourdieu, 'The peasant and photography', *Ethnography*, 5:4 (2003), p. 601.
65. Garrido, 'Home is another country', p. 187.
66. Focus group, 6 February 2013.
67. Focus group, 6 February 2013.
68. Focus group, 6 February 2013.
69. Andrea Louie, 'Reterritorializing transnationalism: Chinese Americans and the Chinese "motherland"', *American Ethnologist*, 27:3 (2000), pp. 657–8.
70. Focus group, 6 February 2013.
71. Participant interview, 25 April 2013.
72. Participant interview, 6 April 2013.
73. Participant interview, 3 April 2013.
74. Matt Hodges, 'The time of the interval: historicity, modernity and epoch in rural France', *American Ethnologist*, 37:1 (2010), p. 121.
75. Participant interview, 3 April 2013.
76. David Lowenthal, *The Past is a Foreign Country* (Cambridge: Cambridge University Press, 1985).
77. Participant interview, 3 April 2013.
78. Robert Hewison, *The Heritage Industry: Britain in a Climate of Decline* (London: Methuen, 1987), p. 144.
79. Participant interview, 14 April 2013.
80. Participant interview, 6 April 2013.
81. Participant interview, 25 April 2013.
82. Focus group, 20 February 2013.
83. Participant interview, 25 April 2013.

12

Home is where the Heart is: Affinity Scots in the Scottish Diaspora

David Hesse

THE KILTED MEN ARE a yearly fixture. Visit the Swiss city of Basel during the three days of carnival – and you will come across the Scots. They will be marching in parades, playing bagpipes, wearing tartan – and often wearing other things as well: demonic masks of papier mâché, oversized heads and noses, garish fantasy costumes. They combine the Scottish pipe and drum band tradition with the local carnival aesthetic. These are the men (and only men) of Schotte Clique; their name quite simply means Scottish krewe or band. Founded in 1947, they have performed every year since without interruption. Many consider Schotte Clique one of the finest and most prestigious carnival krewes in the city; sixty-six active and several hundred passive members wear their Scottish gear with pride and meet regularly throughout the year. Carnival in Basel lasts for only three days, but the cliques provide a social identity that delivers all year round.[1] Schotte Clique change their masks and costumes with every season – the production of such material at home or at the clubhouse is one key aspect of Basel's carnival culture. But every year there will be some Scottish element involved. In February 2014, Schotte Clique marched as a group of kilted Santas, and the year before they were medieval knights, their skirt-like leg wear resembling a Scottish fashion.

The group was not created by Scottish migrants, but by Swiss enthusiasts. Official band history has it that the founders of 1947 took the idea from a decorated shop window in Basel, advertising 'Schottenwoche', a week of prices so low that they would even please a stereotypically mean Scot.[2] The old cliché of the penny-pinching, thrifty Scot continues to resonate across Europe. It stems from the time when sixteenth- and seventeenth-century Scottish merchants and pedlars came to the continent in great numbers and made their name as hard-headed businessmen. The stereotype is still very much alive and often used by retailers when marketing to the parsimonious. In Germany you can find an entire non-food supermarket chain by the name of MäcGeiz – combining the German word for thrift ('Geiz') with a pseudo-Scottish 'Mac'.[3]

In Basel, the tartan-decked shop window apparently inspired a group of young carnivalists to adopt Scottish instruments and costumes. Their first bagpipes were home-made and presumably more for show than for making music. But over the years Schotte Clique became an effective band that was hired whenever pipes were needed. In 1973, they played in the packed football stadium of St Jakob in Basel as the local team FC Basel faced Glasgow Celtic from Scotland during the European Cup. The ironic appropriation of the opponents' costume and musical instruments clearly helped: Basel beat Celtic 3–2.

The Scottish shop window seems to have been the trigger, but there may have been other inspirational forces at work in 1947. The year before, on 11 July 1946, the massed pipes and drums of the 52nd Scottish Infantry Division had been in Basel, playing in front of thousands on the main square, Münsterplatz. The 52nd Infantry Division was at that time stationed in Oldenburg, western Germany, and their pipers and drummers, like other army musical outfits, sometimes left their barracks and went to tour their surroundings. In Basel, the 52nd was met with enthusiasm. A local newspaper noted:

> At the sight of the three drum and pipe majors leading the parade, our boys and girls held their breath. Our carnivalists who had arrived in large numbers had itchy fingertips when they saw how drumsticks whirled through the air with unbelievable precision and virtuosity, only to meet again in a flash under the drummers' noses.[4]

Carnival in Switzerland and the Alps often involves quasi-military fife and drum marching bands – a remnant from the medieval and early modern Swiss mercenary tradition. The newspaper article here suggests that the Scottish military band was instantly recognised as something related – precision drumming, fancy costumes, a martial air.

The Scottish band's appearance was a major event in Basel, and some of the young men who later founded Schotte Clique may have witnessed the military musicians or at least read about them. Also, their early audiences in Basel arguably had some memories of the visiting Scots – memories which could be reactivated by the tartan carnivalists. Schotte Clique's kilted performances then were not merely a re-creation of one shopping centre's marketing campaign, but a colourful re-enactment of Scottish soldiers after the Second World War.

Such military play-acting certainly took place elsewhere in western Europe. In the Netherlands, the town of Tilburg was liberated from

Nazi occupation on 28 October 1944 by the British Army's 15th Scottish Division. To celebrate their victory, the Scots Guards' pipe band paraded through Tilburg city centre, cheered by thousands of bystanders.[5] The image of the kilted Scotsmen stuck. When a couple of years later a group of local boys was eager to set up a youth orchestra, one of the boys' fathers recalled the powerful sight of the Scottish military band. De Scotjes ('little Scots') were set up in 1953 as a homage to the kilted liberators and their bagpipers. The band still exists today, now called the Dutch Pipes and Drums.[6] Early bagpipers in West Germany also report that they were inspired by and even taught by Scottish soldiers stationed there after the war.[7]

But whether motivated by real Scottish soldiers or by a decorated shop window, these early kilted ensembles, Schotte Clique in Basel and the Scotjes in Tilburg, were a success. They were original, unique in their local markets of carnival krewes and youth orchestras, instantly recognisable with their Scottish theme and sound. They built strong followings, outlasted changing tastes and fashions – and continue to perform. Today, however, they are no longer the only Scots around. They face serious competition.

PLAYING SCOTSMEN

At the beginning of the twenty-first century, groups such as Schotte Clique and De Scotjes have become part of a substantial 'Scottish' play-acting subculture. All across north-western Europe, thousands of adult enthusiasts regularly don tartan costumes and perform as Scots.

They do so for pleasure, for the sake of excitement and experience – and sometimes with the hope of educating their audiences about Scotland's history and culture. In many ways, they resemble the hobbyists who enjoy impersonating Native Americans or medieval knights and dames – play-acting communities which, unlike the 'Scots' of Europe, have received considerable scholarly attention.[8] They must be understood as nostalgic and creative role players: imitators and appropriators of a colourful, exotic and largely imagined warrior culture. As Scottish Highlanders, they confront a modernity that they believe is lacking a 'heroic dimension'.[9] Both men and women are active in this Scottish pastime, even if images and ideas of strength and masculinity appear to be at its centre (Figure 12.1).

The self-professed Scots of Europe come in different forms. Many are musicians, drummers and bagpipers – like the Scotjes and Schotte Clique. In the Netherlands alone, some forty kilted pipe and drum bands appeared

Figure 12.1 Re-enacting Scottish soldiers: De Scotjes, Netherlands, 1971. (Photograph by W. Jansen, reproduced courtesy of Regionaal Archief Tilburg, Netherlands)

to be active in 2010. In total, there were at least 230 Scottish-looking bagpipe bands in north-western Europe that year.[10] They could be found in Germany, Austria, Switzerland, France, Belgium, the Netherlands and in all four Scandinavian countries.[11] Lesser numbers were active in Italy, Poland, the Czech Republic and Russia. In some countries, Scottish piping and drumming is remarkably organised; the Bagpipe Association of Germany (BAGEV) holds large-scale competitions.[12]

Most of these Scottish ensembles perform wherever there is demand for bagpipes and the military glamour associated with a marching band – in village parades, commemorative ceremonies, at weddings and at funerals. But there also are growing numbers of specialist bagpipe festivals – often with an explicitly Scottish theme and character. One of the main events for bagpipe fans in Switzerland each year (besides the three carnival days) is the *Basel Tattoo* – a military music spectacle loosely modelled after the Edinburgh Tattoo. The Basel version was set up in 2005 and has since evolved into a two-week-long event, selling 100,000 tickets in 2009 alone.[13]

There are others like it in Europe: the *Fulda Military Tattoo*, Germany, was first held in 2000 as an event 'for all friends of Scottish music and folklore, Royal tradition, and military aesthetic'.[14] The *Kremlin Tattoo* or *Spasskaya Bashnya* was first held (under the name *Zoria*) on Moscow's Red Square in 2007. Its advertisements for the 2009 edition saw the inner city of the Russian capital plastered with huge colour posters showing a Scottish bagpiper.[15] Smaller events include the *Malta Military Tattoo* (established 2003), the *Modena Tattoo*, Italy (1992), the *Luxembourg International Military Tattoo* (2007), and the *International Tattoo Heerlen*, Netherlands (c. 1995). There clearly is demand for pipe bands and kilted aesthetics in continental Europe, and there are festivals to satisfy it.

Other Scottish performers make do without an instrument. Some perform as athletes in a growing circuit of Highland Games strength competitions (Figure 12.2). In 2010, more than 130 'Scottish' Highland Games were held throughout northern and western Europe – most of them in the German- and Dutch-speaking countries, in Germany, Belgium, the Netherlands, Switzerland and Austria. Some of these events were professionally organised and as big as the largest Highland Games in Scotland or North America. The Swiss Highland Games championships at St Ursen (established in 2003) and the Machern Highland Games near Leipzig, Germany, each attracted 18,000 spectators in 2009.[16]

The majority of these European strength contests, however, are small and local events.[17] They take place in the countryside and do not reach national audiences. The Highland Games are part of a rural entertainment circuit and held next to fairs, carnivals, open air music festivals, cattle markets, amateur football tournaments and motorbike conventions. Unsurprisingly, they differ from both the Highland Games in Scotland and those in North America. While there are tournaments which try to tap into an international heavy athletics network with their strict rules, expert referees and single competitions, most Highland Games in Europe are amateur affairs. Often, participants perform in teams of four to six. Athletes wear self-made kilts or kilt-like garments, but nothing that compares to the elaborate and expensive uniforms worn by the pipers and drummers. Men and women compete alike and often at the same time. Many participants are young, the mood is playful, and there is usually a concert stage and a bar on the grounds (see Figure 12.3).

Figure 12.2 Fellow mountaineers – Highland Games athletes at South Tyrolean Highland Games, Falzes, Italy, 2009. (Courtesy of David Hesse)

Figure 12.3 Visitors at South Tyrolean Highland Games, Falzes, Italy, 2009. (Courtesy of David Hesse)

A third group are the re-enactors – the hobbyists who choose to theatrically recreate their favourite moments and characters from Scottish history, wearing tartan, plaid and chainmail (Figure 12.4). There are now some three dozen historical re-enactment clubs on the European continent which specialise in Scottish matters. They are part of a still growing and now well analysed hobbyist re-enactment culture which strives to recreate select historical events for the purpose of entertainment or education.[18]

At living history fairs and similar festivals, the re-enactors perform as Scotsmen and Scotswomen of the past. Most of the re-enactors settle for one historical period. They may come as medieval Scottish warriors, fighting the English alongside Wallace and Bruce in Scotland's Wars of Independence (c. 1296–1328). Anyone who wishes to wear the blue face-paint from the movie *Braveheart* (1995) will be criticised by their more informed colleagues – the historical re-enactment scene is preoccupied with the issue of factual accuracy, an almost self-policing (or peer-reviewed) community.[19]

Then there are Highland mercenaries of the Thirty Years War (1618–48), Jacobite rebels on their way to defeat at Culloden (1745–6), British Highland regiments fighting the French in America (1760s) and at Waterloo (c. 1790–1815). In Germany, one group performs

Figure 12.4 Looking for the Braveheart period: Scottish re-enactors, Aubigny-sur-Nère, France, 2009. (Courtesy of David Hesse)

as a Scottish Confederate militia, combining kilts and battle flags and echoing the long-standing mythology of a 'Scottish' South.[20] There are Scottish soldiers of both world wars, enduring hardship in Flanders and France but ultimately parading victoriously. As in most fields of hobbyist re-enactment, war and the military are the predominant themes here. Women participate either as female soldiers and warriors – or as civilians, in the background (Figure 12.5).

Some may choose to portray a history that never was. One Clan MacMahoon from Germany portrays a band of Highlanders that was driven away from Scotland by a bunch of murderous Orks – no evil landlords or English soldiers but monsters from the Tolkien novels.[21] Here we leave the world of historical re-enactment and enter the domain of fantasy, or live action role play (LARP). These performers create their own past and will not be limited by facts.

Finally, there are commemorators who focus explicitly on Scottish history. They organise festivals and set up monuments to honour characters and events from Scotland's past. They are part of what the historian Jay Winter calls the 'memory boom' of the late twentieth and early

Figure 12.5 Dames and warriors – visitors at Schotse weekend, Alden Biesen, Belgium, 2009. (Courtesy of David Hesse)

twenty-first centuries: a growing public preoccupation with the past, its remembrance and conservation.[22]

Often, these Scotland commemorators focus on moments which connect Scotland and their respective countries. In Flanders, for example, a group of Belgian enthusiasts erected a Celtic cross in August 2007 to honour the many Scottish soldiers who fought and died at Passchendaele during the Great War in 1917. A Flanders Scottish Memorial Day is now held nearby every two years. The project's initiator was a professional Flemish soldier and long-time fan of Scotland and Ireland, a founding member of the kilted Passchendaele 1917 Pipes and Drums. He first had the idea for a Scottish monument after witnessing the reburial of Private John Thomson (of Lochgelly, Fife), a Scottish soldier with the 2nd Bn. Gordon Highlanders who fell in Flanders on 4 October 1917. Thomson's remains were found in 1998 and then officially reburied at Polygon Wood Cemetery, in October 2004.[23] The Flemish soldier was so moved by the ceremony that he decided there should be a monument to 'all Scots who were involved in the Great War'.[24]

These four categories – musicians, athletes, re-enactors and commemorators – often flow together. Kilted pipe and drum bands may perform with military re-enactment units, and commemorative events may involve Scottish Highland Games as a side entertainment. The German town of Schotten, for example, holds a Scottish midsummer festival every year to commemorate the Irish and Scottish missionaries who came to Europe in the early middle ages and apparently gave the town its name.[25] When town officials set up their festival, they decided to give it a decidedly modern Scottish look: they brought in kilted pipe bands and even set up Highland Games. They relied on modern markers of Scottishness.

ORIGINS

What unites all of these activists is their enthusiasm for Scotland – and their will to express this enthusiasm publicly, to dress up in Scottish costume and to parade or perform in what is supposed to be a Scottish manner. Scotland – unlike many other nations – has a highly visible and audible following on the European continent.

To be sure, the 'Scotland' that is on their minds is not necessarily the present-day Scottish nation, the actual place on the map. On the contrary, most of the European musicians and re-enactors appear to be passionate about the Scottish past. They either hope to tap into 'old' Scottish customs such as piping or Highland Games, last remnants of a different age, or they strive to commemorate and even recreate specific historical events in the present.

Their approach to history is selective: nobody (to the author's knowledge) attempts to re-enact Scotland's industrial or mercantile past[26] or to commemorate the recent rise and fall of the Royal Bank of Scotland. Rather, the European hobbyists stick rather firmly to what we can call the Scottish dreamscape – the world of kilts, Celts, clans, tartan and bagpipes.

The Scottish dreamscape is, of course, a well-established romantic fantasy of Scottish history. A largely mythical notion of Scotland as a Celtic warrior society that was dreamed up by novelists, military entrepreneurs and politicians in the late eighteenth and nineteenth centuries.[27] While it contains bits and pieces of genuine Highland history and custom, its modern and familiar form is a historical fantasy.[28] The continental play-actors thus are stuck in a past that never really was. Even when they target real twentieth-century Scottish regiments it is often their pseudo-historical Highland uniforms which excite them and form a key part of the play-acting experience.[29]

European enthusiasm for Scottish performances is a fairly recent phenomenon. It began, as indicated above, after 1945 – much under the impression of the kilted soldiers who fought in Europe during the Second World War or were stationed there afterwards. The first continental imitators were bagpipe musicians inspired by Scottish army bands. Their numbers grew during the European folk music revival of the 1970s, when popular interest in all things 'Celtic' surged and Scottish and Irish folk music came to serve as a template for Europeans who yearned to rediscover and reinvent their own traditional music. In the drone of the Great Highland Bagpipe, some Europeans claimed to hear an echo of their own lost heritage.

The Scottish boom, however, came in the 1990s, when the number of kilted bagpipe bands, re-enactment groups and Scottish festivals multiplied. There were perhaps two or three Highland Games events in Germany before the year 1990 – but fifty-six such events in 2010.[30] One simple reason for this increase in Scottish activity is technological advance: The Internet connected hitherto marginal interests into powerful subcultures. Suddenly, a bagpipe enthusiast could find like-minded people and set up a band.

But there are other reasons as well. First, the mythology of the Scottish Highlander was re-appreciated in popular culture and spread to many corners of the earth. Several successful Hollywood films dealt with kilted Scottish warriors – *Highlander* (1986), *Braveheart* (1995), *Rob Roy* (1995) and later the Disney production *Brave* (2012).[31] In fantasy literature, the American writer Diana Gabaldon had a bestseller with her erotic time travel series *Outlander* (from 1991) which spawned an entire genre of Scottish bodice ripper novels.[32] The Scottish dreamscape was reactivated.

Also, Scotland was arguably more present in the international media during the 1990s and 2000s. Scottish devolution, the reopening of the Scottish parliament in 1999, and the many passionate discussions of what Scottish identity is – this all may have had an impact at a time when other European regions felt disenchanted with their nation states or the European Union and demanded more autonomy, even more identity. Scottish nationalism – with its apparent wealth of symbols and traditions – impressed a number of Europeans.

Finally, the Scottish dreamscape appears to meet a zeitgeist demand. In the age of hobbits and Hogwarts, pre-modern counter-worlds are one again in vogue. I have come to the conclusion – after many interviews with the self-professed Scots of Europe – that the continental Highlanders have a strong interest in heroic European history and that they use Scotland – or rather: dreams of Scotland – to express this interest.

They choose Scotland as a proxy because they consider their own national or regional heritage to be either unavailable (not yet processed by filmmakers and novelists), unexciting (not charged with the mythology of warfare, resistance and rebellion), or too difficult, politically tarnished by past abuse (as in the case of Germany, where Nazi appropriations of certain Germanic symbols made their carefree celebration impossible). The Scottish dreamscape provides a safe playground.

Interestingly, there is nothing quite like the 'Scots' of Europe. No other European nation has its costumes, sports, and songs appropriated by outsiders on this scale. There are no Basque, Slovak or Norwegian festivals that could in any way match the Scottish activity. While Ireland and Wales certainly have their firm place in the long and ongoing history of continental Celtophilia, they, too, fail to mobilise a comparable festive crowd. Yes, there are Irish pubs in almost every larger European city, and at some of them there will be American-style Saint Patrick's Day celebrations on 17 March. But one would be hard-pressed to find several thousand Dutchmen, Austrians or Italians dressing up as Irishmen. How does an Irishman look, anyway? With the Scot, the answer is clear. It is the Scottish mythology's familiarity and availability which heightens its popularity.

AFFINITY SCOTS

One thing that is NOT responsible for the remarkable spread of Scottish enthusiasm across north-western Europe is Scottish emigration. We can say this with some certainty. Playing Highlander is not an expatriate phenomenon. While it is possible to come across the odd biochemical engineer from Kirkcaldy who has joined a kilted pipe and drum band in Geneva or Copenhagen due to reasons of homesickness or sociability, migrants are in no way essential to this Scottish subculture. And most of the kilted activists who set up Highland Games competitions in rural Europe have no family connections to Scotland, the place on the map.

Only very few of the European celebrants justify their activities with Scottish roots. They do not usually claim descent from Scottish ancestors. This phenomenon, then, does not demonstrate a heightened public awareness of the medieval and early modern Scottish migrations to continental Europe.[33] Most of the European play-actors learn about these movements only through their love for Scotland – if at all.

The continental enthusiasm is a form of role play, a masquerade, and openly declared so. The overwhelming majority of the European pipers, dancers, re-enactors do not consider themselves Scottish by either birth or ancestry. This sets them apart from the many tartan activists in North America and Australasia – men and women who dress up in Scottish fashion and hold Scottish events in order to celebrate their known or assumed Scottish ancestors.[34]

Their lack of roots sometimes dismays the Europeans. Unfortunately, I have no Scottish ancestors, they will say in interviews, or, I have not found any yet. Some do their own research and come up with historical links between their home towns and Scotland – links that they hope will add some weight to their performances. For instance, a group of passionate re-enactors from Germany – Mackay's Regiment of Foote – portray Highland mercenaries who fought on German soil for the Swedish king during the Thirty Years War.[35] They choose a moment in Scottish history that somehow connects them to Scotland.

But the 'Scots' of Europe are not Scottish in any legal or ancestral sense. They know this and are usually aware that there is a place on the map called Scotland, populated by modern-day Scots, that the sartorial and musical traditions they celebrate somehow 'belong' to other people, that they are wearing someone else's clothes. Some of the play-actors are slightly worried about this: What will the Scots say if they find out? But most are ready to defend their actions: the problem with the 'real' Scots is that they do so little with their wonderful heritage. One German re-enactor told me how he first flew to Scotland and then felt really out of place in his kilt and gear. 'I landed in Edinburgh and wondered: why am I the only one here wearing a kilt? Have I come to the wrong country?'[36] The 'real' Scots did not live up to his expectations.

Indeed, many of Scotland's most passionate European fans find the actual place a bit disappointing. When I visited a Highland Games event in Strathpeffer, Scotland, in 2010 there were some beautifully dressed Austrians attending. The ladies watched their men compete and told me, 'Yes, it is nice here, but there are no real Highlanders, not like at home.' Scotland is great, but the Austrians do the better Highland Games. The Scottish dreamscape, it appears, is open to all who have the skills to participate.

How then do these friendly impersonators fit into the Scottish 'diaspora'? Scotland, like other nations, has taken a strong interest in her worldwide following in the past decade. Government officials, scholars and entrepreneurs are eager to connect with or find out more about the many millions of people around the world who feel related to Scotland, a part of the nation.[37] The government-orchestrated *Homecoming Scotland* campaigns of 2009 and 2014 were only the most visible symptoms of this heightened interest.[38] Such activity makes sense in times of financial distress, and Scotland is not the only country eager to tap into its migrant networks.[39] Notably, Ireland has had some success with diaspora engagement during the recent economic crisis – a crisis, it must be said, that has seen Irish emigration numbers soar again.[40]

Any approach to the issue of diaspora raises the question of membership and entitlement: Who can be part of the international Scottish community, and who perhaps cannot? Will a government engagement plan exclusively target migrants and their descendants – people who can document their ancestral ties to Scotland? Or should the officials be interested in enthusiasts as well – people who are ready to spend considerable sums on their passion for Scotland, be they related or not?

The Homecoming Scotland organisers realised early on that it would be weird (and perhaps even unpleasant) to have an 'ethnic only' celebration. Everyone should be invited to come and spend money in Scotland. But at the same time they did not want to ruin the diaspora brand. A year of 'Homecoming' should be about more than just tourism. So the Event Scotland agency came up with the term 'Affinity Scots' – people who consider themselves related to Scotland even though they might lack any roots in the place. Homecoming, we were assured, was for everybody.[41]

This makes sense. In the realm of marketing, tourism and perhaps even politics, diaspora must mean people who are passionate about the supposed homeland. The Scottish diaspora campaign targets enthusiasts, people who visibly support and celebrate Scotland and who may want to return, temporarily, as tourists and investors. There is no point in targeting those who carry an old Scottish surname but do not care about that in any way. That would perhaps be an interesting study: people who are descendants but who do not care.

Affinity Scots are the opposite thing: people who have no proven roots but care greatly. And there are plenty of them – and not only in Europe. One group of Affinity Scots that apparently was on the Homecoming organisers' minds hails from the United States: Clan MacBubba, a fictional Scottish clan with the motto 'Big, Bad, and Plaid'.[42] Ethnographers who have looked at the many and sizable Scottish festivals in the United States have suggested that at least some of the tartan-clad celebrants have no roots in Scotland.[43] They join in because they have a love for Scottish history and culture, a partner, friend or neighbour with Scottish roots – or because there was a proficient bagpipe band in their home town and they felt the urge to participate.

In the end, the difference between the European role-players and the American roots enthusiasts may be smaller than expected. It is their love for Scotland – the Scottish dreamscape – that makes them join a kilted band or compete at a Highland Games event. Their Scottishness may have more to do with the things they wear, sing and do than with their family trees. Membership in the Scottish diaspora always requires effort. It never springs automatically from a bloodline.

FUTURE

Some European governments would be thrilled to have an international following like Scotland – roots or not, fantasy or not. But how long will this continental enthusiasm for Scottish custom and costume last? To be sure, many of the clubs, bands and festivals described here will have a limited lifespan. Play-actors grow up or grow tired, shift their attention to the next exciting mythology once they feel that they are 'done' with playing Highlanders. Indeed, some of the self-professed 'Scots' of Europe will tell you what they were before the donned the tartan outfit: Native Americans, medieval knights and dames, Confederate soldiers, live action role play elves and hobbits. Those who exit the Scottish game will only rarely find an heir to keep their pipe bands, re-enactment outfits or Highland Games events alive. True, the kilted Swiss carnivalists of Schotte Clique have been around for seven decades. But the majority of Scottish ensembles and events in Europe appear to come and go like other bands and festivals.

What endures, however, is the dreamscape itself – the rich and seasoned set of Scottish myths and images which continues to enchant and inspire readers, dreamers, and entrepreneurs since at least the late eighteenth century, when the faux-Gaelic poetry of Ossian first stirred European *hommes de lettres* from east to west.[44] The idea of a Scottish counter-world – old, exotic, heroic, threatened but recalcitrant – appears to be an integral part of modern European consciousness.

Scotland has a function as a land of living history, a site of memory for the European north – a back-up archive for those who yearn for the wild past. Long before the first continental imitators started to borrow kilted pipe bands and athletic events, the Scottish Highlander has been embraced as a survivor from the periphery, an important relation and example.[45] Russian writers employed Ossian to formulate their own epic poetry in the early nineteenth century, and German novelists looked to Sir Walter Scott when approaching their own past.[46] The Scottish dreamscape has served as a template in Europe's age of nationalism – and it helps to re-imagine European roots and heritage today.

Of course, the Scottish dreamscape is not a stable set of myths and images. It has constantly evolved, adapted to circumstances and demands. Yet it remains recognisable, familiar and exotic at the same time. Its central themes recur ever since Highland schoolteacher James Macpherson published his first Ossianic verses in 1760. They concern the clash of tradition and modernisation, heroic warfare and resistance, and the need for distinctiveness. These themes are still at the heart of what the 'Scots' of Europe perform and celebrate today.

Distinctiveness may be the key issue. As is well established, the rise and spread of Scotland's Highland mythology in the late eighteenth and nineteenth century was inextricably linked to the nation's political integration into the United Kingdom. Scotland's nineteenth-century elites embraced a faux-Celtic identity to maximise Scottish difference from England – to remain non-English. 'Highlandised Scotland was almost as different as it was possible to be from England', notes Richard Finlay.[47] Scottish military entrepreneurs employed Highland dress and music to create a new and unmistakable brand. Their Highland regiments became a lasting success – in Scotland and beyond.[48]

The issue of distinctiveness perhaps strikes a special chord in Europe today. It appears to be important to many of the continental play-actors that Scotland has 'remained herself' despite more than 300 years of assimilative pressure. The presumed century-old Scottish struggle for identity against an overly dominant neighbour is something that some modern Europeans feel they can relate to. Here are some fairly typical statements from interviews with European Highlanders. Why did they choose to be Scots and not something else?

> [The Scots were] able to survive even 1,000 years neighbourhood to England and Ireland. There is some truth in it, we Luxemburgers are sensitive about that.
>
> (Georges, Neihaisgen, Luxembourg)

> They fight for independence. We have such people too in Holland, in Friesland, they want independence, too. I like this kind of people who fight for something.
>
> (Charles, Alblasserdam, Netherlands)

> Scotland and Flanders have many things in common. The struggle for freedom, independence. We feel the same in Flanders. (Frank, Flanders, Belgium)

> South Tyrol is a logical location for Highland Games. South Tyrol in Italy, that's very much like Scotland and England. There is a distinctive pride in both places. The Scots are a free mountain people – but they are not free.
>
> (Ingemar, South Tyrol, Italy)

These continental Highlanders seem unaware of Scotland's many active roles in both the parliamentary union of 1707 as well as the colonial era of the British Empire. They subscribe to a history of Scottish victimhood and make their costumed performances an act of solidarity with an imaginary Scottish resistance. They clearly seem to be making a statement about their own political situations. Perhaps we must understand at least some of their kilted masquerades as a form of stealth nationalism: they portray Highlanders, but they mean themselves: old, distinctive, renitent.

It remains to be seen whether the Scottish referendum of 2014 has had any effect on the 'Scots' of Europe. Certainly some of the continental groups supported the movement for Scottish independence. But others may have sensed that such a step would leave them with a nation that could no longer be mistaken for a colonised territory. Independence would end the myth of victimhood. Much of the Scottish dreamscape's enduring magic and attractiveness results from Scotland's status as an unfinished nation. It is the struggle for distinctiveness which inspires so many continental (and arguably American and Australasian) Highlanders. If Scotland were to become a proper nation – with all her petty problems and responsibilities – it would perhaps turn into a place like many others and lose some of its bewildering glamour. Some Scots may say it is about time.

NOTES

1. Jeffry M. Diefendorf, 'Princes and fools, parades and wild women: creating, performing and preserving urban identity through carnival in Cologne and Basel', in Jeffry M. Diefendorf and Janet Ward (eds), *Transnationalism and the German City* (New York: Palgrave Macmillan, 2014), pp. 161–72.
2. <http://www.schotteclique.ch> (17 November 2014), and author's interview with Roland Bacher, Schotte Clique (18 July 2009).
3. <http://www.mac-geiz.de> (17 November 2014).
4. 'Unseren Buben und Mädchen verging beim Anblick der drei voranschreitenden Tambour- und Pipe-Majore Hören und Sehen. Unsern Fasnächtlern, die sich in hellen Scharen eingefunden hatten, zuckte es in den Fingerspitzen, als sie sahen, wie die Trommel- und Paukenschlegel mit einer unglaublichen Präzision und Virtuosität durch die Luft wirbelten, um sich dann blitzschnell unter dem Nasenspitz der Tambouren wieder zu vereinigen.' Anon., 'Schotten und Basler voneinander begeistert', *National-Zeitung*, 12 July 1946, p. 5. Several photographs of the concert are held at Staatsarchiv Basel-Stadt, Basel, Switzerland.
5. Regionaalarchief Tilburg holds photographs and newspaper articles documenting the 1944 parade.

6. See the band's fiftieth anniversary publication, *50 Jaar Dutch Pipes & Drums: Opgericht in Mei 1953 as Jeugddoedelzakband de Scotjes* (Tilburg: Vereniging Dutch Pipes & Drums, 2003).

7. David Hesse, *Warrior Dreams: Playing Scotsmen in Mainland Europe* (Manchester: Manchester University Press, 2014), ch. 5.

8. Christian F. Feest (ed.), *Indians and Europe: An Interdisciplinary Collection of Essays* (Aachen: Herodot, 1987); Rayna Green, 'The tribe called Wannabe: playing Indian in America and Europe', *Folklore*, 27 (1988), pp. 30–55; Katrin Sieg, *Ethnic Drag: Performing Race, Nation, and Sexuality in West Germany* (Ann Arbor: University of Michigan Press, 2002); Erwin Hoffmann, *Mittelalterfeste in der Gegenwart: Die Vermarktung des Mittelalters im Spannungsfeld zwischen Authentizität und Inszenierung* (Stuttgart: Ibidem, 2005); Valentin Groebner, *Das Mittelalter hört nicht auf* (Munich: Beck, 2008); Katharina Zeppezauer-Wachauer, *Kurzwîl als Entertainment. Das Mittelalterfest als populärkulturelle Mittelalterrezeption* (Marburg: Tectum, 2012).

9. Charles Taylor, *The Ethics of Authenticity* (Cambridge, MA: Harvard University Press, 1991), p. 4.

10. Hesse, *Warrior Dreams*, ch. 5.

11. On kilted bagpipe bands in Scandinavia, see Mats d' Hermansson, *From Icon to Identity: Scottish Piping and Drumming in Scandinavia* (Göteborg: Göteborg University Press, 2003).

12. <http://www.bagev.de> (17 November 2014).

13. <http://www.baseltattoo.ch> (17 November 2014), and author's interview with Erik Julliard, Basel Tattoo (24 August 2009).

14. 'Das besondere Ereignis für alle Freunde schottischer Musik und Folklore, royaler Tradition und militärischer Ästhetik', <www.military-tattoo.de> (13 March 2010).

15. It appears that the *Zoria* festival was created by the Moscow Caledonian Society, then adopted by the Russian Ministry of Defence. See <http://www.kremlin-military-tattoo.ru/en/about/> (17 November 2014).

16. Numbers are the organisers' estimates and usually based on sold or issued tickets.

17. David Hesse, 'Scots for a day: the Highland Games of Europe', *History Scotland*, 11:3 (2011), pp. 24–30.

18. On historical re-enactment, see Wolfgang Hochbruck, *Reenactment: Formen der Living History. Eine Typologie* (Bielefeld: Transcript, 2013). Ian McCalman and Paul Pickering (eds), *Historical Re-enactment: From Realism to Affective Turn* (Basingstoke: Palgrave Macmillan, 2010).

19. Daria Radtchenko, 'Simulating the past: reenactment and the quest for truth in Russia', *Rethinking History*, 10:1 (2006), pp. 127–48; Stephen Gapps, 'Mobile monuments: a view of historical reenactment and authenticity from inside the costume cupboard of history', *Rethinking History*, 13:3 (2009), pp. 395–409.

20. <http://www.santee-artillery.de> (17 November 2014). On the persistent idea that Scottish migration to the American South created a Celtic-Southern identity, see Rowland Berthoff, 'Celtic mist over the South', *Journal of Southern History*, 52:4 (1986), pp. 523–46.
21. <http://www.macmahoon.de> (17 November 2014).
22. Jay Winter, *Remembering War. The Great War between Memory and History in the Twentieth Century* (New Haven: Yale University Press, 2006).
23. Thomson's remains were identified by his badge and the initials 'J. R. T.' on his pocketknife. The reburial took place on 21 October 2004. Author's communication with Erwin Ureel (21 September 2010). See also CWGC's online archives, <www.cwgc.org> (10 September 2010).
24. Erwin Ureel and John Sutherland, 'A Scottish monument in Flanders', in *Will Ye Come to Flanders* (brochure published by Scottish Memorial in Flanders Campaign, 2007).
25. Author's communication with Tina Ulm, Schotten Tourismus (29 March 2011).
26. With the possible exception of the Dutch town of Veere, where some re-enactors have been concerned with the Scottish wool merchants of the early modern era. See <http://www.veere-schotland.nl> (17 November 2014) and Peter Blom, *Scots Girn about Grits, Gruel and Greens: Four Centuries of Scots Life in Veere* (Veere, Netherlands: Stichting Veere-Schotland, 2003).
27. On the construction of the Scottish dreamscape, see Peter Womack, *Improvement and Romance: Constructing the Myth of the Highlands* (Basingstoke: Macmillan, 1989). On its afterlife, see David McCrone, *Scotland – the Brand: The Making of Scottish Heritage* (Edinburgh: Edinburgh University Press, 1995). Colin Kidd and James Coleman, 'Mythical Scotland', in T. M. Devine and J. Wormald (eds), *The Oxford Handbook of Modern Scottish History, 1500–2010* (Oxford: Oxford University Press, 2012), pp. 62–77.
28. On how customs may be bound into new traditions, see Eric Hobsbawm, 'Inventing traditions', in E. Hobsbawm and T. Ranger (eds), *The Invention of Tradition* (Cambridge: Cambridge University Press, 1983), pp. 1–14.
29. On Scottish military costume, see Thomas Abler, *Hinterland Warriors and Military Dress: European Empires and Exotic Uniforms* (Oxford: Berg, 1999).
30. See Hesse, *Warrior Dreams*.
31. David Martin-Jones, *Scotland: Global Cinema* (Edinburgh: Edinburgh University Press, 2009). These films, of course, built upon a tradition of pseudo-Scottish films; see Duncan Petrie, *Screening Scotland* (London: British Film Institute, 2000).
32. Euan Hague and David Stenhouse, '"A very interesting place": representing Scotland in U.S. romance novels', in B. Schoene (ed.), *The Edinburgh*

Companion to Contemporary Scottish Literature (Edinburgh: Edinburgh University Press, 2007), pp. 354–61.

33. On early modern migrations to Europe, see T. C. Smout, N. C. Landsman and T. M. Devine, 'Scottish emigration in the seventeenth and eighteenth centuries' in N. Canny (ed.), *Europeans on the Move* (Oxford: Clarendon, 1994), pp. 76–111; David Worthington, *Scots in Habsburg service, 1618–1648* (Leiden: Brill, 2004); Steve Murdoch, *Network North: Scottish Kin, Commercial and Covert Associations in Northern Europe, 1603–1746* (Leiden: Brill, 2006); Stephen Conway, 'Scots, Britons, and Europeans: Scottish military service, 1739–1783', *Historical Research*, 82:215 (2009), pp. 114–30; T. M. Devine and David Hesse (eds), *Scotland and Poland: Historical Encounters, 1500–2010* (Edinburgh: John Donald, 2011).

34. Rowland Berthoff, 'Under the kilt: variations on the Scottish-American ground', *Journal of American Ethnic History* (Spring 1982), pp. 5–34; Celeste Ray, *Highland Heritage: Scottish Americans in the American South* (Chapel Hill: University of North Carolina Press, 2001); Paul Basu, *Highland Homecomings: Genealogy and Heritage Tourism in the Scottish Diaspora* (London: Routledge, 2007); T. M. Devine, *To the Ends of the Earth: Scotland's Global Diaspora, 1750–2010* (London: Allen Lane, 2011); Angela McCarthy, *Scottishness and Irishness in New Zealand Since 1840* (Manchester: Manchester University Press, 2011).

35. Mackay's Regiment of Foote, <http://regiment-mackay.de> (17 November 2014).

36. 'Ich bin in Edinburg gelandet und hab mich gewundert, warum ich da der einzige mit einem Kilt war. Bin ich jetzt im falschen Land, oder was?' Author's interview with Helmut Huck, Clan MacConn of Drumfinnan, Germany (12 September 2009).

37. Duncan Sim and Ian McIntosh, 'Connecting with the Scottish diaspora', *Scottish Affairs*, 58 (2007), pp. 78–95.

38. David Hesse, 'Finding neverland: affinity Scots and the Homecoming Scotland campaign', in M. Varricchio (ed.), *Back to Caledonia. Scottish Return Migration from the Sixteenth Century to the Present* (Edinburgh: John Donald, 2012), pp. 220–40.

39. Anon., 'The magic of diasporas', *The Economist*, 19 November 2011. Accessed via <www.economist.com/node/21538742> (17 November 2014).

40. Ciara Kenny, 'Initiatives that put Ireland at top of diaspora engagement', *Irish Times*, 1 November 2014. Accessed via <http://www.irishtimes.com> (17 November 2014).

41. Author's interviews with Leon Thompson, EventScotland (15 May 2009), and Michael Jarvis, VisitScotland (8 April 2009).

42. <http://www.caberdancer.com/MBhome.htm> (17 November 2014).

43. Berthoff, 'Under the kilt'.

44. Dafydd Moore (ed.), *Ossian and Ossianism* (London: Routledge, 2004); Howard Gaskill (ed.), *Receptions of Ossian in Europe* (London: Thoemmes, 2004).

45. Interest in Scotland as a reservoir of European history arguably began before the nation's nineteenth-century Highlandisation. See Martin Rackwitz, *Travels to Terra Incognita: The Scottish Highlands and Hebrides in Early Modern Travellers' Accounts, c. 1600 to 1800* (Münster: Waxmann, 2007).

46. Peter France, 'Fingal in Russia', in H. Gaskill (ed.), *Receptions of Ossian in Europe* (London: Thoemmes, 2004), pp. 259–73; Cairns Craig, 'Scott's staging of the nation', *Studies in Romanticism*, 40:1 (2001), pp. 13–29.

47. Richard J. Finlay, 'Queen Victoria and the cult of Scottish monarchy', in E. J. Cowan and R. J. Finlay (eds), *Scottish History: The Power of the Past* (Edinburgh: Edinburgh University Press, 2002), pp. 209–25, here: p. 150.

48. Robert Clyde, *From Rebel to Hero: The Image of the Highlander, 1745–1830* (East Linton: Tuckwell Press, 1995).

13

What Scottish Diaspora?

David Fitzpatrick

I

FOR EVERY HISTORIAN OF human migration, there surely comes a moment of suspicion that one has been asking the wrong question. Instead of asking why so many people have moved so far, why not ask why so many have failed to do so? Is long-distance migration a perplexing abnormality, or a normal and recurring element of human behaviour? Most studies, whether economic, sociological or psychological, still treat long-distance movement as a disruptive aberration or 'haemorrhage', reflecting structural inadequacies in the home environment or deliberate discrimination against sub-groups within societies or families. The eruption of mass migration is most easily envisaged as a product of catastrophes such as war or famine, or else as a baneful consequence of agrarian or industrial restructuring. Even economic historians, for whom fluctuations in migration are typically explained as rational responses to differential employment opportunities, tend to deplore the regional disparities that forced tens of millions of Europeans to expand the range of rational action beyond home boundaries. Though the outcome of mass migration may be to accelerate globalisation and economic convergence, most economists would still prefer this to be pursued through movements of capital and information rather than labour. While rational, 'enterprising' responses to pull factors are widely admired, similar responses to push factors are treated as regrettable, sometimes tragic consequences of political or managerial failure (a form of 'exile').

Yet, for each individual, movement *almost always* offers the prospect of a better job, a more congenial environment, a happier life somewhere else, whether across the road, the country or the ocean. However good life is, it might be even better elsewhere. From this viewpoint, the central issue for the historian of diaspora is to explain the nature and force of inhibiting factors such as transportation, funding, familial and social ties, aversion to physical or moral risk and fear of isolation. If everyone, or almost everyone, is migratory by disposition, then everyone is more or less motivated by impulses such as a sense of adventure, a desire to grasp novel opportunities and a sense of confinement at home. In pursuing these impulses, whether within the homeland or beyond, migrants will attempt to acquire essential skills such as canniness, enterprise, sensitivity to alien environments, adaptability and versatility. These reputedly quintessential 'Scottish' virtues are no less applicable to Irish migrants, emerging from a very different home culture, and indeed to humanity in general. Most students of national diasporas, including the Irish, marvel at the ingenuity with which so many migrants, often ill-educated and without obviously relevant skills, met the social and economic challenges of being 'strangers in a strange land'. The fact that home skills were often unexportable greatly reduced the comparative advantages of upbringing enjoyed by the Scots or English by comparison with the Irish. If so, background and origin are much less important in defining the dynamics of diaspora than differential opportunities in the host countries.[1]

This raises the issue of national narratives of migration, and how such narratives come to be applied to migrations from different territories. From a global perspective, there is little point in analysing 'Scottish', 'British' or 'Irish' diasporas as if these were distinct and cohesive entities. If human migration results from a universal impulse, then racial and national origins are of limited importance in explaining migratory behaviour. Why then do so many scholars continue to portray mass migrations as unique and distinctive outcomes of national histories, typically highlighting national contrasts and underplaying variations of experience within each national diaspora?

Let me suggest two factors encouraging ethnocentrism in migration studies. First, it is impossible to write coherently about the movements of millions of individuals without both subdividing the human flow and attributing collective characteristics to each subdivision. There is of course a place for studies displaying the infinite variety of the migratory experience and subverting unitary narratives; but such works would have no impact or interest in the absence of unitary narratives worthy of subversion. Thus concentration on peculiarities of the 'Irish' or 'Scottish' or 'British' elements in mass migration is an obvious and effective device for organising multitudinous evidence according to widely recognised categories. The national focus has been reinforced by the practice of official enumerators, whether in North America or Australasia or the United Kingdom, who recorded later nineteenth-century departures and arrivals by 'nationality' (including Irish and Scots) as well as citizenship.

The choice of national origin as the primary discriminant, rather than class or gender or language or religion, also reflects the fact that the study of diasporas is itself an outcome of debates about nationality and ethnicity. These debates generated myths and beliefs about the causes and consequences of mass migration which inspired pioneer scholars in their quest for evidence and explanations. In the Irish case, mass emigration was blamed on the Great Famine and thence misgovernment, a gross simplification which nevertheless still has some academic advocates. The existence of a refutable myth has been a powerful inspiration for revisionist histories of Irish migration, concentrating academic minds on social and economic processes which might otherwise have aroused no more interest than variations in the price of flax or in real wages. The political resonance of the Irish diaspora, and of competing models for explaining its scale and perpetuation, is as strong today as ever.[2] The same surely applies to Scotland, where moral responsibility for emigration associated with the 'Highland Clearances' remains an emotive issue. Should the 'great migration' be depicted as proof of a flawed social and economic structure, or as a triumph of globalisation achieved by Scots taking advantage of imperial and international opportunities?

How successfully have the leading advocates of a 'Scottish diaspora' justified their territorial claim? My perspective is that of an Irishist, always uneasy at attempts to subsume the diasporic Irish as a mere sub-group of 'Britannia's Children', an interesting variant of the 'main English streams' of 'the British diaspora' emerging from the 'British Isles' or 'Archipelago'.[3] In assessing the validity of the Scottish claim to distinctiveness, I shall try to locate the Scottish experience on a scale stretching between the English and Irish diasporas. In many respects, Scotland occupied an intermediate position between Ireland, still predominantly agricultural in the early twentieth century, and England, where urbanisation and industrialisation were most advanced. In its demography, marked by relatively high marital fertility, low nuptiality and substantial out-migration, it has been argued that pre-war Scotland had more in common with Ireland than England.[4] Is this affinity confirmed by comparative study of its diaspora? My analysis concentrates on the 'great migration' out of Europe between the mid nineteenth century and the Great War, bypassing the less measurable diaspora of Scottish capital and 'Scottish religious and secular ideas'.[5]

In evaluating the case for a 'Scottish diaspora', I shall apply a number of tests or questions. First, does the scale of international migration from Scotland rank as an exceptional displacement of population by contemporary European standards? Second, were the economic push factors distinctively Scottish? Third, did the emigrants carry with them a shared national culture likely to affect their human performance elsewhere? Fourth, were the Scots conspicuously 'successful' by comparison with the Irish or the English? Fifth, to what extent did they and their descendants function as an ethnic group in their places of settlement? Finally, has the diaspora had a transformative impact on Scotland itself? Though a positive score in any of these tests might be considered a sufficient condition for classifying Scottish migration as a distinct diaspora, the case for placing the Scots in the same category as the Irish or the Scandinavians seems weak in the absence of a uniformly positive scoreboard. My aim is not to answer these questions myself, beyond exploring some readily available yet neglected statistical sources, but to indicate whether or not convincing answers have been supplied by scholars of the Scottish diaspora. Without international standards of comparison, the notion of a specifically 'Scottish' diaspora must remain a declaration rather than a justification of independence.

II

The most forceful and wide-ranging advocate of 'Scotland's Global Diaspora', Sir Tom Devine, has rightly warned against the 'seductive intellectual traps of exceptionalism and boosterism'. Yet even he, in his zeal to encapsulate and dramatise Scottish traditions of migration, occasionally boosts the scale of Scottish migration beyond credibility. It is technically true that 'Scotland had a higher rate of outward movement ... than virtually any other country' during the great migration, with movement on an 'extraordinary numerical scale'. But is it *really* 'little wonder that Scotland can be regarded as the European country of emigration' between 1825 and 1938? Devine, and other scholars echoing Michael Flinn's statistical survey of *Scottish Population History* (1977), marvel that at least 2.3 million Scots went overseas over that period, and that, in certain decades, net outward movement was equivalent to more than two-fifths of Scotland's recorded natural increase (far more in the 1920s).[6] Marjory Harper maintains that 'Scotland's loss of around 61 per cent of natural increase between 1853 and 1930 reinforced a well-established and self-conscious culture of diaspora'.[7] Flinn, admittedly reliant on a rather haphazard comparison with pre-war Scandinavian ratios, concludes that 'Scotland may well ... come higher than Norway and second only to Ireland in this unenviable championship'.[8] Comparative estimates of European overseas emigration rates confirm Scotland's high ranking (along with Ireland and Norway): top of the league in the 1920s, second in the 1850s and 1900s, third in the 1860s, 1870s and 1880s, and sixth in the 1890s.[9]

Yet, by Irish standards, such rates of movement seem pitiably small. Only by English (and some European) standards did the Scottish 'great migration' seem 'extraordinary' in its scale. The most widely reproduced statistics of gross overseas passenger movement out of Europe indicate that the gap between Irish and Scottish outward movement, hitherto vast, diminished after the 1860s. The Irish were about three times as likely to leave Europe as the Scots in the 1850s and 1860s and twice as likely in the 1880s and 1890s, with a smaller gap in the 1870s and a proportionate excess of Scots in 1901–10. The difference between Scottish and English rates of outward movement was almost invariably smaller, never exceeding a multiple of two.[10] Yet these returns of gross passenger movement greatly understate the true disparity in scale between Irish and Scottish emigration, which is better expressed in estimates of net outward migration. Though no statistical returns of return movement of British subjects by nationality were compiled before 1895, those for the period 1895–1900 indicate that 69 Scots returned from overseas for every 100 Scottish passengers leaving UK ports, compared with 48 for the Irish and 68 for the English.[11] In addition, Irish migration to Britain greatly exceeded that from England and even Scotland to other parts of the United Kingdom. It follows that passenger movement to extra-European ports is a poor proxy for comparative rates of long-term outward migration.

Let us return to the index of net movement most often cited by Scottish historians, based on the difference between 'natural increase' (the excess of registered births over deaths) and the recorded change in population over an intercensal period. Net outward migration from Ireland vastly *exceeded* natural increase in every decade from the 1860s to the 1900s, by a factor of almost three in the 1880s when the corresponding Scottish ratio was 41 per cent. In other words, by this rough and ready measure, the Irish were seven times as likely as the Scots to migrate. As Table 13.1 implies, the multiple was even greater in other decades (6 in the 1860s, 8 in the 1870s, 21 in the 1890s, down to 3 in the 1900s). Over the entire period 1861–1911, the ratios of out-migration to natural increase for Ireland, Scotland, and England were 184, 30, and 8, English net outward migration falling far below the Scottish rate in the 1860s and 1870s.[12] On this scale, the *proportionate* gap between the rates for Scotland and England was only slightly narrower than that between the Irish and Scottish rates.

Table 13.1 Net outward migration from each country in the UK, 1861–1911

Country	Ireland			Scotland			England		
Decade	NOM	NI	Ratio	NOM	NI	Ratio	NOM	NI	Ratio
1861–1871	925	538	161	117	416	28	57	2,703	2
1871–1881	633	396	163	93	469	20	150	3,412	4
1881–1891	727	257	283	218	508	41	619	3,647	17
1891–1901	475	229	207	52	500	10	56	3,581	2
1901–1911	325	256	127	254	543	47	506	4,049	12
Total	3,085	1,676	184	734	2,436	30	1,388	17,392	8

Note: For each country in each decade, the table shows the percentage ratio of estimated net outward migration (NOM) to natural increase (NI), both given in thousands. NOM represents the difference between NI (the excess of registered births over deaths) and the net intercensal increase in population (invariably negative in the case of Ireland). NOM incorporates all movement out of and into each country, whether within the United Kingdom or beyond. Statistics for NI usually refer to the decade ending on 31 December preceding each census year. Since Irish civil registration began only in 1864 and was initially subject to extensive under-registration, my estimates for NI incorporate adjustments for under-registration based on comparison with the censal enumeration of infants; figures for the 1860s are extrapolated from those for 1864–70. Sources: Michael Flinn (ed.), Scottish Population History (Cambridge, 1977), p. 441 (Scotland); B. R. Mitchell and Phyllis Deane, Abstract of British Historical Statistics (Cambridge, 1971), pp. 6, 29–30, 34–5 (England, including Wales); author's computations from reports of Census of Ireland for 1861–1911, and Registrar-General for Ireland for 1864–1910.

Perhaps the clearest indicator of the scale of Scottish emigration is presented in Table 13.2, showing the distribution in about 1911 of those born in Ireland, Scotland, and England in all major destinations. For every 100 natives of England (including Wales) living in the home country, there were 7 living abroad, compared with 23 for Scotland and no fewer than 52 for Ireland. Over a third of expatriate Scots were counted in England or Ireland, a quarter in the United States, almost a sixth in Canada, a tenth in Australia, and smaller but significant proportions in New Zealand, South Africa, the Indian empire, and various British possessions. The English were much less likely to settle elsewhere in the United Kingdom, with relatively large proportions choosing imperial dominions. By comparison with the Scots, the Irish were heavily concentrated in the United States (accounting for three-fifths of the total) with much smaller proportions in most regions of the empire except Australia. The table 'favours' the Scots over the Irish, since Scottish emigration had accelerated over the Edwardian decade while that from Ireland had declined sharply since the 1880s.

The imprint abroad of the three nationalities is more incisively displayed in Table 13.3, which shows their contributions to the UK-born population of each receiving region. By comparison with the Scottish component of the home population (10 per cent), the Scots were over-represented in every region, most conspicuously in other parts of the United Kingdom (31 per cent), New Zealand (23 per cent), Canada (22 per cent), and Australia (16 per cent), but only just above expectation in the Indian empire, British possessions and the United States. The English were considerably under-represented in all regions except South Africa, the Indian empire, British possessions and other parts of the United Kingdom. These proportions have also been converted into scores, showing the propensity of each nationality to choose particular destinations. By comparison with the Irish, the Scots were five times less likely to settle in the United States but almost three times more likely to choose South Africa and twice as likely to choose Canada.

Though less than 4 per cent of expatriates were enumerated elsewhere in the empire, the national origins of this sub-diaspora deserve closer attention in view of Scotland's legendary contribution to imperial expansion and management. Perhaps surprisingly, Scots barely outnumbered the Irish in the vast Indian empire, manned by 123,000 UK-born colonists in 1911. Indeed, India attracted Scots, Irish, and English settlers roughly in proportion to the home populations, though the Scots came top of the table. Elsewhere, the Irish were somewhat under-represented as colonists, contributing 7 per cent of the UK total compared with 11

Table 13.2 Distribution of natives of the United Kingdom, 1911

Location	Thousands				% of Population OHC			
Birthplace	Ire	Scot	Eng	UK	Ire	Scot	Eng	UK
Other UK	552	361	256	1,170	25.0	36.4	10.6	20.6
USA (1910)	1,352	261	960	2,574	61.3	26.3	38.5	45.2
Canada	93	170	523	786	4.2	17.1	21.7	13.8
Australia	139	93	358	591	6.3	9.4	14.9	10.4
New Zealand	41	52	136	229	1.9	5.2	5.6	4.0
South Africa	15	37	130	182	0.7	3.7	5.4	3.2
Indian empire	12	14	97	123	0.6	1.4	4.0	2.2
Colonies	2	4	30	36	0.1	0.4	1.2	0.6
Total OHC	2,207	992	2,491	5,690	100	100	100	100
						Ratio of population OHC:HC		
Home country	4,233	4,362	34,636	43,231	52.1	22.7	7.2	13.2

Note: The table shows the distribution (in thousands) of those returned as natives of Ireland, Scotland and England (including Wales and the islands) throughout the UK, the USA and the empire. The category 'Other UK' refers to residents of the UK living outside their home country (OHC). For each location, the number of each nativity is also given as a percentage of the population of that nativity returned outside the home country (OHC). England includes Wales; Canada includes Newfoundland; USA excludes Hawaii, Alaska and dependencies; colonies include all British dependencies (except the Dominions) for which returns of birthplace are available. Source: 13th Census of the United States for 1910, vol. i, p. 781 (Table 1); Census of England and Wales for 1911, General Report, pp. 352–61 ('Tables relating to the British Empire'), excluding colonies for which no census returns were available by birthplace.

Table 13.3 Distribution of natives of the United Kingdom, 1911

Location	% of Natives of UK			Scores			
Birthplace	Ire	Scot	Eng	Ire	Scot	Eng	% S:I
Other UK	47.2	30.9	21.9	438	306	27	70
USA (1910)	52.5	10.1	37.3	536	101	47	19
Canada	11.9	21.6	66.6	110	214	83	195
Australia	23.6	15.8	23.6	219	156	76	71
New Zealand	17.9	22.6	59.5	166	224	74	135
South Africa	8.0	20.4	71.6	74	202	89	272
Indian empire	10.0	11.3	78.7	92	112	98	121
Colonies	6.8	10.9	82.3	63	108	103	172
Total outside UK	36.6	14.0	49.4	374	140	62	41
Total outside HC	38.8	17.4	43.8	396	174	55	48
Home country	9.8	10.1	80.1	100	100	100	100

Note: For categories and sources, see note to preceding table. For each location, the number of each nativity is given as a percentage of all natives of the UK returned in that location. For each nativity, the score (on the right) gives the % ratio of the proportion for each location to that for persons resident in their home countries (HC), given in the bottom row. The right-hand column shows the % ratio of the Scottish score to the Irish score. The aggregate HC population consists of Irish-born resident in Ireland, Scots resident in Scotland, and English (including Welsh, Manx and Channel Islanders) resident in England (including Wales and islands).

per cent for the Scots and 82 per cent for the English. Proportionate to the home populations, the Scots and English scored 103 and 108 respectively compared with only 63 for the Irish. Yet within the broad category of British colonial 'possessions', there were marked national variations. The most Scottish possession was Basutoland (245), followed by Fiji (225), Johore (204), the Federated Malay States (196), British Honduras (169), Ceylon (164), Barbados (140), the Straits Settlements (131), Uganda (115) and Jamaica (107). The Scots were under-represented in the Maltese islands (76), St Lucia (75), Sierra Leone (73), Cyprus (58) and Ascension Island (53). The possession with the smallest recorded Scottish component was Mauritius (39). The most Irish possessions in 1911 were St Lucia (254), British Honduras (143), Sierra Leone (133) and Fiji (117), the Irish being somewhat under-represented elsewhere. The least Irish possessions were the Straits Settlements (55), Mauritius (54), Jamaica and the Maltese islands (53) and Ascension Island (41). English settlers were far more evenly distributed than the Scots and Irish, with scores varying between 113 (Ascension Island and Mauritius) and 81 (Fiji and St Lucia). Though the imperial impact of the three nationalities cannot simply be measured by the number of settlers, these figures raise significant questions about the fabled pre-eminence of the Scots, at least in the last phase of imperial expansion.

Overall, the disparities between Scottish and English migration rates are minor by comparison with the Scottish–Irish gulf. The numerical comparison, while vindicating Irish 'exceptionalism', leaves the Scottish claim to diasporic independence unresolved.

III

More persuasive is the depiction of Scotland's great migration as a product of industrial revolution, primarily affecting urbanites with more or less 'marketable skills' likely to generate higher earnings outside Scotland. Painstaking calculations of regional variations in migration by Michael Anderson and Donald J. Morse, supplemented by Jeanette Brock, suggest that industrial restructuring was even more important as a push factor in Scotland than in England.[13] Even if the skills possessed by emigrant artisans and workers were often redundant, in the new world as in the old, one would also expect a pronounced difference between the opportunities available to Scottish and Irish emigrants. Scots, emerging from a less impoverished background marked by rapid industrial expansion, were more likely to have prior access to capital than their mainly rural Irish contemporaries, who faced the challenge of accumulating it from scratch. Despite the perennial dream of rags-to-riches, it is obviously easier to display enterprise and amass assets if one has something to invest from the outset. As the Irish case shows, chronic shortage of capital did not inhibit the human flow, but it did restrict the range of occupations which most settlers could hope to secure. This contrast is reflected in the focus of most Irish scholars on strategies of self-betterment adopted by the migratory poor, whereas the Lowland Scottish diaspora is far better served by studies of business and investment strategies. In each case, however, the flip side of mass migration tends to be understudied, with relatively scant attention either to the minority of Irish emigrants with some access to capital, or to the myriad Lowland Scots who migrated with few assets beyond their willingness to work.

IV

Unless those who left Scotland emerged from a distinctive national culture, there would be little reason to package the millions of individuals who left the country as a national diaspora, rather than as a sub-group of the British diaspora, or else as a medley of localised movements with variable cultural baggage. Until quite recently, reputable scholars were shameless in attributing national stereotypes to Scottish emigrants. Thus in *The Enterprising Scot* (1968), an American business historian attributed the success of Scottish investors in the American West to the 'tenacity of the Scot', if not to their inherent 'canniness'.[14] Even Gordon Donaldson, in his pioneering survey of *The Scots Overseas* (1966), affirmed that 'the Scots, in particular, had always had a great gift for assimilation', that 'the Scottish genius for schism went overseas with the emigrants', and that 'the individuality and initiative which were acquired by Lowland Scots earlier than by Highlanders contributed to their success as colonists'.[15] By 1985, R. A. Cage in *The Scots Abroad* was more circumspect, rejecting the possibility or need for a definition of 'Scottishness' or any explanation of Scottish successfulness 'in generic terms'. Yet this was followed by an editorial assertion of Scottish 'clubbishness' and willingness 'to take risks to meet new sets of challenges'. While Eric Richards was firmly dismissive of 'cultural stereotypes', R. H. Campbell suggested that 'the emigrant Scot may have succeeded because his affection for his native land was never allowed to interfere with his commercial judgement'. Bernard Aspinall portrayed the Scots in the United States as embodying the 'Protestant ethic' in their common search for 'an efficient moral social order'.[16]

Even if the term 'Calvinism' has been largely expunged from diasporic discourse, except in quotation marks, it hovers behind more nuanced constructions of Scottishness. In 2004, Harper let slip the view that 'key features of the Scottish psyche became deeply embedded in the culture of the host societies', without questioning the existence of a collective 'Scottish psyche' (akin to the equally dubious 'Irish mind'). No doubt, 'the Scots have always been a restless people' – but which people has not been?[17] These quotations are unfair, because Harper has done more than most to subvert familiar stereotypes, and to document variations and contradictions. Yet they illustrate a problem that affects scholars as much as anyone else when they try to shape and classify human complexity in order to make it comprehensible. In challenging one stereotype, we are always at risk of succumbing to another. A rigorous definition of 'Scottishness' remains as elusive as ever, yet most of us sense that we know perfectly well what it means.

V

Though collective 'success' is widely attributed to Scottish emigrants, this too has been more often asserted than demonstrated through comparative analysis. Despite a multitude of official returns, including the extraordinary dossier compiled for all immigrant groups in the United States by the Dillingham Commission (1907–10), I have not read any sustained comparative analysis of the occupational profile of Scottish immigrants and their children in either the United States or Canada.[18] One test of whether most Scots left home with 'marketable skills' (Harper's term) is whether they actually practised those skills abroad.[19] It might also be enlightening to link samples of probate records with census and passenger returns, in order to correlate heritable assets with birthplace. By documenting career trajectories for samples of Scottish emigrants, historians could avoid excessive reliance on dubious generalisations based on statistical snapshots.

A key test of Scottish 'success' is the extent of intergenerational mobility, which in the Irish case was quite astonishing by 1900.[20] Such studies, comparing Irish, English and Scottish occupations, would clarify the extent to which the three 'ethnic' groups retained the very different occupational profiles recorded at the point of entry. From the Dillingham Commission's analysis of occupations, derived from the census for 1900, it is obvious that Irish immigrants in the United States were much less likely than their English and Scottish counterparts to work in skilled, white-collar, or agricultural occupations. Table 13.4

Table 13.4 Occupational categories by nativity, USA, 1900

Category	Irish			Scottish			English		
	1st	2nd	Ratio	1st	2nd	Ratio	1st	2nd	Ratio
Male									
Agricultural	13.6	16.5	121	18.3	24.4	134	18.1	26.6	147
Professional	1.9	3.7	187	4.5	5.7	128	4.5	4.9	109
Service	30.4	17.0	56	9.9	10.5	106	11.4	10.7	93
Trades	21.6	28.4	131	20.0	25.6	128	18.5	24.3	132
Manufacturing	32.4	34.5	107	47.3	33.7	71	47.5	33.6	71
Female									
Agricultural	2.8	1.4	50	5.0	3.8	76	5.2	3.4	64
Professional	1.9	9.6	515	5.5	18.2	333	6.0	16.0	265
Service	70.4	25.1	36	46.9	25.8	55	40.2	25.9	64
Trades	4.8	18.5	386	11.0	19.7	179	10.5	18.9	180
Manufacturing	20.1	45.4	226	31.7	32.5	103	38.0	35.8	94

Note: Statistics show the proportion of breadwinners aged ten and over in the USA. For each sex and nativity group, the first two columns show the percentage of breadwinners in each of the five broad census categories (agricultural occupations, professional, service, trade and transportation, and manufacturing and mechanical pursuits), for the first generation (born in Ireland, Scotland, or England and Wales) and the second generation (born in the USA with at least one parent born in Ireland, etc.). The third column gives the percentage ratio of the proportion for the second generation to that for the first generation. Source: *Reports of the Immigration Commission* (Washington, DC, 1907–10), vol. i, pp. 821–38 (Tables A, B), based on *12th Census of the United States* for 1900, incorporating unpublished returns.

suggests that 'first-generation' Scots and English had very similar occupational profiles, whereas the Irish were grossly over-represented in the 'service' category for both sexes. The more detailed breakdown in Table 13.5 shows that over half of all occupied Irishwomen were servants cum waitresses, twice the Scottish proportion; while nearly a quarter of occupied Irishmen were labourers, four times the Scottish proportion. Though lower than the proportions of Irish labourers and servants returned in immigrant passenger lists,[21] the census returns confirm the lingering Irish disadvantage by immigrant British standards.[22] Yet the 'new immigrants' from Russia and southern and eastern Europe were typically still more disadvantaged.

Comparable returns for 1910, classified for various 'socio-economic grades', subvert the belief that the Scots excelled the English (excluding the Welsh) in the American occupational hierarchy. They were notably less likely than the English to be 'professional persons', 'proprietors, managers and officials' or 'clerks and kindred workers'. In each of these categories, however, the Scots were far better represented than the Irish. Within the working class, the Scots were more likely than the English (and especially the Irish) to be 'skilled workers and foremen', and less so to be 'semi-skilled workers'. It is noteworthy that the Scots and English were almost equally represented among 'unskilled workers', a group in which the Irish remained slightly over-represented within America's foreign-born white population.[23]

The tables also record the rapidity with which the Irish had 'caught up' with their British rivals, as indicated by the occupations of the 'second-generation' Irish (natives of the United States living with at least one Irish-born parent). Though still somewhat under-represented in agriculture and the professions, and over-represented in the service category, the children of Irish immigrants were more likely than those of English and Scottish immigrants to have employment in manufacturing. Table 13.5 highlights occupations in which the children of immigrants were particularly prominent by comparison with the first generation. Irishmen of the second generation were three times as likely to be accountants or book-keepers, more than twice as likely to be clerks cum copyists, salesmen and agricultural labourers, and more likely to be agents and building workers. Irishmen of the second generation were actually more likely than the Scots or English to be clerks cum copyists and salesmen, though the Scots retained a small advantage among accountants cum book-keepers. The Irish proportion of labourers (down from 22 per cent to 10 per cent between generations) still exceeded that for second-generation Scots and English; yet it is noteworthy that in the British

Table 13.5 Selected occupational groups by nativity, USA, 1900

Category	Irish			Scottish			English		
	1st	2nd	Ratio	1st	2nd	Ratio	1st	2nd	Ratio
Male									
Agricultural labourers	3.2	7.0	220	3.4	7.5	225	3.5	8.6	248
Clerks, copyists	1.8	5.0	286	2.6	4.3	168	2.4	4.2	176
Railroad employees	4.4	4.4	101	2.1	3.0	143	1.9	2.7	141
Salesmen	1.2	2.7	223	2.1	2.9	137	1.7	2.9	169
Draymen, teamsters +	4.3	4.6	107	1.8	2.4	130	1.8	2.4	133
Agents	0.9	1.2	145	1.4	1.7	123	1.5	1.5	101
Farmers, planters +	9.4	8.8	94	12.7	15.4	121	13.1	16.8	128
Merchants, dealers	2.9	2.9	100	3.4	3.9	115	3.5	3.9	112
Accountants +	0.4	1.2	300	1.5	1.7	112	1.3	1.5	117
Labourers (unspec.)	22.3	10.2	46	5.7	6.2	110	6.4	6.9	107
Saloon krs, bartenders	1.9	1.9	101	0.6	0.6	98	0.5	0.5	84
Miners, quarrymen	3.2	2.6	81	7.5	5.6	74	10.2	5.7	82
Iron, steel workers	2.8	2.5	90	2.1	1.5	71	2.6	1.8	70
Building trades	5.9	6.9	117	9.6	6.7	70	7.5	6.3	84
Servants, waiters	1.7	0.9	50	1.0	0.6	63	1.4	0.5	39
Blacksmiths	1.6	1.2	76	2.2	1.2	53	1.5	1.1	72

	Irish			Scottish			English		
Category	1st	2nd	Ratio	1st	2nd	Ratio	1st	2nd	Ratio
Female									
Accountants +	0.4	2.9	783	1.7	7.8	456	1.4	3.2	229
Teachers	1.6	8.9	544	4.2	15.9	375	4.1	13.9	338
Stenographers, typists	0.3	3.0	889	2.0	4.7	237	1.6	4.1	247
Clerks, copyists	0.5	2.9	562	1.7	3.3	191	1.7	3.5	206
Saleswomen	1.2	6.2	511	2.8	4.8	175	2.6	5.1	194
Needle trades	7.5	17.9	239	11.3	15.1	134	13.1	16.2	124
Housekeepers +	3.4	2.3	66	5.2	3.3	64	4.7	3.0	63
Hotel keepers +	2.1	1.1	51	3.0	1.9	63	3.0	1.7	55
Textile mill operatives	7.4	10.4	140	12.8	7.8	61	15.8	9.2	58
Nurses, midwives	2.6	1.6	64	6.7	3.4	50	5.6	2.8	49
Laundresses	6.5	2.9	45	3.0	1.6	53	3.1	1.9	60
Servants, waitresses	54.0	16.0	30	27.5	14.5	53	21.9	15.5	71
Merchants, dealers	1.6	0.7	43	1.6	0.7	42	1.9	0.7	40

Note: Statistics and sources as for Table 13.4. Selected occupational groups are arranged in descending order of the ratio of second to first generation percentages for the Scots. Accountants include book-keepers; draymen and teamsters include hackmen; farmers and planters include overseers; housekeepers include stewardesses; hotel keepers include boarding and lodging house keepers.

case the proportion of labourers was *higher* for the second generation than the first. Otherwise, the direction of Scottish and English intergenerational mobility was fairly similar, except that the second generation were more likely than the immigrants to work in agriculture and less so in the building sector.

The Irish intergenerational advance was even more spectacular for women, for whom the proportion in service declined between generations from 54 per cent to 16 per cent (scarcely above the English and Scottish figures for the second generation). By comparison with the immigrants, second-generation Irishwomen were eight or nine times as likely to be stenographers cum typists and accountants cum bookkeepers, between five and eight times as likely to be clerks cum copyists, teachers, and saleswomen, and more likely to find employment in the 'needle trades' or textile mills. By contrast, the children of Irish immigrants were much less likely than the Irish-born to work as housekeepers, nurses cum midwives, hotel-keepers, and laundresses. Though still rather less prominent in most white-collar categories than the second-generation Scots and English, Irishwomen were proportionately more numerous in needlework and textiles (reversing the contrast for the first generation). By 1900, there was surprisingly little difference between the occupational profile of the children of Irish and British immigrants in the United States. These figures cast doubt on the relative 'success' of second-generation Scots by comparison with their Irish or English counterparts, suggesting that intergenerational upward mobility was far more rapid for the Irish.

Though occupational mobility is an important indicator of ethnic success, suggesting a surprisingly positive outcome for the Irish by comparison with the Scots, it must be balanced by analysis of ethnic failure as indicated by criminality, intoxication and mental illness. Admittedly, only a small minority of emigrants of any nationality were ever classified as criminals, drunks or lunatics, and it is dangerous to impute pathological traits to an entire ethnicity on the basis of aberrant behaviour at the margin. Though the statistical evidence for 'dysfunctional' behaviour by immigrants and their children is seriously distorted by institutional factors, which usually tended to inflate Irish involvement, studies of the Irish diaspora uniformly suggest that the Irish were heavily overrepresented in all three sectors in most countries of settlement. Though no systematic survey exists for the Scottish diaspora, McCarthy's study of immigrants in New Zealand asylums confirms the persistent Irish anomaly, with about 75 per cent more inmates than predicted from the Irish component of the immigrant population. Yet the New Zealand returns also indicate that Scots were slightly over-represented by the early twentieth century, whereas the English were invariably under-represented.[24] Once again, the elaborate survey of 'Immigration and Crime' compiled for the Dillingham Commission deserves renewed comparative analysis, though the comparative ethnic data refer almost entirely to the first rather than second generation.[25]

VI

My fifth test is perhaps the most intractable of all: the extent to which the Scots demonstrably belonged to an ethnic group outside Scotland. Most historians of expatriate Scottish ethnicity have concentrated on the Canadian case, despite the inconvenient fact that the most popular destinations for Scottish emigrants during the half-century preceding the Great War were England and the United States.[26] When asking if there was indeed 'a Scottish diaspora?', Harper states that 'the predominance of Canadian examples in this book is not accidental . . . Scottish identity was far more visible in Canada than in the United States.'[27] Clearly, any comprehensive study of the Scottish diaspora should pay due attention to less 'visible' manifestations, applying appropriate tests of ethnic solidarity to each country of settlement.

At first sight, the case for Scottish ethnicity seems weak by comparison with the Irish diaspora, for which the Roman Catholic Church undeniably played an essential social and political as well as spiritual part in forging self-consciously 'Irish' communities across the globe. Of course, the much vaunted and widely accepted equation between Catholicism and Irishness is deeply flawed, providing revisionists with limitless opportunities to recover and document marginalised emigrant sub-groups such as Protestants, 'perverts' and non-believers. The religious problem is quite different for historians of the Scottish diaspora. Institutional Presbyterianism, so volatile and fragmented by comparison with the 'Church of Rome', cannot be regarded as a unifying factor either in Scotland or in places of Scottish settlement. As Harper observes, 'there was no common religious identity, for Scots exported their sectarianism, while some changed their religion . . . when they emigrated'.[28]

Though 'the Church', whichever it might be, doubtless remained central to the lives of many Scottish emigrants, the extent and force of the connection is much more difficult to assess than Irish adherence to Catholicism. What, for example, is implied by the striking fact that in 1931 three-quarters of Canadians of 'Scottish race' identified themselves as either Presbyterians or followers of the United Church formed in

1925?[29] Since natives of Scotland accounted for less than a fifth of those claiming membership of the 'Scottish race', this might suggest a high level of ethnic solidarity in religious adherence. Yet the very fact that Canadian Presbyterians had pooled their resources with Methodists and Congregationals casts doubt on the extent to which religious affiliation remained an expression of Scottish ethnicity. It is worth noting that the same Canadian census revealed that those claiming 'English race' were far more likely than the Scots or Irish to marry each other. Whereas 70 per cent of the English had married endogamously, the Scottish and Irish proportions were only 45 per cent and 43 per cent respectively. However, since the pool of wives of English race in Canada far exceeded the Scottish and Irish pools, these proportions imply that the propensity for endogamous marriage was greatest for wives of Irish race, followed by the Scots and the English.[30]

The choice of marriage partners, whether defined by religion or ethnicity, is the most potent index of group solidarity. We still know remarkably little about the extent of endogamy among emigrants and their descendants, and systematic comparative studies of Scottish, Irish and English marital behaviour are badly needed. Yet a fundamental problem of interpretation will not be easily solved. The statistical profile of emigration made endogamy far more feasible for the Irish than for either the Scots or the English, wherever they chose to settle. Even though married couples were a relatively small component of Irish emigration, subsequent endogamy was facilitated by three other unique features of the Irish diaspora from the Great Famine onwards. First, the sheer scale of the Irish presence in North America and Australasia, at least by comparison with the Scots, supplied a larger pool of potential ethnic partners. Second, this advantage was reinforced by the fact that the Irish were less geographically dispersed than other ethnic groups. Third, Irishwomen were normally almost as likely to emigrate as Irishmen, whereas virtually all other transoceanic migrations were dominated by men.

The marked preponderance of male Scots ensured that most of them simply could not hope to procure an ethnic partner, regardless of how passionately Scottish they might feel. It was statistically difficult for a male Scot to perform his ethnic marital duty, however many Burns nights and bekilted dances he might attend. In this respect, there was little to distinguish between Scottish and English emigrants. This may be illustrated by a simple comparison of the nationalities of unmarried adults leaving the United Kingdom between 1877 and 1907. For every 100 Irish bachelors there were 98 Irish spinsters; the corresponding ratios for the Scots and the English were 35 and 36 respectively.[31] The critical shortage of British-born women did not, of course, preclude endogamy within religious communities or among those of Scottish or English 'stock' or 'race'. Yet the same factors that curtailed endogamy among British emigrants also restricted the very creation of a 'stock' of native-born descendants overseas.

The demographic imprint of these factors is visible in Tables 13.6 and 13.7, based on the first American census to offer detailed information on the second generation of immigrants, tabulated by parental birth-place. Table 13.6 shows that in 1900, American-born ('native white') children of foreign parents already outnumbered the foreign-born by over 50 per cent. The excess was naturally greatest for countries with a long record of supplying the United States with immigrants. The four regions of the United Kingdom, along with France and Germany, were the only 'countries' for which the second generation exceeded twice the size of the first generation. In this respect, there was little to differentiate Scotland from Ireland, England or Wales. Ireland accounted for 15.6 per cent of immigrants but 23.0 per cent of the second generation, the corresponding figures for Scotland being 2.3 per cent and 3.5 per cent.

The relative shortage of Irish family immigration was responsible for the high proportion of Americans with two Irish parents who were themselves born in America rather than overseas. In addition to enu-merating seven times as many Irish-born as Scottish-born Americans in 1900, drawn from roughly equal home populations, the census recorded two and a quarter million native-born Americans with two Irish parents, *fourteen* times the number with two Scottish parents. As Table 13.7 reveals, only five countries had a native majority among those with two foreign parents, Ireland (56.1 per cent) coming a narrow second to Germany, whereas Scotland (38.9 per cent) scored only thirteenth in the pecking order. The remainder of the second generation were mostly born in America, though about a fifth of the children of 'mixed' foreign marriages were themselves born overseas.[32]

Whereas most second-generation Scottish Americans had only one parent from the homeland, there were more than twice as many Americans with two Irish parents as with mixed Irish and American parentage.[33] The proportion with two parents from the same country was 62.5 per cent for the Irish, 43.6 per cent for the Welsh, 33.3 per cent for the English, and 29.8 per cent for the Scots (only the French and the English Canadians had lower scores). Ireland's high propor-tion of female immigrants was hazily reflected in the disproportion-ate presence of Irish mothers with American partners as against Irish fathers with American partners. In this respect, the Irish scored second

Table 13.6 Native white population with foreign-born parents and foreign-born population, USA, 1900 (in thousands)

Country	FB Parentage	%	FB Population	%	Ratio	Rank
Germany	5,481	34.9	2,647	25.8	206	5
Ireland	3,602	23.0	1,619	15.6	223	3
England	1,702	10.8	842	8.1	202	6
Canada (E)	1,104	7.0	786	7.6	140	9
Sweden	572	3.6	573	5.5	100	13
Scotland	553	3.5	234	2.3	236	2
Norway	508	3.2	337	3.3	151	8
Canada (F)	478	3.0	395	3.8	121	12
Poland	335	2.1	384	3.7	87	14
Russia	301	1.9	424	4.1	71	16
Italy	257	1.6	484	4.7	53	18
France	249	1.6	104	1.0	238	1
Bohemia	216	1.4	157	1.5	137	10
Austria	204	1.3	276	2.7	74	15
Switzerland	203	1.3	116	1.1	175	7
Denmark	201	1.3	154	1.5	130	11
Wales	200	1.3	94	0.9	213	4
Hungary	87	0.6	146	1.4	60	17
Other	497	3.2	565	5.5	88	
Total	15,688	n.a.	10,357	100	151	

Note: For each of eighteen specified countries, the table compares the native white population with one or two foreign-born (FB) parents with the total foreign-born white population of the continental USA, including military and naval personnel abroad. These eighteen countries are arranged in descending order of their share of the total population of foreign parentage. The sum of these percentage shares (106%) exceeds 100% because of the inclusion of persons with parents from two different foreign countries. Since statistics for persons of mixed foreign parentage from individual countries are available only for the total white population, the number for the native white population is estimated from the overall proportion (79.91%). Statistics for Canada include Newfoundland, and are divided between those of 'English' and 'French' origins. The right-hand columns give the percentage ratio of native whites with foreign parentage to the foreign-born, ranked in descending order. Source: *12th Census of the United States* for 1900, vol. i, pp. 810–47 (Tables 38–55).

only to the English Canadians, though the Irish proportion of foreign mothers in these mixed marriages (37.4 per cent) did not much exceed the proportions for England (35.6 per cent), Wales (34.6 per cent) and Scotland (34.1 per cent). These statistics highlight the Irish comparative advantage in generating an ethnic community overseas. By comparison with the Scots and English, the Irish overseas were much better placed to share and replicate their ethnicity through marriage.

Table 13.7 Native white population with foreign-born parents, USA, 1900

| Category | Both parents foreign-born | | | | Mixed parentage | |
Country	% NW	Rank	% of Total	Rank	% of Mothers	Rank
Germany	57.2	1	65.2	9	25.7	12
Ireland	56.1	2	62.5	10	37.4	2
England	41.5	11	33.3	15	35.6	4
Canada (E)	38.5	14	23.7	18	46.9	1
Sweden	41.5	10	72.5	6	35.2	5
Scotland	38.9	13	29.8	16	34.1	9
Norway	51.0	4	68.8	7	34.4	7
Canada (F)	41.9	8	55.6	12	37.1	3
Poland	43.5	6	86.8	1	17.9	17
Russia	37.0	15	82.4	3	18.0	16
Italy	31.0	18	85.1	2	10.7	18
France	41.6	9	28.7	17	22.5	14
Bohemia	51.8	3	78.1	4	34.3	8
Austria	32.7	16	65.6	8	25.4	13
Switzerland	39.9	12	36.9	14	27.0	11
Denmark	43.2	7	57.5	11	28.5	10
Wales	50.1	5	43.6	13	34.6	6
Hungary	31.7	17	76.3	5	18.8	15
Other	*39.9*		*55.8*		*31.1*	
Total	49.1		68.0		33.2	

Note: For each of eighteen countries of origin, the table shows three characteristics of the native white population with one or two foreign-born parents: (1) native whites as a proportion of the entire population with both parents born in each specified country; (2) native whites with two foreign-born parents as a proportion of those with any foreign parentage; (3) mothers as a proportion of all parents (born in each specified country) with native partners. In each case, the eighteen specified countries are ranked in descending order. For source, see note to Table 13.6.

Table 13.8 measures intermarriage between different immigrant groups, some of which would have occurred before departure from Europe. The Scots were particularly prominent in this category, with almost as many products of mixed foreign parentage as of marriages between Scots and 'native' Americans. Unfortunately, detailed cross-tabulation of this interesting sub-group does not distinguish between native-born and foreign-born Americans with particular combinations of foreign-born parents. Even so, since it is known that four-fifths of all white Americans of mixed foreign parentage were natives of the United States, Table 13.8 offers a rough indication of the ethnic preferences and aversions exhibited by each nationality after immersion in the American 'melting pot'.

Table 13.8 Combinations of foreign parentage in USA, 1900

Parental nativity	CE	CF	E	G	I	S	W	OF	All foreign
Fathers born:									
				% of Mothers from each country					
Canada (English)	n.a.	6.3	25.6	8.5	38.3	13.4	0.9	7.0	109,179
Canada (French)	32.8	n.a.	10.3	8.7	27.9	4.1	0.4	15.8	26,342
England	23.2	1.5	n.a.	8.0	36.6	15.1	6.8	8.7	251,085
Germany	7.8	1.2	12.8	n.a.	19.8	2.7	0.5	55.1	215,151
Ireland	30.3	2.3	34.4	6.6	n.a.	19.2	2.0	5.2	222,413
Scotland	25.9	1.3	28.9	3.7	33.4	n.a.	2.0	4.4	131,616
Wales	5.7	0.5	59.1	4.6	16.0	8.6	n.a.	5.6	22,774
Other foreign	1.0	0.6	2.0	12.8	2.5	0.5	0.1	80.5	218,091
All foreign	14.7	2.0	15.6	14.6	19.4	8.1	2.1	23.4	1,340,678
Mothers born:									
				% of Fathers from each country					
Canada (English)	n.a.	4.4	29.5	8.5	34.1	17.3	0.7	5.6	197,619
Canada (French)	25.4	n.a.	13.8	9.5	18.6	6.3	0.4	26.0	26,964
England	13.4	1.3	n.a.	13.2	36.5	18.2	6.4	11.0	209,231
Germany	4.7	1.2	10.3	n.a.	7.5	2.5	0.5	73.3	195,610
Ireland	16.1	2.8	35.3	16.3	n.a.	17.1	1.4	11.0	260,612
Scotland	13.4	1.0	34.6	5.3	39.2	n.a.	1.8	4.8	109,254
Wales	3.6	0.4	61.9	4.2	16.1	9.4	n.a.	4.5	27,612
Other foreign	0.7	0.4	1.9	10.1	1.0	0.5	0.1	85.4	169,720
All foreign	8.1	2.0	18.7	16.0	16.6	9.8	1.7	27.0	1,340,678

Note:: Statistics refer to entire population of mixed foreign parentage, including foreign-born and non-white population as well as persons abroad with the armed services. Figures for 'all foreign countries' include ten other specified countries (listed in Table 13.6) and a miscellaneous category. Source: *12th Census of the United States for 1900*, vol. 1, pp. 850–62 (Table 56).

A third of interbreeding Scottish fathers chose Irishwomen, with slightly smaller proportions marrying English or Canadians. English preference for Irishwomen was even more pronounced, the proportion with Scottish wives being less than half of the Irish figure. As for Irishmen, over a third selected (or were selected by) English partners, while a fifth took the Scottish option. The Scots were markedly less likely to take German wives than the Irish or English, while three-fifths of the Welsh married Englishwomen. Similar contrasts apply to the ethnic choices of women. Again, Irish partners were the favoured choice for both English and Scottish women, while Irishwomen were twice as likely to select English as Scottish men. Otherwise, British and Irish women were less likely than men to choose Canadians and more likely to choose Germans, leading to a noteworthy cluster of families with German fathers and Irish mothers.

Such comparisons are of course distorted by numerical differences in the ethnic populations 'at risk' of interbreeding. Table 13.9 ranks each ethnic combination according to the ratio between the proportions for each country shown in the previous table and the total distribution of foreign parents. Thus the score of 236 for Irishmen with Scottish partners is based on the fact that 19.2 per cent of non-Irish foreign mothers married to Irishmen were Scots, whereas Scottish women comprised only 8.2 per cent of all interbreeding mothers. This index suggests that all English-speaking groups tended to marry among themselves, exhibiting much lower rates of interbreeding with Germans, not to mention those from the countries generating the 'new immigration'. Irish male preferences ranged from 236 (Scottish), 220 (English), and 206 (Canadian English), down to 97 (Welsh) and 45 (German). Irish women were marginally less fond of Scottish men, with scores of 197 (Canadian English), 188 (English), 174 (Scottish), 102 (German) and 82 (Welsh). For Scottish men, the corresponding scores were 185 (English), 176 (Canadian English), 174 (Irish), 96 (Welsh), and 25 (German). Finally, the scores for Scottish women were 236 (Irish), 185 (English), 165 (Canadian English), 106 (Welsh) and 33 (German). The English and Welsh were invariably more than three times as likely to interbreed as predicted from their shares in America's mixed foreign marriage market.[34] These findings are broadly consistent with Eric Richards's assessment that 'there was little friction between the component parts of the British diaspora: they intermingled, intermarried and coexisted without creating serious divisions and subcultures'.[35]

Though illuminating only a fraction of the 'Scottish diaspora', the American data on ethnic family formation suggests affinities as well

Table 13.9 Scores for combinations of foreign parentage in USA, 1900

Mothers born:	CE	CF	E	G	I	S	W	OF	All foreign
Fathers born:	Scores for each combination of countries								
Canada (English)	n.a.	312	164	58	197	165	44	9	100
Canada (French)	222	n.a.	66	59	144	50	20	21	100
England	158	74	n.a.	55	188	185	330	11	100
Germany	53	59	82	n.a.	102	33	26	73	100
Ireland	206	112	220	45	n.a.	236	97	7	100
Scotland	176	64	185	25	174	n.a.	96	6	100
Wales	38	22	379	32	82	106	n.a.	7	100
Other foreign	8	4	15	100	15	7	6	n.a.	100
All foreign	100	100	100	100	100	100	100	100	n.a.

Note: For definitions and sources, see note to preceding table. For each parental nativity, as presented in Table 13.8, the score gives the % ratio of the proportion of mothers from each country to the overall proportion of mothers with partners from all foreign countries, given in the bottom row of the upper section. Note that the logic of this calculation implies that scores for each combination, derived from the lower section of Table 13.8, are identical to those derived from the upper section.

as contrasts between the Irish, Scottish and English ethnic experiences. When these three groups of 'Britannia's children' are examined in isolation, the Irish stand out for the preponderance of the second generation, and, within that second generation, the excess of full-blood American offspring and the relatively high proportion of Irish mothers as against Irish fathers. In most respects, the patterns of Scottish and English family formation and interbreeding resembled each other (apart from the anomalous Welsh). Yet the Irish record seems less remarkable when set in the broader context of European migration. Though still exceptional for the parity between male and female immigrants and the high representation of women in mixed marriages, the Irish preference for endogamous marriage is unusual only by comparison with the British and French patterns.

One of the most exciting aspects of recent scholarship has been the search for non-statistical evidence about the attitudes and collective behaviour of the Scots overseas. As in the Irish case, personal testimony such as letters, diaries and interviews is now accepted as an essential supplement and corrective to sometimes glib hypotheses resting on ambiguous statistics. Angela McCarthy, among others, has done much to establish affinities between the Scottish and Irish diasporas without so far demolishing their distinctive national identities.[36] Equally productive is the documentation of societies and networks involving Scottish emigrants, whether or not these were overtly or uniquely ethnic.[37] What Devine terms 'the Burns Supper School of Scottish History' is no longer supreme, if still flourishing in the vicinity of 'the ends of the earth'.[38] Though initiated in pursuit of specifically ethnic networks, perhaps the most striking outcome of recent work has been to show how adeptly Scottish emigrants exploited multi-ethnic associations, such as friendly societies and the Freemasons, to expand their social and economic connections. The more one studies any national diaspora, the more difficult it seems to disentangle ethnicity from the strategies by which settlers adapted themselves to multi-ethnic environments. Ethnic performances for the benefit of non-ethnic audiences, far from demonstrating clannishness or marginalisation, often betokened what used to be called 'assimilation'.

VII

The ultimate test for a truly national diaspora is surely its impact on the homeland. Even if individual emigrants had little in common and limited enthusiasm for exhibiting Scottishness abroad, they might nevertheless be viewed collectively as a Scottish diaspora if their absence from home and activity abroad had transformative effects. In the Scottish case, this reverse impact has been convincingly demonstrated for the diaspora in its broadest sense, as the global dispersion and circulation of Scottish-raised capital, goods and services. Likewise, attention has been paid to the long-term demographic impact of Scottish migration. Flinn's calculations indicate that, in the absence of emigration, Scotland's population might have approached 7 million by 1939, 40 per cent above the actual figure.[39] Yet I know of no counterpart to the counterfactual studies which have tried to assess the course of Irish economic history in the absence of the Great Famine or mass emigration.[40]

Furthermore, as Devine points out, rather little is yet known about the social and cultural impact of return migration – still less about the diaspora's broader contribution to the Anglicisation, Americanisation, and even Australianisation of Scotland.[41] A study of changes in Scottish idiom, reading habits, recreational preferences and exposure to information on the outside world might enable us to break down the nebulous notion of 'globalisation' into more localised outside influences on Scottish culture. Though personal interaction was not the only agent of cultural change in the period of the 'great migration', direct knowledge of foreigners and alien cultures, along with exposure to eye-witness

reports in letters from relatives and friends, surely had a more powerful impact on Scottish attitudes than the disembodied diffusion of
knowledge through the press or propaganda. In the Irish case, I suspect
that nineteenth-century Americanisation posed an even more insidious
challenge to traditional Irishness than its much execrated competitor,
Anglicisation. Did the same apply to Scotland? Through reports of emigrant experiences overseas, and the need for those at home to visualise
new worlds that they might never visit, the general European trend
towards greater cosmopolitanism was accelerated in highly migratory
societies such as Ireland and arguably Scotland. One awaits a counterpart to Hook's *Scotland and America: A Study of Cultural Relations*
(1975), which ably illuminated Scottish influences on America yet
ignored American influences on Scotland.[42] Like 'cultural relations',
diasporas are best treated as a forum of exchange involving imports as
well as exports, interaction as well as 'dispersion'.

These reflections suggest that Scotland's claim to a distinctive and
coherent national diaspora has yet to be fully tested and vindicated. This
does not diminish the extraordinary achievement of the scholars who,
over the last four decades, have demonstrated the central importance of
migration to the economic and broader history of Scotland itself. Yet
the case for a Scottish diaspora will remain provisional in the absence
of systematic analysis comparing the Scottish outflow with those from
Ireland and England. Apart from exploiting the vast store of nominal
records relating to migration and settlement, many of which are now
digitally searchable, more systematic use should be made of the amaz-
ingly rich and detailed reports of the census and immigration authorities
in most places of settlement. Even Flinn relied mainly on the venerable
compendium of official statistics assembled by Carrier and Jeffery in
External Migration (1953).[43] Perhaps in order to avoid alienating publishers and the public, most leading scholars in the Scottish field have
avoided full statistical analysis even of readily accessible data. There
are probably few surviving historians who share my regret about that
omission! It remains for me to celebrate the achievement of those who
have carved out new territory, explored a vast range of neglected themes
and sources, and synthesised their findings with greater conviction and
power than most English or Irish counterparts. Even if certain aspects
of the case for a Scottish diaspora remain conjectural or contestable,
that case has been presented with impressive erudition and panache.[44]

NOTES

1. For penetrating analysis of the versatility, adaptability, and economic success of Irish emigrants, contrary to a once prevalent stereotype, see numerous studies by Donald Harman Akenson, including *Being Had: Historians, Evidence, and the Irish in North America* (Port Credit, Ontario: P. D. Meany, 1985); *Small Differences: Irish Catholics and Irish Protestants, 1815–1922* (Kingston and Montreal: McGill-Queen's University Press, 1988), chs 3, 4; and *The Irish Diaspora: A Primer* (Toronto: P. D. Meany, 1993).

2. For a brief critique of the Irish case, see David Fitzpatrick, 'How Irish was the diaspora from Ireland?', *British Association for Irish Studies Newsletter*, no. 25 (2001), pp. 5–9.

3. Eric Richards, *Britannia's Children: Emigration from England, Scotland, Wales and Ireland* (London and New York: Hambledon and London, 2004), pp. ix, 6, 14, 307 (note 23).

4. Michael Anderson and Donald J. Morse, 'Fertility decline in Scotland, England and Wales, and Ireland: comparisons from the 1911 census of fertility', *Population Studies*, lii (1998), pp. 1–20; Michael Anderson and Donald J. Morse, 'High fertility, high emigration, low nuptiality: adjustment processes in Scotland's demographic experience, 1861–1914', pts I, II, *Population Studies*, xlvii (1993), pp. 5–25, 319–43.

5. T. M. Devine, *To the Ends of the Earth: Scotland's Global Diaspora, 1750–2010* (London: Allen Lane, 2011), p. xiv. These themes are brilliantly explored in many earlier studies including T. M. Devine, *Scotland's Empire, 1600–1815* (London: Allen Lane, 2003).

6. Devine, *Scotland's Global Diaspora*, pp. 289, xv, 85.

7. Marjory Harper, 'British migration and the peopling of the empire', in Andrew Porter (ed.), *The Oxford History of the British Empire*, vol. I, *The Nineteenth Century* (Oxford: Oxford University Press, 1999), pp. 75–87 (at 85).

8. Michael Flinn (ed.), *Scottish Population History from the Seventeenth Century to the 1930s* (Cambridge: Cambridge University Press, 1977), pp. 448, 22.

9. Dudley Baines, *Migration in a Mature Economy: Emigration and Internal Migration in England and Wales, 1861–1900* (Cambridge: Cambridge University Press, 1985), p. 10 (for further analysis of Scottish emigration, see pp. 61, 304–7).

10. For the most recent reproduction of comparative statistics assembled by Baines, on the basis of returns of outward passenger movement from the United Kingdom along with analagous European returns, see Tanja Bueltmann, Andrew Hinson, and Graeme Morton, *The Scottish Diaspora* (Edinburgh: Edinburgh University Press, 2013), p. 59. For each decade, the annual rates of movement (per 1000 of home population) for each

nationality appear as follows. 1850s: Irish 14.0, Scottish 5.0, English and Welsh 2.6; 1860s: 14.6, 4.6, 2.8; 1870s: 6.6, 4.7, 4.0; 1880s: 14.2, 7.1, 5.6; 1890s: 8.9, 4.4, 3.6; 1900s: 7.0, 9.9, 5.5. These returns refer to the number of recorded passengers of each nationality leaving UK ports for extra-European destinations; from 1877 onwards, nativity was replaced by country of last 'permanent' residence (exceeding one year). Returns include many temporary migrants, and ignore reverse movement (not tabulated by country of intended residence until 1877). 'Permanent' emigration and immigration were not separately tabulated until 1895.

11. The comparison was reversed between 1901 and March 1912, a period of rapidly expanding Scottish and English emigration but sluggish Irish emigration, when the corresponding ratios were 47 for the English and 46 for the Irish, but only 37 for the Scots. For sources and analysis of the scale and composition of Irish return movement, see David Fitzpatrick, 'Emigration, 1871–1921', in W. E. Vaughan (ed.), *A New History of Ireland*, vol. VI (Oxford: Oxford University Press, 1996), pp. 606–52 (at 634–5, 645–7).

12. See also Anderson and Morse, 'High fertility', pt II, 9.

13. Anderson and Morse, 'High fertility', pt I, pp. 8–16; Anderson and Morse, 'High fertility', pt II, pp. 323–4, 341–3; Jeanette M. Brock, *The Mobile Scot: A Study of Emigration and Migration, 1861–1911* (Edinburgh: John Donald, 1999), chs 4, 5. For non-statistical confirmation of the importance and character of economic push-factors, see Marjory Harper, *Emigration from North-East Scotland*, 2 vols (Aberdeen: Aberdeen University Press, 1988); Marjory Harper, *Adventurers and Exiles: The Great Scottish Exodus* (London: Profile, 2003), pp. 104–6; Devine, *Scotland's Global Diaspora*, chs 3, 4.

14. W. Turrentine Jackson, *The Enterprising Scot: Investors in the American West after 1873* (Edinburgh: Edinburgh University Press, 1968), p. vii.

15. Gordon Donaldson, *The Scots Overseas* (London: Robert Hale, 1966), pp. 124, 125, 205.

16. R. A. Cage (ed.), *The Scots Abroad: Labour, Capital, Enterprise, 1759–1914* (London: Croom Helm, 1985), pp. xii, 25, 111, 81.

17. Harper, *Adventurers and Exiles*, pp. 370, 1.

18. For a brief but penetrating analysis, including some Scottish statistics and comparisons, see Brinley Thomas, *Migration and Economic Growth: A Study of Great Britain and the Atlantic Economy* (Cambridge: Cambridge University Press, 1973), pp. 141–52.

19. Harper, *Adventurers and Exiles*, p. 71. Devine likewise maintains that Scottish (and English) emigrants 'often had a decided advantage over the peasant masses that flocked over the Atlantic in their millions from Ireland' and elsewhere: *Scotland's Global Diaspora*, p. 290.

20. David Noel Doyle, *Irish Americans, Native Rights and National Empires: The Structure, Attitudes and Divisions of the Catholic Minority in the Decade of Expansion, 1890–1901* (New York: Arno Press, 1976), ch. 2.

21. For annual returns by occupational category of immigrants from the United Kingdom to the United States (1875–1930), tabulated by each country of birth in the United Kingdom, see Thomas, *Migration and Economic Growth*, pp. 382–6. Comparison between nationalities is clouded by the fact that pre-war immigration returns did not subdivide occupations by sex.

22. Few attempts have been made to analyse the occupations of Scottish emigrants as recorded in passenger lists (beyond occasional references to published official tabulations), though lists for part of 1923 are analysed in Marjory Harper and Nicholas J. Evans, 'Socio-economic dislocation and inter-war emigration to Canada and the United States: a Scottish snapshot', *Journal of Imperial and Commonwealth History*, 34 (2006), pp. 529–52. Charlotte J. Erickson's widely cited article, 'Who were the English and Scots emigrants to the United States in the late nineteenth century?', in D. V. Glass and Roger Revelle (eds), *Population and Social Change* (London: Edward Arnold, 1972), pp. 347–81, offers no separate tabulation for Scottish occupations given in passenger lists for New York (1885–8).

23. Thomas, *Migration and Economic Growth*, 147–52. Thomas, using unpublished returns of the *13th Census of the United States* for 1910, tabulated the occupations of males aged over ten, dividing the proportion in each category for various nativity groups by that for the entire foreign-born white population: ibid. p. 151 (Table 44).

24. Angela McCarthy, 'Exploring ethnicity and ethnic identity in New Zealand asylums, before 1910', in Rosalind McClean et al. (eds), *Counting Stories, Moving Ethnicities: Studies from Aotearoa New Zealand* (Hamilton, NZ: University of Waikato Press, 2012), abstracted in Bueltmann, *The Scottish Diaspora*, pp. 73–4.

25. *Reports of the Immigration Commission*, 36, *Immigration and Crime* (Washington, DC: Government Printing Office, 1911).

26. For the distribution of Scots in 1910–11, see Table 13.2. Comparison of the number of Scots leaving the United Kingdom for the United States, Canada, and Australia between 1861–5 and 1905–9 shows that the United States was the preferred destination in every quinquennium. Australia predominated between 1853–4 and 1860–4, and Canada between 1910–14 and 1925–9: Flinn, *Scottish Population History*, pp. 450–1.

27. Harper, *Adventurers*, p. 369.

28. Ibid. p. 337.

29. Presbyterians and United Church adherents comprised 41.4 per cent and 34.1 per cent respectively of Ontario males of Scottish 'race', the corresponding proportions for females being 38.8 per cent and 35.4 per cent. 19.4 per cent of Ontarians of Scottish race were natives of the United Kingdom. See *7th Census of Canada* for 1931, 4 (Ottawa: Dominion Bureau of Statistics, 1936), pp. 782–3.

30. Returns of intermarriage relate to the parents of children born in Canada

(1929–31), compared with the racial breakdown of all wives aged 15–44 enumerated in the census for 1931. When the observed proportion of wives marrying husbands of the same race is divided by the proportion of all wives belonging to that race, the resultant score, showing the propensity for endogamous marriage, is 394 for the Irish, 351 for the Scots, and only 240 for the English. See W. Burton Hurd, *Racial Origins and Nativity of the Canadian People: A Study based on the Census of 1931 and Supplementary Data* (Ottawa: Dominion Bureau of Statistics, 1937), p. 224.

31. The annual official returns in *Papers relating to Emigration and Immigration* tabulated 'married' and other emigrants aged twelve upwards (1877–1907), leaving the allocation of widowed passengers unclear.

32. Virtually all (98.5 per cent) of the offspring of marriages between one foreign-born and one native-born parent were themselves natives of the United States (99.0 per cent for Irish Americans compared with 97.7 per cent for Scottish Americans), while 79.2 per cent of those with parents from different foreign countries were also native Americans (see note to Table 13.9).

33. Admittedly, even Ireland ranked far behind the countries responsible for the 'new immigration' such as Poland, Italy, and Russia. For each of these ethnicities, native Americans with two foreign parents outnumbered those of 'mixed' parentage by more than five to one.

34. The corresponding failure of Welsh men and women to secure non-English partners, leading to mortifyingly low scores in Table 13.9, may have been exaggerated by the frequency of cross-border marriages prior to emigration.

35. Richards, *Britannia's Children*, p. 302.

36. Angela McCarthy, *Personal Narratives of Irish and Scottish Migration, 1921–65: 'For Spirit and Adventure'* (Manchester: Manchester University Press, 2007).

37. Angela McCarthy (ed.), *A Global Clan: Scottish Migrant Networks and Identities since the Eighteenth Century* (London: Tauris Academic Studies, 2006).

38. Devine, *Scotland's Global Diaspora*, p. 12.

39. Flinn, *Scottish Population History*, p. 22.

40. See Kevin H. O'Rourke, *The Economic Impact of the Famine in the Short and Long Run* (Dublin: University College Dublin, Department of Economics, 1993), *Emigration and Living Standards in Ireland since the Famine* (Dublin: University College Dublin, Department of Economics, 1994), and his many other working papers and articles using general equilibrium models of the Irish economy to measure the impact of major discontinuities.

41. Devine, *Scotland's Global Diaspora*, pp. 290–1.

42. Andrew Hook, *Scotland and America: A Study of Cultural Relations, 1750–1835* (Glasgow and London: Blackie, 1975). This imbalance is not

fully redressed in William R. Brock, *Scotus Americanus: A Survey of the Sources for Links between Scotland and America in the Eighteenth Century* (Edinburgh: Edinburgh University Press, 1982) or Alexander Murdoch, *Scotland and America, c. 1600–c. 1800* (Basingstoke: Palgrave Macmillan, 2009).

43. Norman H. Carrier and J. R. Jeffery, *External Migration: A Study of the Available Statistics, 1815–1930* (London: HMSO, 1953).

44. This impression was confirmed by the high standard of papers and debates at the conference to which I presented a version of this paper on 6 July 2014. I am most grateful to its organisers, Sir Tom Devine, Dr Nick Evans, and Professor Angela McCarthy, for inviting me to discuss 'Historians of the Scottish diaspora: achievements, challenges, opportunities' at the National Museum of Scotland in Edinburgh.

Afterword

Eric Richards

GLOBAL MIGRATIONS LOOKS OUTWARDS from Scotland, searching across four centuries of endeavour. And over this horizon, as so many of the contributors attest, there is a uniting inspiration of the work and example of Tom Devine who has long reached beyond Scotland for wider perspectives. Scotland probably interacted with the outside world, near and far, more than most. It has been a global player for a quarter of a millennium and this basic fact has shaped its evolution and its destiny. But, as Devine himself stresses, most countries claim to punch above their weight, and assertions of historical 'exceptionality' and 'ethnic conceit' are less helpful than the systematic quest for underlying explanations of the current condition of the nation.

In 1966, the English historian Keith Thomas declared chillingly that his own profession, for all its traditional scholarly virtues, had explained remarkably little about the workings of human society. He urged a thoroughgoing infusion of the techniques and theories of 'the social sciences' into historical methods.[1] The subsequent career of both history and the social sciences has been decidedly chequered, and not only in England. In Scotland the challenge was taken up mainly by economic historians and historical demographers; meanwhile historians of Scottish ethnicity and identity have taken over much of the running and there is some tension in the historiography, some of it displayed in these contributions – especially where the urge to measure is met with a counterbalancing emphasis on the incalculable claims of experience and emotion.

The very word 'diaspora' releases hares in all directions, not least on questions relating to the reciprocations of emigration in the form of remittances from abroad, returning migrants to the home country, by investment, trade and human reproduction and most of all in the flows of cultural values and the pervasive matter of 'identity'. John MacKenzie stresses the multiplicity of diasporas in Africa and the rival definitions of 'diaspora'. The re-assertion of Scots identity, especially among the distant peripheries of the Scottish world, has been a feature of recent decades and was probably influential in the nationalist case promoted in 2014–15. The vigour of modern Scottish historiography has, wittingly or not, fuelled the political debate and raised its temperature, and cast an influence over the 2014 Independence Referendum. It is noticeable that the most questioning voices in this volume come from an 'Irishist' and an Australian historian.

Scale is a large issue since the 'diaspora' deals with tens of thousands of Scots people emigrating over many generations, in shifting formations and to a multitude of destinations. In *Global Migrations* we have also rich material about the involvement of Scots in other people's diasporas, overlapping with those of Ireland and England especially. But Scots were further involved in the massive movement of Indians (in the great indenture trade) and in the even greater African diaspora. The entanglement of Scots of the Enlightenment in the slave trade and slave plantations betrayed a deep and lucrative complicity at every level. This is a revelation of recent Scottish historiography, and given special reinforcement in the syntheses of Tom Devine. Meantime, ordinary Scots spread across the Anglo World and beyond, mostly as settlers and workers, but in every capacity. This leaves a trail of historical questions, and the pursuit of patterns, comparisons, lines of causation and of consequences. Not least, of course, are the perennial questions of Scotland's connections with the prime movers of imperialism and colonisation, all touched upon many times in this collection.

The Scottish exodus, on per capita terms, was located high in the league tables during the great age of European emigration. Nevertheless the juxtaposing of the continental experience inevitably prompts questions not only about differences in rates of emigration, but also about the common origins of such remarkable outward movement across the entire continent. Every country would wish to be *sui generis* rather than a subset or a variant, yet the component flows evidently intertwined and also competed in the new environments. The degrees of segregation and integration in the new settings provided the context in which the maintenance of distant identity was forged. The very circumstances of expatriation added greater urgency to the task of sustaining such distinctions, and perhaps especially among émigré Scots. Yet the notion of 'global diaspora' has been further widened, notably in the work of Adam McKeown, Patrick Manning and the brothers Lucassen: they have explored the even larger diasporic phenomena which coexisted with, and even rivalled, the European exoduses. Two other migration systems of the nineteenth century – namely the South East Asia/Indian

Ocean theatre, and the North East Asia/Manchurian system – each yielded approximately 50 million migrants over a similar span of time.[2] Inevitably, emigrating Scots (and multitudinous others) overlapped into all these systems. Perhaps the most infamous case within these intersecting global systems was indeed Scottish: the connections made by Jardine, Matheson and Co. and their associates operating at the very edges of each of these global systems by means of the particularly contentious trade in opium.[3] Matheson ultimately channelled many of his profits into the island of Lewis, again with dislocating consequences.

Of the negative consequences of the Scottish story, some were less visible. As Colin Calloway declares, ironic dimensions of some Scottish emigration were manifested in ways in which 'people who have experienced dispossession and displacement themselves seem to have few qualms about dispossessing and displacing other people'. The North American accounts echo also in the reports from the Scottish-Australian theatre of colonisation. This may suggest a certain insouciant disregard by past emigrants which defies our modern understanding of their mental worlds.

There has been some re-shaping of Scotland's own emigration history. Andrew Mackillop identifies a surprising decline in rates of Scottish emigration in the early eighteenth century, the volume decreasing while the range of destinations increased. Previously Scotland seems to have been prodigal in its export of 'raw humanity', but now there was a change in the export of 'qualitative human capital', much more productive and beneficial for individual Scots and indeed for the country by the end of the century. This qualitative change produced long-term gains, enabling 'massive upward mobility' for many Scots, particularly in colonies of settlement and trade, yielding better returns on emigration and investment, and witnessed also in the purchase of landed estates back in Scotland. It was the 'mobilisation of high-end human capital', especially manifested among Scots in Asia, where small levels of emigration were highly productive and lucrative. In effect there was a critical shift in the character of Scottish emigration, something not captured in the raw figures of population exchanges. It suggests a revised conceptualisation and historical periodisation of Scottish emigration.

Scotland was precocious in many of its modern evolutions, but it was also part of a wider experience which, over more than a century, affected the whole of Western Europe and then moved eastward. The common elements as much as the national variants are best approached by comparisons with, for instance, Norway, Ireland, Catalonia, Sweden or Sicily,[4] some of which has already yielded good results, led as usual by

Devine. In the search for the ultimate secrets of such diasporic phenomena, the American historian Bernard Bailyn has employed the superb Scottish nominal data gathered by the Board of Customs Commissioners in the early 1770s. Bailyn declared that the entire 'Atlantic system' (from Luanda to Shetland, from the Danube to the Mississippi) had been somehow galvanised outwards. He conjured metaphorical tectonic plates set in motion, a universal force affecting the foundations of society, internally and externally, not least in Scotland.[5] The mobilisation of millions of emigrants was an extraordinary moment in European history and suggests deep, even ultimate, causes which perhaps transcended individual national or ethnic cases. But the Scottish component was early and its historiography is contributing greatly to these diasporic mysteries.

The Scottish diaspora at all times entailed a substantial investment of resources, a depletion of its population and capital, though also relieving certain domestic pressures. The replenishment from the returns of overseas investment and settlement was conspicuous at several times in the longer story. The impact of wealth brought back from the Indies, East and West, was profound, notably in the Highlands – shifting the bases of land ownership and the aspirations and demands of new lairds. Remittances back to Scotland were fructifying and can be seen in many mansions across the country. But the narrative is complicated and uneven, and not yet brought into any systematic account.

The Scottish diaspora contained a well-known paradox, namely that of heavy emigration pouring out of this phenomenally successful first industrial nation, through to the twentieth century. This feature is genuinely exceptional to the Scottish case.[6] We now know more about the destinations of most of the emigrants, and the shifts, returnings and sojournings, and their persistence, and the channels which reinforced migrant patterns. The critical paucity of specifically Scottish nominal data means that we are dependent on genealogy for much of the detail of, for instance, skill levels, literacy, human capital and networks. The first requirement of categorising migrants is especially important for understanding the complex Scottish context out of which issued its emigrants.

Nevertheless, the rich description of the people and the infrastructures of the Scottish diaspora have thickened with the capture of much individual experience and their pathways across the globe. The concentration on the domestic stories of emigrants is warranted by the fact that the family was the chief vehicle of migration, and its internal dynamics and strategies are best exposed in individual testimony (oral

or by correspondence). 'The Aspirational Scot', the archetypal economic migrant, sought new ways of improvement for themselves and for
future generations, responding to income differentials which provided
the prime moving force for their emigration. There were, in so many
testimonies, variations on this central theme, adjusting and shaping the
flows over time and region. And the mechanism was subject to coercion
and retention, enhancing and impeding the flow of emigrants, much
complicated by the surrounding context of Scottish industrialisation,
agrarian change and the proximity of England. In a way, migration was
part of the containment, the accommodation to the tensions generated
by these changes.

David Fitzpatrick urges more consideration of the 'nature and force
of inhibiting factors' – the resistance by most people to the lure of
expatriation. In the mid- to late nineteenth century this was the constant plaint of Highland lairds and their factors, who were unable to
comprehend why crofters would not respond to the widening differentials of income, preferring to persist and remain in their poverty, to the
irritation and frustration of the landowners. For figures in authority the
obvious response to poverty was emigration, but most often they were
defied.

Within Scotland, population movements were also tied up with the
regional divergence between the Highlands and the Lowlands from the
late eighteenth century, a localised version of the so-called 'Elephant
Question'.[7] One of the main historical tasks, not least in the Highlands,
is to identify and assess the strength of those forces of retention and
exodus – allowing for the fact that most people simply did not emigrate
at all. England, of course, was the most common destination for most
Scottish migrants. The departures of Scots people, capital and culture
had repercussions which bounced back, in the form of remittances and
profits and of returned migrants too, but they may have depleted the
home country: thus notions of 'haemorrhage' and the draining of home
investment (especially regarding the effect on domestic housing stocks)
continues to reverberate inconclusively in the literature.

The question of 'identity' recurs throughout this volume and Angela
McCarthy is particularly concerned about the danger of 'marginalising'
the matter of ethnicity. Sociologists nowadays claim to have discovered
a defining 'narcissism' in modern times, and thus we insistently ask such
questions as 'Who am I?' and 'Where do I belong?' The effort to capture
the essence of Scottishness is reported in several chapters, evidence of the
'articulation of Scottishness' and nuances of 'the Scottish diasporic consciousness'. We discover the remarkable tenacity of military traditions

in the empire which fed directly upon the vitality of Scottish symbolism across the wide diaspora. It was best exposed in the 'kilted aesthetics' widespread in the Scottish 'memory boom'. Scotland possesses a distinct comparative advantage in the business of ethnic sensibility, and we learn that the Scots/Highland culture even stands as a proxy for other people's lost heritages. It is best witnessed in the astonishing proliferation of pipe bands across Europe and beyond.

These discriminations of identity depend on the angle of view. There can be little doubt about the 'Scots' estimations of themselves', perhaps best exemplified in the patriotic pride of James Taylor in Ceylon and the social cement created by special connections between, for instance, north-east Scotland and India and Ceylon. But in the receiving societies perceptions were less reliable. Thus in Australia, Scots were not distinguishable by their behaviour from the rest of the colonists; Kenyans and other Africans apparently knew the differences between Scots and the English, and some Indian people of North America seemed to acknowledge the distinctions among British immigrants. But the Māori found it impossible to draw intra-British distinctions and tended to lump all Europeans into the catch-all of Pākehā.[8]

Emigrants from the British Isles were not easily differentiated by their social and economic behaviour, habits, trajectories or their levels of assimilation. They shared many common characteristics which are under-researched and such similarities are not much valued; yet the quest for distinctive ethnic markers is now yielding diminishing returns. It may be more fruitful to seek out wider perspectives by comparison with emigrant populations from more distant cultures. For instance, the study of the peoples of the great Chinese diasporas is now yielding rich and fascinating accounts of their expatriation and especially of their homecomings, based on the evidence of emigrant correspondence, artefacts, architecture and the conspicuous consumption habits of returned Chinese emigrants. Such scholarship invites systematic cross-cultural comparisons with Scots and other categories in the widening narrative of modern international migration.[9] As Fitzpatrick declares, Scots, like everyone else, must test their claims of differential endeavour against international standards of comparison. And beyond such tests is the larger question regarding the explanatory functions of the idea of identity and why historians have embraced it with so much enthusiasm.

New ways of thinking about the Scottish diaspora are peppered throughout this volume. In his brisk exposure of the scarcity of systematic measures of the claims to Scottish distinctiveness, Fitzpatrick suggests novel sources and tests of verification. He prods Scottish historians to examine the consequences of return migration which, as his Irish evidence suggests, is more feasible than one might expect. He debunks by way of statistics the fabled pre-eminence of Scots, so dispersing stereotypes in many directions. Often Scots emigrants were distressingly similar to the English (itself an unsatisfactory shorthand for many categories of southern Britons). Statistical rigour is evidently required for all the claims for Scottish 'disproportionality' in the business of empire and globalisation. But the agenda is by no means one-dimensional. Less measurable, less determinate elements keep surfacing. Thus David Alston, wrestling with the apparent illogicality of Scottish investment in Demerara, suggests a behavioural approach to the recurring puzzle of motivation; he tackles the problem of high-risk decision making in remote contexts where his Scottish cases exhibited 'odd and compulsive psychic states'. It becomes clear that many of the dimensions of the Scottish diaspora cannot be measured and leave greater space for speculation. Thus in Ceylon we find 'social capital' embodied in Scottish managers, building a reputation for business.

Linda Colley, critical of London-focused accounts of English history, has also chided Scottish historians for their nationalistic determination to exaggerate the 'mental distance between Scotland and England', causing, she claims, a distortion and simplification of the past: a consequence of national navel-gazing on each side of the border.[10] *Global Migrations* is not so introverted, though it may generally seem to accentuate the positive differences between Scotland and the rest. We might urge the systematic measures of these differentiations, and we might also ask why such an agenda is so dominant in the modern historiography. One thing is clear: wherever one treads Tom Devine has been there before and has left his indelible mark. The debates continue across his Scottish Empire.

NOTES

1. Keith Thomas, 'New ways in history', *Times Literary Supplement*, 7 April 1966; Keith Thomas, 'New ways revisited: how history's borders have been expanded over the past forty years', *Times Literary Supplement*, 13 October 2006.
2. Adam McKeown, 'Global migrations, 1846–1940', *Journal of World History*, 15 (2004), pp. 155–89; Leo Lucassen, 'Migration and world history: reaching a new frontier', *International Review of Social History*, 52:1 (2007), pp. 89–96; Jan Lucassen, Leo Lucassen and Patrick Manning, 'Migration history: multidisciplinary approaches', in Jan Lucassen, Leo

Lucassen and Patrick Manning (eds), *Migration History in World History* (Leiden: Brill, 2010), pp. 3–35.

3. A radical re-interpretation of the effect of opium on the Chinese people is presented by Frank Dikötter, *'Patient Zero': China and the Myth of the Opium Plague* (School of Oriental and African Studies, University of London, 2003), and also Frank Dikötter, Lars Laaman and Zhou Xun, *Narcotic Culture: A History of Drugs in China* (Chicago: University of Chicago Press, 2004). I am grateful to John MacKenzie for drawing my attention to this new research.

4. See, for instance, Graham Tulloch, Karen Agutter and Luciana d'Arcangeli (eds), *Sicily and Scotland: Where Extremes Meet* (Kibworth Beauchamp, Leicester: Troubador Publishing, 2014). In his discussion of the remarkable propensity of the eighteenth-century Highlands to supply manpower to the service of the British armies, Mackillop draws a particularly stimulating comparison with other 'European peripheries or former frontier areas' which also supplied manpower to imperial armies; he cites the example of the deployment of Croatian population to the service of Austria which he describes as something 'akin to a recruiting reservation', part of a 'similar equation of military service with commercial underdevelopment'. The British state anachronistically appealed to the notion of clanship which had already 'imploded'. See Andrew Mackillop, *'More Fruitful than the Soil': Army, Empire and the Scottish Highlands, 1715–1815* (East Linton: Tuckwell Press, 2000), p. 236.

5. Bernard Bailyn, *Voyagers to the West* (New York: Knopf, 1986), ch. 3; see also Bernard Bailyn, *The Barbarous Years* (New York: Knopf, 2012), Preface.

6. See T. M. Devine, 'The paradox of Scottish emigration', in T. M. Devine (ed.), *Scottish Emigration and Scottish Society* (Edinburgh: John Donald, 1992), pp. 1–15. For an alternative perspective, see Angela McCarthy, 'The Scottish diaspora since 1815', in T. M. Devine and Jenny Wormald (eds), *The Oxford Handbook of Modern Scottish History* (Oxford: Oxford University Press, 2012), pp. 510–32.

7. See Paul Henderson Scott, *In Bed with an Elephant* (Edinburgh: Saltire Society, 1985) and *Still In Bed with an Elephant* (Edinburgh: Saltire Society, 1998); and T. M. Devine, 'In bed with an elephant: almost three hundred years of the Anglo-Scottish Union', *Scottish Affairs*, 57 (2006), pp. 1–18.

8. Lachlan Paterson, '"Pākehā or English": Maori understandings of Englishness in the colonial period', in Lyndon Fraser and Angela McCarthy (eds), *Far from 'Home': The English in New Zealand* (Dunedin: Otago University Press, 2012), pp. 123–43. Angela McCarthy informs me that some of the Maori language newspapers recognised differences in their understanding of events back in Britain and Ireland, and she also points out that Matiaha Tiramorehu and Tame Haereroa expressed displeasure in 1856 'with all the men of Scotland'. See Angela McCarthy, 'Scottish

migrant ethnic identities', in John M. MacKenzie and T. M. Devine (eds), *Scotland and the British Empire* (Oxford: Oxford University Press, 2011), pp. 139–40.

9. See, for example, Ding Lixing and Zheng Zongwei (eds), *Chinese Qiaopi and Memory of the World* (Qiaoxiang Culture Research Centre, Wuyi University, Jiangmen, Guangdong, 2014), especially Gregor Benton, 'Documenting the lives of emigrants through their letters: the overseas Chinese case', pp. 484–507.

10. Linda Colley, 'A shared island', *Times Literary Supplement'*, 9 January 2015, p. 8.

Index